Indian Inspired

ALSO BY BHARTI KIRCHNER

The Healthy Cuisine of India

Indian Inspired

A NEW CUISINE FOR THE INTERNATIONAL TABLE

By

Bharti Kirchner

LOWELL HOUSE
Los Angeles

CONTEMPORARY BOOKS
Chicago

Library of Congress Cataloging-in-Publication Data

Kirchner, Bharti

    Indian inspired : a new cuisine for the international table / Bharti Kirchner

       p.   cm.

    Includes bibliographical references and index.

    ISBN 1-56565-200-2

    1. Cookery, International. 2. Cookery, Indic. I. Title.

TX725.A1K54 1993

641.5954—dc20   93-7680

                                                      CIP

Requests for such permissions should be addressed to:

Lowell House

2029 Century Park East, Suite 3290

Los Angeles, CA 90067

Publisher: Jack Artenstein

Vice-President/Editor-in-Chief: Janice Gallagher

Director of Publishing Services: Mary D. Aarons

Text design: Carrington Design

Manufactured in the United States of America

10 9 8 7 6 5 4 3 2 1

For Tom,
my best inspiration

Acknowledgments

· · · · · · · · · · · · ·

Writing this book has brought me in contact with people in remote corners of the globe. Sometimes chance meetings with people have led to valuable cooking tips and insights. There have been numerous others in my hometown who either tested my recipes, eagerly sampled the finished dishes, or critiqued my manuscript; in all cases they provided useful feedback. Still others simply encouraged me by asking, "When will this book be out?" With gratitude and affection I thank them all.

Their names (in no particular order) are: Sukumar Nandi, Tapati Paul, Patricia Kirchner, Dr. Wyveta Kirk, Dick Gibbons and his critique group, Leon Billig and his critique group, Gary Boynton, Mimi Gormezano, Jim Wells, Gela Gibbons, Emma Bernal, Paolo Albuquerque, Meenambigai Sockalingam, Amy Laly, Sri Brennan, and my agent, Doe Coover.

During the long, arduous months of writing, revising, and testing, my editor and able advisor, Janice Gallagher, became a closer friend. Her enthusiasm for this project made the writing process more enjoyable.

Table of Contents

· · · · · · · · · · · · · ·

The Eclectic Indian

What I wanted most when I was in Russia was to drink tea with the local people. The small American group I was traveling with had been treated by Russia's Intourist travel organization like visiting royalty. In St. Petersburg, formerly Leningrad, we marveled at the Czar's summer palace, toured the sprawling city, and dined on shashliks and blinis in lavish hotels that served caviar as the starter course. But no one planned for a simple tea with the Russians.

While visiting the Hermitage museum, I struck up a conversation with a Russian student who invited our group to his university dormitory. Off we went in a taxi, on a December evening, through a maze of small streets swirling with snow. A group of his friends greeted us at the door of a sparsely furnished room that was barely heated. Then the evening passed amid discussions of Castro, consumerism, and rock music.

My clearest memory is the endless cups of tea from an old, dented samovar. Strong and aromatic, the tea suffused our bodies with a pleasant warmth throughout that subzero evening. The accompaniment was simple: boiled potatoes that we peeled and ate as we talked. It was all we could find in the students' nearly empty cupboard. Yet I much preferred it to the opulent meals served at the tourist hotels.

We sang, danced, and improvised on Russian-English tunes well into the early morning. Our farewell was sad and teary-eyed, but I had gained things of lasting value—friendship, a love of samovar tea, and a reminder that the simplest food in the company of friends can be an unforgettable experience.

I learned anew the joy of using whatever is at hand to produce tasty, simple, but pleasurable fare. Numerous adventures such as my Russian visit have shaped my perspective on food, but the roots of this multicultural appetite go back to my childhood.

The doors to the cupboard of the world opened to me in Kalimpong, a mountain town in the Himalayan foothills in eastern India, where Bengali families like ours mingled with people from other Indian states. In their own section of town, hill tribes of non-Indian origin—Lepcha, Gorkha, and Bhutia—maintained their traditional way of life. Each spoke a separate language and had a different diet.

When I was five years old, I watched a barefoot Lepcha child my own age sitting outside a tea shop eating a bowl of a strange grain that was not my beloved rice. It was barley. My young world began expanding, and before long I was enjoying Gorkha potato chutney, snack bars prepared by the Marwaris out of lentils, and Nepalese yogurt pudding.

During my years of schooling in Calcutta, I met students from many parts of the world—Southeast Asia, China, Europe, Africa, and the Caribbean. A Middle Easterner introduced me to bulgur, a staple in her country, a delicious derivative of wheat. A South Indian woman offered me mangosteen and I understood why people get misty-eyed when they speak of this succulent tropical fruit.

I later lived and worked in Europe, the Middle East, and the United States. Traveling for pleasure took me to mainland China, Southeast Asia, and Mexico. In each place I sought out foods that sustained the local people, accompanied their cooks while they shopped, and, as a guest in their homes, watched them lovingly create marvelous dishes from treasured family recipes.

The Chinese taught me the art of combining textures: scallops with green onions, noodles with broccoli, chicken with snow peas. Fresh roasted corn is a favorite street food in India, but it was in the United States that I first tasted cornbread. The Mexicans introduced me to a whole new world of chile peppers—habanero, árbol, and chipotle—varieties quite different from those I had encountered at home in Bengal. Eventually I realized that my approach to cooking had been irrevocably changed and never again would I be able to cook completely within the boundaries of any one culture.

So, although some friends would prefer that I prepare only traditional Indian food, my cooking has evolved into what I call "Indian inspired." I accompany a Bengali fish *jhol* or a Gujarati vegetable stew with a Caribbean sweet and sour plantain sauce, an Indonesian peanut sambal, or a Middle Eastern dried-fruit chutney. A summer brunch might include a turmeric-spiked French ratatouille. A winter supper features a fragrant, cumin-scented vegetable soup served with a Western salad.

On those occasions when an all-Indian dinner seems too richly or predictably spiced, I experiment with ingredients and techniques from other countries. Such meals become adventures in eating where I feel free to try new flavor and textural combinations.

My husband and I love to garden, and often the intensely flavored vegetables we grow guide my efforts in the kitchen. I might invent a blend of herbs and spices to accent the gentle sweetness of baby carrots. Distinctive potato varieties such as Yukon Gold inspire me to serve a dish such as Sweet, Sour, and Smoky Potatoes. Kale, sautéed with warming cumin seeds and balanced by sun-dried tomatoes, provides a lovely triangle of flavors from around the globe.

The recipes in this book are low in fat and create spicy, lively meals. Not all of these dishes have an Indian accent—some are simply tasty and nutritionally rich. But all are intended to be appropriate in a wide variety of dining situations. Many otherwise traditional Indian recipes have acquired a new twist from the use of ingredients and seasonings from other cultures. On some occasions, "Indian inspiration" means complementing a non-Indian meal with one or two everyday Indian dishes such as a chutney or raita.

A wise cooking teacher once said, "There are no culinary absolutes. It's all relative to one's cultural point of view." This cookbook represents my point of view, with dishes based on experience gained both at home and abroad. I invite you to explore this "Indian inspired" cuisine with me. ✳

Before You Begin: Some Tips

• •

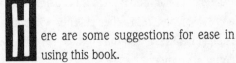ere are some suggestions for ease in
using this book.

* The amount of oil used in each recipe is small, usually a tablespoon or two (15
to 30 ml), with ghee or butter suggested as an option. I have reduced the fat as
much as I feel is possible without compromising the flavor of the dishes, prefer-
ring to rely primarily on the natural flavors of the basic ingredients enhanced by
the use of spices. For this reason, it's crucial not to omit any of the spices called
for in a recipe.

* The total amount of fat in a meal may be reduced even further by teaming a
main dish with steamed, roasted, or wilted vegetables, plain-cooked grains, or
oil-free chutneys or salsas, all of which are essentially devoid of fat. This
approach allows you to enjoy at least one spicy, tasty dish per meal, containing
sufficient fat to develop the flavors, balanced by simple grain and vegetable
accompaniments. The net result is a lowfat meal. This approach is reflected in
the serving suggestions in this book.

* I have provided substitutions whenever possible, but a number of spices and flavorings impart a unique taste and are therefore irreplaceable. Some examples are
tamarind, shrimp paste, and kalonji seeds. All of these items are now available in
ethnic markets and in some well-stocked supermarkets. If you are unable to
locate them in your area, consult the chapter on Food Gathering, Food Shopping: Mail-Order Sources.

* Unless otherwise specified, tomatoes are not peeled. I peel tomatoes only where necessary to substantially improve the texture and/or appearance of a dish. The same applies to other vegetables such as potatoes, sweet potatoes, and squash. I prefer using the whole vegetable whenever I can in order to preserve its maximum nutritional value.

* You will not find instructions for freezing in this book. I refrigerate leftovers but generally don't freeze my dishes. However, you can prepare many of these recipes ahead of time and then freeze them. A word of caution is in order: The texture of some dishes may suffer, and seasonings tend to lose some of their punch after they've been frozen.

* Fresh green chiles play an important role in the Indian-inspired cuisine. I specify jalapeño in these recipes because they are usually available in supermarkets. Jalapeños vary in hotness, and many of them can be very mild. If you run into this problem, substitute serrano, Thai chiles, or other more consistently hot chiles. Don't use larger, mild chiles such as Anaheim, which are meant for stuffing or sautéeing.

If I find that the jalapeños I am using are the mild variety, I increase the amount of heat in a recipe by adding ground red pepper. If you're using serrano or other hotter chiles, consider omitting this item.

* Fresh coriander, which is used extensively in this cuisine as a cooking ingredient and a garnish, is often known by other names, including cilantro and Chinese parsley. Since American supermarkets usually call it cilantro, I have referred to it by that name throughout the book.

* Always peel gingerroot.

* Metric measurements have been rounded off for ease of use. For example, I have specified the metric equivalent of 1 pound as 450 or 500 g rather than 454 g.

* Some recipes call for grinding spices or making a spice paste. I use a mortar and pestle or sometimes a mini-chopper. A mortar and pestle not only saves electricity but often produces a smoother result. When shopping for a mortar and pestle, look for one made of stone with a grainy, rough surface. These are best purchased at Latin American and Southeast Asian markets.

* Servings: Note that the portions here are $1/2$ to 1 cup (125 to 250 ml) servings, except for entrée servings, which are larger. For many recipes, a person will eat more than one serving, so a recipe may serve fewer people than indicated.

* In recipes that call for milk, I use nonfat milk whenever possible. If nonfat milk doesn't produce the desired result, I use lowfat milk and specify it in the recipe.

Nonfat yogurt usually works well, although for a richer taste you can replace it with lowfat yogurt.

✳   The serving suggestions following a recipe are meant only to spur your imagination. These dishes are flexible, and the possible combinations are endless. Feel free to experiment.

Rather than just providing some recipes, I have presented a new way of eating. Fresh, natural ingredients that are imaginatively seasoned are teamed with a multitude of low-calorie, zesty sauces.

Have fun creating these unique dishes and putting together a variety of menus to share with your family and friends.

The International Cupboard: Special Ingredients

ACHIOTE (ANNATTO) • The brick-red seeds of the annatto tree, used for coloring and flavoring food. In Latin America, cooks often color their cooking fat with these seeds, then store it for later use. Sold as seeds, powder, or paste in Latin American markets. In this book, I use the convenient achiote paste, which dissolves readily.

AJWAIN • This seed looks like a celery seed but is slightly larger. Its flavor is faintly reminiscent of thyme, but the difference is great enough so that they are not interchangeable. Used in India in savory dishes. Roast the seeds and sprinkle over potato or macaroni salads or add to yogurt dressings.

ARBORIO • Small, almost round, pearly rice from Italy, used in preparing risotto. It comes in different varieties. For risotto recipes in this book, use *superfino*, which contains the most starch and gives the resulting dish a creamier texture. Refrigerate arborio in a tightly covered container to retain its freshness.

ARUGULA (ROQUETTE) • The long, dark green leaves of this plant have a pungent, peppery flavor. Commonly used in Italy in mixed green salads and pasta dishes, it is becoming increasingly popular in the United States.

ASAFETIDA • Don't be repelled by the strong musky smell of this spice, as its flavor mellows and become rather garliclike when cooked. Asafetida is sold in solid, rocklike chunks or as a powder in Indian groceries and adds a distinctive touch to savory dishes. These recipes use the powdered form.

ASIAN PEAR • One of the oldest of cultivated pears, it is a native of Japan and China, now widely grown in the United States. Shaped more like an apple than a pear, this delightful fruit has a delicate sweet taste and a crisp, juicy texture. It ranges in color from bright yellow to dull russet brown. Although sometimes called "apple pear," it is not a hybrid.

BLACK MUSTARD (BROWN MUSTARD, RED MUSTARD) ▪ Black mustard seeds are widely used in India, both whole and ground. They are considered more flavorful than yellow mustard, common in the West. The whole seeds are sautéed in the beginning of cooking. The ground seeds are moistened with water and allowed to stand for 30 minutes before being added to a dish. This step reduces their pungency and develops a rich flavor.

The leaves of the mustard plant are prized as a vegetable throughout India. Several varieties of mustard grow in the United States; among the best is the delicate Mizuna mustard from Japan.

BLACK SALT (KALA NIMAK) ▪ This salt from India is not black but reddish grey. It has an earthy flavor and adds a distinctive touch to dishes. Indian groceries sell it in lump form or, more conveniently, as powder. There is no substitute.

BOK CHOY ▪ A mild, attractive member of the cabbage family. It does not form a tight head like cabbage and resembles white Swiss chard. The large leaves are dark green and shiny. The thick, white ribs are tender and succulent.

BULGUR ▪ Cracked, parboiled, and dried wheat, popular in the Middle East. Bulgur requires less cooking than plain cracked wheat. Usually it is sufficient to soak bulgur in boiling water for 30 minutes or so.

CARDAMOM ▪ Indian groceries carry these small oval soft-green pods that encase brownish black aromatic seeds; supermarkets carry a less flavorful variety of the pods, creamy white in color. Some recipes optionally call for black cardamom, a larger (about 1 inch [2.5 cm] long) oval-shaped pod that imparts a fine fragrance to rice dishes. These are also sold in Indian groceries, though hard to find at times.

CHAAT POWDER ▪ A mixture of ground spices with a hot, sour, and salty flavor. Chaat may also refer to a spicy salad composed of various fruits and vegetables and dressed with chaat powder, lime, and tamarind. Add a dash of this piquant powder to sliced tomatoes, steamed vegetables (especially potatoes), or to a vegetable or fruit salad. Indian groceries sell it, but if you prefer, you can make it at home.

To prepare chaat powder: Combine $1/4$ teaspoon (1 ml) each of ground cumin, ground coriander, ground ginger, and black salt, $1/8$ teaspoon (0.5 ml) each of black pepper and asafetida, dash red pepper, and $1 3/4$ teaspoons (8 ml) mango powder (*aamchoor*). Grind the mixture to a fine powder in a mortar and pestle or in a spice grinder. Taste and adjust the amount of red pepper, black salt, and mango powder until mixture has a piquant flavor that suits your taste.

CHICK-PEA FLOUR (BESAN) ▪ Prepared by grinding chick-peas and sieving the husks, this flour has a nutty flavor and creamy texture. Used widely in Indian cooking in batters, for thickening, and in breads; available in Indian groceries. Store this perishable flour in the refrigerator. Wheat flour is not a substitute.

CHILES, DRIED ▪ For buying ground red pepper, I usually visit an Asian market. The supermarket variety of cayenne pepper is a substitute, but it's not as piquant. Whole dried red chiles are available in the supermarket spice section in jars. Other whole dried chiles that I purchase from Latin markets are:

Pasilla—Brownish black, long, wrinkled, and very hot. The flesh has a smoky flavor. Also called chile negro. Note that sometimes the dark red, wide anchos are mislabeled as pasillas.

Chipotle—Smoked and dried jalapeños; these are extremely hot.

Chile pequín (chile piquín)—Tiny, bright red, and very hot chiles, sold in Latin markets in the whole form, as powder, or as flakes.

CHILES, FRESH ▪ Fresh chiles are best stored wrapped in plastic in the refrigerator. You will find the following varieties called for in the recipes in this book:

Anaheim (California chile)—A large, light green, mild-tasting chile, commonly used for stuffing. May also be roasted, skinned, cut in strips, and added to dishes.

Habanero—A highly flavored variety reputed to be the hottest of all chiles. It is said to test 100 times hotter than jalapeño and is much prized throughout the Caribbean, Brazil, and Mexico's Yucatán peninsula for its flavor and aroma. The name means "from Havana" in Spanish, though it is rarely used in Cuba now. It is called "goat pepper" in the Bahamas, because it is believed to be too hot for even the goats to eat. The fruit is lantern-shaped and varies from pale yellow through yellowish orange to bright red when ripe. Seed and dice this chile and use sparingly. Look for fresh or dried habanero in fancy supermarkets and Latin American groceries.

Jalapeño—The most common chile in American supermarkets, it is oval, bright green (sometimes greenish black), and has a shiny surface. Though originally extremely hot, the varieties found in supermarkets these days are generally mild.

Serrano—A small, spicy-hot, thin pepper that is a good substitute for jalapeño if you desire a more fiery taste.

Thai chile—A small, thin, and very hot chile that is also known as Japanese chile. It's found in India and in some parts of East Asia as well. You may substitute it for serrano.

CHRYSANTHEMUM LEAVES ▪ Edible chrysanthemum (*shungiku*) is a special variety of chrysanthemum, whose tender, fragrant leaves are used as stir-fry greens in Japan. The young leaves can also be used raw in salads. Arugula is a substitute.

CILANTRO ▪ The leafy greens of the coriander plant, often called Chinese parsley or parsley of the tropics. It is used widely in Asia, Latin and South America, and other parts of the world as a seasoning and as a garnish.

CURRY LEAVES ▪ Small, aromatic leaves sold dried or, occasionally, fresh in Indian groceries. They are indispensable to the cooking of southern and western parts of India. The fresh leaves have more flavor. If you are fortunate enough to find them, use them as soon as possible and refrigerate any leftovers in zip-lock plastic bags. They will last for two or more weeks. You may dry what you can't use immediately by spreading them in a single layer on a tray in a warm spot for several days. Curry leaves are not related to curry powder. There is no substitute.

CURRY POWDER OR CURRY PASTE ▪ The word "curry" is a catchall that British colonials applied to all Indian spice mixes. Now it refers to a jar of spice in the supermarket, which is actually a blend of different ground spices. In East Asia and other countries where Indian cooking influence has spread, curry powder or curry paste, which is a cake of moistened spice mix, is widely used.

Indian cooks don't use such a fixed blend, but instead combine different seasonings for each dish to bring out the flavor of the main ingredient. The blend for potatoes, for instance, is different from that for fish. Because curry powder is now universal, I use it in this book, supplementing it with extra seasonings.

Curry powder in the Western supermarkets comes in mild (less chile) and hot (more chile) blends and contains turmeric (which gives it a characteristic yellow or amber color), and one or more of the following: cumin, fennel, garlic, ginger, fenugreek, cinnamon, cloves, anise, black mustard, and black pepper. In Singapore and Thailand other items are included, notably lemon grass, coriander root, and shrimp powder. Because curry powders and curry pastes are now readily available, I haven't included instructions for preparing them at home.

Selecting curry powder: A large number of brands are available in gourmet shops, supermarkets, and Asian markets, making the selection difficult. The mix should contain at least turmeric, cumin, and coriander. Some Indian groceries now sell freshly ground curry powder, which has more flavor. Don't confuse curry powder with garam masala, a mixture of warming spices such as cardamom, cloves, and cinnamon.

FENUGREEK ▪ Yellow squarish seeds with a slightly bitter maplelike flavor. Used in India in fish and vegetable dishes.

FISH SAUCE (NUOC MUM, NAM PLA, PATIS) ▪ A thin brown sauce made by fermenting salted fish. Its strong taste is mellowed by cooking. Even in small amounts, it adds depth to a dish. There is no substitute. Sold in Asian markets.

FIVE-SPICE (CHINESE) ▪ A ground mixture of cinnamon, clove, fennel, Szechuan peppercorn, and star anise. Sold in Asian markets and some supermarkets.

FIVE-SPICE (INDIAN) ▪ An equal measure of the seeds of cumin, black mustard, fennel, kalonji, and fenugreek. It is not always sold in Indian groceries as a mix, but you can buy the seeds separately and combine them yourself.

GAI LAN (CHINESE BROCCOLI, CHINESE KALE) ▪ A leafy plant, 10 to 14 inches (25 to 35 cm) high, with succulent stems and a small head of white (or sometimes yellow) flowers. The entire plant is edible. Available in Asian markets. When shopping for gai lan, look for unopened flower buds and smooth stalks. Broccoli or broccoli raab can be substituted.

GARAM MASALA ▪ Literally "hot spices," because they raise body heat. This ground mixture consists of cinnamon, cardamom, and cloves and may include black pepper, nutmeg, coriander, and other spices. Added at the last moment, garam masala puts the finishing touch on many dishes. Don't confuse it with curry powder, whose content and use are entirely different. You can buy ground garam masala at any Indian grocery.

Indians also use whole garam masala, a mixture of the hot spices in their whole form—cardamom pods, cinnamon sticks, and whole cloves. The spices are fried in hot oil at the start of cooking to impart aroma to a dish.

GHEE (CLARIFIED BUTTER) ▪ A flavorful cooking medium from India that imparts a distinctive nutty fragrance to dishes. Ghee is made by removing the casein (protein) and other solids from butter. Because of its saturated fat content, I usually specify ghee only as an optional flavoring. Don't substitute vegetable ghee, which contains saturated fat and lacks flavor.

To prepare ghee: Melt 1 pound (450 g) unsalted butter in a heavy-bottomed pan over very low heat and allow it to simmer undisturbed. A smooth white foam will soon cover the surface as the milk solids begin to separate from the fat. The soft foam on the surface will gradually become crusty, turning yellowish initially and then light brown. In 45 to 60 minutes, when the butter has stopped foaming and the sediment at the bottom has turned golden brown, remove from heat. Pour the contents of the pan through four or more layers of dampened cheesecloth pressed into a strainer held over a bowl. Make sure none of the sediment gets through the cheesecloth. Store the golden liquid, ghee, in a covered container in the refrigerator. Discard the sediment.

Soften ghee before using as a cooking medium by placing the covered jar in a pan of hot water. For sprinkling over cooked vegetables or grains, melt it in a small saucepan over low heat. Yields 1^1/$_2$ cups (375 ml).

GINGERROOT ▪ An aromatic rhizome that is an essential ingredient in the cooking of most Asian countries. It has a light brown skin and a pale yellow flesh. In this book, I use peeled fresh gingerroot in most cases and only occasionally ground ginger, which has a milder flavor. When using gingerroot, make sure it is minced or grated. If left in large pieces it will not blend with the sauce. You can also make a paste with ginger-root. This is the form in which it's used in India.

To prepare gingerroot paste: Grind peeled gingerroot in a mortar and pestle until relatively smooth. Or, process it in a food processor or mini-chopper to a paste-like consistency.

INDIAN CHEESE (PANIR) ▪ Soft and crumbly cheese made at home by curdling milk.

To prepare Indian cheese cubes: Bring 4 cups (1 liter) 2% lowfat milk to a full boil in a large pan. (Nonfat milk or 1% lowfat milk will produce a drier cheese with little flavor and is not recommended.) After it boils, lower heat slightly and gradually add 1 to 2 tablespoons (15 to 30 ml) lemon juice, stirring constantly. As soon as the milk separates into milk solids and a soft-greenish liquid, remove from the heat. Drain in a large sieve lined with several layers of cheesecloth. Reserve the liquid for cooking grains or soups. Lay the cheesecloth containing the cheese on a cutting board and place a heavy object like a skillet over it for 45 to 60 minutes to further drain and solidify the cheese. Remove cheese and cut into cubes. It can be stored, covered, in the refrigerator for 2 to 3 days.

To prepare Indian cheese balls: Prepare cheese as above, except place a heavy object over it for 15 to 20 minutes only. The cheese need not be completely solid in this case, but should hold its shape when formed into balls. Add sugar to sweeten it lightly. Tear off a portion and form into a smooth ball, 1 inch (2.5 cm) in diameter, by rolling between the palms of your hand. Serve these balls along with fresh fruits for a snack or as a light dessert.

INDIAN SPLIT CHICK-PEA (CHANA DAL) ▪ The hulled split chick-pea is prized in India for its nutty flavor. It outwardly resembles the yellow split pea commonly found in Western supermarkets, but has a more appealing taste. This versatile dal is featured as the main ingredient in numerous savory soups and stews throughout India. In addition, it is roasted and ground to form chick-pea flour, *besan*, which is widely used by Indi-an cooks as a thickener, in batter, and confections. This dal is available in Indian groceries. Do not substitute yellow split peas.

JACKFRUIT (JAKFRUIT) ▪ Believed to be one of the largest commercially grown fruit in the world; it is found in India and throughout Southeast Asia. The fruit is oval-shaped and has a thick, warty green skin. Both the flesh, which has a sweet, exotic flavor, and the nutlike seeds are edible. The seeds can be eaten roasted or steamed like chestnuts. Fresh jackfruit is not readily available in the West, but may be found dried in well-stocked supermarkets or canned in Asian markets. In either form, jackfruit adds a fine flavor to desserts. Fresh or dried mango is a substitute.

JÍCAMA ▪ A large tuber with a coarse brown skin and edible white flesh that is crunchy, juicy, and faintly sweet, similar in flavor to fresh water chestnuts. Eat it raw in salads (sprinkled with ground red pepper) or use it like a potato. It retains much of its crispness when cooked.

KALONJI SEEDS (NIGELLA) ▪ These blue-black seeds with a peppery, onionlike flavor resemble onion seeds but are not related. They add a distinctive taste and crunch to Indian breads and vegetable preparations. They are most often used whole, occasionally ground.

KASHA (BUCKWHEAT GROATS) ▪ In the United States, "kasha" generally refers to buckwheat, the seed of a plant. In Russia and Eastern Europe, "kasha" means porridge, and can be made with other grains such as bulgur or barley. The nutlike buckwheat, which has a crunchy texture, can be cooked like a grain. Health-food stores and many supermarkets carry kasha.

KEWRA ESSENCE (KEWRA WATER) ▪ Perfumed essence made from the flowers of the screwpine tree, used mostly in flavoring desserts, occasionally in fancy rice dishes. Only a few drops of this highly aromatic liquid are needed. It is sold bottled in Indian groceries.

KOHLRABI ▪ A light green to purplish red vegetable that has a juicy, crisp flesh and resembles a turnip in both flavor and appearance. The leaves are edible and taste like kale. Peel the tough outer woody skin from kohlrabi and steam the flesh or use it in other vegetable preparations as you would potato, turnip, or rutabaga.

LEMON GRASS ▪ A tall grass with a lemony flavor. It is similar to green onions in appearance and is used as a seasoning in Southeast Asia. Discard the tough upper ends of the reedlike stalks and use only the bottom 5 to 6 inches (12.5 to 15 cm). It's available both fresh and dried (called *sereh*) in Asian markets, but for best flavor use only the fresh.

LILY FLOWERS (LILY BUDS, GOLDEN LILIES, GOLDEN NEEDLES) ▪ The golden brown dried lily buds have a subtle, tart flavor, an interesting texture, and are considered nutritious. They are an essential ingredient in Chinese sweet and sour soup. Before adding to a dish, soak in warm water for 10 minutes or until soft. Cut off tough ends, chop into small pieces, or tie into a knot for a decorative look. They are sold in packages in Chinese markets.

LYCHEE (LITCHI) ▪ A thin, bumpy, rosy skin hides the aromatic juicy white pulp of this tropical fruit. Remove the central seed and enjoy the rich flesh as is, in fruit salads, or in certain Chinese meat dishes. Select fruits that are relatively heavy for their size. Since the fresh fruit is not always readily available, buy canned lychee from Asian markets for preparing desserts.

MANGO POWDER (AAMCHOOR) ▪ This light brown powder is used sparingly in various Indian dishes to add a complex tartness. It is made by sundrying green, unripe mangoes and then grinding them to a powder. Do not substitute lemon or lime.

MANGOSTEEN ▪ A tropical fruit, not related in any way to mango. Reddish purple when ripe, it has a snowy white flesh similar in flavor, texture, and appearance to a lychee. It's not yet available fresh in the United States, so buy the canned variety in Asian markets and drain off the syrup before using.

MILLET ▪ Tiny, pale yellow, round, whole grain, one of the oldest cultivated cereals known in the world. It grows well in poor soil and in harsh climatic conditions. It has been used as a staple in Africa, northern China, and some parts of India since ancient times. Though previously used as birdseed and cattle grain in the United States, it is now gaining popularity with people.

MUNG BEAN ▪ A small round bean with a green, black, or brown jacket, familiar in East Asian cooking as bean sprouts. When split, the beans are yellow in color. Either whole or split, the mung bean is one of the most widely used dals (legumes) in India.

MUSHROOMS ▪ Mushrooms add superb flavor, texture, and a rich quality to dishes. To clean these delicate objects, use only a little water. I rely on a mushroom cleaning brush, available in many kitchen stores. Besides the common button mushroom, some exotic varieties are used in this book.

Enoki—A slender-stemmed, delicate white, slightly fruity mushroom with tiny pin-drop caps. Cut off the heavy base, separate the fragile strands, and use them to decorate a salad; or sauté lightly in oil to garnish meat dishes.

Oyster—A fan-shaped and delicate mushroom that acquires a buttery taste when cooked. Sauté lightly with other vegetables.

Shiitake (forest mushroom)—A large, flat, dark brown velvety mushroom that grows on logs. It has a rich, meaty texture and a faintly musky, woodsy flavor. Widely sold dried in Asian markets and fancy supermarkets, it is increasingly available fresh. Separate the stem from the cap and discard its tough base. Cut the cap into slices and add to stir-fries. Chop the stem into small pieces before using.

NAPA CABBAGE (NAPPA, CHINESE CABBAGE, OR CELERY CABBAGE) ▪ This brassica, a Chinese native, is creamy white or pale green in color and barrel-shaped. It is more tender than regular cabbage, cooks more quickly, and has a delicate flavor. Also excellent shredded and served raw in salads.

OILS ▪ Even though the use of oil in this book is minimal, oils provide nutrients essential to health and greatly enhance the flavor of many dishes. Choose them carefully for their taste and nutritional qualities. For maximum flavor, cook with one of the plainer oils; then at the end of cooking splash a few drops of highly aromatic walnut, hazelnut, or avocado oil over the dish and toss to disperse it. To preserve freshness, store all oil in the refrigerator.

You can prepare flavorful infusions by soaking fresh garlic cloves, sun-dried tomatoes, Szechuan peppercorns, or fresh herbs in extra-virgin olive oil or a combination of olive and Chinese sesame or other oils (such as canola or avocado). Use this oil in sautéeing vegetables, in vinaigrettes, or serve warm with crusty bread.

Avocado oil—A clean, light-flavored oil best used in preparing salad dressings; also delightful tossed with freshly cooked pasta. It thickens easily when whisked with vinegar. Look for this oil in well-stocked supermarkets.

Canola oil—This oil is high in both monounsaturates and polyunsaturates, and low in saturated fats. It is relatively flavorless and can be used for general-purpose cooking. Its high smoke point makes it suitable for deep-frying.

Hazelnut oil—This fine-flavored oil is excellent in vinaigrettes, but it would be a waste to use it as a cooking oil.

Olive oil—I use this monounsaturated oil often. It is essental to the cooking of the Mediterranean and the Middle East. Because of its strong aroma and flavor it can clash with Indian spices, but it can be used in selected dishes. Extra-virgin, the finest olive oil, is pressed from fresh ripe olives. This is pale yellow or greenish yellow in color and has a delicate aroma. It's ideal for salad dressings. Subsequent pressings yield lesser quality oils, which can be used for cooking.

Mustard oil—This golden brown aromatic oil from India enhances fish, dal, and vegetable dishes. Indian groceries sell both pure mustard oil, which is stronger, and mustard-flavored blended oil, a milder mixture of mustard and soybean oil. Use them interchangeably in these recipes.

Sesame oil—An oil that comes in two basic forms. A pale yellow oil, very delicate in aroma and flavor, is widely used in South India (where it's known as *gingely*) and the Middle East. A darker form, which is golden brown in color and has a nut-like aroma, is used sparingly as a flavoring in Chinese cooking.

Unrefined safflower oil—A crude, monounsaturated oil that is extracted, distilled, and bottled. The amount of processing that it undergoes is less than that of refined oil. Use in dressings and light cooking.

Walnut oil—An oil with a warm, nutty flavor. Use it in salad dressings and when briefly cooking vegetables.

OLIVES ▪ One of the most ancient of the cultivated fruits, the olive is green when unripe and black when ripe. In this book, I use purple-black Kalamata (Calamata) olives, which are firm, juicy, and flavorful and sold pickled in vinegar in gourmet shops and some supermarkets. Use this intensely flavored fruit in moderation, because of its oil content as well as its propensity to overpower a dish.

PALM HEARTS (HEARTS OF PALM) ▪ Creamy white tender shoots of palm popular in Latin America as a salad ingredient; unlike palm oil, they contain no saturated fat. Sold in cans in fancy supermarkets.

PINE NUTS (PIÑON NUTS, PIGNOLI) ▪ A soft, white, oval nut that looks like a large grain of rice and has a texture and flavor resembling macadamia nuts. Most often lightly toasted and used as a garnish. The longer and thinner variety is more flavorful than the shorter, rounder type.

PLANTAIN ▪ Native to many tropical countries, this is a close cousin to the banana but is slightly larger, has a coarser texture, and a higher starch content. The fruit is not eaten raw, but cooked like a vegetable. When plantain is unripe, the skin is pale green, turning slowly to yellow and then brown with black specks as it ripens. It's available in Latin American markets and well-stocked supermarkets that carry ethnic products.

PLUM SAUCE ▪ A sweet, hot sauce from China, made with plums, chiles, sugar, and spices. It is used as a dip, for brushing on crêpes, or in cooking. Available in Asian markets.

POLENTA ▪ Degerminated yellow (not white) cornmeal that is a staple in northern Italy. You can substitute yellow corn grits, sold in natural-food stores.

POMEGRANATE ▪ A special variety of this fruit yields plump, translucent red seeds, used in the Middle East and India to impart a fragrant sourness to dishes. The seeds are sold packaged in Indian groceries.

QUINOA ▪ A tiny, beige, round ancient grain that comes from Peru and other South American countries. It has one of the highest protein contents of any grain and becomes light and fluffy when cooked. Rinse several times before using to remove a naturally occurring bitter residue called saponin. The bland grain takes on the character of other ingredients in a dish.

RASAM POWDER ▪ Indian groceries sell a ground mixture of cumin seeds, coriander seeds, fenugreek seeds, dried curry leaves, asafetida powder, red pepper, and black mustard seeds. It is used to season *rasam*, a thin, spicy broth from South India that is eaten with rice.

RICE PAPER ▪ Tissue-thin, transparent round sheets made of rice, the size of a tortilla. Sold in packets in Asian markets. Used in Vietnamese cooking for wrapping seafood or vegetables.

SAMBAL OELECK (SAMBAL ULEK) ▪ A ground paste of red chile peppers used not just for hotness, but for flavor. Available in Asian markets, particularly those that carry Indonesian products. My favorite brand is Yeo's, which is not overly hot, so you can use as much as 1 tablespoon (15 ml) for a serving of four. Red chile paste available in Indian stores is a substitute, but can be much hotter. You can also grind seeded, dried red chiles (available on supermarket spice shelves or packaged in Latin American markets) with water. When adding any of these chile pastes to a dish, adjust the amount according to taste.

SEAWEED ▪ The following types, referred to in this book, are sold in Asian markets and natural-food stores:

Kombu (kelp)—A basic ingredient for Japanese soup stock, kombu is used mainly for flavoring. Rinse, chop into small pieces, and add to the broth as it simmers.

Nori—A tender, purple-black seaweed dried in paper-thin sheets, used most commonly in sushi and also as a garnish for rice or soups. Use the seasoned variety and toast it before use.

To toast nori: Place several sheets of seasoned nori on an ungreased skillet over low heat. Within a few seconds, the sheets will change color and become crisper. Remove immediately to avoid burning.

Wakame—A long, curly, dark green dried seaweed that can be softened in water and used as a garnish in soups and salads.

SESAME SEED ▪ Both the black and white seeds are used as a garnish when roasted. Roasted sesame seeds are available bottled in Asian markets, but I find that toasting the raw seeds just before using releases the utmost flavor. Ground sesame seeds flavor and thicken sauces.

To prepare ground sesame seeds: Place white sesame seeds on an ungreased griddle or skillet over medium-low heat. Toast them until they are lightly browned, a few minutes, stirring often. Remove from the heat and grind to a powder in a spice grinder or in a mortar and pestle.

SORREL ▪ An ancient plant used in Europe and the Middle East. The leaves resemble spinach and have a sour, slightly bitter flavor. Best when young and tender, they can be cooked with other vegetables.

SOY MILK ▪ A creamy white liquid made from soybeans. It has the same consistency as dairy milk and can replace cow's milk in many recipes (except where milk needs to be thickened). Because it lacks the natural sweetness of cow's milk, seasonings need to be adjusted. Use it soon after buying as it spoils within a few days.

SPELT ▪ An ancient grain, a type of wheat, much appreciated in medieval Europe. Those who are allergic to the gluten in wheat can often eat spelt. The nutty grain is now reemerging in natural-food stores in the form of flour and pasta.

SZECHUAN PEPPERCORNS ▪ Also called "flower pepper" because they resemble flowers about to open. They are slightly pungent and have a unique flavor. The berries grow on a small tree native to China and are not related to peppers. Asian markets sell them. Roast them on an ungreased griddle until slightly darkened but not burnt. Grind to a fine powder. Freshly ground black pepper can be substituted.

TAMARIND ▪ The tamarind tree bears pods about 8 inches (20 cm) long, which are green when young and dark brown when fully ripe. Inside the pod are shiny seeds surrounded by a brown, intensely sour pulp that is much appreciated in India, Southeast Asia, and Latin America for its complex tart flavor. Asian markets and Indian groceries sell tamarind as a dried block that needs further processing. You can buy the ready-made tamarind concentrate in a jar in Indian groceries. Lemon or lime is not a substitute for tamarind.

To prepare tamarind puree: If tamarind is a major ingredient in a recipe, I prepare tamarind puree from scratch using a block of dried tamarind. The puree has a flavor superior to that of the concentrate. For this purpose, buy a block of tamarind that feels slightly soft to the touch. Chop off a $2\frac{1}{2} \times 1 \times 1$ inch ($6 \times 2.5 \times 2.5$ cm) piece from the block and soak it in $\frac{1}{2}$ cup (125 ml) hot water in a nonmetallic bowl for 5 to 30 minutes. (The amount of time will vary with the hardness of the tamarind.) Using your fingers, extract as much of the pulp as you can. Strain to remove the seeds and fibers, if any, and discard them. Store the puree covered in the refrigerator in a nonmetallic container (to prevent an acidic reaction), but use within a day or two. Yields $\frac{1}{2}$ cup (125 ml).

Tamarind concentrate: If only a small amount of tamarind is needed in a recipe,

I use the concentrate, which requires no preparation. It has a sticky quality but dissolves readily when stirred into hot liquid.

TEMPEH ▪ A cultured soy food with active enzymes to make it more digestible. Tempeh is rich in protein and is one of the few vegetarian sources of vitamin B-12. It has a meaty texture. Tempeh can also be made of other beans and grains instead of soy.

TOFU ▪ Square cakes of fermented soybean that are fragile and have the consistency of custard. Sold as "soft," "firm," or "silken," depending on its texture. Tofu is a protein source for vegetarians.

TURMERIC ▪ A bright yellow root, sold as powder, good for both coloring and flavoring. It is used widely in Indian cooking, especially in fish and vegetable dishes.

URAD DAL ▪ The whole beans have a grayish black jacket and are creamy white inside. They are sometimes called black gram but should not be confused with black beans. The split urad is yellowish white in color and is used both as a legume and as a seasoning. Both are available in Indian groceries.

VINEGAR ▪ The word "vinegar" comes from two French words, *vin aigre,* meaning "sour wine." I use several types of vinegar in this book.

Rice vinegar—This vinegar is distilled from rice and can be either white or red. The white rice vinegar, which has a mild, sweet flavor, is ideal for salad dressings and cooking. My favorite is the Japanese variety (Marukan brand). Sold in Asian markets and some supermarkets.

Balsamic vinegar—This Italian vinegar, which is aged longer than other vinegars, is naturally sweet and has a distinctive flavor. To prepare it, special types of grapes from the Modena region of Italy are placed in wooden casks for two or more years. The casks are changed several times so that the vinegar absorbs the aroma from the woods. Sprinkle this flavorful vinegar over fresh fruits or a green salad as a dressing. Available in well-stocked supermarkets and gourmet food shops.

Raspberry vinegar—A rich red vinegar flavored with raspberries, milder than red wine vinegar. Excellent in salad dressings. Available in gourmet food shops.

WASABI (JAPANESE HORSERADISH) ▪ Asian groceries sell this green powder, which is stronger than the supermarket horseradish. Mix a small amount with a little water and use as a table condiment.

WHITE POPPY SEEDS ▪ The creamy-white seeds of a variety of poppy grown in India. They add texture and a warm nuttiness to fish, meat, and vegetables, and also act as a sauce thickener. Look for them in Indian groceries. Blue-gray poppy seeds, common in European baked goods, are not used in India.

To prepare poppy seed paste: Lightly toast 1 tablespoon (15 ml) white poppy seeds on an ungreased skillet for a few minutes or until slightly darkened. Place in a mortar and pound a few times to crush them slightly. Add 2 tablespoons (30 ml) warm water and grind again to a thick paste.

YUCA (YUCCA, MANIOC, OR CASSAVA) ▪ A root vegetable that is a staple in West Africa and in many parts of Latin America; familiar in its processed form as tapioca. Peel the brittle brown bark and its pink underlayer from the root, and cook the starchy white interior like potato. When cooked, yuca has a soft, sticky, buttery quality.

Breakfast and Light Meals

●●●●●●●●●●●●●●●●●●●●●●●●●●●●●

There's something universally spellbinding about dawn, regardless of where you travel. A lingering darkness, a still mist, the somnolence of the night can all hide the nature of a place—masking vistas and the shapes of buildings, subduing colors and smells. Such similarities of early morning exist whether you're in New Delhi or Newport Beach.

But breakfasts tend to be a unique experience depending on location. While I'm traveling, it's usually the morning meal that reminds me I am away from home. An unfamiliar plate can jolt me to a rude awakening or set a mood of mystery for the day.

In European culture, light, sweet scones, pastries, and croissants are usually favored in the morning. Breakfast is distinct from main meals. Spices are usually absent. To be offered a bowl of chili or chowder in Europe at sunrise would be shocking.

In other parts of the world, however, breakfast is often soup, dumplings, or crêpes, a preview of meals to arrive later in the day. A Japanese breakfast, consisting of small bites of broiled salmon, grated daikon, steamed rice, miso soup, and fresh tropical fruit, is a mini-version of their typical evening meal. Mexicans often greet the day with the same beans, salsas, and fresh tortillas that are standard fare at supper. A Malaysian woman told me she still misses her favorite childhood breakfast of coconut rice and spiced greens now that she lives in the United States. In much of the world, the first meal of the day is likely to include a savory item and at least one protein source, and it usually includes vegetables.

There are as many breakfast habits as types of people. While in Calcutta, I often began each day eating at a small, simple restaurant called The Royal Court. This plebeian eatery is renowned for attracting people from all walks of life with the quality of its food. At breakfast, The Royal Court offers the freshest of flat breads, thick homemade yogurt, chunky potatoes, and a specially brewed spicy tea that is so popular it is served in huge glasses.

I once overheard a man sitting at a nearby table order flat bread and mutton curry. It was 7:00 A.M. and I wondered why he'd eat meat so early. When his dish of hot, steaming bread from the tandoor and fragrant spicy mutton arrived, the man tucked his legs into a lotus position on the chair and devoured with great relish what, to his palate, was clearly a perfect breakfast. For him this was, indeed, a royal court.

Soon, I began approaching breakfast from the same multicultural perspective as dinner. Rather than ethnic tradition, my mood and energy requirements now dictate the food I select. Sometimes I ease into the day with a slice of Date-Nut Squash Bread. If I exercise in the morning, a simple Basmati Rice Congee serves me better. On busy days when the morning sustenance must last until dinner, I breakfast on Tofu-Mushroom Scramble. These recipes can also be used for lunch or dinner.

By varying my first meal of the day, I consume a broader set of nutrients. When the freshness of the dawn combines with such an eclectic menu, breakfast becomes a wonder. ✳

✳ Papaya Porridge ✳
INTERNATIONAL

The porridge that follows is a substantial meal with a delicate note of sweet ripe papaya. It was my usual order at a pleasant eatery on Calcutta's Sudder Street.

Sudder Street is lined with small private hotels, many of which are still run as they were during the days of British occupation. European tourists jam these hotels. In spacious dining rooms, uniformed waiters pour English custard sauce over mango halves, and "Made in England" cottage cream cookies are served with tea. Some say the British never left this street.

On Sudder Street, you will find the Blue Sky Café. This funky café, which caters largely to a youthful Western clientele, serves breakfast, small meals, and tropical fruit drinks. The café is tiny and plain: just one room and a closet-sized adjunct whose only decorations are faded posters advertising scenes of India. But the place is always bustling. You sit where there's room at a crowded table, seeing faces from all over the globe and hearing languages that are just noisy sounds to you. Eventually the waiter takes your order, then hustles to another table for more orders. He doesn't write anything down, but somehow the correct food appears and is placed before you and is so good you can't wait to return. Next morning you arrive earlier, yawning and rubbing your eyes, and the waiter recites what you ordered the day before, turning it into a question.

3 cups (750 ml) water (approx.; check instructions on the cereal package)
1 cup (250 ml) multigrain hot cereal (such as eight- or ten-grain)
2 tablespoons (30 ml) toasted, chopped cashews or other nuts of choice
2 tablespoons (30 ml) raisins or pitted, chopped dates or other dried fruits
1/2 cup (125 ml) lowfat or nonfat milk, or soy milk
1 small ripe banana
Sweetener of choice (regular sugar, palm sugar, honey, brown rice syrup; optional)
1 medium-sized ripe papaya, peeled, seeded, cut in chunks

Bring water to a boil in a steep, medium-sized pan. Add cereal, cashews, and raisins and bring to a boil again. Lower heat, cover, and simmer until all water is absorbed and cereal is tender, 15 minutes or so. (Timing will vary with the type and brand of cereal.) Add milk and heat the mixture through. Peel and slice the banana and add to the cereal. Cook for a minute. Add sweetener. (With certain brands of soy milk, you'll need to sweeten the cereal a bit.) Remove from heat and top with papaya. Best served piping hot.

2 large servings

Serving Suggestions: This porridge is a meal unto itself when served with Honey Ginger Tea (page 292) and fresh-squeezed orange juice.

✳ Noor Jahani Polenta ✳

ITALY

Polenta, a thick, savory puddinglike dish from northern Italy, is made by slowly stirring cornmeal into boiling water. In that simple form, polenta is roughly the equivalent of mashed potatoes. When cooled, it becomes thick enough to cut into squares. These squares are often topped with cheese or tomato sauce and grilled. Polenta often takes the place of bread in an Italian meal, though not usually at breakfast.

In this recipe, I prepare a sweetened version of polenta for breakfast by cooking cornmeal Indian style. I boil the milk until it reduces in volume and thickens before I add cornmeal. Then I incorporate almonds, raisins, and cardamom for further enrichment.

I named the recipe to honor Indian Empress Noor Jahan, "the light of the world." As the consort of seventeenth-century Mogul Emperor Jahangir, she exerted considerable influence in the affairs of the state, and she symbolized beauty, grace, and fine taste during her lifetime.

2 1/2   cups (625 ml) lowfat milk (don't use nonfat)
      Pinch saffron threads, soaked in 1 tablespoon (15 ml) warm water or
         milk for 10 minutes (see *Note 1*)
2 1/2   cups (625 ml) water
  1/2   cup (125 ml) polenta (see *Note 2*)
   1   tablespoon (15 ml) slivered raw almonds or cashew halves
   1   tablespoon (15 ml) golden raisins
  1/4   cup (60 ml) regular sugar, or date or maple sugar (to taste)
  1/2   teaspoon (2 ml) vanilla extract

1. Lightly oil the bottom and sides of a medium-sized, steep-sided pan to prevent milk from sticking. Heat milk over medium to high heat until it comes to a boil. Lower heat slightly and stir vigorously until it subsides. Add saffron. Cook over medium-high heat, stirring often, for 8 to 10 minutes or until reduced to about 1 cup (250 ml). Remove from heat and keep covered.

2. In a separate medium-sized pan over moderate heat, bring 2 1/2 cups water to a boil. Add polenta gradually, stirring continuously. Add almonds and raisins. Cook, stirring, until the mixture thickens and forms a lump around the spoon, 12 to 30 minutes. (Timing will vary with the type of polenta.) Reheat the thickened milk,

add to the polenta, and cook until milk is absorbed, 5 to 8 minutes. Add sugar and vanilla. (If using date sugar, note that this sugar will not dissolve completely but will add an interesting crunch to the finished dish.) Taste for sweetness and if necessary add more sugar. Remove from heat. You can serve it immediately as a pudding.

3. (Optional) Transfer polenta to a 9-inch (22.5-cm) pie tin or an 8-inch (20-cm) square cake pan. Allow to cool to room temperature, then refrigerate for 30 minutes or until polenta is set. Bake at 400°F (200°C, gas marks 6) for 5 to 10 minutes or until thoroughly heated. Cut in squares or wedges and serve warm.

4 servings

Note 1: Saffron will add a distinct bouquet, and is especially inviting if you're serving the polenta as a dessert.

Note 2: Although instant polenta cooks in 5 minutes, it has a soft, mushy quality and a less solid texture than regular polenta. Yellow corn grits, sold in natural-food stores and gourmet shops, have the requisite coarseness and cook in 15 to 20 minutes.

Serving Suggestions: Polenta is portable, and you can carry it on your morning walk or bicycle ride. It makes a delicious brunch when flanked by a savory omelet and home-fries. You can also serve it as a dessert topped with Dream Yogurt (Sweet Variation; page 213) following a vegetarian meal. Take any leftovers to the office for a light lunch.

FRUIT VARIATIONS: If serving polenta as a pudding, try preparing one of these quick fruit sauces for sprinkling on top: Puree fresh mango pulp or strawberries in a blender. Or prepare an apricot sauce by cooking chopped dried apricot in a little water until the fruit softens, then whirling it in a blender until smooth.

VARIATION: POLENTA FLAN An unusual and delicious flan. Follow Step 1 of Shah Jahani Flan (page 270) to coat the bottoms of 6 custard cups with caramelized sugar syrup. (You can do this before you start to prepare the polenta.) Prepare Noor Jahani Polenta up to Step 2. Transfer polenta to a large bowl and allow to cool to room temperature. Take 2 large eggs (or 4 egg whites) and beat lightly in a medium bowl. Add to polenta, beating with a fork until well mixed. Now follow Step 4 of Shah Jahani Flan to bake the polenta. Bake at 350°F (180°C, gas marks 4) for 40 to 45 minutes or until polenta is set. Invert onto a plate as described in the Shah Jahani Flan recipe. Serve at breakfast or for dessert surrounded by fresh ripe peaches or kiwi.

✳ Pongal Pudding ✳

SOUTH INDIA/UNITED STATES

During the harvest festival of Pongal in India's southern state of Tamil Nadu, people place a delicious milk-based pudding composed of mung beans and newly harvested rice before the Sun god as an expression of appreciation for a bounteous harvest.

This protein-rich pudding is high on my list of tasty, nutritious breakfasts. In the recipe that follows, I have replaced rice with quinoa for its higher protein content. Ghee, clarified butter, which is one of the traditional ingredients, is absent. Instead I derive flavors from such American basics as pecans, vanilla, and maple syrup.

Pongal means "exuberance," symbolized by the frothing of the milk. On the day of the festival, in every kitchen in Tamil Nadu you'll find a pot of this simmering milk pudding. People greet each other by asking, "Has it boiled over?" The response is always, "Yes, it has," meaning that it will be a prosperous year.

4   cups (1 liter) 2% lowfat milk (don't use nonfat)
5   whole cardamom pods, bruised
1/4 cup (60 ml) toasted chopped pecans
1   tablespoon (15 ml) golden raisins
2   tablespoons (30 ml) quinoa, rinsed thoroughly several times
1   tablespoon (15 ml) yellow split mung beans, rinsed thoroughly several times
3/4 cup (185 ml) water
1/2 teaspoon (2 ml) vanilla extract
2   tablespoons (30 ml) pure maple syrup (to taste; see *Note*)

Garnish: A few unsalted pistachios, crushed (optional; added for color)

1. To thicken the milk: Lightly oil the bottom and sides of a large, steep-sided pan to prevent milk from sticking. (A pan with a wide surface area will help to cook the milk faster.) Over medium-high to high heat, bring milk to a boil. Lower the heat to stop the milk from boiling over and stir vigorously until the foaming subsides. Add cardamom, pecans, and raisins. Turn heat to medium and bring to a boil again. Cook, uncovered, stirring often to break the skin that forms on the surface, until reduced to about 1 cup (250 ml), 15 to 20 minutes. Keep the milk on the edge of foaming. Watch carefully as it rises over and over again, stirring until the foam subsides. Remove from heat and keep covered.

2. Bring quinoa, mung beans, and water to a boil in a small pan. Reduce heat and simmer, covered, until all water is absorbed and both quinoa and mung beans are tender, 10 to 15 minutes.

3. Reheat the milk to a simmer and add to it the quinoa-bean mixture. Cook, uncovered, for a few minutes to heat the mixture through. Remove from heat. Add vanilla and maple syrup and mix well to disperse flavors. Garnish with pistachios.

4 small servings

Note: Maple syrup will darken the pudding and give it a "cooked cereal" look. When offering Pongal Pudding as a dessert, swirl maple syrup decoratively on top of individual servings rather than mixing it in.

Serving Suggestions: Accompany the pudding with fresh fruits—ripe peaches, strawberries, or raspberries. Try with whole wheat toast or warmed chapati and Mulled Apple Tea (page 291) at breakfast. Enjoy as a light dessert preceded by Roasted Tikka Potatoes (page 243), Gujarati Greens (page 66), and some papads.

✳ Millet Pudding with Cashews and Currants ✳
INTERNATIONAL

When I first arrived in Teheran, Iran, for a year's stay, I immediately began looking for an Indian grocery. A local sent me to a small shop run by a blind Indian man. Every available inch of space in his store was taken up by gunnysacks filled with flour, grains, and dried beans. On the narrow shelves large jars of spices were precariously balanced. I needed an extensive list of ingredients necessary to start an Indian kitchen in my new home; everything from such basics as cumin and turmeric, cashews and dried fruits, to exotics such as saffron and kewra water. The shopkeeper located each item for me using his highly developed senses of touch and smell. I was amazed at his efficiency.

I am invariably reminded of his shop whenever I prepare this millet dish, which is studded with cashews and dried fruit and intensely flavored by saffron and kewra water. Millet is one of the most nutritious of all grains and is easily digestible. This millet pudding is not only delicious but sweet enough to double as a dessert.

    4 cups (1 liter) 2% lowfat milk (don't use nonfat)
    1 teaspoon (5 ml) ground cardamom (see *Note*)
       Pinch saffron threads
  $^1/_2$ cup (125 ml) millet
    2 cups (500 ml) hot water
    1 tablespoon (15 ml) dried currants
  $^1/_4$ cup (60 ml) raw cashew halves, ground to a coarse powder in a blender or
        food processor (measured before grinding)
  $^1/_4$ cup (60 ml) regular sugar, date sugar, or sucanat
       Dash kewra water

1. Lightly oil the bottom and sides of a large, steep-sided pan to prevent milk from sticking. I use a $10 \times 4^1/_2$ (25 × 11 cm) pan; its wide surface area helps evaporate the milk quickly. Heat milk over medium to high heat until it comes to a boil. Stir vigorously until foaming subsides. Add cardamom. Cook over medium-high heat, stirring often. In 18 to 20 minutes the mixture will acquire a chowderlike consistency and will be reduced to about 1 cup (250 ml). Add the saffron threads, making sure they don't tangle. Remove from heat and keep covered. (Saffron will color the thickened milk as it sits.)

2. To toast the millet: Place the grain in a large skillet over medium-low heat. Shake the skillet often so that the grains at the bottom don't burn. Cook for 5 to 7 minutes or until slightly darkened in color.

    Place millet in a large pan and pour the 2 cups (500 ml) hot water over it. Cover and bring to a boil. Lower the heat slightly. Add currants and ground cashews. Cover and simmer for 18 to 20 minutes, or until all water is absorbed and millet is tender and fluffy. Remove from heat.

3. When the millet is ready, reheat the milk to a simmer. Place millet over low heat and pour the milk mixture over it. Stir and cook just until the mixture is heated through. (Overcooking will dry out the millet.) Add sugar. (If using date sugar, note that it doesn't dissolve completely, but adds an interesting crunchiness.) Remove from heat, allow to cool slightly, and stir in kewra water. Best served warm but also good at room temperature. If it's necessary to reheat, dilute the pudding with a little milk.

4 servings

Note: The flavor of cardamom blends particularly well with millet. You can, however, substitute $^1/_2$ teaspoon (2 ml) nutmeg for cardamom.

Serving Suggestions: Top with sliced banana and enjoy at breakfast with a cup of Honey Ginger Tea (page 292). Offer this millet pudding also as a dessert following a vegetarian meal. Some entrée selections that go beautifully are: Bengali Black Beans (page 82); Sweet, Sour, and Smoky Potatoes (page 63); and Greens Ratatouille (page 94).

✳ Sunrise Potatoes ✳

BANGLADESH

These potatoes will open your eyes wide with their mildly spiced, appetite-arousing taste and sunny color. Whip up this easy recipe in the morning or get a head start by doing one of the steps the night before.

The dish comes from Bangladesh. Ask a Bangladeshi what he eats in the morning and the response often is "*rooti, aloo,*" flat bread and potatoes. One man from a Bangladesh village says he is wakened each morning in his hut by the sound of potatoes sizzling in hot oil and the fragrant smell of hot breads baking in a clay oven. He bathes in a nearby lake before sitting down to this simple *nasta,* breakfast.

1 1/2 pounds (750 g) peeled or unpeeled potatoes, about 5 medium, cut into
      1-inch (2.5-cm) cubes (see *Note for the Gardener*)
2 tablespoons (30 ml) mustard oil
2 whole dried red chiles
1/4 teaspoon (1 ml) Indian five-spice
1 cup (250 ml) thinly sliced onion
1/4 teaspoon (1 ml) turmeric
   Salt
2 tablespoons (30 ml) fresh lime juice
   Garnish: Thinly sliced jalapeño (optional)

1. Steam the potatoes 15 to 20 minutes or until tender but not breaking. (You can do this step the night before; refrigerate the potatoes overnight.)
2. Heat oil in a 12-inch (30-cm) skillet over moderate heat until a light haze forms. Add red chiles and five-spice and fry until the seeds start to pop. Add onion and cook until it is translucent. Sprinkle turmeric over the spices. Add potatoes. Cook, turning gently but often, until potatoes and onions are richly browned but not burnt, about 5 minutes. Remove from heat. Discard red chiles. Add salt to taste and sprinkle with the lime juice. Scatter jalapeño slices on top and serve.

4 servings

Note for the Gardener: My favorite potato for this dish is Yukon Gold, a variety that matures quickly and is one of the earlier potatoes in the northern climate where I live. The buttery yellow flesh readily absorbs the delicate lime-turmeric sauce. My husband likes the potato-and-spice combination so much that he calls it "East meets North."

Serving Suggestions: For breakfast, serve with warm tortillas accompanied by a soft boiled or poached egg and Mulled Apple Tea (page 291). (To warm tortillas, place them on an ungreased griddle or skillet over high heat for a few seconds, turning them once. "Touch it, turn it, out," is how a man who had lived in Mexico for many years described this process to me.) For a light vegetarian supper, it is delightful accompanied by jasmine rice (cooked with chopped fresh cilantro and garlic), Eggplant Caponata International (page 78), and Mint-Basil Chutney (page 224).

✳ Basmati Rice Congee ✳

CHINA

Congee (also called *jook*) is a rice soup that is popular throughout East Asia. In southern China, workers consume this thick, flavorful gruel for breakfast, and sip it at midnight as a snack. In Japan, congee is the equivalent of Western chicken soup, a warm home-cure for the ailing.

This versatile congee is traditionally made by slow-simmering rice in plenty of water for hours until the grains disintegrate. Poach slivers of fish or other seafood in this soup during the last few minutes of cooking and it will make a one-dish meal all by itself. Add shredded cooked chicken, duck, or pork to offer yet another set of tastes. To reduce the cooking time, I puree the rice in a blender as soon as it begins to soften. This step surprises my traditional Chinese friends, but they seem to enjoy my version of this breakfast soup. I also substitute Basmati rice for plain white rice to make the dish nutty and chewy. Before serving, I scatter crushed papads on top for an Indian version of croutons, along with the customary gingerroot slivers. The spicy crunch of the papads contrasts with the bland creaminess of the soup.

Once while traveling by train through mainland China, I breakfasted on congee and a small bowl of peanuts around 10:00 A.M. Since then, congee has become my preferred midmorning snack.

$^1/_2$ cup (125 ml) white Basmati rice, rinsed several times, drained

2 cups (500 ml) Chicken Stock (page 44) or a 14$^1/_2$-ounce (411-g) can chicken broth, defatted (see "To defat canned chicken broth," page 45)

1$^1/_2$ cups (375 ml) water

1 tablespoon (15 ml) thinly sliced gingerroot

$^1/_2$ teaspoon (2 ml) low-sodium soy sauce (or more, according to taste)

Salt

Garnish:

2 scallions, green part only, thinly sliced

2 papads (preferably chile and garlic flavored), baked, crushed (see *Note*)

Chopped cilantro (optional)

Combine rice, chicken stock, and $^1/_2$ cup (125 ml) water in a large, steep pan. Cover and bring to a boil. Lower heat slightly; simmer, covered, until the rice is soft, 15 to 18 minutes. Process the mixture in a blender or food processor using the remaining 1 cup (250 ml) water until relatively smooth. You may need to do this in batches. Return to the pan and add gingerroot. Cover and bring to a simmer. Remove from heat. Add soy sauce and salt to taste. Serve immediately, garnished with scallions, crushed papads, and cilantro. If allowed to stand, the soup will thicken. Dilute slightly with water before reheating.

4 small servings

Note: To bake papads: Place the papads, non-overlapping on an ungreased cookie sheet. Bake in a 350°F (180°C, gas marks 4) oven for 6 to 15 minutes or until crisp. The timing will vary with the type of papad and the number being baked simultaneously. Check frequently and don't let them burn.

Serving Suggestions: Serve at breakfast topped with a poached or soft-boiled egg or baked tofu cubes. Or offer as a first course at a main meal, accompanied by one or more of the following condiments: chopped arugula and Five Fundamental Seasonings (page 203); Peanuts, Seaweed, and Red Chile Flakes (page 220); or Toasted Baby Sardines and Caramelized Peanuts (page 261).

✳ Tofu-Mushroom Scramble ✳

CHINA

Here, tofu and mushrooms become a brunch dish, strikingly reminiscent of scrambled eggs but with a fraction of the cholesterol because only one egg is required. Fish sauce, the ubiquitous condiment of Southeast Asia, seasons the combination.

The Chinese often cook tofu and mushrooms together in vegetable dishes. The silky, neutral tofu blends particularly well with the woodsy mushrooms commonly used in China. The texture and appearance of tofu remind me of Indian cheese, *channa*, although the tastes are not the same and they can't always be interchanged. But both are good sources of protein.

If you breakfast lightly on weekdays but want a substantial brunch on the weekend, try this hearty scramble.

      14-ounce (396-g) carton of firm tofu, drained, rinsed
2   teaspoons (10 ml) fish sauce (preferred; or low-sodium soy sauce to taste)
1   large egg or 2 egg whites, lightly beaten
1¹/₂   tablespoons (22 ml) Indian sesame oil (*gingely*)
¹/₄   teaspoon (1 ml) asafetida powder
      4 to 6 large garlic cloves, minced
1   tablespoon (15 ml) minced gingerroot
6   ounces (175 g), fresh button mushrooms, about 15, thinly sliced
      Salt
      Dash Chinese sesame oil
      Chaat Powder (page 8; start with ¹/₈ teaspoon [0.5 ml])

Garnish:
2   scallions (green part only), thinly sliced
      Chopped cilantro

1. To press water out of tofu: Wrap tofu in a heavy kitchen towel or place it between several layers of paper towels on a cookie sheet. Put a heavy weight such as an iron skillet on top. Let stand at room temperature for 30 minutes. Remove the weight and the towel(s). (With much of the water drained this way, tofu acquires a more solid texture.) Mash tofu with a fork in a medium bowl. Stir in fish sauce and egg. The mixture will be somewhat lumpy.

2. Heat oil in a large skillet over moderate heat. Sprinkle asafetida over the oil. Add garlic and gingerroot and fry until they are lightly browned. Add mushrooms and

stir a few times. Add the tofu mixture. Lower heat slightly. Cover and simmer 6 to 10 minutes. The tofu will resemble scrambled eggs and a thin sauce will form at the bottom. Remove from heat. Add salt and sesame oil and sprinkle with Chaat Powder. Serve garnished with scallions and cilantro.

2 large servings

Serving Suggestions: At the table, pass around extra sesame oil and fish sauce, a tray of Five Fundamental Seasonings (page 203), and chopped fresh seasonal herbs, such as dill and tarragon. For brunch serve with a cup of green tea and garlic toast, a hard roll, or warm whole wheat pita wedges and papaya slices. Or try as a dinner entrée accompanied by brown rice, fresh sliced tomatoes and cucumbers drizzled with Curry-Walnut Dressing (page 234), and Sweet Potato Salad with Sesame-Tamarind Dressing (page 242).

✳ Eggs in a Spinach Nest ✳
INDIA/UNITED STATES

This dish was inspired by the Parsees, followers of Zarathustra, or Zoroaster, who is believed to have lived in the seventh century B.C. in Persia, which is now Iran. More than 1,200 years ago, Parsees immigrated to the west coast of India because of religious differences with the rulers of Iran. Their cuisine is a unique and interesting blend of influences from both ancient Persia and India.

Parsees frequently breakfast on a spicy egg-scramble called *ekoori*. Scrambled eggs look and taste best when they form large, moist, tender curds. Western cooks have shown me that achieving this result requires an extra measure of attention. I cook my eggs over low heat, handling them gently until they have nearly reached the desired consistency. At this point I remove them from the heat and let the residual heat of the frying pan complete the cooking process.

Cilantro is the leafy green preferred in *ekoori*. I have chosen to give this dish an American accent by using spinach.

The spinach:
1½ tablespoons (22 ml) mustard oil or canola oil
¼ teaspoon (1 ml) Indian five-spice
1½ cups (375 ml) thinly sliced onion

1   tablespoon (15 ml) minced gingerroot
1/2 jalapeño, seeded and chopped (to taste)
2   teaspoons (10 ml) ground cumin
1   teaspoon (5 ml) chick-pea flour, *besan* (no substitute)
     Ground red pepper (to taste; start with a scant pinch; best if there is a hint
       of hotness)
2   cups (500 ml) fresh spinach leaves, rinsed well and shredded (see *Note for
       the Gardener*)
     Salt

The eggs:
6   large eggs
     Salt and freshly ground black pepper
1   tablespoon (15 ml) mustard oil, ghee, or butter

Garnish:
     Red bell pepper strips
     Chopped cilantro

1. To prepare the spinach: Heat 1 1/2 tablespoons (22 ml) oil in a steep skillet or pan over moderate heat. Fry five-spice. Add onion, gingerroot, and jalapeño and cook until onion is translucent and slightly soft, about 2 minutes. Add cumin, chick-pea flour, and red pepper and mix well. Turn heat to low. Add spinach. Cook, uncovered, until spinach is just wilted, 2 to 3 minutes. (Don't overcook, as spinach will lose its color.) Remove the spinach mixture to a medium bowl. Add salt. Cover and keep warm. Rinse and wipe out the skillet.

2. To prepare the eggs: Whisk eggs with salt and pepper and set aside. Heat oil in the same skillet over moderate heat until a light haze forms. If using a gas stove, turn heat to very low; if using an electric burner, switch to another burner that has been set to low heat. Pour eggs into the skillet. When the egg mixture begins to set, gently lift it up and over with a large spoon several times. This will help form large curds. Do not over-stir. While part of the mixture is soft and still runny, remove from heat. The eggs will continue cooking from the remaining heat in the skillet. Let stand several minutes to finish setting the eggs. Adjust seasoning.

3. Arrange the spinach mixture on a platter or on individual serving plates, hollowing it out like a nest. Top with the eggs. Serve garnished with bell pepper and cilantro.

4 servings

Serving Suggestions: Serve with warm pita triangles or toasted slices of Date-Nut Squash Bread (see below) for breakfast. Pair with Noor Jahani Polenta (page 24) for a Sunday brunch.

Note for the Gardener: You can use other garden greens besides spinach. In spring, when you thin your rows of Swiss chard, kale, or collard, use the tender leaves in a dish like this rather than throw them away. Because of their high water content, steam them first for a minute or two, which will drain out some of the water. In Step 2, cook them just long enough to mix with the spices.

These tender greens are also splendid when sautéed with shiitake mushrooms, fresh or dried (reconstituted by soaking in warm water for 20 to 30 minutes), and served as a side dish at brunch or dinner.

✳ Date-Nut Squash Bread ✳

UNITED STATES

During autumn and winter when squashes and fresh pumpkins are plentiful, I prepare this pretty orange-colored bread. Gingerroot, cardamom, cinnamon, and dates make it extraordinary. Sliced and toasted, it makes an excellent breakfast. When wrapped in foil, this dense, moist bread keeps well in the refrigerator for several days.

  1   pound (500 g) butternut squash (or fresh pumpkin or other nonfibrous
        winter squash such as Hubbard), seeded and cut into 1-inch (2.5-cm)
        cubes (see *Note*)
  2   teaspoons (10 ml) coarsely chopped gingerroot
 $1/2$ cup (125 ml) canola oil
 $3/4$ cup (185 ml) firmly packed dark brown sugar
  2   large eggs or 4 egg whites
  1   cup (250 ml) plain nonfat yogurt
 $1^1/2$ cups (375 ml) unbleached white flour
 $1^1/2$ cups (375 ml) whole wheat flour
  2   teaspoons (10 ml) baking powder
  1   teaspoon (5 ml) baking soda
  1   teaspoon (5 ml) ground cardamom
 $1/2$ teaspoon (2 ml) ground cinnamon
 $1/4$ cup (60 ml) chopped pitted dates
 $1/2$ cup (125 ml) chopped pecans, toasted

1. Steam the squash cubes for 12 to 18 minutes or until tender. Process squash, gingerroot, oil, sugar, eggs, and yogurt in a blender or food processor until smooth.
2. Preheat oven to 350°F (180°C, gas marks 4). Sift together white and wheat flours, baking powder, and baking soda. Add cardamom, cinnamon, dates, and pecans. Add the squash puree to the flour mixture, stirring with a fork to moisten the ingredients. Pour into an oiled loaf pan. Bake for 50 to 65 minutes or until a toothpick inserted in the middle comes out clean. Best served while still warm, but also good at room temperature.

10 servings

Note: If using butternut squash, I leave it unpeeled. The peel blends with other ingredients and renders the bread rich in fiber and nutrients. I peel Hubbard or other hard-skinned squashes and pumpkins.

Serving Suggestions: Try at breakfast with unsweetened hot cereal. Serve for dessert with frozen vanilla yogurt, or toasted and spread with peanut butter or Dream Yogurt (Sweet Variation; page 213) on top. I also enjoy gift-wrapping the bread and giving it to friends.

✳ Fragrant Hot Bread with Creamy Thick Yogurt ✳

THE MIDDLE EAST

While living in Iran, I shopped daily for fresh *barbari*, an oval-shaped flat bread. It's similar to Italian focaccia without any topping. Iranians prepare *barbari* around the clock in special bread shops. The men knead the dough, allow it to rise slightly, and slap it into a searing hot, ancient stone oven, using a long-handled wooden spatula. An earthy fragrance fills the air. People jam the shop to buy this steaming-hot bread, and leave carrying huge unwrapped pieces under their arms and in baskets. I'd usually buy two, and finish eating a large part of one by the time I reached home.

You can occasionally find *barbari* in Middle Eastern stores, although it will not be fresh. A good substitute is a simple focaccia made with herbs and olive oil that is now available fresh in many Italian delicatessens. Similar options are chapati or pita bread. Any of these flat breads taste delicious with thickened yogurt and bring a delightful combination of flavors and textures to your kitchen.

Labne, thick yogurt seasoned with onion and perhaps a little olive oil, is a common accompaniment to flat bread at breakfast time in many parts of the Middle East. I thicken commercial yogurt by draining it overnight in a sieve.

> Dream Yogurt (page 212)
> Olive oil or Olive Oil and Fresh Herb Dip (page 235) for drizzling
> 1/2 small, mild red or other sweet onion, cut into rings
> Sprinkling of chopped fresh (or dried) basil or oregano
> 2 focaccia, chapati, or whole wheat pita breads

1. Spread the yogurt on a medium-sized platter with raised edges so that the yogurt looks like a pizza. Drizzle a little olive oil over the surface. Sprinkle with the onion and basil. If not ready to serve yet, refrigerate. Warm the bread by placing briefly on an ungreased heated griddle and serve with the yogurt sauce on the side.

2 small servings

Serving suggestions: Accompany at breakfast with a cup of Soy Chai (page 293). Add tomato wedges, chopped cucumbers, scallion halves, and Kalamata olives for lunch.

✸ Runner's Rice ✸

GREECE

The assertive flavor of Chinese sesame oil and the crunchiness of toasted pumpkin seeds make this rice and spinach casserole enticing. The simple but substantial dish eliminates food cravings for hours, making it a perfect post-workout breakfast.

The original idea for this recipe came from a runner friend of Greek ancestry. We frequently exchanged food tips during our runs together. One morning she reminisced about a meal of rice and spinach she prepared in her homeland. After the run, I went home and tested her recipe. I ended up using brown rice after I discovered that it goes especially well with spinach.

- 1 cup (250 ml) brown Basmati rice, rinsed thoroughly
- 2 cups (500 ml) hot water
- 1 cup (250 ml) fresh spinach leaves, rinsed thoroughly and shredded
  Salt
  Chinese sesame oil

Garnish: Toasted pumpkin seeds

Place rice and water in a medium pan. Cover and bring to a boil. Lower heat, cover, and simmer until all water is absorbed and rice is tender, 40 to 50 minutes. (See *Do-ahead Note.*) Add spinach during the last 5 minutes of cooking. Remove from heat. Fluff with a fork, mixing in the spinach with the rice. Add salt. Sprinkle with sesame oil. Garnish with pumpkin seeds and serve at once.

2 large servings

Do-ahead Note: You can prepare the rice alone the day before. Next day, sprinkle water over the rice, top with spinach, and reheat. The added water will turn into vapor, steaming the spinach and reconstituting the rice simultaneously.

Serving Suggestions: Serve at breakfast alone or topped with a poached egg (or some steamed tofu) and accompanied by Mulled Apple Tea (page 291). Enjoy at dinner with Shrimp Sancoche (page 70) or Spicy Seoul Cucumber (page 76), and Mint-Basil Chutney (page 224).

Starter and Main-Course Soups

•••••••••••••••••••••••••••••••

In an old World War II movie, a group of weary refugees arrived at a shelter. Many were too weak to digest anything but liquid after a long journey on foot without food or water. They were given bowls of soup. With each slow, trembling sip they took, their weary faces brightened.

There's something magical and elemental about a bowl of steaming soup. It has soothed and comforted people since ancient times. In cold weather, soup will often prepare your palate for the entrée. However, in scorching Eastern India where I grew up, a separate soup course would not serve that purpose. I didn't understand the cooking concept until I had lived in the West for several years. Now I'm a convert.

On busy days a soup can be the entire meal. One need look no further after lifting the cover of the tureen and finding a fragrant broth brimming with noodles, fish, meat, or vegetables.

In India, a broth or sauce often accompanies the main meal. South Indians delight in *rasam*, a thin, tart soup flavored with lentils, tomatoes, chile, or tamarind. I now use *rasam* as a base for more substantial soups. As an adult, I have rediscovered other legumes of my childhood—whole mung beans, split chick-peas, and black urad dal—and have incorporated them into my diet as main-course soups.

Many of the ideas for combining ingredients and spices that I have applied here come from India. Whole dried red chiles simmer with the soup and add flavor, not heat. As a topping, browned onions garnish and enrich a soup. A dash of garam masala at the end of cooking completes the spicing process. Rice or flat bread is always eaten with any soup-type legume dish in India, but in the West I am as likely to serve quinoa, kasha, or millet.

Indian cooking makes limited use of stocks. On special occasions, a meat broth can enhance a lavish one-dish meal made with rice. A good soup base is vital because the flavor of soup depends on the richness of its stock.

Some years ago I discovered a food stall in Granville Market in Vancouver, British Columbia, that sold freshly prepared stocks—perhaps the first such store in North America. So many kinds of stock, each in an individual container, ignited my imagination. Back in my own kitchen, I began to come up with various ways of preparing stock.

In the process, I incorporated tips from many cultures. Japanese cooks use kombu, a seaweed that adds nutrients and flavor to *dashi*, a broth base for noodles. The French pick herbs from the garden, including watercress, to add a sprightly taste to soups. My own experiments revealed other methods. I often place the damaged outer leaves of a head of lettuce, those not suitable for salad, on top of a simmering broth to add nutrients and freshness. Sometimes I save the water used in cooking pasta to make a rich starter for soups. A number of Indian staples, such as asafetida, gingerroot, or whole cardamom pods, add distinction to the stock.

For the most part, soups are simple. And, unlike a fancy fish bake or a deliberate pilaf, a hearty soup pleases the mighty and the humble alike. Soup is both timeless and universal. ❋

Stock Answers

* When preparing soups or stocks, use filtered or bottled spring water rather than tap water for improved taste.
* To increase the vitamin-mineral content of the stock and for savor, use leafy greens (such as lettuce, collard, kale, or mustard greens) and/or sea vegetables (such as kombu) as ingredients.
* To prepare flavorful vegetable stocks without using meat bones, I first roast selected vegetables using a little oil. (Roasting imparts a rich aroma to the resulting broth.) Then I put a substantial amount of herbs, spices, and other vegetables, along with water, in the pot. Whenever possible, I use the nutrient-rich water left from steaming vegetables, simmering beans, soaking sun-dried tomatoes, reconstituting dried mushrooms, or cooking pasta as my base for vegetable stocks.

✳ Increase the nutritional content of a dish by replacing the water in the recipe with stock. Fish stock enhances a fish or vegetable preparation. Vegetable stock adds flavor to grains, vegetable casseroles, and stews, and can also be used in preparing bread doughs.

✳ Combine different stocks for a more complex taste. For example, when making a fish soup, combine fish stock with vegetable stock or vegetable stock with the broth left over from steaming clams or mussels.

✳ Once the stock is prepared, reduce it for a richer flavor as described in the recipes. This is especially important for vegetable stocks.

✳ Store stock in the refrigerator and use within a week. Or freeze individual portions in containers.

✳ Vegetable Stock ✳

INTERNATIONAL

This recipe calls for some conventional stock ingredients such as carrots, celery, and onion, and a few new ones—gingerroot, dried red chiles, and lettuce leaves. It produces a gently fragrant broth that can enrich any grain or vegetable preparation. Try one of the variations for a different flavor.

1 1/2 tablespoons (22 ml) olive oil
2 whole dried red chiles (optional; see *Note*)
1 medium onion, quartered
4 large cloves garlic, slivered
1-inch (2.5-cm) piece gingerroot, slivered
1 large carrot, about 3/4 pound (375 g), diced
2 stalks celery, leaves included, coarsely chopped
A handful of cilantro or parsley sprigs
A few romaine or other lettuce leaves
9 cups (2.25 liters) water or canned vegetable broth

1. Heat oil in a large stockpot over medium heat. Add red chiles and fry until the chiles blacken. Add onion, garlic, gingerroot, and carrot. Cook uncovered stirring often, until the vegetables are richly browned, 5 to 7 minutes. Add celery, cilantro, lettuce, and water and bring to a boil. Lower heat; cover and simmer for

30 minutes. Strain by pouring through a sieve. As you do so, press on the vegetables with a slotted spoon to extract the residual juices. Reserve the stock and discard the vegetables.

2. For best results, reduce stock: cook uncovered 10 to 15 minutes over moderate heat or until reduced by 1 cup (250 ml).

Yields 8 cups (2 liters)

Note: Dried red chiles add a gentle smoky aroma and, if hot, a pleasant background heat. To control the amount of hotness, lift them off the stock and discard a few minutes after the stock has started to simmer.

NONFAT ALTERNATIVE: Omit oil from the list of ingredients and don't brown the vegetables in Step 1.

VARIATION: ASIAN STOCK Rinse and add a long piece of kombu (or kelp, another seaweed) to the pot along with cilantro.

VARIATION: SUMMER STOCK During summer, I make an unorthodox vegetable stock using the season's bounty—zucchini, summer squash, and fresh herbs. This stock has a delicate sweet taste and is especially good for cooking grains, poaching chicken, or imparting flavor to vegetable dishes. After the stock has simmered for 10 minutes, add 1 pound (500 g) each of zucchini, pattypan squash, and yellow crookneck squash, each sliced crosswise into thick rounds.

✳ Fish Stock ✳
INTERNATIONAL

Preparing fish stock may seem daunting to many cooks, but the method is actually easy. The stock has many uses: in fish soups, for poaching fish or vegetables, and in fish stews. The best fish to use are rich, firm-fleshed varieties such as salmon, halibut, tuna, and sea bass.

1¹/₂   pounds (750 g) fish trimmings
  6   cups (1.5 liters) water
  2   bay leaves
  2   toasted dried red chiles

 1   medium onion, peeled
 6   large cloves garlic, halved
      3-inch (7.5-cm) lemon grass stem, bottom part only (optional)
6 to 8   fresh cilantro or parsley sprigs (see *Note for the Gardener*)

1. Place fish trimmings and water in a large, deep pot. Add the remaining ingredients, cover, and bring to a boil. Simmer, covered, 30 minutes. During this period, remove the cover occasionally and turn the ingredients. (See *Money-Saving Tip.*) Drain in a colander lined with several layers of cheesecloth. As you do so, press on the fish and vegetables with a slotted spoon to extract the residual juices. Discard the vegetables; reserve the fish for use in other dishes.
2. This stock is usually rich and shouldn't need much reducing. You can, however, reduce it slightly. To do so, bring it to a boil over moderate heat. Lower heat and cook, uncovered, about 10 minutes.

Yields 5 cups (1.25 liters)

Note for the Gardener: If you grow herbs, snip some fresh dill and add to the pot for a delicate tang.

Money-Saving Tip: After 10 minutes of simmering, remove a few of the bones to a large bowl and pull off the flesh (about ¼ cup [60 ml]), which will be cooked by now. Return bones to the pot. Allow the flesh to cool. Use this fish to prepare the delicious Fish Aïoli (page 227) or add it to a potato salad. If using salmon bones, prepare a dish such as Salmon-Pasta Salad International (page 250).

VARIATION: SALMON BROTH Use this highly concentrated broth in place of water when preparing fish or shellfish dishes and you'll get a most flavorful result. If salmon isn't available, use any rich, firm-fleshed fish such as grouper, Atlantic cod, tuna, or halibut. Use 1½ pounds (750 g) salmon bones, but only 4 cups (1 liter) water. Also use a medium peeled onion, studded with 5 whole cloves. Add 5 whole cardamom pods, bruised. The rest of the ingredients are the same as in Fish Stock. When reducing the broth, cook uncovered 18 to 22 minutes or until reduced to about 1 cup (250 ml).

Yields 1 cup (250 ml)

✹ Chicken Stock ✹

INTERNATIONAL

I once had a yoga teacher who instructed his students to do everything "with atten-tion." I believe this concept applies as well to cooking. The chef's level of commitment shows in a finished dish. When the ingredients have been rightly seasoned, cooked just the right amount of time, and garnished to perfection, a dish will be excellent. And, like excellence at sports, art, or music, a perfected meal is inspiring.

Preparing outstanding chicken stock requires an unhurried mind just as making bread does. The steps are quite simple and concentrating on the process can be relaxing.

Use this stock in preparing soups, poaching chicken or vegetables, or in cooking grains. (Because of its richness, I dilute it slightly with water when cooking grains.) Prepare it the day before you need to use it so there will be time to defat it.

2 to 3   pounds (900 g to 1.5 kg) chicken necks, bones, wings, and back (see *Money-Saving Tip*)

1   medium carrot, rutabaga, turnip, or kohlrabi, about ¹/₂ pound (500 g), coarsely chopped

1   medium onion, quartered

4   large cloves garlic, coarsely chopped

8   cups (2 liters) water

The spices:

2   bay leaves

A few black peppercorns

5   whole cardamom pods, bruised

A handful of fresh herbs such as tarragon, cilantro, oregano, sage, parsley (see *Note*)

1   whole jalapeño (optional)

2   whole dried red chiles (optional)

In a large stockpot, place chicken, carrot, onion, and garlic. Add water and the spices. Cover and bring to a boil. Lower heat and simmer for 4 hours. Strain by pass-ing through a sieve placed over a large bowl. Defat the stock before using (see instructions below).

Yields 7 cups (1.75 liters)

Note: Fresh herbs impart aroma to the stock, so use generously.

Using a crock pot to prepare chicken stock: If you don't want the long simmer to tie you to the kitchen, consider using a crock pot. The size of the crock pot is a factor. Use no more than 2 pounds (1 kg) chicken in a standard 3 1/2-quart (3.5-liter) crock pot.

Bring the ingredients to a boil in a stockpot as before. Remove from heat and transfer to the crock pot. Make sure the top surface of the chicken and the liquid lies at least 2 inches (5 cm) below the top rim of the crock pot. This is to ensure that the stock will not seep out of the pot as it bubbles and foams. If necessary, reduce the amount of liquid.

Cook on "High" for 3 hours. Strain. Defat before using.

To defat chicken stock: Allow the stock to cool to room temperature. Place the stock in a large, wide-mouthed bowl and store in the refrigerator overnight. (Using a wide bowl helps in removing the congealed fat.) The fat will float to the surface and form a solid layer. Using a spoon, carefully remove the solidified fat in pieces. The stock is now ready for use.

To defat canned chicken broth: Place the unopened can in the refrigerator for 45 minutes or longer. When you open it, you'll find globs of fat floating on top. Remove the fat with a spoon and discard. The broth is now ready to be used.

To add flavor to canned broth: You can add flavor to canned chicken or vegetable broth by simmering it with 2 bay leaves, 1 onion (diced), 4 garlic cloves (slivered), 1 medium carrot (diced), a few kale leaves, 2 cilantro sprigs, and 4 cardamom pods for 20 to 30 minutes. Strain and use this fragrant broth in soups, in vegetable dishes, and in cooking grains. Measure it before adding to a recipe.

Money-Saving Tip: You can use the chicken meat for other dishes. For this purpose, buy chicken pieces of your choice. Remove chicken from the pot after it has simmered for 20 to 30 minutes. (The timing will vary with the type of meat; chicken breast will take the lesser amount of time.) When cool enough to handle, remove skin and pull the meat off the bones. Return the skin and bones to the pot and continue to cook as in the recipe. You can use the chicken meat to prepare Tarragon-Poached Chicken with Sauces (page 128).

VARIATION: TENDER GREENS AND CHICKEN STOCK Leafy greens add aroma and nutrients to the stock. Shred a large handful of mustard, kale, or other greens of your choice. Gardeners can harvest turnip, beet, kohlrabi, or other edible greens. Add in Step 1 along with other ingredients.

✳ South Indian Gazpacho ✳
SOUTH INDIA/SPAIN

Rasam ("essence") is a highly flavored broth from South India that is almost a staple in that tropical region. It comes in many varieties. Some are legume-based, others have tomato or tamarind as the main ingredient. *Rasam* is tasty alone; however, the custom in South India is to eat it with rice as a second course. A woman from South India told me that on busy days, she often cooks only *rasam* and rice.

Here I use *rasam* as a base for gazpacho, a chilled soup from Spain well known in the Western world. This spicy, tamarind-tinged gazpacho provides a lively alternative to the original version, one that can be served with pride.

The rasam:
- 1   teaspoon (5 ml) tamarind concentrate
- 1   cup (250 ml) water
- 1/4   teaspoon (1 ml) ground cumin
- 1/4   teaspoon (1 ml) ground coriander
-     Salt
-     Ground red pepper (to taste; start with a scant pinch; best if there is a hint of hotness)
- 2   teaspoons (10 ml) mustard oil
- 1/4   teaspoon (1 ml) black mustard seeds
- 5   large cloves garlic, minced
- 1/2   jalapeño, seeded, chopped

The vegetables (see *Note for the Gardener*):
- 1/2   pound (250 g) Roma tomatoes, seeded, finely chopped
- 1   large green bell pepper, finely chopped
- 1/2   large cucumber, peeled, seeded, finely chopped
- 1   medium mild red or other sweet onion, finely chopped
-     Salt
-     Ground red pepper (to taste; start with a scant pinch)

Garnish: Chopped cilantro or parsley (see *Note*)

1. To prepare *rasam:* Mix tamarind with 1/4 cup (60 ml) water in a large nonmetallic bowl until smooth. Add the remaining 3/4 cup (200 ml) water. Add cumin, coriander, salt, and red pepper and stir to dissolve the spices. Place this mixture in a medium-sized nonmetallic pan. Cover and bring to a boil. Lower heat and simmer for a few minutes. Remove from heat.

2. Heat oil in a small skillet over moderate heat. Add mustard seeds and fry until the seeds start to pop. (Keep the pan partially covered to prevent the seeds from flying out.) Add garlic and jalapeño and fry until garlic is lightly browned. Remove from heat and add this mixture to the *rasam*. Allow *rasam* to cool to room temperature.

3. Combine tomatoes, bell pepper, cucumber, and onion in a large bowl. Take ³⁄₄ cup (185 ml) of this mixture and ¹⁄₂ cup (125 ml) of *rasam* and process in a blender or food processor until relatively smooth. This puree will add body to the soup. Return to the large bowl containing the vegetables. Pour the rest of the *rasam* into the same bowl. Add salt and red pepper. Refrigerate for at least 30 minutes. Adjust seasoning. Garnish with cilantro and serve cold.

4 starter course or 2 entrée servings

Note for the Gardener: Since the vegetables in this soup are used raw, their freshness is crucial. I prepare this soup in August when I can harvest from an abundant garden. Instead of green bell peppers, I sometimes use pale yellow Hungarian sweet peppers, which look beautiful next to the bright red Romas.

Note: Garnishing is important here, as the soup can acquire a darker color when you puree part of the vegetables. Make sure that a few tomatoes show through the top; sprinkle cilantro or parsley over the surface. You'll have a lovely soup for warm summer days.

Serving Suggestions: Serve in a chilled cup and enjoy while you're barbecuing meat or preparing an entrée such as Garlic-Glazed Tofu (page 67) or Soy- and Mirin-Glazed Salmon (page 99). Accompany with French bread topped with Roasted Garlic Spread (page 221) or offer some warmed chapatis. On another occasion, serve as a main course with a side dish of Sweet, Sour, and Smoky Potatoes (page 63).

✳ August Tomato Soup ✳
HUNGARY

During late summer when tomatoes ripen almost overnight in my Pacific Northwest garden, I know it's time to invite friends for a soup-and-bread meal. This smooth, delicate soup gets a boost from the innovative seasoning of ground warm spices—cinnamon, cardamom, and cloves. The creamy texture belies its lowfat base. If possible, use vine-ripened tomatoes for this dish.

6   cups (1.5 liters) sliced tomatoes (see *Note*)
1   small, peeled onion, stuck with 4 whole cloves
3   large cloves garlic, coarsely chopped
1   bay leaf
1   whole jalapeño
    Dash Hungarian sweet paprika
1/4 cup (60 ml) water
    Salt and freshly ground black pepper
1   tablespoon (15 ml) olive oil
1   tablespoon (15 ml) all-purpose flour
1   cup (250 ml) 2% lowfat milk (don't use nonfat)
1/2 teaspoon (2 ml) garam masala

Garnish: Chopped cilantro

1. Bring tomatoes, onion, garlic, bay leaf, jalapeño, paprika, and water to a boil in a large pan. Lower heat and simmer, covered, 25 to 30 minutes or until tomatoes are thoroughly dissolved. Discard bay leaf and onion. Puree in a blender or food processor until smooth. Pass the mixture through a sieve to eliminate any seeds or bits of skin. Salt and pepper to taste. Keep warm.

2. In a separate medium-sized pan over moderate heat, heat oil. Add flour gradually and stir constantly until it browns. Slowly mix in milk, stirring constantly. Cook over gentle heat until the mixture thickens slightly, stirring often. Remove from heat. Pour over the tomato soup a little at a time, stirring constantly. Mix in garam masala and garnish with cilantro. Adjust seasoning.

4 starter course or 2 entrée servings

Note: If tomatoes are canned or not fully ripe, add 1 to 2 teaspoons (5 to 10 ml) sugar along with salt and pepper in Step 1.

Serving Suggestions: Serve with a baked potato or pasta salad, chunks of steamed corn on the cob, and Piquant Salad in Shades of Green (page 258) tossed with Cumin Vinaigrette (page 233). A basketful of crusty Italian or French bread for dunking will complete the meal.

✳ Sweet and Nutty Carrot-Turnip Soup ✳

EASTERN EUROPE

This is a great opportunity to get acquainted with turnips. Blended with carrots to create a unique soup, the turnip adds a subtle sweetness and delicate background flavor. This bright orange soup with its sensuous smoothness and gentle warmth was just what I needed the first time I tried it in a Chicago restaurant on a near-zero winter evening. Root vegetables like carrots and turnips are particularly appealing during winter. They bind us closer to the earth.

Developing my own recipe, I found that carrots have a particular affinity for cumin, a spice nearly as common in North Indian cooking as black pepper in the West.

The soup:

- 2 cups (500 ml) sliced carrots, about 2 large (see *Note 1 for the Gardener*)
- 1 cup (250 ml) turnip, cut in French-fry–type strips (see *Note 2 for the Gardener*)
- 1/2 cup (125 ml) coarsely chopped onion
- 1 tablespoon (15 ml) coarsely chopped garlic
  Several sprigs cilantro
- 3 cups (750 ml) water
- 1 teaspoon (5 ml) sugar
- 1/4 cup (60 ml) evaporated skim milk
  Salt

The spices:

- 1 to 1 1/2 tablespoons (15 to 22 ml) olive oil
- 1/4 teaspoon (1 ml) cumin seeds
- 1 cup (250 ml) finely chopped onion
- 8 to 10 pecans, toasted, chopped

1. To prepare the soup: Bring carrots, turnip, 1/2 cup (125 ml) onion, garlic, cilantro, and water to a boil in a large, steep-sided pan. Cover and simmer 40 to 45 minutes or until carrots are tender. Add sugar. Puree, in batches, in a food processor or blender. Return to the pan. Add milk and salt. Return to heat, bring to a simmer, then keep warm.

2. To prepare the spices: Heat oil over moderate heat in a medium skillet. Add cumin seeds and fry until they are lightly browned. Add 1 cup (250 ml) onion and fry, stirring often, until it is richly browned, 10 to 15 minutes. Remove from heat. Gently float the onions over the soup so that they form a decorative pattern. Serve garnished with pecans.

4 starter course or 2 entrée servings

Note 1 for the Gardener: Since carrots are the main ingredient, the younger and fresher they are, the tastier the soup will be. Consider harvesting baby carrots for this soup.

Note 2 for the Gardener: If you grow turnips, you can benefit doubly from the nutritious greens, which are not sold in supermarkets. Use them in any recipe that calls for kale, collard, or Swiss chard.

FISH OR SHRIMP VARIATION: Poach fresh shrimp or pieces of fish (tuna, halibut, catfish) in the soup just before adding the spiced onion mixture. Use 1/2 pound (250 g) fish or shrimp, cut into bite-sized pieces, and cook for a few minutes until done (a toothpick inserted in the thickest part of the fish or shrimp should show an opaque color in the piece).

SPICY VARIATIONS: For a richer and more exotic soup, consider using one or more of these seasonings: Add a pinch of saffron threads, soaked in 1 tablespoon (15 ml) warm milk, to the carrot mixture after it has been blended. Toast 1 tablespoon (15 ml) dried sweetened flaked coconut and sprinkle over the finished soup. Add a dash of red chile paste or sambal oeleck to the finished dish. Swirl in a few drops of ghee at the end for a fine flavor.

Serving Suggestions: Good accompaniments include couscous or bulgur tossed with chick-peas, or Shrimp and Orzo Pullao (page 149), Gai Lan with Balsamic Vinaigrette (page 70), or Gujarati Greens (page 66).

✳ Fresh Squash Soup with Orzo and Red Pepper ✳
THE MEDITERRANEAN

O rzo, a rice-shaped pasta common in the Eastern Mediterranean countries, is a welcome change from rice and the usual forms of pasta. In this soup, orzo absorbs the flavor from fresh vegetables, making it even tastier. Gingerroot brings an Indian touch to the New World ingredients of squash and pepper. Chunks of sweet red pepper and finely chopped cilantro make an exciting contrast to the rich orange-colored broth made from squash. The soup serves well as a complete meal or as a starter for a formal dinner.

The vegetables:

 1 pound (500 g) butternut squash (or other winter squashes such as Hubbard)
    cut into $^1/_2$-inch (1-cm) cubes (see *Note* and *Note to the Gardener*)
 4 cups (1 liter) Chicken Stock (page 44) or two 14$^1/_2$-ounce (411-g) cans
    chicken broth, defatted (see "To defat canned chicken broth," page 45)
 1 tablespoon (15 ml) minced gingerroot
 1 jalapeño, seeded, minced
 1 large red bell pepper, seeded, cut into $^1/_2$-inch (1-cm) pieces
 1 cup (250 ml) cooked navy beans or chick-peas
    Salt

The orzo:

 4 cups (1 liter) water
$^1/_4$ pound (100 g) orzo, about $^3/_4$ cup (185 ml)
 2 tablespoons (30 ml) finely chopped cilantro (or a combination of cilantro
    and arugula)
 2 tablespoons (30 ml) fresh lime or lemon juice

Garnish: Honey-Glazed Onions (page 218)

1. Put squash, stock, gingerroot, and jalapeño in a large pan and bring to a boil. Lower heat and simmer, covered, 16 to 20 minutes or until the squash is tender but firm. Puree about $^3/_4$ of this mixture in a blender or food processor. Return to the pan. Bring to a simmer over low heat. Add bell pepper, beans, and salt. Cook for 3 to 5 minutes. The pepper need not be thoroughly cooked at this point. (Up to this point, you can prepare ahead of time, but preferably the same day.) Remove from heat.

2. To cook orzo: Bring about 4 cups (1 liter) water to a boil in a pan at least 2 quarts (2 liters) in size. Add orzo and cook over medium heat for 9 to 12 minutes. Stir often to prevent sticking to the bottom of the pan. Adjust heat to prevent boiling over. The best way to check for doneness is to taste. Orzo should be tender to the bite but not too soft, as it will cook slightly longer in the soup in Step 3. Drain, reserving the orzo. Save the water for cooking soups, grains, or vegetables.

3. Bring the soup to a simmer over moderate heat. Add orzo and mix well. Remove from heat. Sprinkle with cilantro and lime juice. Adjust seasoning if necessary. Serve garnished with onions. If allowed to stand, orzo will thicken the soup and lessen its volume by absorbing some of the liquid, although the soup will still be tasty.

4 starter course or 2 entrée servings

Note: If using butternut squash, you can leave it unpeeled. If using Hubbard or other thicker-skinned squash, you will need to peel it. Since the peel is pureed, its color and texture affect the final appearance of the dish.

Note to the Gardener: To cut a large Hubbard, which has an especially thick skin, my husband uses a keyhole saw with a soft and flexible blade.

Serving Suggestions: A crisp green salad, sourdough bread, and fresh seasonal fruits complete the evening meal. Serve at a luncheon with a wild rice salad and some papads.

ORECCHIETTE VARIATION: Instead of orzo alone, use $1/2$ cup (125 ml) orzo and $1/4$ cup (60 ml) orecchiette. Orecchiette, a beret-shaped pasta, provides a lovely contrast to the vegetable cubes. If unavailable, use medium-sized shell pasta that are $1/2$ to 1 inch (1 to 2.5 cm) across, about the size of the squash cubes. Cook these two pastas the same way as in Step 2, but add orecchiette first. After 2 to 3 minutes, add orzo. Cook until both are tender to the tooth. Optionally, add $1/4$ teaspoon (1 ml) turmeric to the water before bringing it to a boil to tint the pastas a pleasant yellow.

✳ Peanut Soup with Kasundi Dip ✳
WEST AFRICA/EASTERN INDIA

This soup comes from West Africa, where eating peanuts is practically a way of life. Because it bears fruit below the ground, the Africans call the peanut the groundnut. A man from Ghana told me that in his country roasted peanuts and bananas often serve as lunch for farm workers, and in affluent homes the noon meal consists of peanut soup or stew enriched by curry spices. The latter was introduced by East Indian immigrants. African cooks grind fresh peanuts before preparing this soup. Peanut butter will do the job, but because it improves the flavor, I occasionally roast and grind raw peanuts. Below you'll find instructions for using each.

This thick soup has a comforting quality. It's good alone but is even tastier with Kasundi Dip, a zesty sauce from India. Kasundi is based on black mustard seeds and is generally eaten with rice. Here I prepare a Westernized version using the more common yellow mustard seeds. Each guest can season the soup to taste with a sprinkling of this sharp condiment.

   2   tablespoons (30 ml) canola oil
   1   cup (250 ml) finely chopped onion
   4   large cloves garlic, minced
   1   tablespoon (15 ml) minced gingerroot
 1/4   teaspoon (1 ml) turmeric
 1/2   pound (250 g) Roma tomatoes, seeded, chopped
 1/4   cup (60 ml) water
   1   cup (250 ml) peanut butter, pureed with 2 cups (500 ml) water in a blender
       or food processor (see *Note*)
1 to 2   tablespoons (15 to 30 ml) sambal oeleck
 1/2   teaspoon (2 ml) sugar
       Salt
       Ground red pepper (to taste; start with a scant pinch)
       Juice of 1 lime

Garnish: Chopped scallions (green part only)

Heat oil in a large pan over moderate heat. Add onion and fry, stirring often, until it is richly browned but not burnt, 8 to 15 minutes. Stir in garlic, gingerroot, and turmeric. Add tomatoes and water. Cover and bring to a boil. Simmer, covered, 5 minutes. Add the peanut butter mixture, sambal oeleck, and sugar. Cover and simmer 15 minutes. During this period, remove the cover occasionally and stir, adding a little water if the soup is too thick. Add salt. Increase hotness, if desired, by adding red pepper. Remove from heat. Sprinkle with lime juice, garnish with scallions, and serve immediately. If allowed to sit, the soup will thicken. Dilute it slightly with hot water before reheating to avoid burning.

4 starter course or 2 entrée servings

Note: Peanut butter bought at a supermarket may contain added oil, salt, and sugar, which will affect the flavor and texture of the soup. If possible, buy peanut butter that contains only peanuts. This is available in natural-food stores.

Serving Suggestions: Tear off a piece of a warmed chapati, scoop up a bit of the soup, top with chopped sweet onion and shredded lettuce, and enjoy as a main course. Or accompany with Chicken-Flavored Baby Potatoes (page 244), sautéed green beans, and Honey-Glazed Onions (page 218).

RAW PEANUT VARIATION: Though peanut butter is easier to use, for best results, buy raw peanuts from natural-food shops or bulk stores and roast them at home. Place

1 cup (250 ml) red-skinned peanuts on a cookie sheet in a 350°F (180°C, gas marks 4) oven for 12 to 15 minutes or until a nutty aroma emanates from the oven. At this point, the skin will have acquired a darker color and the peanuts will be crunchy. Don't overbake, as the nuts will burn and become bitter. Grind to a relatively smooth powder in a blender or food processor. Mix with 2 cups (500 ml) water and proceed as in the recipe. This will result in a slightly coarser soup. If desired, return the water and the peanut mixture to the blender and puree to a smoother consistency.

✳ KASUNDI DIP ✳

4 teaspoons (20 ml) yellow mustard seeds, ground to a powder, or
   1 tablespoon (15 ml) dry mustard
5 tablespoons plus 1 teaspoon (80 ml) raspberry vinegar or red
   wine vinegar

Combine mustard and vinegar in a medium bowl. (You can substitute dry mustard, though it will not be as fresh.) At the table, mix with soup, a little at a time, according to taste.

✳ Fragrant Whole Red Lentil Soup ✳
EASTERN INDIA/UNITED STATES

Red lentils, *masoor dal*, are used both whole and split throughout India. India's northwestern neighbors from Pakistan rate *masoor dal* as their favorite legume. Lentils that are whole have a brownish color, whereas the common split variety is salmon pink. Although whole red lentils take longer to cook, they are heartier and have a warm, earthy flavor. In the following recipe, I prepare whole red lentils Bengali style and thicken them in Western fashion with mashed potatoes. Ginger and cardamom impart an exotic flavor to this dish.

4 cups (1 liter) water
1 cup (250 ml) whole red lentils, rinsed
1 whole jalapeño
$1/2$ teaspoon (2 ml) turmeric

$^1/_2$ cup (125 ml) water

1 cup (250 ml) mashed potato (see *Note*)

$^3/_4$ teaspoon (3 ml) salt

2 tablespoons (30 ml) mustard oil

5 whole cardamom pods, bruised

1 cup (250 ml) finely chopped onion

2 tablespoons (30 ml) minced gingerroot

1 tablespoon (15 ml) minced garlic

2 teaspoons (10 ml) ground cumin

Ground red pepper (to taste; start with a scant pinch)

1 teaspoon (5 ml) garam masala

2 tablespoons (30 ml) fresh lime juice

2 tablespoons (30 ml) finely chopped cilantro

A sprinkling of ghee (optional)

Garnish: Lime wedges

1. Bring water to a boil in a large, deep pot. Add lentils and bring to a boil again. Lower heat slightly. Add jalapeño and turmeric. Simmer, covered, until the lentils are very soft, about 40 minutes. (When pressed between the thumb and the index finger, the lentils should break easily.) Remove from heat. Discard jalapeño. Puree $^1/_2$ cup (125 ml) of this mixture with the $^1/_2$ cup (125 ml) of water in a blender or food processor. Return to the pot. Stir in the mashed potato and salt and mix until potato is dissolved.

2. Heat oil in a medium skillet over medium heat. Fry cardamom for a few seconds. Cook onion, stirring constantly, until it is richly browned but not burnt, 8 to 15 minutes. Add gingerroot, garlic, cumin, and red pepper and cook until gingerroot and garlic are lightly browned, another 1 or 2 minutes. Pour the contents of this skillet over the lentil mixture.

3. Return lentils to heat and simmer for a few minutes. Remove from heat. Discard cardamom pods. Stir in garam masala, lime juice, and cilantro. Adjust seasonings. Sprinkle with ghee, garnish with lime wedges, and serve piping hot.

4 starter course or 2 entrée servings

Note: Cut a large baking potato in chunks and steam until tender. Peel and mash with a fork until smooth. Use any leftovers for use in other vegetable dishes.

Serving Suggestions: For a winter meal, serve with Saffron-Scented Millet (page 172) and a side dish of Anchovy Mustard Greens (page 93). Also good during spring and summer with chapatis or tortillas and Piquant Salad in Shades of Green (page 258).

✳ Chick-pea Ragout ✳
EASTERN INDIA/CHINA

In Bengal, red lentils and mung beans are everyday legumes, but flavorful *chana dal*, Indian split chick-peas, occupy center stage on festive occasions. Bengali cooks prepare this robust legume like meat. They first fry whole spices such as cardamom, cinnamon, and cloves, then add onions for sautéeing, and finally the chick-peas, which simmer slowly in water.

I once served this dish to a Chinese friend who asked for soy sauce. I was appalled. But to my surprise, the soy-infused dal tasted delicious. Since then I regularly season dal dishes with soy sauce and a dash of Chinese sesame oil in East Asian fashion.

Chick-peas cook slowly even split, so I soak them overnight. Cabbage contributes a sweet, crunchy contrast to the softened legume.

The dal:

- 1 cup (250 ml) Indian split chick-peas (*chana dal*), soaked overnight in 5 cups (1.25 liters) water
- 1/4 teaspoon (1 ml) turmeric
- 1 whole jalapeño
- 1/2 pound (250 g) Roma tomatoes, seeded, chopped
- 2 teaspoons (10 ml) ground cumin
- Ground red pepper (to taste; start with a scant pinch)
- Salt
- 3/4 teaspoon (3 ml) sugar

The spices:

- 1 1/2 tablespoons (22 ml) mustard oil
- 1 bay leaf
- 1 whole dried red chile
- 5 whole cardamom pods, bruised
- 2-inch (5-cm) cinnamon stick
- 2 whole cloves
- 1/4 teaspoon (1 ml) asafetida powder
- 2 cups (500 ml) finely shredded cabbage
- 1/4 cup (60 ml) water
- 1/2 teaspoon (2 ml) low-sodium soy sauce (to taste)
- 1/2 teaspoon (2 ml) garam masala
- 2 tablespoons (30 ml) fresh lime juice
- A sprinkling of ghee or Chinese sesame oil

Garnish:
> Lime wedges
> Chopped cilantro

1. Bring *chana dal* and the soaking water to a boil in a large pot. Lower the heat slightly. Add turmeric, jalapeño, and tomatoes. Simmer, covered, about 1 hour or until the dal is very soft and breaks easily when pressed between two fingers. During this period, uncover and stir often, adding 1 to 2 tablespoons (15 to 30 ml) of hot water if the dal starts to stick to the bottom. Add cumin, red pepper, salt, and sugar. With the back of a spoon, mash some of the dal to further thicken the sauce. Keep warm.

2. Heat oil in a large skillet over moderate heat. Fry bay leaf and red chile until the chile blackens. Fry cardamom, cinnamon, and cloves for a few seconds. Sprinkle asafetida on top of the spices. Add cabbage and stir a few times. Add water. Without lowering the heat, cook covered 3 to 6 minutes or until cabbage is tender. Pour this vegetable mixture over the dal and gently heat the mixture through. (If the soup is too thick, add a little hot water and bring to a simmer again.) Add soy sauce. Remove from heat. Discard whole spices using a slotted spoon (if desired). Add garam masala and lime juice and mix well. Adjust seasoning if necessary. Sprinkle with ghee. Serve garnished with lime wedges and cilantro.

4 entrée servings

Serving Suggestions: This dish needs no other accompaniment than brown Basmati rice or plain pasta, some sliced tomatoes drizzled with Sesame-Tamarind Dressing (page 233), and Five Fundamental Seasonings (page 203).

✳ Tart Fish Soup ✳
VIETNAM

One night I noticed a Vietnamese restaurant in a dilapidated section of San Francisco's Mission district. Peeking through the window and seeing people seated on bar stools under dim lights in the smoke-filled room, I didn't go in. But I later returned at a lunch hour and discovered the delightful seafood dishes, especially this light, limey, fragrant fish soup.

At my insistence, the owner let me observe as she prepared the delicacy. Later, when I reconstructed it, I experimented with the Indian technique of rubbing the fish with turmeric and salt. This coating tinted the soup a pleasant yellow color and further enhanced its taste.

    ¹/₄ teaspoon (1 ml) salt
    ¹/₂ teaspoon (2 ml) turmeric
  1¹/₂ pounds (750 g) firm-fleshed fish, such as halibut, cod, or salmon, cut into
         bite-sized pieces
      1 tablespoon (15 ml) canola oil
         8-ounce (227-g) can unsweetened pineapple chunks, undrained
      1 whole dried red chile
      2 stalks fresh lemon grass, bottom 6 inches (15 cm) only, cut into 2-inch (5-cm)
         pieces (optional), or ¹/₄ teaspoon (1 ml) grated lemon peel
      6 cups (1.5 liters) Fish Stock (page 42)
    ¹/₂ large green or red bell pepper, cut in chunks
      1 cup (250 ml) mung bean sprouts
      2 tablespoons (30 ml) rice vinegar
    ¹/₄ cup plus 1 tablespoon (75 ml) fresh lime juice
      4 teaspoons (20 ml) sugar
         Salt
      1 tablespoon (15 ml) chopped cilantro

Garnish:
         Honey-Glazed Onions (page 218)
         Chopped fresh basil

1. Combine salt and turmeric in a medium bowl. Toss the fish pieces in this mixture so that each piece is well-coated. Heat oil in a 10-inch (25-cm) skillet over moderate heat. Fry the fish for a minute or so, just until opaque, turning the pieces once or twice. Transfer to the same bowl.

2. Drain the pineapple and save the juice. Bring red chile, lemon grass, fish stock, and pineapple juice to a boil in a large pan. Lower heat slightly. Add bell pepper. Cover and simmer for 3 to 5 minutes or until the bell pepper is slightly tender. Add fish and pineapple chunks. Cover and simmer gently for another 3 to 5 minutes or until fish is done (a toothpick inserted in the thickest part and pushed to one side should show an opaque color in the fish).

3. Add bean sprouts. Remove from heat and add vinegar, lime juice, sugar, and salt. Adjust seasoning so that the soup has a pleasantly tart and a mildly sweet taste. Add cilantro. Pour into individual soup bowls and sprinkle with the onion and basil garnishes.

6 to 8 starter course or 4 entrée servings

Serving Suggestions: Perfect with white Basmati rice at lunch or at supper. For a heartier meal, pour over a bowl of cooked rice or cellophane noodles and follow with Hot Punjab Eggplant (page 80) and Peanutty Napa Cabbage (page 90).

VARIATION: TART TOFU SOUP Vegetarians can enjoy the tofu version of this delicious soup. Replace fish stock with canned vegetable broth if desired. Take half of a 14-ounce (396-g) carton of firm tofu and cut into 1-inch (2.5-cm) cubes. Press the water from the tofu by placing the pieces between a kitchen towel or several layers of paper towels and placing a weight, such as a skillet, on top for 30 minutes. In Step 1, optionally sauté the tofu until lightly browned. Add tofu to the broth along with pineapple chunks in Step 2.

✸ Indian Chicken Soup ✸
UNITED STATES

Chicken soup in America is synonymous with a quick recovery from assorted ailments and is said to work only if "someone brings it to you." The American version is simple. The chicken broth is seasoned with garlic, onion, celery, carrots, bay leaves, and a dash of black pepper. This Indian version is enlivened with asafetida, cilantro, dill, and red pepper. Serve it to your loved ones in both sickness and in health.

    6   cups (1.5 liters) Chicken Stock (page 44); or three 14 1/2-ounce (411-g) cans
            chicken broth, defatted, plus 1 cup (250 ml) water (see "To defat canned
            chicken broth," page 45)
  1/4   teaspoon (1 ml) asafetida powder
    1   medium onion, diced
    1   medium carrot, turnip, or rutabaga, about 1/2 pound (250 g), diced
    1   medium boiling potato, about 1/4 pound (100 g), unpeeled, cut into 1-inch
            (2.5-cm) cubes
    1   cup (250 ml) shredded Swiss chard
6 to 8 snow peas
    1   tablespoon (15 ml) chopped cilantro
    1   tablespoon (15 ml) chopped fresh dill, or 1 teaspoon (5 ml) dried dill
        Salt
        Ground red pepper (to taste; start with a scant pinch)

Bring stock to a boil. Reduce heat and add asafetida, onion, carrot, and potato. Simmer, covered, 15 to 18 minutes or until the vegetables are almost done. Add Swiss chard and snow peas. Simmer, covered, a few more minutes or until all the vegetables are done. Remove from heat. Add cilantro, dill, salt, and red pepper. Serve hot.

4 to 6 starter course servings

Serving Suggestions: For a light meal, serve Asian style with a bowl of white rice. At lunch, team with a pita (or chapati) sandwich filled with Salmon-Pasta Salad International (page 250), prepared without the noodles. For a late-night supper, serve with Quick Indian Pizza (page 195) and Winter Salad (page 259).

GLOBAL VARIATIONS: Throw in a few spoonfuls of kasha or pastina (tiny pastas) after the soup has come to a boil. Simmer until the kasha or pastina softens. Another terrific variation is to add fresh peas 6 to 8 minutes before finish, and chopped scallions and Honey-Glazed Onions (page 218) on top at the end.

Vegetable Specialties and Side Dishes

●●●●●●●●●●●●●

On a cold, foggy night in San Francisco, a noted Bengali cook invited several of us expatriate Indians for dinner. The moment we walked through the door, we were transported to our native Bengal by warm greetings in the mother tongue and by the air, redolent with rich spices of home. Our hostess intended her centerpiece of the meal to be roasted chicken and lamb kebabs, but we devoured her exquisite vegetables first. Here was cauliflower, chunky, juicy, and tender, with just the right touch of chile and cumin. A simple sauté of spinach was made fragrant with five-spice. And the sweet and sour pumpkin made us long for home.

"This happens every time," she sighed. "My guests only want the vegetables."

It's easy to understand why. Indian vegetable dishes come in an array of richly satisfying flavors. Combined with grains, they provide a balanced meal. There's little desire for anything else.

But even Indian vegetarian cooking can benefit from other culinary influences. Indians tend to overcook their vegetables both for reasons of sanitation and to develop complex flavors. Here in the West, I've learned to cook my broccoli, Brussels sprouts, and winter squashes al dente.

Once while visiting Bangkok, I meandered off a main road and found a simple cafeteria-style eatery. It was not the type of restaurant that a tourist guidebook would recommend, though definitely one where locals congregated. A wide variety of tantalizing vegetable preparations awaited me, some topped with a garnish of fresh red chile slivers or whole chile "flowers." There were stir-fried leafy greens, bean sprouts tangled with carrot sticks, and eggplant glazed with a deep brown sauce. The food was delicious. The two women managers didn't speak English, but I communicated via the universal language of hunger—an empty plate and a happy smile. I left respecting Thai cuisine even more.

Although Korea is known for its beef dishes, vegetables are no less significant. When cooking with cucumber, Koreans add part of the cucumber in the early stages of cooking for a tender texture, and the remainder toward the end, locking in fresh flavor. They work culinary magic with fragrant pine mushrooms, marinating them in a mixture of soy and sesame, then grilling them to succulent tenderness.

While living in France, I became acquainted with the leek, a member of the onion family. Though the French dote on it, this elegant vegetable is not widely used in the United States and is unknown in India. One evening I ordered dinner from the fixed menu at a Paris bistro. The first course was vegetables, not the customary fish. Two whole leek stalks, their delicate white color shaded into muted green, reposed on an oval platter. Braised simply with butter, salt, and black pepper, they tasted soft and creamy, yet resilient. Soon I began to cook this versatile vegetable with grains, potatoes, or, when in a Mediterranean mood, with eggplant. In late summer, I snip off the tender leek tops in my garden and use them in place of chopped onion.

My vegetable repertoire has grown to include many new marinating, cooking, and garnishing techniques. In the Indian fashion, I still include a variety of vegetables on the dinner plate, sometimes combining several in one dish. But I am likely to select vegetables unknown in India, such as gai lan, yuca, or oyster mushroom. I find that fresh Mediterranean herbs, such as oregano and tarragon, mix surprisingly well with Indian-spiced vegetable dishes. Indian combinations, such as black mustard seeds and curry leaves, invigorate Swiss chard and broccoli. These vegetable dishes can be as elegant as the fanciest seafood or meat dinners. They enrich the millennia-old Indian vegetarian cookery.

The preparation of such exquisite vegetable dishes requires skill. That makes vegetable cooking a challenge and an adventure, and the result, a source of pride. ✳

Vegetable Matters

✳   The concept of an entrée does not exist in an Indian meal. Many dishes work in concert to provide flavor, texture, and nutrition in a meal. However, Indian-inspired vegetable dishes that are hearty and substantial can be served as a main course in the West. The serving suggestions for those recipes will indicate so.

✳ *Flavoring steamed vegetables:* When steaming vegetables to serve as an accompaniment, place raw onion slices and fresh herbs such as mint, tarragon, or sage on top for flavor. Flavor-absorbing vegetables such as potatoes, cauliflower, and rutabaga are especially good this way.

✳ To satisfy the needs of different types of vegetarians such as lacto-ovo or vegan, I have included some dishes without dairy products, a few with eggs, and still others with fish or shrimp-flavored sauces for those who are not strict vegetarians.

✳ Sweet, Sour, and Smoky Potatoes ✳
WESTERN INDIA

When Spain's conquistadors arrived in South America, they found the Incas growing a tuber that they called *battato*. In English that became "potato." The Portuguese traders introduced the potato to India, where it was enthusiastically adopted. This subtly flavored vegetable easily absorbs other stronger flavors, making it a perfect foil for the highly spiced dishes of India. In the centuries since that time, Indians have developed countless ways of preparing the potato.

This potato dish comes from the western Indian state of Gujarat, where, not too surprisingly, potatoes are called *batata.* I enhance the sweet and sour flavor combination, so loved by Gujaratis, by smoking part of the potatoes using a stove-top smoker. If you don't have a smoker, omit this step; the dish will still be fabulous.

For a different taste adventure, try Yellow Finn or Yukon Gold potatoes. These varieties have a natural buttery flavor and respond well to the touch of chile, cumin, and coriander.

2	tablespoons (30 ml) mustard oil
1/2	teaspoon (2 ml) black mustard seeds
1/4	teaspoon (1 ml) cumin seeds
2	tablespoons (30 ml) minced gingerroot
1	jalapeño seeded, finely chopped (to taste)
2 1/2	pounds (1.25 kg) peeled or unpeeled potatoes, about 8 medium, cut into 1 1/2-inch (4-cm) cubes
1	tablespoon (15 ml) ground cumin
1	tablespoon (15 ml) ground coriander
3/4	teaspoon (3 ml) turmeric
3/4	cup (185 ml) water

1 tablespoon (15 ml) finely chopped cilantro

1 teaspoon (5 ml) salt

1 tablespoon (15 ml) sugar

2 teaspoons (10 ml) tamarind concentrate

Garnish: Chopped cilantro

1. Heat oil in a 12-inch (30-cm) steep-sided skillet over moderate heat until sizzling. Add mustard and cumin seeds and fry until the mustard seeds pop and the cumin seeds are lightly browned. Add gingerroot and jalapeño and fry until gingerroot is lightly browned. Add potatoes and stir well to coat with the oil and spices. Fry for 2 minutes over medium heat, stirring often. Combine cumin, coriander, turmeric, and water in a small bowl and whisk until smooth. Pour this spice paste over the potatoes and mix well. Add cilantro, salt, and sugar and bring to a boil.

2. Simmer, covered, 25 to 35 minutes or until the potatoes are tender. During this period, uncover a few times and turn the potatoes. Add a little water if the skillet is too dry. Stir in tamarind. Cook, uncovered, for a few minutes to thicken the sauce. Remove from heat.

3. To smoke the potatoes (optional): Take 6 to 9 (or more if you desire) potato cubes out of the skillet and smoke them in a stove-top smoker following manufacturer's directions. Return them to the skillet and mix in gently with the other potatoes.

4. Serve hot or at room temperature garnished with cilantro.

4 entrée or 6 to 8 side dish servings

Serving Suggestions: Accompany with warmed tortillas (or chapati, Syrian, or pita bread) and Mint-Basil Chutney (page 211) for a light vegetarian meal. To serve as a side dish, partner with Soy- and Mirin-Glazed Salmon (page 99), Lime-Grilled Chicken (page 125), or Garlic-Glazed Tofu (page 67). Serve these potatoes also at teatime or at a brunch or buffet; the flavors blend perfectly with a fruity bread or a rich, sweet cake such as Spicy Apple Cake (page 277).

✳ Gujarati Potato Boats ✳
WESTERN INDIA

Gujaratis, many of whom are vegetarians, excel in blending unique spice mixes in vegetable dishes. An example is the stuffing for this dish, which comes from Indu Patel, an expert cook in Philadelphia. Her fabulous filling contains sesame seeds, chick-pea flour, coconut, gingerroot, and green chile. She insists that it takes "a bit of oil." I substitute chicken broth for oil to reduce fat and calories and to achieve a lighter taste. Though the spicing is Indian, the dish is baked and presented in a Western manner.

I had to include both of these Gujarati potato recipes in this chapter because they are so different from each other and so good.

The spice paste:

1   tablespoon (15 ml) coarsely chopped gingerroot

1   jalapeño, seeded, coarsely chopped (to taste)

1   teaspoon (5 ml) dried flaked sweetened coconut

3   tablespoons (45 ml) water

3   tablespoons (45 ml) toasted and ground sesame seeds

The filling:

1   tablespoon (15 ml) canola oil

¹/4   teaspoon (1 ml) turmeric

1   cup (250 ml) chicken broth, defatted (see "To defat canned chicken broth," page 45)

1   teaspoon (5 ml) chick-pea flour, *besan* (no substitute)

2   teaspoons (10 ml) Cream of Wheat (no substitute)

1¹/4   teaspoons (6 ml) sugar

¹/4   teaspoon (1 ml) salt

2   pounds (1 kg) new potatoes, 20 small (about 2 inches [5 cm] in diameter), peeled or unpeeled (see *Note for the Gardener*)

Canola oil for brushing

Salt and freshly ground black pepper for dusting

Cilantro Splash (page 223)

1. To prepare the spice paste: Using a spice grinder, a food processor, or a mortar and pestle, pound gingerroot, jalapeño, coconut, and water to a relatively smooth paste. Combine with sesame powder in a small bowl.

2. Preheat oven to 450°F (230°C, gas marks 8). To prepare the filling: Heat oil in a small skillet over moderate heat until it sizzles. Add turmeric. Add the spice paste and cook until it is lightly browned. Add chicken broth, chick-pea flour, Cream of Wheat, and sugar. Cook, uncovered, until the mixture thickens, stirring often. Add salt. Remove from heat and allow to cool to room temperature.

3. Cut the potatoes in half crosswise. Brush the outside surface lightly with oil, then dust with salt and pepper. If you like, scoop out some of the flesh from the cut side of each half to make room for the filling. (Use these potato bits in other vegetable dishes.) Put the two halves together and arrange the potatoes on an ungreased roasting pan or cookie sheet. Bake for 35 to 45 minutes or until done (a toothpick inserted in the middle easily goes all the way through).

4. Spread some filling evenly on the cut side of each half. Layer with Cilantro Splash. Place under the broiler, sauced side up, for 2 to 3 minutes to brown very lightly. Best served warm, but can be served at room temperature.

4 to 6 side dish servings

Serving Suggestions: Toothpick the two halves together and place on a buffet table. Or serve cut side up and use as a pretty side dish to Indian Chicken Soup (page 59) or Anchovy Mustard Greens (page 93).

Note for the Gardener: Any of the following finely flavored potato varieties are suited for this dish: Desiree, red-skinned with pale yellow flesh; Bison, a red-skinned, white-fleshed tuber with a smooth, firm texture; Yukon Gold, whose yellow interior takes on a golden-brown tone with baking; and Butte, a high-protein baking potato with a smooth texture.

VARIATION: MIDDLE EASTERN VEGETABLE MEDLEY For a stunning visual effect and taste sensation, stuff a combination of vegetables with this spicy filling in Middle Eastern style. Choose onion, eggplant, zucchini, or mild chiles such as Anaheim. Prepare as above up to Step 4, then spread with a variety of sauces such as Chilied Mango Chutney (page 205), Tamarind-Date Chutney (page 208), or Roasted Tomato-Chile Salsa (page 216). Top the sauce with toasted dried fish, sweet onion, roasted peanuts, or Five Fundamental Seasonings (page 203). You can also stuff hard-boiled egg halves (with the yolks removed). They would be ready to serve immediately. These stuffed vegetables and eggs can be an interesting appetizer or part of a buffet dinner.

VARIATION: GUJARATI GREENS The savory filling becomes a sauce base for hearty greens. Even people who don't like greens enjoy this dish. Prepare the filling in a large (10-inch [25-cm]), steep-sided skillet. In Step 2 before adding salt, add 1/2 pound (250 g), about 5 cups (1.25 liters) of chopped kale, collard, Swiss chard, fresh spinach leaves, or a combination. Cook, covered, 6 to 8 minutes or until the greens are tender to the bite but still retain their color. If using spinach alone, cook only 3 to 5 minutes. Remove from heat and add salt.

4 side dish servings

Serving Suggestions: Be sure to place a tray of Five Fundamental Seasonings (page 203) on the table. For a grain dish, choose Bengali Crab Risotto (page 170) or, for the vegetarians, Basic Pilaf with Nutty Vermicelli Threads (page 177). Sweet and Sour Plantain Sauce (page 222) is a perfect accompaniment.

✳ Garlic-Glazed Tofu ✳
INTERNATIONAL

My husband Tom is not particularly fond of tofu, but this custard-like soybean derivative is so rich in calcium and other nutrients that I strive to make it tasty. One day I served some marinated and broiled tofu, and he called it "the best tofu dish ever." The creamy white tofu triangles became irresistible dipped in an aromatic soy, garlic, and gingerroot marinade and roasted to a deep brown color. "Almost like a flan, only darker," is how Tom described it.

14-ounce (396-g) carton firm tofu, drained, rinsed

The marinade:
- 1/4 cup (60 ml) low-sodium soy sauce
- 1/2 cup (125 ml) mirin, Japanese cooking wine
- 2 teaspoons (10 ml) grated gingerroot or gingerroot paste (see page 12)
- 3 garlic cloves, forced through a garlic press
- Ground red pepper (to taste; start with a scant pinch)

The topping:
- 2 teaspoons (10 ml) canola oil
- 4 to 8 large cloves garlic, minced (to taste)

Garnish (don't omit):
- Chopped cilantro and thinly sliced scallions

1. To cut tofu into triangles: Turn tofu on its side and cut in half. Cut each half into quarters and then slice each quarter diagonally into triangles. When you finish, you should have 16 triangles.
2. To press water out of tofu: Wrap tofu pieces in a heavy kitchen towel or place between several layers of paper towels on a cookie sheet. Put a heavy weight such as an iron skillet on top. Let stand at room temperature for 30 minutes. Remove the weight and the towel(s).

3. Meanwhile, combine soy sauce, mirin, gingerroot, garlic, and red pepper in a small saucepan. Bring to a boil over moderate heat, then lower the heat slightly. Cook, uncovered, 8 to 15 minutes until the mixture thickens and is reduced to about ¹/₄ of its volume, stirring often. Transfer to a large bowl and allow to cool to room temperature.

4. To prepare the topping: In hot oil in a small 6-inch (15-cm) skillet over moderate heat, fry garlic until it is medium brown in color and emits an aroma, 3 to 5 minutes, stirring often. Don't let it burn. Tranfer to a small bowl.

5. When tofu is ready, preheat oven to 350°F (180°C, gas marks 4). Dip 2 or 3 pieces of tofu at a time in the marinade, making sure each piece is well-coated. Lift with a slotted spoon and place on a cookie sheet or baking pan lined with aluminum foil. (Do this just before broiling, otherwise the water still being secreted by the tofu could dilute the marinade.) Return any extra marinade to the small saucepan. Bake tofu for about 10 minutes. Then place under the broiler for 4 to 6 minutes or until the color is darker and the texture is slightly harder. Remove from the broiler. Meanwhile, reheat the marinade and spoon a little over each tofu triangle. Place a bit of garlic on top of each. Serve garnished with scallions and cilantro. (Garnishing is essential to offset the dark color of this dish.)

2 entrée or 4 side dish servings

Serving Suggestions: Serve as a main dish at a vegetarian meal along with a side dish of Gujarati Greens (page 66) and Summer Squash Ragout (page 89). Sweet (short-grain, glutinous) brown rice, which cooks to a sticky mass, is perfect as the grain-mate. (This rice is sold in natural-food stores. Or substitute plain brown rice.) Offer the garlic lovers a small bowl of Toasted Garlic Crumbs (see page 245), which is delicious sprinkled over both the tofu and the rice. On another occasion, try these tofu triangles as an appetizer; or pack them in a lunch box with a spinach salad and Hindi Croutons (page 259).

✳ Sweet and Spicy Sancoche ✳
LATIN AMERICA

*S*ancoche or *sancocho*, a filling and nutritious soup-stew, originated in Latin America. The name loosely means "a mixture of everything," because it's a dish that can contain beef, pork, pickled meat, or fish, mixed with various vegetables. This vegetarian version brims with root vegetables such as yuca (or cassava) and sweet potato. Yuca is the tuber of choice in Brazil, where it's used much like potato. Indeed, you can substitute potato for yuca in this dish.

The gentle sweetness of the sauce results from the melting of the sweet potato pieces. Annatto (achiote) paste, a Latin favorite derived from brick-red annatto seeds, is the seasoning that gives the stew its color and zip. With the addition of cumin, gingerroot, turmeric, and tamarind, this stew speaks with a slightly Indian accent.

Chop all vegetables into 1-inch (2.5-cm) cubes:

1	medium sweet potato, about $^1/_2$ pound (250 g), peeled, cubed
1	tablespoon (15 ml) canola oil
$^1/_4$	teaspoon (1 ml) cumin seeds
1	cup (250 ml) thinly sliced onion
5	large cloves garlic, slivered
1	tablespoon (15 ml) grated gingerroot or gingerroot paste (see page 12)
1	jalapeño, seeded, chopped (to taste)
$^1/_4$	teaspoon (1 ml) turmeric
1	teaspoon (5 ml) ground cumin
2	cups (500 ml) water
$^3/_4$	teaspoon (3 ml) annatto paste mixed with 2 teaspoons (10 ml) water (see *Note 1*)
1	small yuca (cassava), about $^1/_2$ pound (250 g), outer bark and inner mauve layer removed, cubed; or 2 medium unpeeled potatoes, cubed (see *Note 2*)
$^3/_4$	pound (375 g) butternut squash, peeled, cubed
$^1/_4$	cup (60 ml) raw cashew halves
$^1/_2$	cup (125 ml) chopped cilantro
2	teaspoons (10 ml) tamarind concentrate
	Salt

Garnish:

2	hard-cooked eggs, quartered
	Chopped cilantro

1. Mince 3 or 4 sweet potato cubes, so that they will dissolve in the sauce and thicken it.
2. In hot oil in a large, deep-sided pan over moderate heat, fry cumin seeds. As soon as they turn light brown, add onion and cook until it is translucent, about 2 minutes. Add garlic, gingerroot, jalapeño, turmeric, and ground cumin and stir a few times. Add water and annatto paste and bring to a boil.

3. Add yuca, squash, cashews, and cilantro. Lower heat slightly. Simmer, covered, 20 to 30 minutes or until vegetables are tender. Add tamarind and salt. Remove from heat. If the gravy is still thin, thicken it by mashing a few squash pieces with the back of a spoon and mixing in with the sauce. Garnish with eggs and cilantro and serve hot.

2 to 4 entrée or 6 side dish servings

Note 1: Annatto paste, available in Latin American markets, is easier to use than the conventional annatto seeds. (The seeds are ground to a powder, then mixed with oil, which is then used to impart the characteristic red-orange annatto color and flavor to a dish.) Some brands of annatto paste might contain a few other ingredients such as salt and oregano, but they don't detract from the flavor of this dish.

Note 2: If you like the taste of yuca, you can serve it in another meal simply steamed. Peel and cube this tuber as in this recipe, then steam for 15 minutes or until tender. Serve as a potato substitute, tossed with lime juice, salt, black pepper, ground red pepper, and a little olive oil or avocado oil.

Serving Suggestions: Enjoy a meat-free meal with Quinoa Uppama (page 180) and Mint-Basil Chutney (page 224). You can please the fish eaters by serving this stew with Steamed Fish in Lime-Ginger Sauce (page 101); brown Basmati rice that has been cooked with garlic, cilantro, cashews, and raisins; and Sweet and Hot Peanut-Lime Sambal (page 219). Use any leftovers as a sandwich filling for toasted pita bread.

VARIATION: SHRIMP SANCOCHE Create a taste adventure for nonvegetarians by adding shrimp to this dish. Use 1/2 pound (250 g) fresh shrimp or thawed frozen shrimp. Add in Step 2 during the last 5 minutes of cooking.

✳ Gai Lan with Balsamic Vinaigrette ✳

CHINA

Gai lan, a dark green vegetable also known as Chinese broccoli, is a common item featured in Chinese restaurants in the United States. Chinese chefs call gai lan "the king of vegetables." When cooked it retains its lovely color and doesn't shrink like other greens.

All parts of this nutritious vegetable—the leaves, succulent stalks, and white or yellow flowers—are edible. It needs little cooking; I find steaming or simmering to be the best way of releasing its bold flavors. The rest is equally simple: just splash with a mixture of balsamic vinegar and olive oil, or sprinkle with a little balsamic ghee. The elegant gai lan provides a wonderful accompaniment to spicier dishes.

$^1/_4$ cup (60 ml) olive oil, ghee, or butter

1$^1/_2$ tablespoons (22 ml) balsamic vinegar

Dash black salt

$^1/_4$ teaspoon (1 ml) salt

1 bunch gai lan, at least 1 pound (500 g) (see *Note for the Gardener*)

1. To prepare the sauce: If using ghee or butter, melt it over very low heat. (I use a small Turkish coffee maker with a spout for both cooking and serving. You can use a small saucepan.) Stir in vinegar. If using olive oil, drizzle vinegar slowly over the oil while beating lightly with a wire whisk to thicken the mixture.

2. To prepare gai lan: Steam gai lan until the cut end turns pale green, 5 to 8 minutes. Alternatively, cook it the Chinese way, simmered in water mixed with a little oil. This method allows you to check each stalk individually for doneness, and the oil gives a beautiful sheen to the vegetable. To do this, fill a large, steep-sided pan slightly less than halfway with water. Add a teaspoon (5 ml) of canola or other oil of choice. Bring water to a boil, lower heat, and add gai lan. Gai lan should lie immersed in water. Cook, uncovered, 5 to 8 minutes, checking the cut ends for a pale green color. (Use a pair of chopsticks to do this.) Remove each stalk as soon as it's done to a heated serving platter. Overcooking will destroy the succulence of the vegetable and discolor it. Reserve the water and use in preparing stocks. Serve gai lan drizzled with the balsamic vinaigrette, black salt, and salt, or let guests add their own.

4 side dish servings

Note for the Gardener: Gai lan is easy to grow. I plant it every spring at the same time I plant mustard greens and spinach. I harvest it before the buds open, when the vegetable is at its tender best.

Serving Suggestions: When gai lan is on the menu, bring out the chopsticks. To continue with the Asian theme, lay the table with jasmine rice and Blackened Chicken (page 126). Tamari-Wasabi Dressing (page 234) could be an alternative or addition to the Balsamic Vinaigrette. Fresh fruit—papayas, lychees, mandarin (or regular) oranges—are an ideal end to such a meal. Gai lan is versatile and you can serve it as a side dish to most other meat, seafood, or vegetarian meals as well.

* Braised Leeks with Elephant Garlic *

FRANCE

Leeks are as elegant as asparagus and a superb treat in winter. Asafetida and elephant garlic bring out the delicate flavor of the leeks in this dish as they are braised. Elephant garlic, actually a type of onion, is used in two ways: minced as a seasoning and cubed as a vegetable.

  4 ounces (100 g) elephant garlic, about 2 cloves
1 1/2 pounds (750 g) leeks
1 1/2 tablespoons (22 ml) olive oil, ghee, or butter
  1/2 teaspoon (2 ml) asafetida powder
  2 tablespoons-plus (30 ml) chicken broth, defatted (see "To defat canned chicken broth," page 45)
     Salt and freshly ground black pepper

1. To prepare the elephant garlic: Peel the cloves. Mince half of them; chop the remainder into 1/2-inch (1-cm) cubes.
2. To prepare the leeks: Trim off the roots and the coarse top, leaving as much of the tender green section as you can. Slice leeks in rounds 1 inch (2.5 cm) thick or, for a better presentation, leave them whole. In either case, make sure you have removed the soil that sometimes can be found buried down the stalks. (Soaking them briefly in a bowl of water can draw out this soil.)
3. In a large, steep-sided skillet in sizzling hot oil, cook asafetida and the minced and cubed garlic until garlic is lightly browned. Stir constantly to prevent sticking to the bottom of the skillet. Add chicken broth and bring to a boil. Lower the heat slightly and add leeks. Cover and simmer until the leeks and the garlic cubes are tender, 5 to 7 minutes. Don't overcook, as the leeks will lose their color and texture. Salt and pepper to taste.

4 side dish servings

Serving Suggestions: White Basmati rice is a good accompaniment to this dish, along with Salmon-Pasta Salad International (prepared without the noodles, page 250). Some papads (preferably those flavored with cracked black pepper) and Green Mango Chutney (page 206) will complete a vegetarian meal. You can also serve these leeks as an appetizer to precede a seafood dinner.

✳ Satay Apples and Bok Choy ✳

INDONESIA/WESTERN INDIA

The western state of Maharashtra in India has a distinct regional cuisine that makes frequent use of peanuts, a New World transplant that grows well in that region. Coconut is also a favorite flavoring in that coastal state. In fact, Marathi cooks believe that "no sauce is complete without a touch of coconut." Both of these ingredients are also used widely in Indonesia. Satay, an Indonesian peanut-coconut sauce, is known all over the world. It is most often served with skewered meat.

Here bok choy bathes in a robust peanut butter sauce that has subtle overtones of coconut. The versatile apple, treated as a vegetable, adds a pleasant sweetness.

$1/4$ cup (60 ml) peanut butter (see *Note*)
$1/2$ cup (125 ml) water
   1   tablespoon (15 ml) Indian sesame oil (*gingely*), or canola oil
   1   whole dried red chile
   1   tablespoon (15 ml) minced gingerroot
   1   jalapeño, seeded, chopped (to taste)
$1/4$ teaspoon (1 ml) turmeric
$1/2$ teaspoon (2 ml) ground cumin
$1/2$ teaspoon (2 ml) ground coriander
$1/2$ teaspoon (2 ml) sugar
      Salt
      Ground red pepper (to taste; start with a scant pinch)
$3/4$ pound (375 g) bok choy, coarsely shredded crosswise
   1   medium tart apple, about $1/2$ pound (250 g), cored but not peeled, cut into
         slices $1/4$ inch (6 mm) thick
$1/4$ teaspoon (1 ml) garam masala
$1^1/2$ tablespoons (22 ml) fresh lime juice
   1   tablespoon (15 ml) dried, flaked, sweetened coconut

1. Combine peanut butter and water in a medium bowl. Stir with a fork or whirl in a blender until smooth.
2. Heat oil in a 12-inch (30-cm) steep-sided skillet over moderate heat. Fry red chile until it blackens and a pungent smell rises from the skillet. Add gingerroot and jalapeño. Add turmeric, cumin, coriander, sugar, salt, and red pepper. Add the peanut butter mixture. As soon as it comes to a boil, lower heat. Add bok choy and

apples. Simmer, covered, 5 minutes or just until the vegetables are tender. At this point the bok choy will still retain its beautiful green color, and the apple slices, tinged light yellow with turmeric, will hold their shape. Remove from heat and gently mix in garam masala and lime juice. Adjust seasoning if necessary. You can mix in coconut at the same time or sprinkle it on top for a lovely snowflake effect.

4 side dish servings

Note: The common supermarket brands of peanut butter may contain salt, sugar, and preservatives. If possible, buy peanut butter made only with peanuts, sold in natural-food stores and some supermarkets.

Serving Suggestions: Serve as part of a hearty supper with plain kasha topped with Honey-Glazed Onions (page 218), sautéed carrots, and Roasted Tikka Potatoes (page 243).

✳ Indian Spiced Brussels Sprouts ✳

UNITED STATES

In this recipe, I use Eastern spicing with Brussels sprouts, a Western vegetable, and it's an excellent match. Indian five-spice, cumin, and coriander accent the cream-colored yogurt sauce. Since the fragrance of coriander permeates the dish, I roast and grind coriander seeds just before cooking rather than using the store-bought powdered spice.

- 2 tablespoons (30 ml) mustard oil or canola oil
- 1 pound (500 g) Brussels sprouts (about 18), tough ends trimmed, quartered (see *Note*)
- 1 bay leaf
- 2 whole dried red chiles
- 1/4 teaspoon (1 ml) Indian five-spice
- 1 tablespoon (15 ml) grated gingerroot or gingerroot paste (see page 12)
- 1 jalapeño, seeded, chopped (to taste)
- 1/4 teaspoon (1 ml) turmeric
- 1/2 teaspoon (2 ml) salt
- 1/2 teaspoon (2 ml) sugar
- 2 teaspoons (10 ml) ground cumin

1   tablespoon (15 ml) ground coriander
¹/₃ cup (75 ml) water
2   tablespoons (30 ml) plain nonfat yogurt, lightly beaten until smooth and
     mixed with ¹/₄ teaspoon (1 ml) all-purpose flour
1   tablespoon (15 ml) fresh lime or lemon juice

Garnish: Toasted cashew halves or toasted slivered almonds

1. Heat 1 tablespoon (15 ml) oil in a large skillet over moderate heat until sizzling.
   Sauté the Brussels sprouts for a few minutes, stirring often. They will absorb the
   oil quickly. When they start to turn brown at the edges, remove with a slotted
   spoon and set aside.

2. Heat the remaining 1 tablespoon (15 ml) oil in the same skillet over moderate
   heat. Fry bay leaf and red chiles until the chiles are blackened. Add five-spice. As
   soon as the spices start popping, add gingerroot, jalapeño, turmeric, salt, and sugar
   and stir several times. Combine cumin, coriander, and water in a small bowl and
   stir until smooth. Pour this spice paste over the other spices in the skillet; stir.

3. Add the Brussels sprouts. Bring to a boil. Simmer, covered, until the vegetables are
   tender but not mushy, 12 to 18 minutes. Don't overcook Brussels sprouts, as they
   will discolor and develop an odor.

4. If using a gas stove, turn heat to low. If using an electric stove, transfer to a second burner that has been set to very low heat. (This is so that the yogurt will not
   curdle from excessive heat.) Gently mix in yogurt. When the mixture is heated
   through, remove from heat immediately. Taste for salt. Let stand, covered, for a
   few minutes to help develop flavor. Just before serving, sprinkle with lime juice.
   Serve garnished with cashews.

4 side dish servings

Note: You can shred Brussels sprouts thinly and use in place of cabbage in most cabbage recipes. You can also substitute them in cauliflower recipes.

Serving Suggestions: Celebrate Thanksgiving by serving this unusual but highly nutritious cruciferous vegetable along with Sweet and Nutty Carrot-Turnip Soup (page
49). On another occasion, serve a hearty vegetarian dinner by accompanying with
brown Basmati rice (or warmed chapatis), Gujarati Potato Boats (page 64), and
Green Mango Chutney (page 206). You can also serve these Brussels sprouts slices
as an appetizer.

✸ Spicy Seoul Cucumber ✸

KOREA

I first experienced these soy-and-sesame-drenched cucumber pieces in Seoul, where they were served as a garnish. I developed an immediate and lasting craving for the garnish even though I no longer remember the entrée they accompanied. In reconstructing the recipe, I include a touch of asafetida, which adds depth to the sauce and a subtle hint of things Indian.

This sauté is tasty enough to stand on its own as a side dish. Don't limit its use to a garnish.

   1   medium-sized cucumber or $1/2$ large English cucumber, about $1/2$ pound
         (250 g)
   1   tablespoon (15 ml) low-sodium soy sauce
 $1/2$ teaspoon (2 ml) Chinese sesame oil
 $1/2$ teaspoon (2 ml) toasted and ground sesame seeds
 $1/2$ teaspoon (2 ml) sugar
   1   tablespoon (15 ml) unrefined safflower oil or canola oil
 $1/4$ teaspoon (1 ml) asafetida powder
        Salt

Garnish: Toasted white sesame seeds

1. Peel, halve, and seed the cucumber and thinly slice into semicircles about $1/8$ inch (3 mm) thick. (If using an English cucumber, you don't need to peel or seed.)
2. Combine soy sauce, sesame oil, ground sesame, and sugar in a small bowl. Heat oil in a medium skillet over moderate heat. Sprinkle asafetida over the oil. Add cucumber. Cook for a few minutes until cucumber softens and turns slightly pale. Add the soy sauce mixture and cook just until the mixture is heated through. Add salt. Remove from heat, garnish with sesame seeds, and serve.

4 side dish servings

Serving Suggestions: Enjoy these spicy cucumbers with plain-cooked millet or brown rice and a legume dish such as Bengali Black Beans (page 82). Or serve as a topping for any grain dish.

* Savory Sprouts Stir-Fry *

UNITED STATES

My first experience with sprouts was as a young student when I had to sprout a chick-pea and draw its picture for a botany class. The bean was amazing as it sent out shoots. It needed no soil, only air and water; yet this tiny bean represented a flow of life. I learned that a seed contains the plant's supply of vitamins, minerals, and protein. This vital energy increases as it is transmitted to the sprout, which then becomes a most desirable food.

A variety of sprouts are available in American supermarkets. While the gentler alfalfa and radish sprouts are ideal for salads, the stronger lentil and pea sprouts are best if briefly cooked. I prefer to quick-fry these cooking sprouts with a few Indian staple spices. This browns the sprouts and seals in their flavor while retaining some of the crunchiness. To add texture and body to the dish, I add Brussels sprouts and toasted cashews.

I find myself devouring this simple dish, joyfully ignoring the rest of the meal.

1/4	pound (100 g) Brussels sprouts (about 4), tough ends trimmed
6	ounce (175 g) mixed sprouted lentils, azuki beans, and sweet peas (or other cooking sprouts)
1 to 1 1/2	tablespoons (15 to 22 ml) olive oil
1/4	teaspoon (1 ml) cumin seeds
3 to 5	large cloves garlic, minced
1/2	cup (125 ml) thinly sliced onion
2	tablespoons (30 ml) toasted cashew halves
1/4	teaspoon (1 ml) black salt
	Salt
	A few drops of ghee (optional)
2	tablespoons (30 ml) fresh lime juice

1. Steam Brussels sprouts 12 to 20 minutes or until tender but not too soft. Take care not to overcook. Cut them in halves. Steam the cooking sprouts for 3 to 5 minutes or until they are tender to the bite.
2. Heat oil in a small skillet or a wok over moderate heat. Add cumin seeds and fry until the seeds are lightly browned. Add garlic and fry until it is lightly browned. Add onion and cook until onion is translucent. Lower the heat slightly and add the cooking sprouts, Brussels sprouts, and cashews and cook, uncovered, for a minute

or two to heat the mixture through. Add black salt and regular salt. Remove from the heat. Sprinkle with ghee and lime juice. Best served immediately.

2 entrée or 4 side dish servings

Serving Suggestions: Provide each guest with a mixture of sambal oeleck, Chinese sesame oil, and fish sauce in a small saucer to pour over the vegetables. Team this dish with brown rice and Onion Yogurt Relish (page 209) for supper. For a delightful lunch, toss with cooked pasta that has been moistened lightly with olive oil; season to taste with Five Fundamental Seasonings (page 203) and finely chopped arugula leaves. On another occasion, accompany with Velvet Fish (page 111) and Curried Quinoa, Olive, and Romaine Salad (page 179).

✳ Eggplant Caponata International ✳

ITALY

Caponata is a Sicilian specialty. Its base is eggplant and sometimes other vegetables. Apparently in medieval times, it was accompanied by a sweet and sour sauce, but my version of caponata has been expanded to include a variety of flavors from around the world. Using a tip from an Italian chef, I first roast the sliced eggplant. Then I coat the pieces with a choice of sauces: red chile paste; black bean paste; a blend of plum sauce and tamarind concentrate; an herb chutney. Next I broil the sauced pieces briefly and finally drizzle them with a vinaigrette. Guests feast from my colorful caponata platter that bespeaks many cultures.

    1   medium eggplant, about 1 pound (500g)
        Olive oil for brushing
        Black salt for dusting

The sauces (choose from one or more according to taste):

For a sweet-tart flavor

    1   teaspoon (5 ml) plum sauce
    1/4 teaspoon (1 ml) tamarind concentrate

For a warm flavor

    1   teaspoon (5 ml) sambal oeleck
        Dash black salt

For a fiery flavor
  1 teaspoon (5 ml) black bean sauce with chile

For a fresh herb flavor
    Cilantro Splash (page 223) or Mint-Basil Chutney (page 224)

For a sweet, sour, and hot flavor
  1 teaspoon (5 ml) tamarind concentrate
  1 teaspoon (5 ml) water
 $^1/_2$ teaspoon (2 ml) sugar
 $^1/_4$ teaspoon (1 ml) ground cumin
    Dash Chaat Powder (see page 8)
    Ground red pepper (to taste; start with a scant pinch)
    Dash black salt

The vinaigrette:
  2 tablespoons (30 ml) olive oil
  2 tablespoons (30 ml) avocado oil
  4 teaspoons (20 ml) rice vinegar
  2 teaspoons (10 ml) fresh chopped tarragon (or a combination of fresh herbs
      such as tarragon, thyme, and oregano), or $^1/_2$ teaspoon (2 ml) dried tarragon
 $^1/_8$ teaspoon (0.5 ml) black salt
    Salt

1. Preheat oven to 450°F (230°C, gas marks 8). Slice the unpeeled eggplant crosswise in rounds $^1/_2$ inch (1 cm) thick. Halve the wider rounds from the middle of the eggplant into two semicircles if you like. Prick the top surface of each piece with a fork several times so that the oil and spice can penetrate. Brush the top surface generously with oil and dust lightly with black salt. Place the pieces on an oiled baking sheet and bake for 22 to 32 minutes or until tender and golden brown. (A toothpick inserted in the middle should go through easily and show a translucent color in the flesh.) Don't let the rounds get too brown.

2. To prepare sauces (you can do this while the eggplant is baking): Place the ingredients for each sauce in a small bowl and mix with a fork until smooth.

3. Layer the top surface of each eggplant piece with a teaspoon (5 ml) or so of one of the sauces. Broil for 2 to 5 minutes or until the sauce is bubbly. Watch carefully so the pieces don't burn. Cover and keep warm.

4. To prepare the vinaigrette: Combine all the ingredients except regular salt in a screw-top jar. Add salt. Close the top and shake the jar; the dressing will thicken.

Place the eggplant pieces on a large platter. Drizzle with the vinaigrette so that each piece is well-covered, or let the guests add dressing to suit their individual tastes. Best served warm. If not serving immediately, pour the vinaigrette over the eggplant pieces and let them marinate for several hours at room temperature or covered in the refrigerator. Don't reheat, but bring to room temperature before serving.

4 side dish servings

Serving Suggestions: Serve as an appetizer or as part of a main meal with Barley, Wild Rice, and Azuki Beans Khichuri (page 181). For vegetable accompaniments, try some steamed asparagus or green beans and a baked yam or browned potatoes (see "To brown potatoes" on page 113). Sun-Dried Tomato and Sweet Red Pepper Cream (page 226) would be a lovely addition to the meal. Pack any leftovers for lunch with Noor Jahani Polenta (page 24).

✳ Hot Punjab Eggplant ✳
CHINA / NORTH INDIA

One summer my husband and I shared a large rented house in Honolulu with friends from different parts of the mainland. This was a rare opportunity for us to be together, and we soon discovered how different our eating habits were. Among us were teenagers, an athlete in training who had strict dietary needs, and several vegetarians. While cooking for such a diverse group posed several problems, this eggplant dish was pleasing to everyone. I roasted the eggplant in the North Indian fashion, and its smoky flavor blended perfectly with the rich, fiery sauce inspired by the cuisine of China's Szechuan province.

In this dish, asafetida imparts a garlicky flavor, while the garlic cloves, cut into large slivers, act as a vegetable. They turn mellow during cooking and taste delicious.

- 14-ounce (396-g) carton firm tofu, cut into 1-inch (2.5-cm) cubes
- 1/2 cup (125 ml) chopped cilantro
- 1 medium eggplant, about 1 1/2 pounds (750 g)
- 1 1/2 tablespoons (22 ml) Indian sesame oil (*gingely*), or canola oil
- 1/2 teaspoon (2 ml) asafetida powder
- 5 large garlic cloves, halved lengthwise
- 1 tablespoon (15 ml) low-sodium soy sauce

$^1/_2$ teaspoon (2 ml) black bean sauce (available in Asian markets; see *Note*)

$1^1/_2$ teaspoons (7 ml) plum sauce (available in Asian markets)

  2 tablespoons (30 ml) chopped cilantro

    Salt

    Ground red pepper (to taste; start with a scant pinch; best if there is a hint
       of hotness)

Garnish:

    Red bell pepper strips

    Cilantro sprigs

1. To press water out of tofu: Wrap tofu pieces in a heavy kitchen towel or place
   them between layers of paper towel on a cookie sheet. Put a heavy weight such as
   a skillet on top. Let stand at room temperature for 30 minutes. Remove the
   weight and the towel(s). Set tofu aside.

2. To broil the eggplant: Cut the eggplant in half lengthwise and arrange the halves,
   flat side down, on a cookie sheet lined with aluminum foil. Broil until the flesh
   softens, skin chars, and a smoky aroma is emitted, 10 or more minutes. The
   amount of time will vary with the size and thickness of the eggplant. Check often,
   as overbroiling will dry the flesh. Allow to cool. Discard skin and coarsely chop
   the flesh.

3. Heat oil in a 12-inch (30-cm) skillet over moderate heat. Sprinkle asafetida over
   the oil. Add garlic and fry until lightly browned. Lower the heat slightly. Add eggplant and soy sauce and mix well. Stir in black bean sauce and plum sauce. Add
   tofu. (Handle gently from this point so that tofu doesn't break.) Simmer, covered,
   5 minutes. Add cilantro, salt, and red pepper. Remove from heat. Serve hot, decorated with bell pepper strips and cilantro sprigs.

2 entrée or 4 side dish servings

Note: Or use black bean sauce with chile, another bottled sauce. The chile-added
version is more flavorful but can be very hot, so use it in moderation.

Serving Suggestions: This assertive dish is a match for Hazelnut Kasha with Red Pepper Cream (page 173) topped with Mint-Tamarind Pesto (page 225). Or serve as a
side dish to Orecchiette with Swiss Chard and Indian Cheese (page 146). Prune and
Date Chutney (page 207) will complete the evening meal.

✳ Bengali Black Beans ✳

EASTERN INDIA/LATIN AMERICA

Black beans, a Latin American favorite, are not available in India. The first time I prepared them Indian style, my husband told me they were "made to order for Indian spices." So I continued experimenting with them and found these strongly flavored beans easily accommodate a lot of aromatics and spices. A final blend of garam masala gives the tamarind-tart sauce a rich, fragrant overtone.

2   tablespoons (30 ml) unrefined safflower oil or canola oil
1   cup (250 ml) finely chopped onion
4   large garlic cloves, forced through a garlic press
1   tablespoon (15 ml) minced gingerroot
1   jalapeño, seeded, chopped (to taste)
1   tablespoon (15 ml) ground cumin
1   tablespoon (15 ml) ground coriander
$1/2$ teaspoon (2 ml) turmeric
3   tablespoons (45 ml) water
1   pound (500 g) tomatoes (2 large tomatoes or 9 medium Roma tomatoes),
      unpeeled, chopped
1   cup (250 ml) liquid from cooked or canned black beans
2   cups (500 ml) fresh cooked or canned black beans, drained (see *Note*)
1   teaspoon (5 ml) sugar
    Salt
$1 1/2$ teaspoons (7 ml) tamarind concentrate
$1/4$ teaspoon (1 ml) garam masala

Garnish:
     Sweet onion rings
     Chopped cilantro

1. Heat oil in a 12-inch (30-cm) steep-sided skillet over moderate heat. Add onion and cook, stirring often, until richly browned but not burnt, 8 to 15 minutes. Add garlic, gingerroot, and jalapeño. Combine cumin, coriander, turmeric, and water in a small bowl. Add this spice paste to the skillet and stir several times. Add tomatoes and $1/2$ cup (125 ml) of the bean liquid. Cover and bring to a boil.

Lower heat and simmer, covered, 10 to 15 minutes. During this period, remove the cover occasionally and mash the tomatoes with the back of a spoon to mix in with the sauce.

2. Whirl $1/4$ cup (60 ml) of the black beans in a blender or food processor with the remaining $1/2$ cup (125 ml) bean liquid until smooth. Add this puree and the remaining beans to the skillet. Cover and simmer for 3 to 5 more minutes to heat the mixture through. Stir in sugar, salt, and tamarind. Remove from heat and add garam masala. Let stand for a few minutes to develop the flavors. Serve garnished with onion rings and cilantro.

4 entrée servings

Note: Freshly cooked black beans are far more flavorful than the canned variety. They take a long time to soften, but require minimum attention when cooked in a crock pot. To cook black beans using a crock pot: Soak the beans overnight. Next morning bring them to a boil in a kettle on the stove, then transfer them to a crock pot. Allow them to cook for several hours until they become tender.

Serving Suggestions: Although in India a bean dish is usually served with rice, I find a baked sweet potato goes just as well. Top the sweet potato with Onion Yogurt Relish (page 209). You might want to include some leafy greens in this meal, such as a spinach and arugula salad tossed with Sesame-Tamarind Dressing (page 233).

VARIATION: BLACK BEAN "COBBLER" (LATIN AMERICA/ITALY)

This tasty cobbler—savory rather than sweet—has spicy black beans as base and polenta as topping. Prepare Bengali Black Beans and place in an ovenproof casserole or cake pan. Prepare Savory Indian Polenta (page 198) up to Step 2, or if short of time, plain polenta (polenta cooked in water and seasoned to taste). Allow polenta to stand for 20 minutes or so to stiffen it a bit, then layer it on top of black beans. Let rest in the refrigerator for 30 minutes or so or until polenta is set. Bake in a preheated 400°F (200°C, gas marks 6) oven for 5 to 10 minutes or until thoroughly heated.

✳ Cuban-Indian Cassoulet ✳

CUBA/INDIA/FRANCE

Cassoulet is a celebrated bean-and-meat stew from the country kitchens of France. The name comes from the word *cassole*, which is an earthenware pot traditionally used on the farm when preparing this dish. The ingredients include Great Northern beans and (one or more of) sausages, lamb, duck, goose, and pork. Each region of France has its own variation.

This vegetarian version, made with black beans, has a decidedly Latin character. Black beans are a favorite in Cuba, where they're typically served with rice at Christmas. "You can tell what's special to people by looking at their Christmas menu," a Cuban chef once told me. A combination of Indian spices—cumin, coriander, turmeric, gingerroot, and garlic—heightens the taste of black beans in this recipe.

The best part of a cassoulet to me is its toasty, crumbly top. Here the rich brown crust is enhanced by the garlic flavor of asafetida.

Bengali Black Beans (page 82)

The crumb topping:
- 2　tablespoons (30 ml) Indian sesame oil, *gingely* (see *Note 1*)
- 1/2　teaspoon (2 ml) asafetida powder
- 2　cups (500 ml) bread crumbs (see *Note 2*)
- 1/2　cup (125 ml) chopped cilantro
- Salt and freshly ground black pepper

1. Prepare Bengali Black Beans, but increase the amount of bean liquid to 1 1/2 cups (375 ml), supplementing with water if necessary. Place the finished beans in a large, deep, ovenproof casserole or a cake pan such as a 9 x 12 x 2 inch (22 x 30 x 5 cm) pan. Preheat oven to 350°F (180°C, gas marks 4).

2. To prepare the topping: Heat oil in a medium skillet over moderate heat. Sprinkle asafetida over oil. Add the bread crumbs and cilantro and cook for a minute. Add salt and pepper. Remove from heat and transfer to a medium bowl.

3. To prepare the cassoulet: Sprinkle about 1/3 of the crumb mixture on top of the beans. Bake for 10 minutes, then push the crumb layer down with the back of a spoon and sprinkle another 1/3 of the crumb mixture on top. After another 10 minutes, repeat procedure using the remaining crumbs. Bake for 10 minutes, then place under the broiler for a few minutes to brown the top.

4 entrée servings

Note 1: I have used a small amount of oil. For a richer flavor add more oil, which the bread crumbs will soak up quickly. You can also use ghee.

Note 2: To prepare bread crumbs, cut 8 slices (each ¼ inch [6 mm] thick) whole wheat or white bread into small cubes. Place on an ungreased baking sheet in a 300°F (150°C, gas marks 2) oven and bake until dry and crumbly, 15 to 25 minutes. Don't let them burn. Grind them to small crumbs in a blender or food processor. For a bolder flavor, substitute rye bread for wheat. Yields 2 cups (500 ml).

Serving Suggestions: Serve with French or Italian country bread (or any other crusty bread, such as sourdough) and Herbed Butter-Oil Dip (page 235). Pureed rutabaga, turnip, or carrots topped with Rustic Salsa Pasilla (page 214) would be an appropriate accompaniment. For a starter, try Piquant Salad in Shades of Green (page 258).

✳ Sesame Arugula and Squash ✳

NEPAL

Nepalese cuisine has always intrigued me because of its creative use of a limited number of ingredients and its similarity to Bengali cooking. The latter is not surprising, given the social and cultural exchanges between the two areas through the millennia. Scholars, adventurers, and traders have long traversed the rugged Himalayan terrain that divides Nepal and Bengal, carrying both scriptures and a wide variety of goods for trade—seeds, spices, flavorings. So I wasn't surprised to find a Nepali dish whose thick, rich, sesame-enriched sauce reminded me of my Bengali heritage.

In Nepal, this dish is made with potatoes, one of the primary staples of that country. But this native American version is composed of winter squashes and has a lovely yellowish-orange color with a hint of sweetness. Some of the herbs that the Nepalis use for this dish are unavailable in the West, so I substitute arugula, whose slight bitterness heightens the taste.

2   pounds (1 kg) butternut or Hubbard squash, peeled, cut into 1-inch (2.5-cm) cubes; or about 8 medium potatoes, peeled, cubed (see *Note 1 for the Gardener*)

2   tablespoons (30 ml) mustard oil or canola oil

¼   teaspoon (1 ml) fenugreek seeds

2   tablespoons (30 ml) grated gingerroot or gingerroot paste (see page 12)

½   teaspoon (2 ml) turmeric

$^3/_4$ teaspoon (3 ml) salt

$^1/_2$ teaspoon (2 ml) sugar

3 tablespoons (45 ml) sesame seeds, roasted and ground to a powder (see
    page 17)

$^1/_4$ cup (60 ml) water

$^1/_4$ cup (60 ml) thinly shredded arugula or cilantro (see *Note 2 for the Gardener*)

2 tablespoons (30 ml) fresh lime juice

Garnish:

Lime wedges

1 teaspoon (5 ml) sweetened flaked coconut (optional)

1. Steam the squash for 10 to 15 minutes or until tender but not breaking. (If using
   potatoes, steam for 15 to 18 minutes or until tender.)

2. Heat oil in a large skillet over moderate heat until sizzling. Add fenugreek seeds
   and fry for a few seconds until lightly browned. (Overcooking will make them bitter.) Add gingerroot and fry until it is lightly browned. Stir in turmeric. Whisk salt,
   sugar, and sesame powder with $^1/_4$ cup (60 ml) water and add to the skillet. (If
   using arugula, add at this time.) Add squash and gently mix in with the spices.
   Cook, uncovered, for 2 to 3 minutes to heat the mixture through. Remove from
   heat. Add cilantro and lime juice. Adjust seasonings. Serve hot, garnished with
   lime wedges and sprinkled with coconut.

4 entrée or 6 to 8 side dish servings

Note 1 for the Gardener: Freshly unearthed potatoes, which are more tender than
supermarket potatoes, cook more quickly, so adjust your timing accordingly. Both
Yukon Gold and Bison are good choices here.

Note 2 for the Gardener: Instead of arugula, you can use sorrel, a leafy green that
has a lemony bite. Sorrel needs little care, grows quickly, and produces early in
spring. Best time to use sorrel is when the leaves are young. They are a bit too strong
for salads, but delightful combined with other leafy greens in vegetable dishes. The
lemony flavor reduces the need for salt in cooking.

Serving Suggestions: Long-grain brown rice is my preferred grain for this dish. You
can also choose a grain salad such as Tabbouleh Plus (page 176). Tamarind-Date
Chutney (page 208) is perfect as a condiment. When serving as a side dish, add some
hearty beans such as Cuban-Indian Cassoulet (page 84). Or take the opportunity to
try a meat appetizer—Date and Nut-Filled Meatballs (page 135).

✳ Golden Squash Cream ✳

UNITED STATES

In India simmered, thickened milk, *khoya*, is used not only in confection-making but also in savory dishes. In that ancient cuisine, the rich *khoya* takes the place that sour cream or *crème fraîche* occupies in the Western world. Traditionally rice and meat dishes require this, but I also combine a lowfat version of *khoya* with vegetables for a pleasant creamy sauce.

It is a privilege to spoon this golden sauce on my dinner plate while watching the warm, yellow sunset colors that fill the Pacific Northwest sky.

2   cups (500 ml) lowfat or nonfat milk

1   pound (500 g) yellow pattypan squash or yellow crookneck squash
      (about 2 medium)

1   tablespoon (15 ml) mustard oil

$1/4$ teaspoon (1 ml) kalonji seeds

1   medium onion, thinly sliced

$1/4$ teaspoon (1 ml) turmeric

1   jalapeño, seeded, chopped (to taste; see *Note*)
      Salt

Garnish: Chopped fresh mint leaves

1. Lightly oil the bottom and sides of a large, deep pan to help prevent milk from sticking. Add milk and bring to a boil over medium to high heat. Stir vigorously until the foaming subsides. Lower the heat to medium and continue to cook until reduced to about $1/4$ cup (60 ml), 15 to 20 minutes. Watch carefully during this period, as the milk will rise from time to time. Stir often and mix in any milk solids as they accumulate on the sides and bottom of the pan. Remove from heat and transfer to a medium bowl.

2. Steam squash until tender, 10 to 15 minutes. Remove from the heat, place in a large bowl, and mash with a fork.

3. Heat oil in a large skillet over moderate heat. Add kalonji and fry for a few seconds. Add onion and cook until it is translucent, about 2 minutes, stirring often. Stir in turmeric and jalapeño. Add squash puree and the thickened milk. Cook, uncovered, for a few minutes to heat the mixture through, stirring often. Add salt. Serve garnished with mint.

4 side dish servings

Note: For a special taste treat, use habanero chile, which has a matching yellowish-orange color and an unusual flavor. Because this variety is extremely hot, use it in very small amounts.

Serving Suggestions: Turn your dinner plate into a color palette by serving plain kasha along with steamed beets and asparagus (or gai lan). You can serve Sesame-Tamarind Dressing (page 233) as a dip for the vegetables. For dessert, let the family nibble on kiwi slices and ripe papaya cubes, plain or dusted with Chaat Powder (see page 8).

✳ Simple Pleasure Zucchini Sauté ✳

UNITED STATES

I especially enjoy preparing this simple dish in June, when tiny zucchinis first form behind the blossoms in our garden. Slicing a freshly harvested zucchini—so dense and moist—is a treat; it's almost like cutting through a stick of butter. The natural juices that accumulate in the pan during cooking are so delicate that I need to use only a small amount of oil and can omit the salt entirely.

$1^1/_2$ tablespoons (22 ml) olive oil or avocado oil

$^1/_4$ teaspoon (1 ml) asafetida powder

$^1/_4$ teaspoon (1 ml) kalonji seeds

1 medium onion, thinly sliced

$^1/_2$ pound (250 g) tomatoes (2 large Roma tomatoes or 1 large vine-ripened tomato), sliced

1 pound (500 g) zucchini (about 2 medium), cut into cubes or french-fry type strips (see *Note*)

Salt

Garnish:

Toasted pine nuts

Chopped cilantro

Heat oil in a large skillet over moderate heat. Sprinkle asafetida over the oil. Add kalonji seeds and fry for a few seconds. Add onion and cook until it is translucent, about 2 minutes. Add tomatoes and zucchini. Lower the heat. Cover and cook just until zucchini is fork-tender, 6 to 8 minutes. Add salt. Serve topped with pine nuts and cilantro.

4 side dish servings

Note: In spring, gourmet produce markets sell baby zucchini and pattypan squash with the blossoms still on. Buy these if you can. If you garden, harvest some baby zucchinis for this dish. My husband calls them "the zucchini equivalent of new potatoes."

Serving Suggestions: This colorful dish looks lovelier when surrounded by Saffron-Scented Millet (page 172) and Garlic-Glazed Tofu (page 67).

VARIATION: SUMMER SQUASH RAGOUT For a riot of colors and a larger number of helpings, bring together an assortment of squashes in this dish: pattypan, crookneck, as well as zucchinis. In this case, in addition to the zucchini, add 2 medium pattypan squash (1 pound [500 g]), or 1 pattypan and 1 small yellow crookneck squash (combined weight 1 pound [500 g]). Chop all the vegetables into the same size. Increase the amount of tomatoes to 1 pound (500 g).

8 side dish servings

✳ Crispy Snow Peas ✳
INTERNATIONAL

Snow peas are delicious, cooked or raw, any time during the year, but especially in spring when freshly harvested. They need minimum cooking and very little spicing. This fat-free but elegant dish has colors of green, white, and deep red. It can be a family treat or a dish for company.

- 1/4 cup (60 ml) Chicken Stock (page 44) or chicken broth, defatted (see "To defat canned chicken broth," page 45)
- 1/2 cup (125 ml) finely chopped onion
- 1/2 jalapeño, seeded, chopped (to taste)
- 1/2 pound (250 g) snow peas, stems trimmed, or sugarsnap peas, with the string removed from the tougher end (see *Note 1* and *Note 2 for the Gardener*)
- 1 tablespoon (15 ml) dried tomato bits (see *Note*)
- Salt

Bring chicken broth to a boil in a small pan over medium heat. Add onion. Lower heat and simmer, covered, for a minute or two. Add jalapeño, snow peas, and dried tomato bits. Simmer, covered, 4 to 7 minutes or until the snow peas are tender to the bite. Don't overcook, as they will lose some of their color. Add salt.

2 side dish servings

Note 1 for the Gardener: The dark green sugarsnaps, which are crunchy and sweet, work especially well in this dish.

Note 2 for the Gardener: Both the pods and the vines on which the snow peas grow are edible. The vines are considered to be a choice stir-fry green in East Asia. A plate of young pea tips is a delicacy served in many Chinese restaurants, although it's found less often on English menus. Chinese chefs gather young pea shoots when they are approximately 1 foot (30 cm) long for quick-frying.

Note: These are sold in jars and require no presoaking. If not available, blanch and chop 2 to 3 sun-dried tomatoes.

Serving Suggestions: This vegetable dish can go alongside most meals. At a buffet, place next to Shrimp and Scallop Vatapa (page 115). At a brunch, accompany with Peanut Soup with Kasundi Dip (page 52) and Quinoa Uppama (page 180). Use these snow peas also as a topping for plain Basmati rice or other plain cooked grains.

✳ Peanutty Napa Cabbage ✳
CHINA

When visiting Beijing one autumn, I noticed Chinese cabbages piled everywhere: in markets, on trucks, stashed in restaurant kitchens, and even on balconies of apartment buildings. A Chinese man told me that this cabbage, easily preserved, was being stored for the long winter months when fresh vegetables become scarce. He added that this cabbage served their need for fuel-efficient foods as it required very little cooking. I found Chinese cabbage to be lighter and sweeter in taste than regular cabbage.

The most common variety of the many Chinese cabbages available in the United States is Napa cabbage. Readily enhanced with Indian seasonings, it is especially tasty with this blend of cumin, peanut butter, and gingerroot.

  1   cup (250 ml) water
  5   tablespoons (75 ml) peanut butter (see *Note 1*)
  1/2   teaspoon (2 ml) low-sodium soy sauce (to taste; see *Note 2*)
  1 1/2   tablespoons (22 ml) canola oil
  1/2   teaspoon (2 ml) cumin seeds

   1   cup (250 ml) onion, thinly sliced

   2   tablespoons (30 ml) minced gingerroot

   2   tablespoons (30 ml) minced garlic

   2   teaspoons (10 ml) ground cumin

       Ground red pepper (to taste; start with a scant pinch; best if there is a hint of hotness)

   1   medium-sized red bell pepper, thinly sliced

1 1/2 pounds (750 g) cabbage—1 small head Napa cabbage, or a small head regular cabbage, finely shredded

       Salt

Garnish: Chopped peanuts

1. Add water, a little at a time, to peanut butter in a small bowl, stirring with a fork to form a smooth sauce. Add soy sauce.

2. Heat oil in a 12-inch (30-cm) skillet over moderate heat. Add cumin seeds and fry until the seeds become lightly browned. Add onion and cook until it is translucent, about 2 minutes. Add gingerroot, garlic, ground cumin, and red pepper and mix well. Add bell pepper and peanut butter mixture. Simmer, covered, 3 minutes. Add cabbage. Simmer, covered, 3 to 5 more minutes (5 to 10 minutes if using regular cabbage) or until cabbage is tender but not too limp. (Uncover and add a little water once or twice if cabbage sticks to pan.) Overcooking will destroy the texture of the cabbage and discolor it. Remove from heat. Add salt. Taste for red pepper. Serve garnished with chopped peanuts.

4 to 6 side dish servings

Note 1: For a leaner dish, reduce the amount of peanut butter to 3 tablespoons (45 ml).

Note 2: If you're not a strict vegetarian, replace soy sauce with fish sauce for a sharper taste. With either of these sauces, you can taste and add more at the end of cooking if you like. Also pass these sauces around at the table to add according to taste.

Serving Suggestions: Sop up the nutty sauce with warmed flour tortillas or crusty French bread. Or serve with orzo tossed with a little olive oil and topped with Roasted Tomato-Chile Salsa (page 216). You can offer sautéed tempeh or hard-boiled eggs for protein. Finish with a platter of sliced Asian pears, dried persimmons or mangoes, and black dates (or regular dates).

✳ Shrimp-Scented Cabbage ✳

SOUTHEAST ASIA

Growing up in Bengal I discovered a kinship between shrimp and cabbage. Bengali cooks often include a handful of shrimp when braising cabbage. Later when traveling in Southeast Asia, I noticed Malaysian cooks seasoning their vegetables with shrimp paste, which is a thick gray sauce with a powerful flavor. I was inspired to experiment adding shrimp paste to my own South Indian–style cabbage dish. The touch of shrimp so intensified the flavor that I now serve this cabbage to my most special guests.

1	tablespoon (15 ml) canola oil
6 to 8	curry leaves, crushed
1/4	teaspoon (1 ml) black mustard seeds
1	tablespoon (15 ml) grated gingerroot or gingerroot paste (page 12)
1	jalapeño, seeded, chopped (to taste; retain some seeds for a hotter taste)
1/2	teaspoon (2 ml) turmeric
1	teaspoon (5 ml) shrimp paste
1/2	cup plus 2 tablespoons (155 ml) chicken broth, defatted (see "To defat canned chicken broth," page 45)
1	medium head cabbage, about 1 3/4 pounds (875 g), finely shredded
2	tablespoons (30 ml) dried, sweetened, flaked coconut
	Salt

Heat oil in a large skillet over moderate heat. Add curry leaves and mustard seeds and fry just until the seeds start to pop. Add gingerroot, jalapeño, and turmeric and stir a few times. Add shrimp paste and chicken broth. Add cabbage and coconut. Simmer, covered, until cabbage is tender, 10 to 15 minutes. Add salt.

4 to 6 side dish servings

Serving Suggestions: Start the meal with Tart Fish Soup (page 57) or, for the vegetarians, Tart Tofu Soup (page 59). Follow with Tabbouleh Plus (page 176) and Fresh Mango Brûlée (page 274). For a simpler meal, accompany this tasty sauté with roasted new potatoes or jasmine rice cooked with saffron and Cilantro Splash (page 223).

* Anchovy Mustard Greens *

INTERNATIONAL

The often overlooked leafy greens of the mustard family are a nutritional treasure-house of vitamins A and C and calcium. Since the natural flavor of these greens is especially strong, they require special seasoning to mellow the taste. I automatically think of anchovy. The Italians incorporate this powerful condiment into many of their pasta sauces. You'll find it a delicious addition to these assertive greens.

        1   tablespoon (15 ml) canola oil
     $1/4$ teaspoon (1 ml) asafetida powder
     $1/2$ teaspoon (2 ml) cumin seeds
   3 to 4   large garlic cloves, slivered
            2-ounce (50-g) can anchovies, drained, rinsed, and mashed with a fork
     $1/4$ pound (125 g) Roma tomatoes, thinly sliced
            About $3/4$ pound (375 g), 8 cups (2 liters) mustard greens (or kale, collard, or
              Swiss chard), thinly shredded, stems diced if desired (see *Note* and *Note*
              for the Gardener)
            Salt

Heat oil in a 12-inch (30-cm) skillet over moderate heat. Sprinkle asafetida over the oil. Add cumin seeds and garlic and fry until both are lightly browned. Stir in anchovies and tomatoes. Add mustard greens. Cover and simmer 5 to 10 minutes or until the greens are tender to the bite but still retain their color. Add salt.

4 side dish servings

Note: To quickly shred mustard or other greens, stack several leaves on top of each other. Cut lengthwise along the central rib. Then cut crosswise into strips 1 inch (2.5 cm) or narrower.

Note for the Gardener: Miike Giant, a Japanese variety of mustard, is a good choice for this dish. The large, attractive, purple-veined leaves of the plant stand out on my vegetable bed. The flavor is that of mustard but with a hint of sweetness.

Serving Suggestions: Think of a few mildly seasoned dishes as mates, such as plain polenta topped with Honey-Glazed Onions (page 218) along with sautéed tempeh, grilled fish, or roast chicken. Baked butternut or other winter squashes, drizzled with a little Garlic Ghee (page 236), will complement these greens nicely. Serve any left-overs over cooked pasta that has been tossed lightly with Chinese sesame oil.

✳ Greens Ratatouille ✳

FRANCE/ITALY

Ratatouille is a French stew, highly preferred in summer, usually containing eggplant, tomato, zucchini, and other warm-weather vegetables. While living in France, I once served *baingan bharta*, a roasted eggplant and tomato puree from India, to a French resident, who described it as being "a bit like ratatouille." We compared the two dishes and found a similarity—both used tomato as a base. We decided that nearly anything else compatible with tomatoes might suit the French casserole. I concluded that the content of ratatouille is more a personal preference than a specific recipe. As with many things French, it is a state of mind.

I now prepare ratatouille with many different vegetables, including leafy greens. In my opinion, this is one of the best ways to prepare greens. Besides fresh tomatoes, the smooth sauce contains creamy ricotta cheese and an Italian veil of sun-dried tomatoes.

About $3/4$ pound (375 g), 8 cups (2 liters) shredded greens (choose one or
　　more of: kale, collard, Swiss chard, beet greens, fresh spinach leaves)
1　tablespoon (15 ml) canola oil
$1/4$　teaspoon (1 ml) ajwain seeds or cumin seeds (see *Note 1*)
1　cup (250 ml) thinly sliced onion rings
$1/4$　teaspoon (1 ml) turmeric
1　jalapeño, seeded, chopped (to taste; see *Note 2*)
4　ounces (100 g) Roma tomatoes, peeled, seeded, and coarsely chopped
6　sun-dried tomatoes, soaked in boiling water to cover for 5 to 10 minutes or
　　until soft, then chopped finely
2　tablespoons (30 ml) water
1　tablespoon (15 ml) fresh chopped dill, or $1 1/2$ teaspoons (7 ml) dried dill (see
　　Note for the Gardener)
1　tablespoon (15 ml) capers, drained, rinsed, chopped
$1/4$　cup (60 ml) lowfat or part-skim ricotta cheese
　　Salt (optional)

Garnish: Toasted pine nuts

1. Steam the greens until they are tender to the bite, 5 to 10 minutes. If using spinach alone, steam only 3 to 5 minutes. Keep covered.

2. In hot oil in a large skillet, fry ajwain seeds until lightly browned. Add onion and cook until it is translucent, about 2 minutes. Add turmeric, jalapeño, Roma tomatoes, sun-dried tomatoes, and water. Lower heat, cover, and simmer for 5 to 7 minutes. (During this period, remove cover once or twice, stir, and add a little water if sticking.) Add greens and cook covered to heat the mixture through. Combine dill, capers, and ricotta cheese in a small bowl and stir until smooth. Pour over the greens. As soon as the cheese is thoroughly mixed with the sauce, remove from heat. Taste for salt. Serve garnished with pine nuts.

6 side dish servings

Note 1: This dish works well with either cumin or ajwain seeds. In general, however, these two spices are not interchangeable.

Note 2: For a taste variation, omit jalapeño and add a dab of sambal oeleck, a red chile paste that is sold in jars in Asian markets, along with the cheese in Step 2. Taste and add more if you like.

Note for the Gardener: In India, fenugreek leaves are considered health-giving and are often added to vegetable preparations and flat bread doughs to impart a nutty, slightly bitter flavor. The seeds are available in health-food stores and Indian groceries. Fenugreek grows in my garden and I harvest some of the leaves along with other greens to give a peppery taste to this dish.

Serving Suggestions: For a glamorous dinner, start with Fresh Squash Soup with Orzo and Red Pepper (page 50). Wild rice (cooked with chicken or vegetable broth) and Green Mango Chutney (page 206) could follow. On another occasion, serve with Siamese Ceviche with Jícama (page 98) and millet.

Fish and Seafood

●●●●●●●●●●●●●●●●

Of all the culinary attractions that impress travelers to Bengal, by far the most notable is fish. In my childhood, I tasted a wide variety, most so freshly caught they would be flopping and quivering at the fishmongers' stalls. My mother prepared them in a delicious, thick black mustard puree, a cashew-enriched gravy, or a robust green chile sauce. Such elegant meals laid a foundation for me to appreciate the profusion of outstanding seafood creations I encountered when I ventured eastward.

Singapore's restaurants are reputed to prepare the world's finest chile crab, so when I arrived in that fabled crossroads of the world, I searched for the delicacy. A hotel clerk told me to go to Newton Circus, where he promised I'd find the best. Newton Circus is a large, open-air food center with dozens of tiny booths offering specialties from all over Asia. In a particularly crowded stall, a bearded young chef prepared his chile crab. I watched, somewhat mystified. In Bengal, the crab would be braised in turmeric, ground cumin, coriander, and possibly yogurt. This man stir-fried the meat in a sizzling wok with gingerroot and hot green chiles, then doused it with a rich tomato sauce. The pungent aroma made my mouth water.

The chef served the crab meat on a large oval platter, garnished with green pepper strips and sweet onion slices. Each morsel of that succulent seafood was a pocket of flavors. Although the preparation of crab is well understood in Bengal, in this one worthwhile afternoon I garnered a brilliant new idea for saucing it.

In Pinang, an island city in Malaysia, I tasted an outstanding prawn dish with a soy-based sauce. As custom dictated, I savored this rich-gravied dish while watching the tropical sun set over the Strait of Malacca.

While visiting Bangkok, I tried Thai-style seafood. In a restaurant on Sukhumvit Road I first "shopped" for the food by choosing among fish either swimming in tanks or nestled on beds of ice. I eventually settled on a small, handsome catfish lookalike. When I pointed out my choice, the waiter asked, "What type of sauce?" I ordered chile sauce with a bit of yellow curry, knowing that Thai cooks create magic with their version of that pungent blend of spices.

The fish arrived, veiled in a shimmering golden gravy amid patterns of cilantro and slivered red chiles. It was the best fish dish I had tasted outside of Bengal, making it another worthy entry in my ever-growing seafood repertoire.

When I toured the coastal region of Normandy with a group of French nationals, we stopped one afternoon for a meal at an oceanside restaurant. While enjoying the first course of a shellfish *gratin*, we discussed our favorite seafood. For one man it was trout. A Breton woman, claiming to be a *fille de la mer*, said she liked them all. But conversation stopped with the arrival of mussels steamed in wine and garlic sauce. My French friends extracted the delicate meat, relishing every bite and making sure no edible morsel was left in the shells. The only sounds were those of the waves, the silverware, and smacking of lips.

Mussels are rarely served in India and I'd never tasted them before. I left dreaming of ways to prepare them Indian style—on a bed of rice, perhaps, or in a light turmeric-onion broth.

The recipes in this chapter embrace principles from all culinary traditions and are combined with ideas of my own. I use many different cooking methods. Sometimes I steam fish to accentuate its natural flavor; at other times I grill it to give it a rich glaze. I note the cooking time carefully; fish must not be overcooked. I may also marinate fish in lime juice for many hours to pickle it, an alternative to cooking.

Selecting seafood can test the skills of any cook. It's important to find the seafood variety that complements each sauce. In my recipes I list several choices. I may supplement a lean fish with a flavorful sauce, but I grill the rich, oily types of fish. And as in Bengal, I select sauces to match the taste and texture of the seafood. But clearly the most vital quality is freshness.

It doesn't matter if fish is eaten under the tropical Singapore sun or under your own kitchen lights. A simple steamed fish or an elaborate chile crab raises the aesthetic standard of any meal. ✳

✳ Siamese Ceviche with Jícama ✳

MEXICO

Ceviche is a popular Latin American fish appetizer that is believed to have originated in Peru. It consists of raw fish, marinated in lime juice for several hours. During this time the fish is "cooked" by the acid of the citrus. Its flesh turns opaque white and it acquires a cooked taste. The end result, somewhere between steamed fish and sashimi, is delightful.

In this recipe, the marinated fish is covered with a dressing that has a sharp, tart Indo-Thai flavor derived from blending chile, lime juice, vinegar, cilantro, and asafetida. This ceviche makes a delightful luncheon entrée, appetizer, or even a light evening meal.

 1 pound (500 g) firm-fleshed fish such as cod, snapper, or halibut, deboned, cut into bite-sized pieces (see *Note 1*)

1 to 1 1/4 cups (250 to 310 ml) fresh lime juice (juice of about 7 limes)

The dressing:

 1/2 cup (125 ml) rice vinegar

 2 tablespoons (30 ml) fresh lime juice

 1/4 teaspoon (1 ml) asafetida powder

 2 tablespoons (30 ml) sugar

 1/2 jalapeño or Thai chile, seeded, chopped (see *Note 2*)

 1 tablespoon (15 ml) finely chopped cilantro

 2 large cloves garlic, forced through a garlic press

The vegetables:

 1/4 cup (60 ml) thinly sliced mild sweet onion

 1 cup (250 ml) paper-thin sliced jícama

 1/2 medium red bell pepper, cut into thin strips

Garnish: Chopped Thai basil or regular fresh basil

1. Marinate fish in lime juice in the refrigerator for at least 5 hours or until fish is opaque (indicating the fish is "cooked"), turning several times.
2. Meanwhile, mix all the dressing ingredients in a small bowl and chill. An hour or so before serving, combine the vegetables in a large bowl and pour the dressing over them. Before serving, drain fish and discard marinade. Combine fish with the marinated vegetables. Serve garnished with basil.

4 entrée servings

Note 1: Since heat is not used to prepare this dish, pay attention to selecting the highest quality, freshest fish, as the marinating process will not destroy any bacteria or parasites that may be present in low-quality or spoiled fish. Buy your fish from a reputable seafood dealer; Japanese seafood markets are particularly careful in this respect.

Note 2: This dish tastes best if slightly hot. You can substitute a tiny amount of habanero chile for jalapeño. Habanero has a lovely yellowish orange color and an exotic flavor but is extremely hot; used sparingly and chopped extra fine, it is *the* chile pepper to use in a ceviche, according to many Latin Americans.

Serving Suggestions: For a colorful presentation, serve on cup-shaped whole radicchio or romaine leaves; or serve on corn tortillas that have been baked until crisp. An attractive combination is this salad accompanied by Quinoa Uppama (page 180) and Gai Lan with Balsamic Vinaigrette (page 70).

VARIATION: SIAMESE CEVICHE WITH TURMERIC POTATOES AND JÍCAMA Cooking fish with potatoes is an Indian technique that I simply couldn't resist mentioning here. These attractive, yellow-tinted potatoes are simply delicious with the tart fish and juicy, crisp jícama.

Once the fish is ready in Step 1, prepare the potatoes: Peel $1/2$ pound (250 g) new or Yellow Finn potatoes (about 2 medium potatoes) and cut into 1-inch (2.5-cm) cubes. Boil in water that is lightly salted and tinted with $1/4$ teaspoon (1 ml) turmeric. Drain, immediately add 2 tablespoons (30 ml) lime juice, and toss gently until absorbed. Let cool to room temperature. Remove with a slotted spoon (discarding the excess lime juice) and add to the fish and vegetables in Step 2.

You can use the potato water in making vegetable stocks (the color will be yellow) or when cooking vegetables Indian-style.

✳ Soy- and Mirin-Glazed Salmon ✳

JAPAN

In Japan, a combination of mirin (Japanese cooking sake) and soy sauce is used to marinate fish and meat to sweet and salty perfection. The Indian technique of rubbing fish with turmeric and salt to prevent sticking and to remove any fishy flavor before marinating produces a superior dish. A pinch of dill adds a subtle Western nuance to this savory blend of South and East Asian ingredients.

My favorite local fish in the Pacific Northwest is Alaskan Copper River King salmon, available only in the spring. The deep red flesh and the buttery quality of this legendary fish when glazed with rich brown spices make a memorable dish. Other salmon varieties such as coho also work well; or substitute any other rich fish.

2 pounds (1 kg) fish (salmon, lake trout, halibut, sturgeon, tuna, or rich fish of your choice), cut into 2 x 2 inch (5 x 5 cm) pieces
1/2 teaspoon (2 ml) turmeric
1/4 teaspoon (1 ml) salt

The marinade:
1 tablespoon (15 ml) Chinese sesame oil
1/4 cup (60 ml) mirin
2 tablespoons (30 ml) low-sodium soy sauce
1 tablespoon (15 ml) minced garlic
2 tablespoons (30 ml) fresh lemon juice
1 tablespoon (15 ml) chopped fresh dill, or 1 1/2 teaspoons (7 ml) dried dill

1. Rub fish with turmeric and salt so that each piece is well-coated. Combine all the marinade ingredients in a large bowl. Toss fish in this marinade, making sure each piece is well-coated. Store, covered, in the refrigerator for at least 30 minutes, turning once.
2. Preheat oven to 375°F (190°C, gas marks 5). Remove fish with a slotted spoon and place on a roasting pan, preferably one with a removable rack. Reserve the marinade. Bake fish for 12 to 18 minutes or until a toothpick inserted in the middle and pushed to one side shows an opaque color in the fish. The timing will vary with the thickness and type of fish. Check often and take care not to overcook. Leave fish in the pan and broil for 2 to 3 minutes or until slightly brownish on top. Turn, baste fish with the reserved marinade, and broil for 2 to 3 more minutes or just until medium brown in color. Remove from the broiler and keep covered.
3. Drain off the liquid from the roasting pan and place in a small pan along with the reserved marinade. Bring to a boil over medium-high heat. Reduce heat slightly and cook uncovered for 3 to 5 minutes until the sauce thickens. Place fish on a heated serving platter, pour sauce over it, and serve.

6 to 8 entrée servings

Serving Suggestions: Surround the fish platter with brown Basmati rice, topped with toasted, shredded nori (purplish-black seaweed) for color and extra nutrients. Other side dishes and condiments that complement this lovely fish dish include Eggplant Caponata International (page 78), Simple Pleasure Zucchini Sauté (page 88), and Cilantro Splash (page 223).

✳ Steamed Fish in Lime-Ginger Sauce ✳

CHINA

Steaming is the preferred method of cooking fish in China and some parts of India, because the fish retains its moistness and flavor as it cooks over indirect heat. Steamed black cod is a delicacy that I often order in the Chinese restaurants in the Pacific Northwest. The fish becomes tender and buttery in the vapor and the Chinese wisely keep the spicing simple. A Chinese cook told me that timing is critical especially when steaming a whole fish: the skin must not be broken and the fins and tail should remain intact.

In this recipe, a lean marinade of lime juice, gingerroot, garlic, cilantro, mustard oil, and a hint of turmeric lends an Indian accent to the fish. It's well-suited for salmon, halibut, cod, or any other firm-fleshed fish.

3	tablespoons (45 ml) coarsely chopped gingerroot
2	tablespoons (30 ml) coarsely chopped garlic
1/4	cup (60 ml) coarsely chopped fresh cilantro (see *Note*)
1	jalapeño, seeded, coarsely chopped (to taste)
2	tablespoons (30 ml) mustard oil (preferred), or canola oil
1/4	teaspoon (1 ml) turmeric
1/2	teaspoon (2 ml) salt
3	tablespoons (45 ml) fresh lime juice
1 1/2	pounds (750 g) firm-fleshed fish, cut into 2 x 2 inch (5 x 5 cm) pieces

1. Using a food processor or a mortar and pestle, grind together gingerroot, garlic, cilantro, and jalapeño until a relatively smooth paste results, adding a little water if necessary. Add oil, turmeric, salt, and lime juice and mix well. Toss the fish pieces in this marinade, making sure each piece is well-coated. Cover and refrigerate for at least 30 minutes, turning once.

2. Just before serving: Place the fish and the marinade on a piece of heavy-duty aluminum foil, large enough to make a steaming pouch (or two pouches) for the fish. Draw the edges of the foil over the fish and seal them tightly so that no water can seep in during the cooking process. Place this pouch in a steamer basket. Steam fish gently for 7 to 12 minutes or until a toothpick inserted in the thickest part of the fish and pushed to one side shows an opaque color in the piece. (The cooking time will vary with the thickness and type of fish.) Adjust seasoning.

4 entrée servings

Note: For a sharper flavor, replace cilantro with 12 to 14 fresh curry leaves (don't use dried curry leaves, sold in packages). Many Indian groceries now sell these leaves fresh.

Serving Suggestions: My favorite way to enjoy this wholesome steamed fish is after a pasta course such as Karhi-Sauced Penne (page 154) or with a grain dish such as Picnic Squash Pullao (page 169).

VARIATION: LIME-GINGER CHICKEN This sauce tastes excellent with chicken breast or other parts of chicken (preferably boneless). Skin and cut 1 to 1 1/2 pounds (500 to 750 g) chicken into serving size pieces. With a knife, make a few surface slits in the chicken, about 1/4 inch (6 mm) deep, for the marinade to penetrate. In Step 2, place the chicken with the marinade in a large skillet over low heat. Cover and simmer 15 to 30 minutes or until chicken is done. (A toothpick inserted in the meat and pushed to one side should show an opaque color in the center of the piece.)

❋ Fish Swimming in Three Flavors ❋
INDIA

In India, chutneys are not only made of fruits and vegetables but also of fish and shellfish. This fish chutney is usually served in small amounts as a condiment. For my husband Tom, the intriguing combination of tart, pungent, and rich, sweet flavors was irresistible and I now serve it as a main course.

Firm-fleshed fish that hold their shape during cooking, such as swordfish, tuna, yellowtail (hamachi), and halibut, are particularly good choices.

2	tablespoons (30 ml) mustard oil or canola oil
1	whole dried red chile
1	cup (250 ml) thinly sliced onion
1	tablespoon (15 ml) minced gingerroot
1	jalapeño, seeded, chopped (to taste)
1/4	teaspoon (1 ml) turmeric
	Ground red pepper (to taste; start with a scant pinch)
	Salt
1/4	teaspoon (1 ml) sugar
1 1/2	pounds (750 g) fish, cut into 2 × 2 inch (5 × 5 cm) pieces
1/4	cup (60 ml) rice vinegar

Garnish: Chopped cilantro

Heat 1 tablespoon (15 ml) oil in a large skillet over moderate heat. Add red chile and fry until it blackens. Add onion and cook, stirring constantly, until it is richly browned but not burnt, 5 to 8 minutes. Add gingerroot, jalapeño, and turmeric, and stir several times. Add red pepper, salt, sugar, fish, and vinegar. Simmer, covered, until fish is done, 5 to 7 minutes. (A toothpick inserted in the thickest part and pushed to one side should show an opaque color in the piece.) As it simmers, uncover and turn the fish once, adding a little water if the skillet is too dry. Adjust seasoning. Remove from heat immediately. Serve garnished with cilantro.

4 entrée servings

Serving Suggestions: To accompany, I suggest white or brown Basmati rice, Gujarati Greens (page 66), and lime pickle (available in Indian groceries). This fish dish is also delightful served over very fine pasta, such as angel-hair. Serve as a chutney at room temperature on a buffet table with Peanuts, Seaweed, and Red Chile Flakes (page 220), Sweet and Spicy Sancoche (page 68), and some warmed chapatis.

✳ Fragrant Fish Pullao ✳

INDIA

Fish and rice are a happy combination at any meal, but especially so in this dish from India in which a cloud of steam from the rice floats over the fish as it's served. The fish is prepared separately so it will not be overcooked and then is combined with the rice during the last stage. Any fish will work, but halibut, sturgeon, or salmon produces exceptional results.

The fish:

$1/2$ teaspoon (2 ml) turmeric

$1/2$ teaspoon (2 ml) salt

$1/2$ pound (250 g) fish, cut into 1-inch (2.5-cm) cubes

$1/4$ cup (60 ml) coarsely chopped onion

2 tablespoons (30 ml) coarsely chopped gingerroot

1 jalapeño, seeded, coarsely chopped (to taste)

1 tablespoon (15 ml) mustard oil or canola oil

1 tablespoon (15 ml) white poppy seeds made into a paste (see page 20)

$1/2$ cup plus 1 tablespoon (140 ml) water

2   tablespoons (30 ml) plain nonfat yogurt, mixed with $\frac{1}{4}$ teaspoon (1 ml)
      all-purpose flour

$\frac{1}{2}$ teaspoon (2 ml) garam masala

The rice:

2   tablespoons (30 ml) mustard oil or canola oil

1   cup (250 ml) coarsely chopped onion

2   tablespoons (30 ml) raw cashew halves

2   bay leaves

5   whole cardamom pods, bruised

1   black cardamom pod (optional)

1   cup (250 ml) white Basmati rice (rinsed several times and drained)
      or long-grain white rice

$1\frac{1}{2}$ cups (375 ml) water

$\frac{1}{2}$ teaspoon (2 ml) salt

$\frac{1}{2}$ teaspoon (2 ml) sugar

$\frac{1}{2}$ teaspoon (2 ml) garam masala

1   tablespoon (15 ml) finely chopped cilantro

Garnish: Red bell pepper strips

1. Combine $\frac{1}{4}$ teaspoon (1 ml) of the turmeric and $\frac{1}{4}$ teaspoon (1 ml) of the salt
   in a bowl. Toss fish in this mixture, making sure that each piece is well-coated.
   Set aside.

2. To prepare the fish: Place onion, gingerroot, and jalapeño in a blender or food
   processor and process to a smooth puree. Sauté the pureed mixture in hot oil in a
   large skillet over moderate heat for 2 minutes. Add the remaining $\frac{1}{4}$ teaspoon
   (1 ml) turmeric and the remaining $\frac{1}{4}$ teaspoon (1 ml) salt. Add poppy-seed paste
   and water. Lower heat and simmer, covered, 20 to 25 minutes. (This slow simmer removes the raw taste from the pureed onion and gives it a warm, mellow
   flavor.) Add fish and simmer, covered, 3 to 6 minutes or until fish is done. (A
   toothpick inserted in the thickest part and pushed to one side should show an
   opaque color in the piece.) Don't overcook. Remove fish with a slotted spoon to a
   warm bowl and cover to retain the heat. Pour the sauce remaining in the skillet
   into a large bowl and mix in yogurt and garam masala, stirring until smooth. This
   liquid will be used in Step 4.

3. To prepare the rice: Heat 1 tablespoon (15 ml) oil in a large pan over moderate
   heat. Add onion and fry until it is lightly browned, 3 to 5 minutes, stirring

constantly. Add cashews and fry until they are lightly browned, about 2 minutes, stirring often. (Watch carefully and don't let either the onion or the cashews burn. If some of the onions start to burn, remove those pieces immediately.) Remove onions and cashews with a slotted spoon and set them aside.

4. In the same pan, heat the remaining 1 tablespoon (15 ml) oil over moderate heat. Fry bay leaves, cardamom, and black cardamom for a few seconds. Add rice and cook until it turns opaque, about 2 minutes, stirring constantly. Add water, salt, and sugar and bring to a boil. Simmer, covered, 10 to 15 minutes, or until rice is nearly tender. Pour the reserved fish liquid over the rice but don't stir the rice.

5. Simmer, covered, another 8 to 10 minutes. Remove from heat. Add garam masala and cilantro. Let stand, covered, 5 minutes to help develop flavor. During this time, place the reserved fish in a warm oven briefly (3 to 5 minutes) in preparation for serving.

6. Fluff rice with a fork and pile on a large preheated platter. Arrange the fish pieces over the rice. Sprinkle with the onion and cashews, decorate the top with bell pepper strips, and serve.

2 entrée servings

Serving Suggestions: Side dishes that showcase this pullao are Indian Spiced Brussels Sprouts (page 74) or Artichoke and Sweet Red Pepper Salad (page 249), Chicken-Flavored Baby Potatoes (page 244), and Mint-Tamarind Pesto (page 225).

VARIATION: This fish is so tasty that I sometimes prepare and serve it without the rice pullao. To do so, add the garam masala to the sauce along with the yogurt at the end of Step 2. Then return the fish and the sauce to the skillet, and heat gently over very low heat until sauce begins to bubble. Remove from heat immediately, garnish with cilantro, and serve.

❋ Many Splendored Smelts ❋
EASTERN INDIA

In the Bengal region of India, small fish resembling smelt are a favorite both for their delicate flavor and the endless spicy sauces that accompany them. "A plate of *pooti maach* [baby catfish] and some rice, and I am in heaven," is an oft-heard phrase in Bengal. In America, any freshwater pan fish such as lake perch, blue gills, or sunfish are suitable, if there is a fisher in your family. If these are not available, your favorite firm-fleshed fish will do. This recipe is an excellent reason for not throwing the small fish back, but the tart sauce is also delightful with larger fish.

I apply the Bengali technique of sautéeing the fish briefly in a little mustard oil before adding it to the sauce. Doing so seals in the flavor and makes the fish more succulent. The use of mustard oil imparts a unique Bengali fragrance to the dish.

$2^1/2$ tablespoons (37 ml) mustard oil

2 pounds (1 kg) smelt or other small fish, or salmon, halibut, sturgeon, or tuna cut into 2 × 2 inch (5 × 5 cm) pieces

2 whole dried red chiles (see *Note for the Gardener*)

$1/4$ teaspoon (1 ml) black mustard seeds

$1/4$ teaspoon (1 ml) turmeric

$1/4$ teaspoon (1 ml) salt

1 teaspoon (5 ml) sugar

$3/4$ teaspoon (3 ml) tamarind concentrate

$1/2$ cup (125 ml) water

Garnish: 1 jalapeño, seeded, slivered

1. Heat $1^1/2$ tablespoons (22 ml) oil in a steep-sided pan or skillet, at least 10 inches (25 cm) in diameter, over moderate heat. Add fish and cook for about 1 minute or just until opaque, turning the pieces once. Remove with a slotted spoon and set aside.

2. Add the remaining 1 tablespoon (15 ml) oil to the same skillet and heat over moderate heat. Add red chiles and fry until they blacken. Add black mustard seeds. As soon as the seeds start popping, stir in turmeric, salt, and sugar. (Cover the skillet partially to prevent the seeds from flying out.) Stir in tamarind concentrate and water and bring to a boil. Reduce heat slightly.

3. Simmer, covered, 5 minutes. Add fish and any accumulated liquid. Cover and simmer 3 to 5 more minutes or until fish is done. (A toothpick inserted in the thickest part and pushed to one side should show an opaque color in the fish.) Serve sprinkled with jalapeño slivers.

6 to 8 entrée servings

Note for the Gardener: The cayenne pepper plants in my garden bear profusely every summer. I don't harvest them all while they are still green. I let some peppers stay on the plant to ripen to a red color, then dry them in a food dehydrator following the manufacturer's directions. I use these aromatic dried red chiles for the remainder of the year.

Serving Suggestions: Spend an evening in India by serving Picnic Squash Pullao (page 169), Cilantro Splash (page 223), and some steamed cauliflower. End the meal with Lychee Swirl (page 287) and a cup of Soy Chai (page 293).

✳ Kale Spiced with Fish ✳
EASTERN INDIA/UNITED STATES/EAST ASIA

Cooking fish with greens is quite common in Bengal. Here in the West, I use kale because it's an easy-to-prepare, tasty vegetable that is high in calcium, iron, and B vitamins. But I also find kale's taste is too strong for many people. The assertive flavor of these greens can be masked by cooking them with canned or smoked fish.

For buying highly flavored canned fish, my first choice is Asian markets, where I can find roasted eel, sauries, or mackerel preserved in fermented bean sauce or teriyaki sauce. If these are not available, you can substitute canned smoked sardines or mussels or any smoked fish.

2   tablespoons (30 ml) canola oil
1/4   teaspoon (1 ml) cumin seeds
1   cup (250 ml) thinly sliced onion
1   jalapeño, seeded, chopped (include some seeds for hotness)
1/2   teaspoon (2 ml) curry powder (see "Selecting curry powder," page 10)
1/4   cup (60 ml) chicken broth, defatted (see "To defat canned chicken broth," page 45)
3/4   pound (375 g) kale or mustard greens, thinly shredded, stems chopped and added if desired (see *Note for the Gardener*)
4   ounces (100 g) canned fish, drained, cut into small pieces (see *Note*)
    Salt (optional)

Heat oil in a large skillet over moderate heat. Add cumin seeds and fry until they are lightly browned. Add onion and fry until slices turn medium brown, 6 to 10 minutes. Stir in jalapeño and curry powder. Add broth and bring to a boil. Add kale. Cover and simmer until kale is tender to the bite, 10 to 15 minutes. (Overcooking will discolor the greens.) Add fish, cover, and cook 2 to 3 minutes until the mixture is heated through. Remove from heat and serve piping hot.

2 entrée servings

Note: If available, use canned fish preserved in fermented beans or teriyaki sauce. Other options are canned smoked oysters or mussels, Norway sardines, and kippered herrings. Another alternative is to use 2 ounces (50 g) smoked fish, cut into thin slivers.

Note for the Gardener: My husband and I plant kale of different colors in our Pacific Northwest garden where this easy-to-grow, hardy brassica overwinters. Our favorite is a type with large red-veined leaves variously known as Red Russian or Winter Red. I harvest the leaves just before cooking. They become wonderfully sweet and tender as they are braised. If allowed to sit after harvesting, kale becomes tough, as is often the case when it's purchased at supermarkets.

Serving Suggestions: Warm up with Gujarati Potato Boats (page 64) and some steamed and pureed beets drizzled with Tamari-Wasabi Dressing (page 234). Then cool down with Onion Yogurt Relish (page 209) and some fresh papaya slices.

✳ Fish Korma ✳

EASTERN INDIA

Yogurt is widely used in Indian cooking because of its ability to produce thick, rich sauces that disperse the essence of spices. This style of sauce, known as *korma*, is much favored by the Moslems. In this recipe from Bengal, the fish is napped in a creamy yogurt *korma* that is accented by both garlic and gingerroot. The absence of turmeric has caused this dish to be nicknamed "white-sauced fish." Though the dish is traditional, I serve it with accompaniments of quinoa or millet and a salsa, which are unknown in India.

Most fish work well, but salmon, halibut, black cod, or catfish is especially good and creates a simple but impressive dish.

The marinade:

   2   tablespoons (30 ml) grated gingerroot or gingerroot paste (see page 12)
3 to 5   large garlic cloves, forced through a garlic press
  1/2   cup (125 ml) plain nonfat yogurt, lightly beaten until smooth and mixed
          with 1/2 teaspoon (2 ml) all-purpose flour
  1/2   teaspoon (2 ml) salt
   1   teaspoon (5 ml) sugar
        Ground red pepper (to taste; start with a scant pinch)

The fish:
- 2 pounds (1 kg) fish, cut into 2 × 2 inch (5 × 5 cm) pieces
- 2 teaspoons (10 ml) mustard oil
- 1 bay leaf
- 5 whole cardamom pods, bruised
  - 2-inch (5-cm) cinnamon stick
- 2 whole cloves

Garnish: Chopped cilantro

1. Combine the marinade ingredients in a large bowl. Add fish, tossing gently to coat each piece with the marinade. Cover and refrigerate for at least 30 minutes.
2. Heat oil in a skillet over moderate heat. (If you're using an electric stove, turn a second burner to low heat at this time. This is to prevent the yogurt from curdling while being simmered later in this step. The texture of the fish is also better if cooked over low heat.) Fry bay leaf, cardamom, cinnamon, and cloves for a few seconds until they emit a pleasant smell. (Since the amount of oil is small, place the spices in those places in the pan where the oil accumulates.) If using gas, turn heat to very low. If using electricity, place skillet over the second burner. Add the fish and marinade. Simmer, covered, until fish is done, 8 to 15 minutes. (A toothpick inserted in the thickest part and pushed to one side should show an opaque color in the piece.) During this period, remove cover and turn the fish pieces once or twice. Remove from heat. Let stand covered for a few minutes to help develop the flavor further. Serve garnished with cilantro.

6 entrée servings

Serving Suggestions: Quinoa or millet is a good base for this tangy sauce. Prepare the eggplant sauce from the recipe Soba Noodles with Tahini Eggplant (page 158) and serve as a vegetable side dish. Rustic Salsa Pasilla (page 214) or Prune and Date Chutney (page 207) will complete the meal.

✳ Mango-Marinated Fish with ✳ Dried Tomato Sauce

INDIA/ITALY

Using mango powder is one of the ways Indian cooks add tartness to a dish. To create this taste, unripe, green mango is dried and crushed. The synergy of mixing this powder with dried tomato, an Italian specialty, creates the base for this fish braise. The sauce tastes rich and mellow, yet it has no added fat.

The marinade:

- $1/2$ cup (125 ml) plain nonfat yogurt
- $1/4$ teaspoon (1 ml) turmeric
- $1/2$ teaspoon (2 ml) mango powder (*aamchoor*)
- $1/4$ teaspoon (1 ml) ground ginger
- $1/2$ teaspoon (2 ml) all-purpose flour
- $1/2$ teaspoon (2 ml) ground cumin
- $1/2$ teaspoon (2 ml) salt
  Ground red pepper (to taste; start with a scant pinch)

The fish:

- $1^1/2$ pounds (750 g) fish (salmon, halibut, sturgeon, or other fish of your choice), cut into 2 x 2 inch (5 x 5 cm) pieces
- 1 tablespoon (15 ml) dried tomato bits (see *Note*)
- 2 tablespoons (30 ml) fresh lime or lemon juice
- 1 tablespoon (15 ml) chopped fresh mint leaves

1. Whisk all the marinade ingredients together in a large bowl. Toss fish in this marinade, making sure each piece is well-coated. Refrigerate for at least 30 minutes.
2. Place fish and marinade in a large skillet over low heat. Sprinkle with tomato bits. Cover and cook 6 to 10 minutes or until fish is done. (A toothpick inserted in the middle and pushed to one side should show an opaque color in the fish.) Remove from heat. Adjust seasoning. Sprinkle with lime juice and mint leaves and serve immediately.

4 entrée servings

Note: Dried tomato bits are sold in jars in gourmet stores and some supermarkets and require no presoftening. If they are not available, blanch 2 to 3 sun-dried tomatoes in boiling water for 5 to 10 minutes, drain and pat dry, and then chop finely.

Serving Suggestions: This faintly tart dish becomes the focal point of a meal when surrounded by Saffron-Scented Millet (page 172), Crisp Potato and Wilted Spinach Salad (page 246), and Chilied Mango Chutney (page 205).

❋ Velvet Fish ❋

INDIA

Raita, a tangy salad, can be a cooling conclusion to an Indian meal. It's easily prepared by combining yogurt with spices and a main ingredient of fruit, vegetable, or, more rarely, fish. In this raita recipe, fish swims in a pool of velvety yogurt sauce—a merger of sweet and hot flavors along with a touch of tamarind tartness. In the West, it makes an excellent main dish. Swordfish, tuna, or halibut is especially appropriate here.

    2   teaspoons (10 ml) mustard oil (preferred) or canola oil
    2   whole dried red chiles
 1/4   teaspoon (1 ml) asafetida powder
 1/4   teaspoon (1 ml) turmeric
    1   teaspoon (5 ml) black mustard seeds, ground to a powder, mixed with
            1 tablespoon (15 ml) water and allowed to stand 30 minutes
 1/4   cup (60 ml) water
1 1/2   pounds (750 g) fish, cut into 2 x 2 inch (5 x 5 cm) pieces
 3/4   teaspoon (3 ml) salt
    1   teaspoon (5 ml) sugar
          Ground red pepper (to taste; start with a scant pinch)
 1/2   teaspoon (2 ml) tamarind concentrate
    1   cup (250 ml) plain nonfat yogurt, lightly beaten until smooth and mixed with
            1/2 teaspoon (2 ml) all-purpose flour

Garnish: Chopped cilantro

1. Heat oil in a large skillet over moderate heat. Add red chiles and fry until they darken. Sprinkle asafetida over the chile. Add turmeric and mustard-seed paste and stir a few times. Add water, cover, and bring to a boil. Simmer, covered, 5 minutes.
2. Add fish, salt, sugar, and red pepper. Simmer, covered, another 4 to 7 minutes or until fish is done. (A toothpick inserted in the thickest part and pushed to one side

should show an opaque color in the piece.) Add tamarind and stir gently so as not to break the fish pieces. If using a gas stove, set the burner to low heat. If cooking on an electric range, transfer to another burner with low heat. Add yogurt. As soon as the yogurt thins and forms a sauce, remove from heat. (Prolonged cooking over high heat can curdle yogurt and destroy the texture and appearance of the sauce.) Let stand covered for 10 minutes to help thicken the sauce and develop the flavor further. Sprinkle cilantro on top and serve.

4 entrée servings

Serving Suggestions: For a glamorous dinner, team with Sesame Arugula and Squash (page 85), Basic Pilaf with Nutty Vermicelli Threads (page 177), and Mint-Basil Chutney (page 224).

✳ Broiled Fish and Browned Potatoes ✳ in Bengali Sauce

EASTERN INDIA

In Bengal, black mustard seeds are a popular sauce ingredient, especially in fish preparations; white poppy seeds are prized as a thickener and for their nutty aroma; and coconut is used frequently to add richness and flavor to both fish and vegetables. This unique recipe combines all three ingredients.

Instead of simmering fish and potatoes in the sauce as is the custom back home, I cook each separately and let my guests help themselves to the sauce. This way one can enjoy the individual flavors of the fish, the potatoes, and the sauce.

The sauce:

    1   tablespoon (15 ml) mustard oil (preferred) or canola oil
    1   cup (250 ml) finely chopped onion
  1/4   teaspoon (1 ml) turmeric
    1   teaspoon (5 ml) black mustard seeds, ground to a powder, mixed with
            1 tablespoon (15 ml) water and allowed to stand for 30 minutes
    1   cup (250 ml) water
    1   tablespoon (15 ml) white poppy seeds, made into a paste (see page 20)
    1   tablespoon (15 ml) sweetened flaked coconut, reduced to a coarse
            powder in a blender or food processor
    1   teaspoon (5 ml) sugar
        Salt

The potatoes:

> 1   pound (500 g) potatoes, about 4 medium (Yellow Finn, if possible), peeled or unpeeled, cut into 1 1/2-inch (4-cm) cubes (see *Note for the Gardener*)
>
> 1 to 2   tablespoons (15 to 30 ml) ghee, mustard oil, or olive oil
>
> Salt and freshly ground black pepper

The fish:

> Ghee (melted) or mustard oil for brushing
>
> Asafetida powder
>
> Salt and freshly ground black pepper
>
> 1 1/2   pounds (750 g) fish (salmon, tuna, swordfish, or shark), cut into 2 × 2 inch (5 × 5 cm) pieces

1. To prepare the sauce: Heat oil in a skillet over moderate heat until a light haze forms. Add onion and cook until it is translucent, about 2 minutes. Sprinkle turmeric over the onion and stir. Add mustard-seed paste and water. Cover and bring to a boil. Lower the heat, cover, and simmer for 5 minutes. Stir in poppy-seed paste, coconut, sugar, and salt. Cover and simmer 10 to 15 more minutes. Remove from heat.

2. To brown potatoes: Steam the potatoes until tender but not breaking, 12 to 18 minutes. Heat oil in a medium to large skillet over medium heat. Add potatoes and cook until richly browned, 8 to 12 minutes, turning often but carefully to brown all sides. Add salt and pepper. Transfer to a medium bowl and keep covered.

3. To prepare the fish: Combine ghee, asafetida, salt, and pepper in a large bowl. Brush fish with this mixture, making sure each piece is well-coated. Broil for 5 to 8 minutes or until fish is done and is browned on top. (A toothpick inserted in the thickest part and pushed to one side should show an opaque color in the piece.) The timing will vary with the thickness and type of fish. Remove from the broiler and keep covered.

4. Reheat sauce briefly and transfer to a sauce boat. If necessary, warm up the fish and potatoes briefly in a warm oven, then arrange them on a large heated platter. Put the sauce boat on the side and serve hot.

4 to 6 entrée servings

Note for the Gardener: Both Yukon Gold and German Butterball are exciting potato varieties to grow. The fine-skinned Yukon Gold is buttery yellow, moist, and creamy inside. German Butterball also has a yellow flesh but is slightly crisper in texture. If you grow either variety, try them in this recipe.

Serving Suggestions: Accompany with Satay Apples and Bok Choy (page 73). Some warmed chapatis or tortillas and a bowl of Salsa Maharaja (page 213) would also be appropriate here.

✳ "Southern" Shrimp and Cauliflower "Gumbo" ✳
SOUTH INDIA/SOUTHEAST ASIA

A Western friend told me that when she first started using shrimp paste she had to open her windows to dissipate the strong aroma, but that with time she began to appreciate both its scent and pungent flavor. I cook often with shrimp paste and fish sauce, another bold condiment, and find that both of these Southeast Asian staples mellow when added to this recipe of "Southern" Indian origin. The result is an atypically thin but robust dish, which bears some resemblance to a traditional Louisiana gumbo.

2	tablespoons (30 ml) Indian sesame oil (*gingely*), or canola oil
2	whole dried red chiles
1	cup (250 ml) finely chopped onion
4	large garlic cloves, forced through a garlic press
2	tablespoons (30 ml) grated gingerroot or gingerroot paste (see page 12)
1	jalapeño, seeded and made into a paste by processing in a mini-chopper or by pounding in a mortar and pestle
1/2	teaspoon (2 ml) turmeric
1	teaspoon (5 ml) ground cumin
1	pound (500 g) Roma tomatoes (about 4 large), chopped
1/2	teaspoon (2 ml) shrimp paste
1/4	teaspoon (1 ml) fish sauce
1 1/2	cups (375 ml) water
3/4	pound (375 g) cauliflower, 1/2 a medium head, cut into florets
1	inch (2.5 cm) in diameter
1	pound (500 g) fresh shrimp, deveined, or frozen shrimp, thawed
	Salt

Garnish: Chopped cilantro

1. Heat oil in a large skillet over moderate heat. Add red chiles and fry until they blacken. Add onion and fry until richly browned but not burnt, 10 to 12 minutes.

Stir in garlic, gingerroot, jalapeño, turmeric, and cumin. Add tomatoes, shrimp paste, fish sauce, and water. Bring to a boil. Add cauliflower, then cover and simmer for 10 to 12 minutes. Remove cover occasionally and stir, mashing the tomatoes with the back of a spoon to mix in with the sauce.

2. Add shrimp. Cover and simmer for 5 or so more minutes or just until shrimp is done. (A toothpick inserted in the middle and pushed to one side should show an opaque color in the shrimp.) Add salt. Garnish with cilantro and serve hot.

4 entrée servings

Serving Suggestions: Plain white Basmati rice is the ideal accompaniment to this gumbo. To complete the meal, serve one or more of the following vegetable dishes: Sweet Potato Salad with Sesame-Tamarind Dressing (page 242), Greens Ratatouille (page 94), or Hot Punjab Eggplant (page 80). Consider serving Onion Yogurt Relish (page 209) as a cooling condiment.

VEGETABLE VARIATION: EGG AND CAULIFLOWER WHIMSY A splendid dish for vegetable lovers. Cauliflower has an affinity for eggs, and their union is a Bengali country favorite.

Omit shrimp in Step 2, but arrange 4 hard-cooked eggs (or 8 hard-cooked egg whites), halved or quartered, over the sauce just before serving.

* Shrimp and Scallop Vatapa *
BRAZIL

The first time I tasted *vatapa*, an extravagant seafood stew from Brazil, I knew I'd discovered a lifetime favorite. The dish originated in Bahia, a colorful region in the northeast, known for its folk costumes and its cuisine. This cuisine was enriched by African slaves who were brought over by the Portuguese in the sixteenth century to work on the sugar and coffee plantations. The result was a unique blend of African, European, and local influences.

The ingredients for *vatapa* are exotic: fish, fresh and dried shrimp, coconut milk, peanuts, *dênde* oil (a palm derivative), and manioc (cassava flour). I omit palm oil and add only a small amount of coconut milk. Chick-pea flour, *besan*, known for its nutty aroma, is my substitute for cassava flour. True to my Bengali origin, I am unable to resist dusting the fish with a little turmeric both for its pungent flavor and the lovely yellow color it imparts. My altered version is a lighter soup that seems to me every bit as delicious as the original recipe.

   5   cups (1.25 liters) Fish Stock (page 42)
 1/2 cup (125 ml) unsalted, skinless, dry-roasted peanuts, ground to a coarse
          powder in a blender or food processor
   1   tablespoon (15 ml) shrimp powder (optional; available in Latin and
          Asian markets)
   1   tablespoon (15 ml) chick-pea flour, *besan*, toasted (see *Note*)
   1   tablespoon (15 ml) canola oil
   1   cup (250 ml) thinly sliced onion
   1   tablespoon (15 ml) minced garlic
 1/2 teaspoon (2 ml) turmeric
   1   jalapeño, seeded, chopped (to taste)
   1   pound (500 g) fresh shrimp, preferably with shells intact
   1   pound (500 g) scallops
 1/2 cup (125 ml) unsweetened coconut milk, fresh or canned, stirred until
          evenly mixed
       Salt

Garnish:
       2 scallions, thinly sliced (green parts only)
       chopped cilantro

1. Combine 4 cups (1 liter) fish stock, ground peanuts, shrimp powder, and chick-pea flour in a large, deep pot and bring to a boil. Simmer, uncovered, over medium heat until thick and creamy, 18 to 25 minutes. Cover and keep warm. (Up to this point the recipe can be made ahead and refrigerated.)

2. Heat oil over moderate heat in a large skillet. Cook onion and garlic until onion is translucent, about 2 minutes. Stir in turmeric and jalapeño. Add the remaining 1 cup (250 ml) fish stock and bring to a boil. Lower heat slightly and add shrimp and scallops. Cover and simmer until the seafood is done, 5 to 7 minutes. (A toothpick inserted in the middle and pushed to one side should show an opaque color in the seafood.) Remove from heat.

3. Reheat the 4 cups (1 liter) fish stock if necessary to bring to a simmer. Add the seafood and vegetables and bring to a simmer again. Turn heat to very low. Add coconut milk and cook, uncovered, for a few minutes. (Too much heat might curdle the coconut milk.) Add salt. Remove from heat, garnish with scallions and cilantro, and serve piping hot.

4 entrée servings

Note: Don't substitute regular flour. *Besan* has a warm, nutty taste that adds to the flavor of the broth. To toast *besan*, place in an ungreased skillet over low heat for 3 to 6 minutes or until lightly browned, stirring constantly. You'll notice a warm aroma. Don't let the flour burn.

Serving Suggestions: Plain white rice is a good complement. So is Italian bread such as panini, when spread with Fish Aïoli (page 227). During summer, I slice vine-ripened tomatoes into rounds, drizzle with a little olive oil and balsamic vinegar, sprinkle lightly with asafetida powder and fresh basil, and serve as a salad. During winter, I steam potatoes, cauliflower, and snow peas and serve Rustic Salsa Pasilla (page 214) as a dip.

VARIATION: FISH AND SHRIMP VATAPA OR FISH VATAPA
Substitute 1 pound (500 g) fish, cut into bite-sized pieces, for scallops. *Vatapa* can also be prepared with fish alone. In this case, omit both shrimp and scallops. Use 2 pounds (1 kg) fish, cut into bite-sized pieces. Salmon, halibut, tuna, and snapper are good choices, or use any firm-fleshed fish you like.

VARIATION: CAULIFLOWER AND POTATO VATAPA
If you don't fancy fish, treat yourself to this delightful vegetable version. Both cauliflower and potatoes taste delicious when simmered in the *vatapa* broth. Cut 1 pound (500 g) peeled or unpeeled potatoes, about 4 medium, into 1-inch (2.5-cm) cubes. Add to the pot when the fish broth comes to a boil in Step 2. Simmer, covered, 10 minutes. Add a medium head of cauliflower, about 1½ pounds (375 g), cut into small florets. Simmer, covered, another 10 to 12 minutes or until both potatoes and cauliflower are fork-tender. Continue with the rest of the recipe.

✳ Quinoa-Bedded Clams ✳

SPAIN

The clams in this dish look stunning nestled on a bed of tiny plump grains, and the quinoa kernels become more flavorful as they soak up the clam juice.

This simple but lovely preparation owes its origin to paella, the saffron-flavored rice and seafood casserole said to be one of the prized dishes of Spain. Paella can contain a variety of seafood—shrimp, mussels, squid—and is equally superb with chicken and sausage. This lighter and spicier Indian version requires fewer ingredients and is well-suited for serving at dinner parties.

The clams:

1 to 1 1/2	tablespoons (15 to 22 ml) mustard oil or canola oil
1	whole dried red chile
1/4	teaspoon (1 ml) asafetida powder
1/2	teaspoon (2 ml) black mustard seeds
1	tablespoon (15 ml) minced gingerroot
1	jalapeño, seeded, chopped (to taste)
1/4	teaspoon (1 ml) turmeric
1	teaspoon (5 ml) ground cumin
2	teaspoons (10 ml) ground coriander
1/2	pound (250 g) Roma tomatoes (2 large), seeded, sliced
1/2	cup (125 ml) water
	Pinch saffron threads, ground to a powder and soaked in 1 tablespoon (15 ml) water for 10 minutes (optional)
2	pounds (1 kg) clams (manila, butter, or steamer clams) (see *Note*)

The quinoa:

1 1/2	tablespoons (22 ml) canola oil
1	cup (250 ml) finely chopped onion
1	cup (250 ml) quinoa, rinsed several times and drained
1/2	cup (125 ml) fresh peas or thawed frozen peas

Garnish: Chopped cilantro

1. To prepare the clams: Heat oil in a large, deep-sided pan over moderate heat. Fry red chile until it blackens. Sprinkle asafetida over the chile. Add black mustard seeds. As soon as the seeds start popping, add gingerroot and jalapeño. Cook until gingerroot is lightly browned. Stir in turmeric, cumin, and coriander.

2. Add tomatoes, water, and saffron. Cover and bring to a boil. Add clams. Cover and raise heat to medium-high. After 4 to 5 minutes, uncover and remove the clams that have started to open slightly. (Cooking time will vary based on the type of clams used.) The clams need not open entirely, since they will be cooked more later. To avoid overcooking, remove them immediately as soon as they open slightly and set them aside in a large bowl. Cover the pan again for a minute or so, then repeat this process. When you have removed all of the clams from the pan, turn off heat. (A few clams that remain closed may open later.) Pour the remaining liquid with its spices and bits of tomato into a large measuring cup. Add enough water to equal 2 cups (500 ml).

3. Wash and wipe out the pan. Heat 1 tablespoon (15 ml) oil in this pan over moderate heat. Add onion and cook until it is translucent, about 2 minutes, stirring often. Add quinoa and cook for 1 to 2 minutes, stirring often. Pour the clam liquid over the quinoa and bring to a boil. Simmer, covered, 25 to 35 minutes or until all liquid is absorbed and quinoa is tender and fluffy. (If using fresh peas, add on top during the last 5 to 6 minutes of cooking.) Don't stir the grains. When quinoa is ready, arrange frozen peas on top. Place the clams over the peas and pour any accumulated liquid over them. Cover and simmer for another 2 to 3 minutes, just until heated through. Don't overcook. At this point discard any clam that hasn't opened. Serve sprinkled with cilantro on top.

2 entrée servings

Note: This dish requires no salt because the clam juices provide ample salinity.

Serving Suggestions: Magnificent as a luncheon course, followed by Egg and Cauliflower Whimsy (page 115), acorn squash (baked with a dab of ghee and honey and sprinkled before serving with lime juice), and Mint-Basil Chutney (page 224).

VARIATION: MUSSELS BEDDED ON SAFFRON RICE Replace clams with mussels and quinoa with Basmati rice. Saffron is mandatory in this case as its flavor goes particularly well with mussels. Separate the mussels, trim beard from each, then scrub with a brush under cold running water to remove any extraneous matter from the shells. Rinse the rice several times and drain. In Step 2, remove cover after 3 to 4 minutes. Some of the mussels will be fully open. Also, later in this step, measure liquid to come up to 1¾ cups (435 ml). In Step 3, cook rice for a shorter length of time, 15 to 20 minutes, or until all liquid is absorbed and rice is tender and fluffy.

✳ Chile and Yogurt-Sauced Crab ✳

SOUTHEAST ASIA

Chile crab is one of Singapore's most famous dishes. After returning to the United States, I prepared a crab Singapore-style, but instinctively added Indian spices and yogurt. To me the crab tasted even better, and this easy recipe became one of my favorites.

The dish has a rich, complex flavor and offers a number of variations.

  2   tablespoons (30 ml) mustard oil or canola oil
  1   medium onion, coarsely chopped
  2   tablespoons (30 ml) grated gingerroot or gingerroot paste (see page 12)
  1   jalapeño, seeded, chopped (to taste)
 1/4   teaspoon (1 ml) turmeric
  1   teaspoon (5 ml) ground cumin
  1   teaspoon (5 ml) ground coriander
 1/2   teaspoon (2 ml) sugar
  1   teaspoon (5 ml) sambal oeleck (to taste)
  2   tablespoons (30 ml) tomato ketchup (see *Note*)
  2   tablespoons (30 ml) Heinz chili sauce or equivalent
2 to 3 pounds (1 to 1.5 kg) fresh crab, cleaned and cut into serving size pieces
  3   tablespoons (45 ml) plain nonfat yogurt, lightly beaten until smooth and
       mixed with 1/4 teaspoon (1 ml) all-purpose flour
       Salt (optional)

Garnish: Chopped cilantro

1. Heat oil in a large, steep-sided skillet over moderate heat. Add onion, ginger-root, and jalapeño and cook until onion is translucent, 1 to 2 minutes, stirring constantly.

2. Stir in turmeric, cumin, coriander, and sugar. Add sambal oeleck, ketchup, and chili sauce and heat until the mixture bubbles. Add the crab pieces and stir to coat with the sauce. Do not lower the heat but cover tightly and braise the crab for 7 to 10 minutes, or until done. Cooking time will vary according to the size of the pieces. To test for doneness, break open a large piece. If the meat is flaky and opaque, it's done.

3. If using a gas burner, turn heat to very low. If using an electric stove, transfer to another burner that has been set to low heat. Stir in yogurt. As soon as yogurt has been incorporated into the sauce, remove from heat. At this point, sample the sauce and add salt if necessary. Arrange crab on a heated serving platter and pour the sauce over it. Scatter cilantro on top.

2 entrée servings

Note: In Singapore the cooks use a local variety of ketchup-type tomato sauce. The combination of American ketchup, chili sauce, and Indian spices punches up the flavor of this dish.

Serving Suggestions: Complete a delicious supper with white or brown Basmati rice, Gai Lan with Balsamic Vinaigrette (page 70), and baked butternut squash sprinkled with lime juice, maple syrup, and minced gingerroot.

OTHER SEAFOOD VARIATIONS: For a delicious fish dish, replace crab with $1^1/2$ pounds (750 g) firm-fleshed fish. I prefer salmon or halibut, but cod, snapper, or other similar fish will also produce a good result. In Step 2 before adding the fish, lower the heat. Cover and simmer gently for about 5 minutes or until done. (A toothpick inserted in the thickest part and pulled to one side should show an opaque color in the fish.) Other seafood options are scallops and lobster. Cook scallops as you would fish. For lobster, follow recipe for crab.

TOFU VARIATION: Another terrific alternative. Use a 14-ounce (396-g) carton of firm tofu. Drain and rinse. Cut tofu in triangles and press water out of the pieces by following instructions in Garlic-Glazed Tofu (page 67). In Step 2, simmer for about 5 minutes.

✳ Peppery Squid ✳

INTERNATIONAL

An oft-heard word in India is *masala*, spice or spice mixture. Few Indian dishes are complete without *masala*. To use a small amount of spice sparingly and yet produce a fine result is the mark of a good cook. Indians shop for *masala* with as much care as when choosing fish, meat, or vegetables. It's not unusual to run into a friend on the street who says, "I have to get some *masala* for the fish tonight." This typically results in a pleasant delay while you exchange tips about where to buy the freshest.

This light squid dish contains a few spices, such as cumin seeds and turmeric, to enhance the taste of the sauce.

2 large red bell peppers
1 tablespoon (15 ml) olive oil
1/4 teaspoon (1 ml) cumin seeds
4 large garlic cloves, minced
1/4 teaspoon (1 ml) turmeric
4 teaspoons (20 ml) sambal oeleck (to taste)
1 pound (500 g) cleaned, fresh whole squid
1 tablespoon (15 ml) chopped cilantro
Salt

1. Roast the bell peppers by placing them under the broiler for 7 to 10 minutes or until the skin is mostly charred. Remove from the broiler. Place the peppers in a paper bag and close the top. Let stand for 10 to 12 minutes. When cool enough to handle, peel off the skin and remove the seeds, inner membranes, and any charred flesh. Whirl the remaining flesh in a blender or food processor to a smooth puree.

2. Heat oil in a large skillet over moderate heat. Add cumin seeds and fry for a few seconds. Add garlic and fry until lightly browned. Sprinkle turmeric over the spices. Add the pepper puree, cover, and heat the mixture to boiling. Reduce heat and add sambal oeleck and squid. Cover and simmer for 10 to 20 minutes or until squid is opaque but tender. Squid will turn rubbery if overcooked; check frequently after 10 minutes. Add salt. Remove from the heat immediately and add cilantro.

4 entrée servings

Serving Suggestions: Perfect with white Basmati rice, steamed asparagus drizzled with Tamari-Wasabi Dressing (page 234), and some steamed beets. Shah Jahani Flan (page 270) is just the right dessert.

Poultry and Meat

•••••••••••••••

An aroma will bring back memories to me more than any other sense. One childhood winter evening after we had dined on a big pot of lamb stew, redolent of onion, garlic, and cardamom, my mother put the still-warm stewpot against my feet when I went to bed. The pot toasted my toes and I fell asleep with the fragrance of spices floating up to my head. Whatever I dreamt that night was pleasant. Any smell of highly spiced meat today draws me back to that cozy room, to that carefree time, to that blissful state of mind.

Yet the portion of meat on our dinner plate was quite small. Indians have traditionally served meat in small amounts because of its scarcity and price. They stretch the servings by combining it creatively with other ingredients. They braise meat with potatoes or cauliflower in a spicy, aromatic gravy, allowing the vegetables to absorb the rich flavors and become as tasty as the meat. Or they prepare numerous rice dishes to which meat is added in small quantities to enhance the flavor of the grains.

Meat has traditionally been an important item in the diet of most cultures. In Asia, a Thai salad composed mainly of fresh raw vegetables may be accented with thin slices of beef. The Chinese are experts at extracting the maximum flavor from the smallest sliver of meat by including it in a stir-fry or letting it simmer slowly in a hot pot with tofu, shellfish, and vegetables. Although meat continues to be popular in the West, increased awareness of the connection between diet and health is leading people to serve smaller portions of meat. Meat is appearing more in a supporting role rather than as the central character, as a flavor enhancer rather than the main ingredient.

I once saw a celebration of meat in a Seoul restaurant where two Korean men with whom I shared a table showed me how to prepare *bulgogi*, "fire beef," or beef cooked barbecue style. First they braised paper-thin slices of beef, marinated in soy sauce, garlic, and sesame oil, over a tiny gas burner set right in the table. Then they wrapped fresh lettuce and edible chrysanthemum leaves around the meat and popped it into their mouths. The amount of meat was moderate, and at least five vegetable side dishes surrounded the meat platter, balancing the nutrition while adding taste and texture. These two men told me this Korean national dish is a legacy of their nomadic Mongol ancestors, who grilled meat over an open fire.

Here in the United States, I watched a Japanese-American friend set up *shabu shabu* for her guests. An electric skillet filled with simmering hot broth took up the center of the table. Then she placed platters of thinly sliced meat, carrot strips, cabbage leaves, mushrooms, and scallions in front of the guests. Each diner was invited to pick up a morsel and swirl it gently in the simmering broth until cooked to his or her individual taste. After a while, the broth became rich with the flavors of the meat and vegetables that had been simmered in it. And it was time to end the meal with a savory cup of the steaming broth. My friend called this type of serving a "gathering of everything," and it made food that evening's entertainment.

In this chapter I present an array of dishes that embody concepts from around the world, but I return to my Indian background often for ideas, such as allowing a rich, thick sauce to compensate for smaller-than-usual portions of meat. In India, meat is usually marinated or rubbed with a mixture of spices before cooking. This allows the spices to penetrate the meat better, and a marinade often helps to tenderize the meat. Indians skin a chicken before cooking, a technique I apply also to chicken dishes from other countries. To compensate for the smaller portions of poultry or meat, I offer as accompaniment plenty of grains or vegetables, as is the custom in India.

Among the recipes that follow, cubes of chicken meat nestled on fresh leafy greens form a vibrant main course. Plain poached chicken served with a mélange of exciting sauces will stand out at any buffet. Extra-lean ground beef simmered with vegetables and spices is just the sort of homey dish to share with the family. In this fashion, one can continue to enjoy meat in a spirit of moderation. ✳

✳ Lime-Grilled Chicken ✳

AFRICA/FRANCE

Yassa is a chicken dish that Africans serve when entertaining a large number of guests. The chicken is marinated in lemon juice for several hours, and the host grills the chicken as the guests arrive. Later, all share a large platter of the citrus-glazed meat served with grilled juicy onions and rice.

In this recipe, I use lime instead of lemon and season the meat with red pepper and black salt for a more complex flavor. Fresh tarragon, so beloved by the French, goes particularly well with this chicken. The sauce is quite tart, so add lime juice gradually to the marinade, tasting occasionally; stop when the flavor suits you.

1 1/2 pounds (750 g) chicken breasts or other pieces, skinned, cut into serving size pieces
1 tablespoon (15 ml) olive oil
  Ground red pepper (to taste; start with a scant pinch)
1/4 teaspoon (1 ml) black salt
  Salt and freshly ground black pepper
2 tablespoons (30 ml) chopped fresh tarragon, or 2 teaspoons (10 ml) dried tarragon
1 cup (250 ml) fresh lime juice, juice of 7 to 8 limes
1 medium onion, cut into rings 1/4 inch (6 mm) wide

Garnish: 2 scallions, chopped (green part only)

1. With a sharp knife, make slits 1/4 inch (6 mm) deep across the grain of the meat to allow the marinade to penetrate. In a large bowl, combine oil, red pepper, black salt, regular salt, black pepper, and tarragon. Stir in lime juice a little at a time, adjusting according to taste. (The flavor will mellow somewhat with cooking.) Coat chicken and onion rings in this marinade. Cover and let stand in the refrigerator for at least 30 minutes. Turn the chicken a few times during this period.

2. Preheat oven to 350°F (180°C, gas marks 4). Bake chicken, onion, and the marinade for 20 to 30 minutes or until done. (Insert a fork in the thickest part of the meat and pull the meat apart. If it is opaque all the way through to the bone, it is done.) Remove from the oven. Drain marinade and place it in a small saucepan. Arrange chicken and onion on top of a rack that stands on a broiler or baking pan. Broil for 2 to 5 minutes or until medium brown; halfway through broiling, turn the chicken pieces over. Remove each chicken or onion piece as it's done. (The

onion may take less time.) Take care not to burn either of them. Remove from the broiler and keep covered to retain heat.

3. Heat marinade over moderate heat. When it starts to bubble, lower heat. Cook, stirring often, until the sauce thickens. Remove from heat. Adjust seasonings. Arrange chicken on a large heated platter and place the onion rings around it. Pour the sauce over the chicken and serve garnished with scallions.

4 entrée servings

Serving Suggestions: Accompany with brown Basmati rice, cooked with golden raisins and pistachios; Gai Lan with Balsamic Vinaigrette (page 70); and Sweet and Sour Plantain Sauce (page 222).

TOFU VARIATION: Vegetarians need not miss the tasty *yassa* sauce. Instead of chicken, use a 14-ounce (396-g) carton of firm tofu. Cut tofu into triangles $1/2$ inch (1 cm) thick, then press water out of the pieces. (See Steps 1 and 2 of Garlic-Glazed Tofu on page 67 on how to slice and press the tofu.) In Step 1, dip tofu in marinade just before baking. (You need not marinate it for a period of time in the refrigerator.) Bake for 15 or so minutes. In Step 2, broil for 1 to 3 minutes or until lightly browned on top.

✳ Blackened Chicken ✳

KOREA

In Korea, garlic, gingerroot, soy sauce, and sesame form a tasty marinade for fish and meat dishes. In this recipe, garam masala gives an extra depth to this seasoning mix, which has a rich black color reminiscent of Cajun blackened fish. The preparation is easy, but this dish is delicious. And as a Korean woman once laughingly shared, "We've been using garlic and gingerroot for generations. Now we're finding they are good for your health."

2   tablespoons (30 ml) grated gingerroot or gingerroot paste (see page 12)
2   tablespoons (30 ml) minced garlic
1   tablespoon (15 ml) toasted and ground sesame seeds
1   jalapeño, seeded, finely chopped (to taste)
$1/4$ teaspoon (1 ml) freshly ground black pepper
$1/3$ cup (75 ml) low-sodium soy sauce

  2   tablespoons (30 ml) Chinese sesame oil
 ¹/₂   teaspoon (2 ml) salt
  1   teaspoon (5 ml) sugar
 ¹/₂   teaspoon (2 ml) garam masala
1¹/₂   pounds (750 g) chicken breasts or other pieces, skinned, cut into
       serving size pieces
  1   scallion, finely chopped

Garnish:
       Chopped scallion (green part only)
       Chopped cilantro
       Mild onion rings

1. Combine all ingredients except chicken, scallion, and garnishes in a large bowl. With a sharp knife, make a few slits in the chicken, approximately ¹/₄ inch (6 mm) deep across the grain of the meat to allow the marinade to penetrate. Toss chicken in this marinade, making sure each piece is well-coated. Add scallion. Cover and store in the refrigerator for at least 30 minutes; an hour or so is better.
2. Preheat oven to 350°F (180°C, gas marks 4). Bake chicken for 20 to 30 minutes or until done. (Insert a fork in the thickest part of the meat and pull the meat apart. If it is opaque all the way through to the bone, it's done.) Some varieties of soy sauce and sesame oil will produce a darker color than others. You may also broil the chicken at this point for a few extra minutes, which will make the sauce darker. Don't let the chicken burn. Adjust seasonings if necessary. Garnish generously with scallions, cilantro, and onion rings to contrast with the dark color of the chicken and serve piping hot.

4 entrée servings

Serving Suggestions: This sesame-flavored chicken is a hit when served with rice, a crisp green salad, and another Korean winner, Spicy Seoul Cucumber (page 76). Continue with the Korean theme by offering a cup of ginseng tea afterward.

✳ Tarragon-Poached Chicken with Sauces ✳

INTERNATIONAL

Poaching meat is a simple, healthful, and energy-efficient way to cook. My recipe evolved from a suggestion from a man from mainland China who placed a whole chicken and water in a covered pot, brought it to a boil, and then turned off the heat. When he returned home hours later, the chicken would be cooked tender from the vapor.

In this recipe, chicken is prepared in a similar fashion and is infused with fresh herbs. I serve it with a series of sauces and let my guests choose from a number of flavor sensations.

The chicken:

1   cup (250 ml) Chicken Stock (page 44), Basic Vegetable Stock (page 41), or
     $^1/_2$ a 14$^1/_2$-ounce (42-g) can of chicken broth, defatted (See "To defat
     canned chicken broth," page 45)
2   tablespoons (30 ml) chopped fresh tarragon or 2 teaspoons (10 ml) dried
     tarragon
1$^1/_2$ pounds (750 g) chicken breasts or other pieces, skinned, cut into serving
     size pieces

Place stock and tarragon in a large skillet and bring to a boil. Lower heat and add chicken. Cover and simmer 20 to 30 minutes or until chicken is done. (Insert a fork in the thickest part of the meat and pull the meat apart. If it is opaque all the way through to the bone, it's done.) Remove chicken with a slotted spoon. Reserve the stock to use as a base for chicken or vegetable soup. Pull meat off the bones in large pieces and cut into even sizes. Serve topped with one or more of the sauces below. Double or triple the sauce recipes if preparing only one or two sauces.

The sauces:

(1) For a nutty, hot flavor:

2   tablespoons (30 ml) Chinese sesame oil
4   teaspoons (20 ml) sambal oeleck (or red chile paste)
$^1/_8$ teaspoon (0.5 ml) Chaat Powder (see page 8; to taste)
2   tablespoons (30 ml) finely chopped onion
2   scallions (green part only), thinly sliced
     Chopped cilantro

Place sesame oil and sambal oeleck in a medium bowl and stir with a fork until smooth. Add Chaat Powder. Sprinkle with onion, scallion, and cilantro.

(2) For a tart flavor:

  4   teaspoons (20 ml) tamarind concentrate
  8   teaspoons (40 ml) low-sodium soy sauce
  4   teaspoons (20 ml) unrefined safflower oil or canola oil
  4   teaspoons (20 ml) sugar
1/4 cup (60 ml) finely chopped onion
  2   scallions (green part only), thinly sliced
     Toasted sesame seeds

Mix tamarind and soy sauce in a medium bowl with a fork until tamarind dissolves. Stir in oil and sugar. Adjust the ingredients for a tart, faintly sweet flavor. Sprinkle with onion, scallions, and sesame seeds.

(3) For a peanut flavor:

     Sweet and Hot Peanut-Lime Sambal (page 219)
  2   scallions (green part only), thinly sliced

Combine the peanut sauce and the scallions in a medium bowl.

(4) For a garlicky flavor:

     Roasted Garlic Spread (page 221)
  2   scallions (green part only), thinly sliced

Sprinkle the garlic sauce with the scallions.

4 entrée servings

Serving Suggestions: Serve as a main course with millet, Winter Salad (page 259), and Roasted Tikka Potatoes (page 243). For a terrific brown bag lunch, stuff toasted multigrain (or whole wheat) pita with shredded romaine, grilled eggplant or zucchini slices, and some of these sauce-dipped chicken pieces.

✳ Chicken Chaat with Potatoes, ✳ Palm Hearts, and Salsa

INTERNATIONAL

Chaat is an Indian fruit-and-vegetable salad that is flavored with a special blend of spices called chaat powder. Here I apply that tart, hot powder to leftover chicken and potatoes. Palm hearts, a delicacy from South America that is available in the United States only in canned form, is an honored foreign guest. A dollop of Roasted Tomato-Chile Salsa, almost an afterthought, finishes this elegant and exciting salad.

4   cups (1 liter) shredded romaine or butterhead lettuce (see *Note 1*)
$1/4$ teaspoon (1 ml) Chaat Powder (see page 8; to taste)
1   cup (250 ml) cubed cooked chicken meat
      Chicken-flavored Baby Potatoes (page 244; see *Note 2* for a speedy, nonfat alternative)
      Roasted Tomato-Chile Salsa (page 216)
$1/4$ cup (60 ml) finely chopped palm hearts (or artichoke hearts)

On individual serving plates or a deep platter, form a bed with the shredded greens. Dust Chaat Powder over chicken cubes. Arrange the meat and the potatoes over the greens. Pour salsa over, top with palm hearts, and serve at once.

2 entrée servings

Note 1: You can add arugula, tender Mizuna mustard, spinach, or other piquant greens. When preparing a salad, I usually shred lettuce by hand, but here I cut it with a knife for an even and uniform look. I don't dress the greens, but if you like, you can moisten them lightly with Cumin Vinaigrette (page 233), or sprinkle them with lemon juice, salt, and black pepper.

Note 2: Instead of the richer-tasting chicken-flavored potatoes, you can prepare an easier version that uses no oil. Steam $1/2$ pound (250 g) potatoes, about 2 medium, unpeeled and cut into 1-inch (2.5-cm) cubes, for 15 minutes or until tender. Immediately add 3 tablespoons (45 ml) fresh lime juice, $1/4$ teaspoon (1 ml) Chaat Powder (see page 8; to taste), a dash of black salt (or regular salt), and ground red pepper (to taste; start with a scant pinch). Drain off excess lime juice before using.

Serving Suggestions: Complete a light supper with Sweet and Nutty Carrot-Turnip Soup (page 49) and some Spicy Biscuitsticks (page 197).

VARIATION: POTATO PALM HEART SALAD Vegetarians can omit the chicken and serve this as a spicy vegetable salad. Arrange some hard-cooked egg slices on top and sprinkle with toasted pecans.

✷ Indian Chicken Salad ✷
JAPAN/UNITED STATES

$\int$urprisingly, the inspiration for this Indian-style chicken salad came from a San Francisco–based Japanese woman who annually hosts a lavish New Year's Day party in the Japanese tradition. The dish that most appealed to me was her simple but elegant shredded teriyaki chicken, attractively arranged on a bed of crisp greens. Although surrounded by fancier dishes, I found this Western style salad to be far superior. For years I thought of making my own version, and the following recipe is the result. It is an excellent way of savoring meat in moderate amounts.

The chicken is so tasty that you can also prepare it alone to serve as a main course.

The spice paste:

1¹/₂ to 2 tablespoons (22 to 30 ml) ghee (melted), olive oil, or canola oil
  1 teaspoon (5 ml) asafetida powder
  1 teaspoon (5 ml) garam masala
   4 to 5 large garlic cloves, forced through a garlic press
  ¹/₂ teaspoon (2 ml) salt
   Ground red pepper (to taste; start with a scant pinch)
   Juice of ¹/₂ lime

The salad:

  1¹/₂ pounds (750 g) chicken breasts or other pieces (or 1 pound [500 g]
    boneless chicken breasts), skinned, cut into serving size pieces
   Red leaf, butterhead, or romaine lettuce, or a mixture (see *Note 1*)
   Cumin Vinaigrette (page 233)
  8 cherry tomatoes, halved (see *Note 2*)
  ¹/₂ medium-sized mild red or other sweet onion, cut into rings
   Chopped cilantro
   Juice of ¹/₂ lime

1. Preheat oven to 350°F (180°C, gas marks 4). Combine ghee, asafetida, garam masala, garlic, salt, red pepper, and lime juice. If the mixture is too thick, add a teaspoon (5 ml) or so of water so that it has a spreadable consistency.
2. Using a sharp knife, make slits in the chicken, approximately 1/4 inch (6 mm) deep across the grain of the meat to allow the spices to penetrate. Rub the spice paste into the chicken pieces, making sure to force some of the paste into the slits. Bake for 20 to 30 minutes or until done, turning the pieces once halfway through baking time. (Insert a fork in the thickest part of the meat and pull the meat apart. If it is opaque all the way through to the bone, it's done.) Broil for 2 to 5 minutes or until browned. Don't let chicken burn. Remove from the broiler.
3. When cool enough to handle, gently separate the meat from the chicken bone in pieces as large as possible. Cut the meat into equal-sized pieces, 1 to 1 1/2 inches (2.5 to 4 cm) in length. Sprinkle with half of the lime juice.
4. Shred lettuce, dress it with the Cumin Vinaigrette, and place on 4 large individual serving plates. Arrange chicken meat over the lettuce. Place tomatoes around the meat and scatter onion rings on top. Sprinkle with cilantro and the remaining lime juice, and serve.

4 entrée servings

Note 1: Use several types of lettuce or other salad greens for a mix of colors and a variety of textures.

Note 2: If available, buy a few yellow mini-pear tomatoes.

Serving Suggestions: Serve at a buffet. Or offer as a starter course accompanied by a grain dish such as Barley, Wild Rice, and Azuki Beans Khichuri (page 181) and a condiment such as Salsa Maharaja (page 213).

VARIATION: INDIAN FISH SALAD Instead of chicken, use 1 pound (500 g) firm-fleshed fish, such as halibut, salmon, sturgeon, shark, or tuna, cut into 1-inch (2.5-cm) cubes. In Step 2, bake for 12 to 15 minutes or until done. (A toothpick inserted in the thickest part and pushed to one side should show an opaque color in the piece.) Broil for a minute or two. Omit Step 3 and go directly to Step 4.

VARIATION: INDIAN TEMPEH SALAD Replace chicken with 2 packages (each 6 ounces [180 g]) of soy tempeh, cut into 1-inch (2.5-cm) cubes. In Step 1, heat ghee (or butter or oil) in a large skillet. Sprinkle asafetida over oil. Cook the garlic until lightly colored. Brown the tempeh and allow it to puff up a bit. (You may need a bit of extra oil.) Add garam masala and red pepper to taste. Remove from heat and sprinkle lemon juice on top. Omit Steps 2 and 3 and go directly to Step 4.

❋ Parsee Chicken in Fragrant Coconut Gravy ❋

WESTERN INDIA/MEXICO

Parsees have a distinctive cuisine in India characterized by the use of coconut, curry leaves, and plenty of chiles. Traditionally the myriad other flavorings that compose this fragrant gravy were ground by hand. This version is an "instant" one, because the seasonings are quickly processed in a blender. The secret to the thick, savory sauce lies in simmering it slowly, allowing the spices to develop their flavors. Many Parsees are known to cook the sauce over low heat for hours.

Amy Laly, a filmmaker of Parsee origin now living in the United States, gave me the inspiration for this recipe. In re-creating this dish, I have reduced the amount of meat but have added more vegetables. Another adaptation is a touch of heat from the Mexican chipotle chile (smoked hot jalapeño). Even though the ingredient list is long, the dish is quite easy to prepare.

The spice paste:

1	pound (500 g) Roma tomatoes, about 9 medium, peeled and seeded, or 14 1/2-ounce (411-g) can peeled Italian-style tomatoes
1/2	teaspoon (2 ml) turmeric
2	teaspoons (10 ml) ground cumin
2	teaspoons (10 ml) ground coriander
1/4	teaspoon (1 ml) ground cloves
1/4	teaspoon (1 ml) ground cinnamon
1/2	teaspoon (2 ml) ground cardamom
1/4	teaspoon (1 ml) freshly ground black pepper
5	large garlic cloves, coarsely chopped
	1-inch (2.5-cm) piece gingerroot, coarsely chopped
8 to 10	fresh mint leaves or 1 teaspoon (5 ml) dried mint
1/2	cup (125 ml) unsweetened canned coconut milk, stirred to mix the thin and thick parts
1	cup (250 ml) water
1/2	cup (125 ml) coarsely chopped cilantro
1	tablespoon (15 ml) rice vinegar
2	teaspoons (10 ml) sugar
1/4	teaspoon (1 ml) chipotle chile in adobo sauce (see *Note*) or ground red pepper (to taste; start with a scant pinch)

The chicken:

  2 tablespoons (30 ml) mustard oil or canola oil
6 to 8 curry leaves, crushed
  1 cup (250 ml) finely chopped onion
  4 pounds (2 kg) chicken breasts or other pieces, skinned, cut into serving
      size pieces
  1 small head cauliflower, 1 to 1½ pounds (500 to 750 g), cut into florets
  ¼ pound (125 g) green beans, cut into 2-inch (5-cm) pieces
    Salt

1. In the container of a blender or food processor, place the tomatoes followed by the remaining spice paste ingredients. Process until smooth. The puree will be thin.
2. To prepare the sauce: Heat oil in a 12-inch (30-cm) steep-sided skillet over moderate heat. Fry curry leaves and onion, stirring often, until onion is richly browned but not burnt, 12 to 15 minutes. Add the spice paste and bring to a simmer, keeping the skillet uncovered. Adjust heat so that it stays at a simmer; don't let it boil vigorously. Cook, uncovered, at least 30 minutes, an hour if time allows, stirring occasionally. The sauce will thicken. Add a little water from time to time if the sauce sticks to the bottom of the skillet.
3. Add chicken. Simmer, covered, 30 to 40 minutes or until done. (Insert a fork in the thickest part of the meat and pull the meat apart. If it is opaque all the way through to the bone, it's done.) Remove chicken with a slotted spoon to a large bowl and keep covered. Add cauliflower and green beans to the sauce in the skillet. Simmer, covered, 12 to 15 minutes or until the vegetables are fork-tender. (Because of the thickness of the sauce, both the meat and vegetables will cook more slowly than usual.) Return chicken to the skillet. Cook for a few minutes, just until heated through. Add salt. Adjust the amount of hotness by adding a bit more chipotle if necessary.

8 entrée servings

Note: This sauced chipotle is sold in ready-to-use form in cans in Mexican grocery stores. Or, soak a dried chipotle in warm water for 1 hour or until soft; chop into small pieces. In either case, add sparingly. Taste and add more if you would like it hotter.

Serving Suggestions: Splendid on a buffet table with plain cooked rice, millet, quinoa, or barley. To offset the rich spiciness, offer a large bowl of Piquant Salad in Shades of Green (page 258). For a condiment, choose Cilantro Splash (page 223) or Mint-Tamarind Pesto (page 225).

VEGETARIAN VARIATIONS: For a delicious one-dish meal, omit chicken but add ¼ pound (125 g) cooked rice noodles or fettuccine at the end.

If you want to try different vegetables, other choices are: 1 small head of broccoli (instead of cauliflower), cut into florets, and 2 cups (500 ml) shredded cabbage instead of green beans. Replace rice noodles with vermicelli.

✳ Date and Nut-Filled Meatballs ✳

THE MIDDLE EAST

Here I season ground meat in the Indian manner with gingerroot, cilantro, and garam masala. I then stuff the meatballs with dates and nuts, a technique employed in the Middle East. Spicy, sweet, hot, and luscious best describes this dish. You can either deep-fry the meatballs or bake them oil-free.

The meatballs:

    1   cup (250 ml) minced onion
    4   large garlic cloves, forced through a garlic press
 1½   tablespoons (22 ml) grated gingerroot or gingerroot paste (see page 12)
    1   tablespoon (15 ml) minced cilantro
  ½   teaspoon (2 ml) turmeric
    2   teaspoons (10 ml) ground coriander
    1   teaspoon (5 ml) garam masala
  ⅛   teaspoon (0.5 ml) freshly ground black pepper
  ½   teaspoon (2 ml) salt
        Ground red pepper (to taste; start with a scant pinch)
    1   tablespoon (15 ml) plain nonfat yogurt
    2   tablespoons (30 ml) fresh lime or lemon juice
    1   pound (500 g) lean ground lamb or beef

The stuffing:

    2   tablespoons (30 ml) finely chopped pitted dates
    2   tablespoons (30 ml) finely chopped toasted slivered almonds
        Canola oil for deep-frying (optional)

1. In a large bowl, combine all the ingredients for the meatballs except ground meat. Mix in ground meat, handling it as little as possible so as not to squeeze out the moisture.

2. In a separate small bowl, combine the stuffing ingredients. Pinch off a portion of the meat mixture and shape into a ball about 1 1/2 inches (4 cm) in diameter. With your little finger, make a small indentation about halfway into the center of the ball and stuff with about 1/8 teaspoon (0.5 ml) of the date-almond mixture. Carefully close the ball around the stuffing.

3. If baking: Preheat oven to 350°F (180°C, gas marks 4). Place a rack on top of a broiler pan or cookie sheet. Arrange the balls on top of the rack. (This is so that the fat from the meat can drain out.) Bake for 12 to 15 minutes or until the balls are cooked. (A toothpick inserted in the middle and pulled gently to one side should show an opaque color in the meat.) Raise heat to 450°F (230°C, gas marks 8). Bake the balls an additional 3 to 5 minutes or until they are lightly browned. Watch carefully and do not let them burn.

4. If deep-frying: Heat oil in a deep-fat fryer or a pan to 375°F (190°C, gas marks 5). Heat oven to no more than 200°F (100°C, gas marks 1/4). Carefully lower 3 or 4 balls into the oil using a large slotted spoon. Remove them as soon as they turn medium brown on all sides, usually about a minute. Drain on paper towels. Serve immediately or place in the warm oven until all of them have been fried.

Makes 25 croquettes, 4 entrée servings

Serving Suggestions: This recipe makes a delightful potluck dish served with Cilantro Splash (page 223) and Green Mango Chutney (page 206). Or serve as a main course over rice (or quinoa), with side dishes of Vegetable Sunburst (page 254) and steamed Brussels sprouts.

✳ Kheema with Kale and Chinese Five-Spice ✳

INDIA/CHINA

This recipe for *kheema*, a word that means a ground meat preparation, requires simple ingredients like ground meat and leafy greens that are elevated to culinary art by the careful use of Indian spices. Cooking with spices has always been important in India. When the seventh-century Indian philosopher Sukracharya listed 64 types of art, he included cookery and spices among them.

This recipe also employs the Chinese flavor principle of simmering meat with five-spice powder. Five "heavenly" spice is an equal measure of star anise, fennel, cinnamon, cloves, and Szechuan pepper. Its aroma and warmth remind me of garam masala. Kale, the bold brassica, blends well with the meat seasoned with these Eastern exotics.

    2 tablespoons (30 ml) olive oil
    1 cup (250 ml) minced onion
    1 tablespoon (15 ml) minced gingerroot
    1 teaspoon (5 ml) minced garlic
    1 jalapeño, seeded, chopped (to taste)
  $1/2$ teaspoon (2 ml) turmeric
    2 teaspoons (10 ml) ground cumin
    2 teaspoons (10 ml) ground coriander
  $1/2$ teaspoon (2 ml) Chinese five-spice powder
  $1/4$ cup (60 ml) water
    1 pound (500 g) extra-lean ground beef or lamb (preferably ground round or
        ground leg of lamb)
    1 medium tomato (preferably vine-ripened), peeled, seeded, and coarsely
        chopped, or $2^{1}/2$ tablespoons (37 ml) tomato paste
  $1/2$ teaspoon (2 ml) sugar
    4 cups (1 liter) finely shredded kale, collard, or cabbage (see *Note*)
  $1/4$ cup (60 ml) thawed frozen peas
       Salt
       Ground red pepper (to taste; start with a scant pinch)
Garnish:
       Red bell pepper strips
       Chopped cilantro

1. Heat oil in a large 12-inch (30-cm) steep-sided skillet over moderate heat. Add onion and fry, stirring often, until it is richly browned but not burnt, 8 to 15 minutes. Add gingerroot, garlic, and jalapeño and stir several times. Add turmeric, cumin, coriander, and Chinese five-spice and mix well. Add water. Lower the heat slightly. Add meat, breaking it up gently with a spoon. Add tomato and sugar; stir gently.
2. Simmer, covered, 10 to 15 minutes or until the meat has turned opaque. During this period, uncover once and stir, adding a tablespoon (15 ml) of water if the mixture starts to stick to the bottom of the pan. Stir gently to break up any lumps. Add kale. Simmer, covered, until kale is tender, 10 to 12 minutes. (Overcooking will darken its color.) Add peas and simmer, covered, 2 more minutes. Remove

from heat. Add salt and red pepper to taste. The sauce may be slightly thin at this point. It can be served this way, or you can thicken it. To do so, remove meat and vegetables with a slotted spoon into a large bowl, leaving the sauce in the skillet. Cook the sauce, uncovered, over medium heat for 3 to 5 minutes or until thick. Return meat and vegetables to the pan. Garnish with red pepper strips and cilantro and serve immediately. If allowed to sit longer the kale might darken, although it will still taste good.

4 entrée servings

Note: For this dish, kale should be fresh and tender. If not available, use cabbage or collard.

Serving Suggestions: A grain dish such as Basic Pilaf with Nutty Vermicelli Threads (page 177) and steamed or sautéed carrots will make a well-balanced meal. For dessert I recommend Halwa Delight (page 275).

✳ Coconut-Sauced Beef ✳

THAILAND

This recipe combines a Thai-style coconut sauce with Indian marinating and spicing techniques. It offers a progression of flavors: first a spicy sweetness, then a richness, and finally a background heat of chile. This dish is an excellent choice when entertaining.

The marinade:

- 5 large cloves garlic, forced through a garlic press
- 2 tablespoons (30 ml) grated gingerroot or gingerroot paste (see page 12)
- 1/4 teaspoon (1 ml) freshly ground black pepper
- 1/2 teaspoon (2 ml) turmeric
- 1/4 teaspoon (1 ml) salt
- 1/4 cup (60 ml) finely chopped cilantro

The meat:

- 2 pounds (1 kg) beef (filet mignon, boneless sirloin, T-bone steak with bones removed, New York strip, or round steak) or leg of lamb, cut into serving size pieces
- 2 tablespoons (30 ml) canola oil

1 cup (250 ml) finely chopped onion

1 jalapeño, seeded, chopped (or to taste)

$^1/_2$ teaspoon (2 ml) salt

$^3/_4$ teaspoon (3 ml) sugar

2 tablespoons (30 ml) water

$^3/_4$ cup (185 ml) unsweetened canned coconut milk (stirred until evenly mixed)
or a mixture of $^1/_2$ cup (125 ml) coconut milk and $^1/_4$ cup (60 ml)
lowfat milk

$^1/_4$ teaspoon (1 ml) garam masala

Garnish:

Red bell pepper strips

Chopped cilantro

1. Combine all the marinade ingredients in a large bowl. Toss meat in this marinade, making sure each piece is well-coated. Let stand, covered, in the refrigerator for at least 30 minutes.

2. Heat oil in a large skillet over moderate heat. Add onion and fry, stirring constantly, until it is richly browned but not burnt, 8 to 15 minutes. Add jalapeño, salt, sugar, meat, and water. Lower the heat slightly and simmer, covered, 30 to 45 minutes or until meat is tender. (Uncover occasionally and stir, adding a little water if sticking.)

3. Remove from heat. With a slotted spoon, transfer meat to a bowl. Add coconut milk to the skillet and return to very low heat (low heat is to prevent the coconut milk from separating). Cook uncovered, stirring often, for about 15 minutes, until the sauce thickens slightly. (Make sure the heat stays low and the sauce does not boil.) Remove from heat. Add garam masala. Return meat and accumulated juices to the skillet. Taste for salt. Let stand, covered, for a few minutes to help develop the flavor further. Scatter red bell pepper strips and chopped cilantro on top and serve.

4 entrée servings

Serving Suggestions: Accompany with Basmati rice, Satay Apples and Bok Choy (page 73), steamed beets, and Lychee Swirl (page 287).

✳ Universal Vindaloo ✳

SOUTH INDIA

Vindaloo, originally a Portuguese-influenced dish from Goa, is one of the better known Indian meat dishes outside that country. The word vindaloo is believed to derive from *viande*, meat, and *aloo*, potatoes. Little or no water is used in preparing the dish, which is characterized by a thick, clinging, hot-and-vinegary sauce. Prized all over South India, the dish is prepared in different ways. In this universal variation, meat plays a small part, assisting in enhancing the flavors. Tofu and potatoes absorb the rich, meaty sauce while adding bulk and important nutrients. Even people who are in transition to a vegetarian diet can enjoy this dish, serving themselves only the tofu and potatoes.

Though the ingredient list may seem long, this dish is actually quite easy to prepare.

The marinade for the pork:

- 1/4 cup (60 ml) coarsely chopped onion
- 3 large garlic cloves, coarsely chopped
- 2-inch (5-cm) piece gingerroot, coarsely chopped
- 1/2 jalapeño, seeded, coarsely chopped
- 1/4 teaspoon (1 ml) salt
- 2 tablespoons (30 ml) rice vinegar
- 1/2 pound (250 g) boneless pork loin chops, cut into 1-inch (2.5-cm) cubes

The marinade for tofu:

- 2 tablespoons (30 ml) rice vinegar
- 1 tablespoon (15 ml) hoisin sauce
- 14-ounce (396-g) carton firm tofu, drained, rinsed, and cut into 1-inch (2.5-cm) cubes
- 1 1/2 to 2 1/2 tablespoons (22 to 37 ml) Indian sesame oil (*gingely*), or canola oil
- 1/2 medium onion, cut into rings 1/4 inch (6 mm) thick
- 1/2 pound (250 g) potatoes, about 2 medium, peeled and cut into 1-inch (2.5-cm) cubes
- 1/4 teaspoon (1 ml) kalonji seeds
- 1/4 teaspoon (1 ml) fennel
- 2-inch (5-cm) cinnamon stick
- 5 whole cloves

1   teaspoon (5 ml) ground cumin

$^1/_2$ cup (125 ml) water

$^1/_2$ teaspoon (2 ml) sugar

$^1/_2$ teaspoon (2 ml) low-sodium soy sauce

$^1/_2$ teaspoon (2 ml) tamarind concentrate

Honey-glazed Onions (page 218) (optional)

Salt

Ground red pepper (to taste; start with a scant pinch)

Garnish:

Sweet onion rings (optional)

Chopped cilantro

1. To marinate the pork: Place onion, garlic, gingerroot, jalapeño, salt, and rice vinegar in a blender or food processor. Process until smooth, adding a little water if necessary. Toss pork in this marinade, making sure each piece is well-coated. Cover and refrigerate for at least 30 minutes; an hour or two is even better.

2. To marinate the tofu: Combine rice vinegar and hoisin sauce in a large bowl. Add tofu and marinate, covered, in the refrigerator for at least 15 minutes.

3. Heat 1 tablespoon (15 ml) oil in a small, 7-inch (17.5-cm) skillet over moderate heat until a light haze forms. Cook onion rings until they are translucent and soft but still slightly crunchy, 2 to 4 minutes. Remove with a slotted spoon and set aside. Heat 1 tablespoon (15 ml) oil in a large skillet over medium-high heat. Add potatoes and cook for a few minutes until lightly browned, 5 or so minutes. Remove with a slotted spoon and set aside. (To lower the fat content of this dish, you can omit sautéeing the potatoes in oil. They will be cooked later in Step 4.)

4. Heat the remaining $^1/_2$ tablespoon (7 ml) oil in the large skillet over moderate heat. Add kalonji seeds, fennel, cinnamon, and cloves and fry until fennel is lightly browned. (Keep the skillet partially covered to prevent the seeds from flying out.) Lower the heat. Add pork and the marinade and mix well with the spices. Add cumin, water, and sugar. Cover and bring to a boil. Lower the heat slightly and simmer, covered, for 10 minutes. Add potatoes. Simmer, covered, 15 to 25 additional minutes or until both pork and potatoes are almost done. During this period, remove cover occasionally and stir, adding a little water if the mixture sticks to the bottom. (Up to this point, this dish can be prepared ahead of time and refrigerated. Bring to room temperature and reheat, adding a little water if necessary.)

5. Drain tofu and discard the marinade. Add tofu to the skillet. Simmer, covered, 3 to 5 more minutes. Uncover and gently remove pork, potatoes, and tofu with a slotted spoon to a serving platter. Add soy sauce, tamarind, and the Honey-Glazed Onions to the sauce in the skillet and mix well. The sauce should be thick. If it's still watery, cook uncovered for a few minutes to thicken. Add salt and red pepper. Adjust seasonings for a tart, hot taste. Remove from heat and discard whole spices. Pour sauce over the pork mixture. Serve garnished with the onion rings and cilantro.

4 entrée servings

BEEF VARIATION: Instead of pork, use boneless beef sirloin.

Serving Suggestions: Consider serving this meal Indian-style in a *thali*, a stainless steel circular tray with matching small bowls, sold in Indian groceries. Mound Basmati rice cooked with garlic in the center of the tray. Fill the bowls with two or more of the following side dishes and sauces: Gujarati Greens (page 66), Golden Squash Cream (page 87), Savory Sprouts Stir-Fry (page 77), Chilied Mango Chutney (page 205), or Onion Yogurt Relish (page 209).

Pasta and Noodles

Pasta has a distinguished history in China and Italy, where it has long been a staple. In India, however, where rice and wheat form the basis of the diet, it is used sparingly. For the past several centuries, Indian homemakers have used vermicelli, a thread-thin pasta, for preparing festive puddings and have added thick chick-pea noodles to various savory snacks; rarely have they considered using pasta as a substitute for rice or bread. Now as modern Indians become more interested in foreign cuisines, pasta is finding its way into the country's cupboards. When I visit India, I'm frequently asked, "How do you make tomato sauce for pasta?"

During one such visit, I watched a street vendor in Calcutta cooking pasta. It was the monsoon season, and the man's faded gray shirt matched the somber sky, but his eyes danced and his pasta shimmered. A crowd gathered as he filled little saucers with the steaming noodles and topped them with a ladle of spicy sauce. He did a brisk business.

On a trip to Singapore and Malaysia, I saw another example of noodles seasoned in an Indian manner. Singapore is noted for its Nonya cuisine, developed in the nineteenth century when immigrant Chinese workers took Malay wives. To please their men, these wives, *nonyas*, adopted Chinese ingredients such as noodles. They cooked them with spices, some native and others brought to Malaysia by Hindu invaders centuries earlier. Thus was born *laksa lemak*, noodles in coconut gravy spiked with turmeric, chile, and lemon grass. This dish can be traced in part back to India and has become popular in Singapore, Malaysia, and even in the West.

Living in America, where pasta is prominent on the menus of Thai, Chinese, and Italian restaurants, I began to see it as a potential ingredient in Indian cooking. I enjoy both pasta and Asian noodles, and often can think of no quicker or more satisfying dinner. Fresh pasta cooks in minutes. Like rice and potatoes, pasta assumes a different character dependent on the sauce it's dressed with. Noodles can be made from rice, buckwheat, or mung beans, as well as wheat. Their shapes and flavors vary enormously. The endless ways of using pasta in Indian dishes became clear when I began combining it with a wide variety of spices, flavorings, and chutneys. It opened an exciting new set of culinary possibilities for me.

An Italian once told me he started all his meals with pasta, which to him was like a plate of jewels. For me, pasta is the best of two worlds: the tasty carbohydrate provides the muscle fuel I need as a runner, while the spicy Indian sauces enchant me as a food lover.

The pasta and sauce combinations in this chapter are some of my favorites. They run the gamut from udon, a hearty wheat noodle from Japan, spread with a thick lentil sauce, to rotini swimming in a coconut-mustard *malai* sauce. In our household, eating hasn't been the same since this happy marriage of East and West. *

Pointers for Perfect Pasta

1. Have the sauce ready before starting to cook the pasta. As soon as the pasta is cooked, combine it with the sauce or toss it with a little oil so it will not be sticky.

2. Read directions for Asian noodles. Each variety is cooked differently. Follow package instructions.

3. One pound ($^1/_2$ kg) of pasta will yield 4 entrée or 8 side dish servings. You'll need about $^1/_2$ cup (125 ml) of sauce per serving.

4. Bring enough water to a rapid boil. For one pound ($^1/_2$ kg) of pasta you need 4 quarts (1 liter) of water. For 2 pounds (1 kg), 5 to 6 quarts (1.25 to 1.5 liters) of water is sufficient. Contrary to conventional wisdom, I don't add oil or salt to the water. Done correctly, it needs neither at this stage.

5. Ease pasta into the water all at once. Stir it one time around with a long spoon. Push the long strands down until they are submerged. Don't cover the pot, as the water might boil over. When the water returns to a boil, lower the heat slightly.

6. Cook for as long as package directions indicate—generally 3 to 4 minutes for fresh pasta and 7 to 12 minutes for dry pasta. Stir from time to time to prevent sticking.

7. Tasting it is the best way to judge whether pasta is ready. Pasta should be firm but not rigid.

8. Drain off water, but don't rinse unless you're making a cold pasta salad.

9. Reserve some of the pasta water. You may need it to dilute the sauce. I also use this enriched water when preparing vegetable soups, stocks, and sauces.

Pasta Permutations

* Pasta makers in recent times have begun flavoring this product with a wide variety of additives; tomato, spinach, and squid ink, to name a few. Try combining two or more of these varieties in a dish—tomato pasta with spinach pasta, for example. Cook them separately if their cooking times are different.

* Serve pasta with two sauces side by side for a contrast in color and taste: a tomato-based sauce over one half and Mint-Tamarind Pesto (page 225) on the other. Or use with Mint-Basil Chutney (page 224) along with the sauce from Soba Noodles with Tahini Eggplant (page 158).

* I generally serve plain pasta as a foil for richly seasoned sauces. However, pastas that are colored or flavored look beautiful when served with a sauce that has a contrasting color, if the flavors don't clash. Examples are yellow saffron pasta served with a tomato sauce, or smoky squid ink pasta topped with a creamy white sauce. These and other pasta varieties can present a brilliant color contrast for your favorite sauce without competing in the flavor arena. Roasted garlic pasta, on the other hand, has a pronounced flavor of its own and goes well with delicate seafood or vegetable preparations. Pastas that have an attractive shape, such as rotini, in any color, enhance the appearance of a dish.

* Most pastas go with most sauces, but be aware of some basic rules. Linguine, fettuccine, the tubular penne, and the various saucer-shaped shell pastas trap thick sauces better. Spaghetti and the finer angel-hair pasta can be served with thin sauces.

* If you wish to sprinkle Parmesan or other hard cheeses over the sauce, buy them in blocks and then grate them at the table. The flavor will be fresher and the cheese will keep longer.

✳ Orecchiette with Swiss Chard and Indian Cheese ✳

INDIA

In India leafy greens and fresh cheese are combined in a classic green-and-white dish called *saag panir*. The greens are finely minced and the cheese is cut into small cubes. The tasty abalone-shaped orecchiette ("little ear") pasta is a perfect receptacle for this savory green puree, and its curvy shape contrasts with cheese cubes. In this version, finely chopped green beans add body to the sauce. The final touch of spice comes not from the customary garam masala but from hot and tart Chaat Powder.

4 cups (1 liter) lowfat milk, made into Indian cheese (see page 12)

The spice paste:

1/4   teaspoon (1 ml) turmeric
1   tablespoon (15 ml) ground cumin
1   tablespoon (15 ml) ground coriander
1/4   teaspoon (1 ml) ground nutmeg
   Ground red pepper (to taste; start with a scant pinch)
3 tablespoons (45 ml) water

The sauce:

2   tablespoons (30 ml) mustard oil
1/4   teaspoon (1 ml) cumin seeds
1   cup (250 ml) finely chopped onion
4   large garlic cloves, minced
1/2   pound (250 g) Roma tomatoes, finely chopped
1   teaspoon (5 ml) sugar
2   tablespoons (30 ml) water
1/4   pound (100 g) green beans, finely chopped
   About 3/4 pound (375 g), 7 cups (1.75 liters) finely shredded Swiss Chard (or beet greens or kale; see *Note*)
   Salt
1   teaspoon (5 ml) Chaat Powder (see page 8)
1/2   pound (250 g) orecchiette or shell pasta

1. Slice Indian cheese into 1/2-inch (1-cm) cubes. Crumble a few of the cubes for garnish.
2. To prepare spice paste: Combine the spices and water in a small bowl and stir until smooth.

3. In a 12-inch (30-cm) skillet, fry cumin seeds in hot oil until lightly browned. Add onion and garlic and cook, stirring often, until onion is medium brown in color, 8 to 10 minutes. Add tomatoes, sugar, spice paste, and water and bring to a boil. Lower heat slightly. Add green beans and simmer, covered, 3 to 5 minutes. Stir in greens. Simmer, covered, 6 to 8 minutes or until the vegetables are tender to the bite. Add salt and Chaat Powder and remove from heat. If allowed to sit, the sauce will lose some of its color, although it will still taste good.

4. Cook and drain pasta. Mix with the sauce. Arrange cheese cubes on top and serve sprinkled with the reserved crumbled cheese on top.

4 to 5 entrée servings

Note: You can chop the stems and include them. The succulent Swiss chard stalks are especially tasty this way. Cut any leftover stems in french-fry sizes, steam them until tender, then serve with a dip of Tamari-Wasabi Dressing (page 234).

Serving Suggestions: This Indian pesto of sorts is complete as a supper dish, but I like to accompany it with Golden Squash Cream (page 87) or Sweet Potato Salad with Sesame-Tamarind Dressing (page 242). Orecchiette is also delicious cooked alone and tossed with Herbed Butter-Oil Dip (page 235; especially the East Asian Variation) and sautéed fresh button mushrooms.

✳ Fettuccine and Crab in Silky Black ✳ Mustard-Poppy Seed Sauce

EASTERN INDIA

In Bengal, black mustard and white poppy seeds are blended for making a delicious silky sauce. Mustard lends pungency, and poppy thickens the gravy while imparting its nutty sweet taste. I use this sauce as a base for fettuccine. The dish is best when fiery-hot, so I use either a hotter jalapeño or an incendiary habanero chile.

Pinkish-red crab meat and brilliant green snowpeas make this an elegant and attractive presentation.

2 teaspoons (10 ml) mustard oil or canola oil
2 tablespoons (30 ml) minced gingerroot
1 jalapeño, seeded, chopped (to taste)
1/4 teaspoon (1 ml) turmeric

$^1/_2$ teaspoon (2 ml) sugar

$^2/_3$ cup (150 ml) water

   2   teaspoons (10 ml) black mustard seeds, ground to a powder, mixed with
          2 tablespoons (30 ml) water and allowed to stand 30 minutes

   2   tablespoons (30 ml) white poppy seeds, made into a paste (see page 20)

2$^1/_2$ cups (625 ml) snow peas, stem ends trimmed, strings removed

 12   ounces (375 g) cooked crab meat

      Salt

   1   pound (500 g) fettuccine

Garnish:

      Chopped cilantro

      Thin-cut sweet onion rings

1. In hot oil in a 10-inch (25-cm) skillet, fry gingerroot and jalapeño until the ginger-
    root is lightly browned. Stir in turmeric and sugar. Add water and mustard-seed
    paste. Bring to a boil. Lower heat and simmer, covered, 6 to 8 minutes.

2. Add poppy-seed paste. Simmer, covered, another 6 to 8 minutes. Add snow peas.
    Add a little water if the sauce sticks to the bottom of the skillet. Simmer, covered,
    2 to 3 more minutes or until the vegetables are almost done. Add crab meat and
    salt, and simmer, covered, 2 to 3 minutes to heat the mixture through. (Over-
    cooking will discolor the pea pods.) Remove from heat. Let stand covered for a
    few minutes to allow the sauce to thicken more and the flavor to develop further.

3. Cook and drain pasta. Pour sauce over it and garnish with cilantro and onion rings.

4 entrée servings

Serving Suggestions: This pleasantly spicy crab dish calls for a crisp green salad
topped with tender enoki mushrooms and toasted sesame seeds. Carrot sticks, jícama
slices, and Tamarind-Date Chutney (page 208) will go nicely together in an appetizer
tray. For additional vegetable side dishes, consider lightly sautéeing cauliflower florets
that have been steamed until fork-tender. The sauce is also excellent served with
plain Basmati rice instead of pasta and accompanied by Sesame Arugula and Squash
(page 85).

VARIATION: FISH IN SILKY BLACK MUSTARD-POPPY SEED SAUCE Serve this delicious and
pretty fish variation as a substitute for crab with either pasta or rice. Use 1$^1/_2$ pounds
(750 g) fish, cut into 2 × 2 inch (5 × 5 cm) pieces. If serving with pasta, cut fish into
1-inch (2.5-cm) cubes. Replace snow peas with a large red bell pepper, cut into thin

strips. Add bell pepper along with the poppy-seed paste in Step 2. Simmer, covered, 5 to 7 minutes, then add fish. Simmer, covered, 5 to 7 more minutes or until fish is done. (A toothpick inserted in the thickest part and pushed to one side should show an opaque color in the piece.)

✳ Shrimp and Orzo Pullao ✳

GREECE

Like most pastas, orzo, the Greek tear-shaped pasta, adapts well to Indian spices and cooking techniques. Here I season the pullao (pilaf) with asafetida and black mustard seeds, then sprinkle on a spoonful of toasted urad dal (split black lentils), which are South India's favorite spices for adding flavor to grains and vegetables. Shrimp and orzo have an affinity that I find lacking in rice-based shrimp pilafs.

4 cups (1 liter) water
1 1/2 cups (375 ml) orzo
1 tablespoon (15 ml) olive oil
1/4 teaspoon (1 ml) asafetida powder
1/4 teaspoon (1 ml) black mustard seeds
1 tablespoon (15 ml) urad dal (if available; optional)
1/2 cup (125 ml) finely chopped onion
1/4 teaspoon (1 ml) turmeric
1/2 teaspoon (2 ml) salt
1 jalapeño, seeded, chopped (to taste)
1/2 pound (250 g) fresh or thawed frozen bay shrimps
1/2 cup (125 ml) thawed frozen peas

Garnish: 2 tablespoons (30 ml) toasted raw cashew halves

1. To cook orzo: Bring water to a boil in a medium-sized pan. Add orzo, lower heat slightly, and cook, uncovered, stirring often, for 8 to 12 minutes or until firm-tender. The best way to check for doneness is to taste. Drain and set aside.
2. Heat oil in a 12-inch (30-cm) skillet (see *Note*). Sprinkle asafetida over the oil. Fry mustard seeds and urad dal until the seeds start to pop. (Hold the cover over the skillet to prevent the seeds from flying out.) Add onion and fry until it is translucent, 2 to 3 minutes. Add turmeric, salt, and jalapeño. Add shrimp and

cook just until they turn pink. Add peas and orzo and mix well. As soon as the mixture is heated through, remove from heat. Adjust seasoning. Serve sprinkled with toasted cashews.

4 to 6 side dish servings

Note: If you have a paella pan, cook and serve this pullao in it for a dramatic presentation.

Serving Suggestions: The springtime flavors of this dish seem to call for fresh vegetables and fruits as side dishes. Offer steamed green beans, a baked yam topped with plain nonfat yogurt and a dash of ground cinnamon, and shredded red leaf lettuce bathed in Sesame-Tamarind Dressing (page 233). End with fresh sweet pineapple slices lightly dusted with ground red pepper (or for the brave, a scant pinch of ground chile pequín, available in Latin American markets) and black salt or regular salt.

✳ Scallops, Rotini, and Vegetables Malai ✳
INDIA

In India, *malai* means a thick and creamy sauce. A *malai* is usually coconut-based but can also be made with thickened milk. Indian cooks open a fresh coconut for this purpose, and use shrimp or another shellfish for the main ingredient. Such a dish often begins a festive event—a wedding or an anniversary.

This reduced-fat recipe uses less coconut milk and remains stupendous. Scallops, a seafood not used in India, add richness to the lush sauce. Potatoes soak up the flavors. Rutabaga, also known as Swedish turnip, is a tan-colored vegetable that looks attractive in this *malai* and accentuates the sweetness of the shellfish with its mild turnip-like taste. If you've always bypassed the nutritious rutabaga, here's a chance to try it in a new way. Pasta is as natural a mate to this dish as the traditional rice.

1   small rutabaga, about 1/2 pound (250 g), hairy parts peeled, cut into 1-inch (2.5-cm) cubes (see *Note 1*)

The spice paste:

2   tablespoons (30 ml) coarsely chopped onion

1   tablespoon (15 ml) coarsely chopped garlic

1   tablespoon (15 ml) coarsely chopped gingerroot

1/2 jalapeño, seeded, coarsely chopped (to taste)

The sauce:

2 to 2¹/₂   tablespoons (30 to 37 ml) mustard oil (or a combination of oil and ghee)

   1   pound (500 g) scallops, larger pieces cut in halves (see *Note 2*)

  ¹/₄   teaspoon (1 ml) turmeric

   1   teaspoon (5 ml) black mustard seeds, ground to a powder, mixed with
      2 teaspoons (10 ml) water and allowed to stand 30 minutes

   1   medium new potato, about ¹/₄ pound (100 g), peeled and cut into 1-inch
      (2.5-cm) cubes

  ³/₄   cup (185 ml) Salmon Broth (page 43), Fish Stock (page 42), or water
      (see *Note 3*)

  ³/₄   cup (185 ml) unsweetened coconut milk, stirred until evenly mixed (see
      Note 4 for lowfat alternative)

  ³/₄   teaspoon (3 ml) sugar

     Salt

     A sprinkling of ghee (optional)

   1   pound (500 g) rotini (spiral pasta; preferably multicolored)

Garnish: Chopped cilantro

1. Steam rutabaga for 15 minutes. It will not be tender at this stage, but presteamed this way it will cook at about the same time as potato in Step 3.

2. To prepare the spice paste, place the ingredients in a blender and whirl to a smooth puree. Heat 1 to 1¹/₂ tablespoons (15 to 22 ml) oil (or oil-and-ghee combination) over moderate heat in a 12-inch (30-cm) skillet. Sauté scallops until lightly browned on all sides, 2 to 3 minutes, turning them once. Remove with a slotted spoon to a medium bowl and set aside.

3. Heat 1 to 1¹/₂ tablespoons (15 to 22 ml) oil over moderate heat in the same skillet. Add the spice paste and fry until lightly browned, 3 to 5 minutes. Add turmeric, mustard-seed paste, rutabaga, potato, and fish broth and bring to a boil. Cover and simmer until the vegetables are tender, 18 to 25 minutes. During this period, uncover and add a little water if the skillet is too dry. If using a gas burner, turn heat to low. If using an electric stove, switch to another burner that has been set to low heat. Add coconut milk and sugar. From this point on, keep heat low and don't bring the sauce to a boil, as the coconut milk might curdle. Add scallops and any accumulated liquid. Add salt. Cook until the scallops are done, about 5 minutes. (A toothpick inserted in the middle and pushed to one side should show an opaque color in the scallop.) Sprinkle ghee over sauce. Keep covered until ready to serve.

4. Cook and drain pasta. Serve sauce atop pasta, garnished with cilantro.

4 entrée servings

Note 1: You can substitute a turnip or kohlrabi for rutabaga if you like.

Note 2: Crab or lobster are other choices.

Note 3: If time allows, prepare Salmon Broth, which gives the sauce a stunning effect.

Note 4: As a lowfat alternative, substitute a mixture of ¹/₂ cup (125 ml) coconut milk and ¹/₄ cup (60 ml) nonfat milk. The sauce will be slightly thinner and less in volume but will still be tasty. To thicken the sauce, use a slotted spoon to remove scallops and vegetables from the skillet at the end of Step 4. Over very low heat, cook sauce, uncovered, for a few minutes until slightly thicker. Return scallops and vegetables to the skillet.

Serving Suggestions: This makes a gorgeous main dish for a dinner party when served with Crispy Snow Peas (page 89) and a spinach salad tossed with Sesame-Garlic Vinaigrette (page 232). Conclude with Exotic Fruits with Sweet Pecans and Sauce (page 285).

✳ Curried Pasta and Fagioli ✳

ITALY/THAILAND

Pasta e fagioli, "pasta and beans," is a popular dish in Italy, and each town is said to have its own favorite version. In a new twist to this old classic, navy beans, the traditional legume for New England baked beans, are dressed in a tomato sauce and spiked with cumin seeds and Thai curry paste. In India, such a dish would be liberally garnished with tomato and mild sweet onion and savored with rice. Farfalle ("butterfly") pasta makes just as good a base and the same garnish works wonderfully. In Italian this variation would be spelled "*delizioso*."

1¹/₂ to 2   tablespoons (22 to 30 ml) olive oil
¹/₄   teaspoon (1 ml) cumin seeds
1   cup (250 ml) finely chopped onion
3   large garlic cloves, forced through a garlic press

1 tablespoon (15 ml) grated gingerroot or gingerroot paste (see page 12)
1 tablespoon (15 ml) Thai yellow curry paste
1 jalapeño, seeded, chopped (retain a few seeds for a hint of hotness)
³/₄ pound (375 g) Roma tomatoes, peeled, seeded, chopped
1 cup (250 ml) bean liquid or water
3 cups (750 ml) cooked navy beans or two 15-ounce (425-g) cans navy or Great
   Northern beans, drained, cooking or can liquid reserved
¹/₂ teaspoon (2 ml) garam masala
   Salt
2 tablespoons (30 ml) fresh lime or lemon juice
1 pound (500 g) farfalle pasta

Garnish:
   Sweet onion rings
   Zippy Tomato Relish (page 228) or chopped Roma tomatoes and chopped
      cilantro

1. In a large, steep-sided skillet in hot oil, fry cumin seeds until the seeds are lightly browned. Add onion and cook until it is medium brown, 7 to 10 minutes, stirring often. Add garlic, gingerroot, curry paste, and jalapeño and stir several times. Add tomatoes and bean liquid. Cover and bring to a boil. Lower heat and simmer, covered, until a thick sauce forms, 15 to 18 minutes.

2. Add the beans and raise heat slightly to bring back to a simmer. When the mixture is heated through, remove from heat. Stir in garam masala, salt, and lime juice. (If using canned beans, which are salty, you will need less salt.) Keep warm.

3. Cook farfalle and drain. Serve sauce over farfalle, garnished with onion rings and Zippy Tomato Relish.

4 entrée servings

Serving Suggestions: Potatoes and beans are considered an ideal combination in India, so serve with Roasted Tikka Potatoes (page 243). Another perfect vegetable mate is English cucumber slices (or peeled and thinly sliced regular cucumber) tossed with Chile-Lime Dressing (page 231). The bean sauce (prepared without the pasta) makes a filling supper when served with Quinoa Uppama (page 180) and Prune and Date Chutney (page 207).

✳ Karhi-Sauced Penne ✳

WESTERN INDIA

K*arhi*, a cooling, savory yogurt soup or sauce, is prepared in many parts of India. It is served with rice. In the western state of Gujarat, it's slightly sweet, while further north, it will be more tangy. The consistency of this sauce is that of buttermilk; so, in the United States I substitute buttermilk for yogurt, which results in a finer *karhi*. Pureed squash, a native American vegetable, thickens my sauce and imparts a saffron-like color to it. While looking for a creamy base for pasta without much fat, I discovered that *karhi* tastes just as good with pasta as with rice. Any pasta will do, but penne ("quill") pasta, which allows the sauce to run through its interior, is particularly good.

$1/2$ pound (250 g) butternut (or Hubbard) squash, peeled, cubed

$1/2$ cup (125 ml) water (or water left from steaming squash)

$1^1/2$ cups (375 ml) lowfat buttermilk

 1   tablespoon (15 ml) chick-pea flour, *besan* (no substitute; see *Note 1*)

 2   tablespoons (30 ml) olive oil

 2   whole dried red chiles

$1/2$ teaspoon (2 ml) black mustard seeds

$1/4$ teaspoon (1 ml) fenugreek seeds

$1/2$ teaspoon (2 ml) cumin seeds

 1   cup (250 ml) finely chopped onion

 3   large cloves garlic, forced through a garlic press

 1   tablespoon (15 ml) grated gingerroot or gingerroot paste (see page 12)

 1   jalapeño, seeded, chopped (to taste)

$1/4$ teaspoon (1 ml) turmeric

 1   teaspoon (5 ml) ground cumin

$1/2$ teaspoon (2 ml) ground coriander (see *Note for the Gardener*)

$1/2$ teaspoon (2 ml) sugar

  Salt

$3/4$ pound (375 g) penne (see *Note 2*)

Garnish: Chopped fresh mint (or cilantro)

1. Steam the squash until very tender, about 15 minutes. Process squash and the water in a blender or food processor until smooth.

2. Pour a small amount of buttermilk gradually over chick-pea flour in a medium bowl, stirring to remove any lumps. When the mixture is smooth, add the remaining buttermilk.

3. Heat oil in a 10-inch (25-cm) skillet over moderate heat. Add red chiles and fry until they turn black. Add mustard seeds, fenugreek seeds, and cumin seeds and fry until the mustard seeds pop. Hold cover over the skillet to avoid splattering. Add onion, garlic, and gingerroot and fry until onion is translucent and slightly soft, 2 to 3 minutes. Add jalapeño, turmeric, ground cumin, coriander, and sugar; stir. Add squash puree and cook uncovered 3 to 4 minutes, stirring often.

4. If using a gas burner, turn heat to low. If using an electric stove, switch to another burner that has been set to low heat. Add the buttermilk mixture. Cook uncovered, stirring constantly, just until the sauce bubbles and is heated through, 5 to 8 minutes. If the heat is too high or if cooked too long, the sauce could separate and lose its appearance. Remove from heat. Discard red chiles. Add salt. Let stand, covered, for a few minutes to thicken the sauce further and develop its flavor.

5. Cook and drain pasta. Mix with the sauce. Serve garnished with mint.

4 entrée or 6 side dish servings

Note 1: Chick-pea flour adds a warm, nutty taste to the sauce that cannot be duplicated by wheat flour.

Note 2: If penne is not available, or if you want a taste variation, try one of the roasted garlic pastas. The flavor of garlic goes particularly well with this sauce.

Note for the Gardener: Late in autumn, my cilantro plants start to seed. I collect the seeds, then toast and grind them (sieving, if necessary, to remove any husks) for use in a dish like this.

Serving Suggestions: Bring a burst of color and fresh herb taste to the table by bordering the sauced pasta with Mint-Basil Chutney (page 224). Offer a basket of warm Italian bread and some roasted elephant garlic. For protein, serve Steamed Fish in Lime-Ginger Sauce (page 101) or Lime-Grilled Chicken (page 125). For vegetables, serve steamed broccoli and a crisp green salad. You can serve the *karhi* sauce (prepared without the pasta) alongside most grain dishes.

✳ Pasta Puttanesca International ✳

ITALY

*P**uttanesca*, or "Ladies of the Night" pasta, is featured in most Italian restaurants in the United States. It is said that these women can quickly assemble this tasty pasta dish while taking a "break."

This adaptation has an international flavor that begins with a special trip to an Asian market for fresh Thai basil. You can substitute fresh or dried regular basil. Mango powder imparts a zip to the thick tomato sauce, which is already infused with cumin and turmeric. I occasionally add a touch of mustard oil to liven the traditional olive oil foundation. The result is a most flavorful sauce that can be enjoyed anytime.

2 tablespoons (30 ml) olive oil, or 1 tablespoon (15 ml) each olive oil and
mustard oil

¹/₄ teaspoon (1 ml) asafetida powder

2 tablespoons (30 ml) minced garlic

¹/₂ teaspoon (2 ml) turmeric

1 teaspoon (5 ml) ground cumin

2 pounds (1 kg) Roma or regular tomatoes, peeled, seeded, and chopped,
or 28-ounce (794-g) can Italian-style pear tomatoes, undrained,
chopped (see *Note 1*)

6 sun-dried tomatoes, blanched, chopped (see *Note 2*)

¹/₂ a 2-ounce (50-g) can anchovies, drained and slightly mashed (see
Vegetarian Variation)

¹/₂ teaspoon (2 ml) mango powder (*aamchoor*)

¹/₈ to ¹/₄ teaspoon (0.5 to 1 ml) red pepper flakes to taste (best if the dish is
slightly hot; see *Note 3*)

5 Kalamata olives, pitted, slivered

¹/₂ to 1 tablespoon (7 to 15 ml) capers, drained, rinsed, and chopped (use the
larger amount for a more intense taste)

¹/₄ cup (60 ml) chopped fresh Thai or regular basil, or 2 teaspoons (10 ml)
dried basil

Salt and freshly ground black pepper

¹/₂ cup (125 ml) chopped cilantro

1 pound (500 g) spaghetti, gemelli ("twins," a twined pasta), or linguine

1. Heat oil in a large, steep-sided skillet over moderate heat. Sprinkle asafetida over hot oil. Add garlic and fry until garlic is lightly browned. Add turmeric and cumin and stir several times. Add tomatoes, sun-dried tomatoes, anchovies, dried basil (if using), and mango powder. Adjust the heat to keep the sauce to a simmer. If using fresh tomatoes, simmer, uncovered, just until a thick sauce forms, 12 to 15 minutes. (Overcooking will destroy the fresh flavor.) If using canned tomatoes, simmer uncovered for 25 to 30 minutes or until the sauce is quite thick. Stir often during this period. Remove from heat. Add red pepper flakes, olives, capers, fresh basil, salt, black pepper, and cilantro. Let stand, covered, until pasta is ready.

2. Cook and drain pasta. Pour sauce over pasta and serve.

4 entrée servings

Note 1: The quality of tomato really shows in this dish, so choose the best. If available, use vine-ripened tomatoes.

Note 2: For richness, use sun-dried tomatoes that have been stored in olive oil. These are sold in gourmet food shops. Drain thoroughly before using. These tomatoes don't require presoaking.

Note 3: For a bold, smoky flavor, replace red pepper flakes with a roasted whole dried red chile. Roast the chile on an ungreased skillet over low heat. When blackened on all sides, discard the seeds and the inner ribs and chop the flesh finely. Add in Step 1, adjusting the amount according to your taste.

Serving Suggestions: Rustic Italian bread is almost a must with this dish, as well as a crisp green salad and Spicy Apple Cake (page 277). For an atypical presentation, pair with a Chinese partner—Gai Lan with Balsamic Vinaigrette (page 70) or baby bok choy, stir-fried with garlic and black bean sauce. Steamed cauliflower can be a second vegetable side dish in either case. You can prepare the *puttanesca* sauce alone and serve over cooked grains, roasted or baked potatoes, or steamed kale, or use as a sauce for pizzas.

VEGETARIAN VARIATION: Omit anchovies, but increase the amount of sun-dried tomatoes to 8. Consider using the larger amount of capers in this case.

✳ Soba Noodles with Tahini Eggplant ✳

THE MIDDLE EAST

Roasting and grilling are believed to have come to India from her Central Asian neighbors and invaders. I can picture Genghis Khan getting off his horse in a dusty Himalayan plateau and demanding a full meal of grilled meat and vegetables from his retinue.

In India, eggplant is considered to be the choice vegetable for roasting, because it acquires a smoky flavor while the flesh turns buttery during the process. *Baingan bharta*, the best known Indian eggplant dish, is seasoned with cumin, tomatoes, and garam masala. It is served with rice or flat bread. This classic eggplant sauce is ideal over pasta and goes especially well with the earthy flavor of soba noodles, slender buckwheat noodles from Japan. Roasted tomatoes impart mellowness, and tahini sauce contributes a touch of that classic Middle Eastern eggplant dish, *baba ghanouj.*

If you choose a young eggplant whose flesh is still white and tomatoes that are deep red, the sauce will have a pleasant brownish-orange color. (Older eggplants have a pale yellowish tone to their flesh, which could darken the sauce.) The pretty garnishes further accent the color of the dish.

1	medium eggplant, about 1 1/2 pounds (375 g), unpeeled
1	pound (500 g) tomatoes, preferably vine-ripened
1/2	teaspoon (2 ml) sugar
2	tablespoons (30 ml) sesame tahini (see *Note*)
	Ground red pepper (to taste; start with a scant pinch)
2	tablespoons (30 ml) mustard oil
1	cup (250 ml) finely chopped onion
	Salt
1/2	teaspoon (2 ml) garam masala
2	pounds (1 kg) soba noodles

Garnish:

Chopped cilantro

Red bell pepper strips

Sweet onion rings

1. To broil the eggplant: Cut the eggplant in half lengthwise and arrange the halves with the flat side down on a cookie sheet lined with aluminum foil. Place under the broiler. Broil until the flesh softens, skin chars, and a smoky aroma is emitted, 10 or more minutes. The amount of time will vary with the size and thickness of the eggplant. Check often as overbroiling will dry the flesh. Allow to cool. Peel and discard the skin and coarsely chop the flesh.

2. Broil the tomatoes 6 to 12 minutes or until the skin is charred in places. Allow to cool.

3. In a blender or food processor, combine the eggplant pulp, the broiled tomato and any accumulated juice, sugar, tahini, and red pepper. Process until smooth.

4. Heat oil in a large, steep-sided skillet over moderate heat. Add onion and fry, stirring often, until richly browned but not burnt, 8 to 15 minutes. Add eggplant mixture and salt and cook, uncovered, for a few minutes to heat the mixture through. Add a little water if the sauce is too thick. Mix in garam masala. Taste for salt. Keep warm until pasta is ready.

5. Cook soba noodles according to package directions. Pour sauce over the noodles. Serve garnished with cilantro, bell pepper strips, and onion rings.

2 entrée or 4 to 6 side dish servings

Note: I use the Westbrae brand of Natural Toasted Sesame Tahini, sold in natural-food stores, which contains hulled, toasted organic sesame seeds. This tahini has a roasted flavor and is superior to raw tahini made with ground hulled raw sesame seeds.

Serving Suggestions: Serve this all-purpose sauce over baked potatoes, as a dip for papads, or as a hot dressing for shredded cabbage or steamed greens. It will also work as a pizza sauce. For an unusual potato salad, toss with a mixture of steamed potatoes, sweet onion rings, chopped arugula, and slivered olives. When serving over pasta, border with Cilantro Splash (page 223). If the pasta is to be a side dish, the tart kick of Mango-Marinated Fish with Dried Tomato Sauce (page 110), the freshness of a shredded Napa cabbage salad dressed with Curry-Walnut Dressing (page 234), and a cup of *hojicha* (roasted green tea) will turn this into a memorable meal.

VARIATIONS: For a flavor punch, add sambal oeleck or sweet chili sauce (both Yeo's brand), available in Asian markets. Start with a teaspoon (5 ml) and adjust according to taste. Add this sauce along with garam masala in Step 5. For extra color and crunch, separately sauté a thinly slivered red bell pepper until crisp-tender and add with the eggplant mixture in Step 4.

✳ Hearty Lentils and Udon ✳

UNITED STATES/JAPAN

In India, *dal* is the generic name for lentils, peas, and beans. It is spiced in many tasty ways and eaten daily as a soup or stew with rice or bread. For many vegetarians, it is the protein component of the meal. I widened my pasta repertoire the day I sauced pasta with dal, a greenish-brown lentil that can be obtained in supermarkets. Although this variety is unavailable in India, it takes well to Indian seasonings. The thick, spicy sauce tastes delicious with many types of pastas, but my favorite is udon, thick wheat noodles from Japan, similar to linguine.

This dish is especially warming during winter.

$1^1/2$ cups (375 ml) lentils

5 cups (1.25 liters) water

$1/2$ teaspoon (2 ml) turmeric

2 whole jalapeños

$1/4$ pound (100 g) Roma tomatoes, unpeeled, coarsely chopped

2 tablespoons (30 ml) mustard oil or canola oil

$1/4$ teaspoons (1 ml) Indian five-spice

1 cup (250 ml) thinly sliced onion

Salt

2 tablespoons (30 ml) fresh lime or lemon juice

A sprinkling of ghee (optional)

1 pound (500 g) udon (wider rather than a thinner variety), soba noodles, or linguine

Garnish:

Chopped cilantro

Honey-Glazed Onions (page 218; see *Note*)

1. Bring lentils and water to a boil in a large, deep pan. Add turmeric, jalapeños, and tomatoes and simmer covered for 30 to 40 minutes or until the lentils are tender to the bite. Discard jalapeños and process the mixture in a blender or food processor until smooth, adding a little extra water if necessary. Return to the pan, cover, place over low heat and bring to a gentle simmer. Remove from heat.

2. Heat oil in a 7-inch (17.5-cm) skillet over moderate heat. Add five-spice and fry until the seeds pop. Add onion and cook, stirring intermittently, until it is richly browned but not burnt, 8 to 15 minutes. Remove from heat and add this spice mixture to the lentils. Add salt. Stir in lime juice and the optional ghee.

3. Cook udon according to package directions. Pour sauce over udon, garnish with cilantro and Honey-Glazed Onions, and serve.

4 entrée servings

Note: Don't omit these onions as they enhance the taste of the sauce.

Serving Suggestions: To go with the strong flavors of this pasta dish, you need simpler accompaniments such as a large helping of Crisp Potato and Wilted Spinach Salad (page 246) or Winter Salad (page 259). Some steamed rutabaga (or carrots), snow peas, and beets topped with Roasted Garlic Spread (page 221) will also go nicely. For condiments consider grated daikon and Five Fundamental Seasonings (page 203).

✳ Shanghai Noodles with Mung Beans, ✳ Zucchini, and Lily Flowers

CHINA

Mung beans are an everyday dal dish in India, and this sauce laced with dried lily flowers and tossed with tasty Shanghai noodles is quite exotic. Long, slender lily buds, which the Chinese use in their hot and sour soup, add a woody flavor and a contrast in textures.

Gingerroot is used generously here, as it is in many dal dishes in India, and it lends its zing to the overall dish. A batch of whole green chiles adds flavor but not heat and is discarded at the end. I also apply the Indian technique of "final spice garnish," which is to fry a few whole spices in a little oil at the end of cooking and add them to the sauce. The spices retain their maximum flavor this way and further augment the appeal of the dish.

The mung beans:

1	cup (500 ml) yellow split mung beans, rinsed thoroughly
4	cups (1 liter) water
1/4	teaspoon (1 ml) turmeric
3	tablespoons (45 ml) minced or grated gingerroot
3/4	pound (375 g) tomatoes, unpeeled, chopped
2 to 3	whole jalapeños, serranos, or Thai chiles
6 to 8	dried lily flowers, each tied in a knot for decoration, soaked in warm water to cover for 10 minutes (if available; optional)

The vegetables:

   1   tablespoon (15 ml) mustard oil
   1   bay leaf
 ¹/₄   teaspoon (1 ml) Indian five-spice
   3   large cloves garlic, forced through a garlic press
   1   small zucchini, about ¹/₄ pound (100 g), cut crosswise in pieces ¹/₂ inch
         (1 cm) wide, or ¹/₂ pound (250 g) leeks cut similarly
       Salt
       Ground red pepper (to taste; start with a scant pinch)
   2   tablespoons (30 ml) fresh lime juice
       A sprinkling of ghee (optional)
       12-ounce (375-g) package Shanghai noodles or other wheat noodles

Garnish: Thinly sliced scallion (green part only)

1. Bring mung beans and water to a boil in a large pan over medium heat. Lower
   heat. Remove foam from the top with a slotted spoon or let it subside in the liquid. Add turmeric. Simmer, covered, 15 minutes. Add gingerroot, tomatoes,
   jalapeños, and lily buds. Simmer, covered, another 15 minutes or until the mung
   beans are very tender. (During this period, uncover occasionally and stir, adding
   1 to 2 tablespoons (15 to 30 ml) of hot water if the beans start to stick to the bottom.) You can discard the jalapeños at this point. Keep at a low simmer.

2. Heat oil in a small skillet over moderate heat. Add bay leaf and five-spice and fry
   until the spices start crackling. Add garlic and fry until it is lightly browned. Lower
   the heat slightly. Add zucchini and stir to mix with the spices. Remove from heat.
   Pour this spice mixture over the mung beans. Simmer, covered, until zucchini is
   tender, 6 to 10 minutes. (Overcooking will make the vegetables mushy.) Add salt
   and red pepper to taste and mix in lime juice. Sprinkle with ghee.

3. Cook Shanghai noodles according to package directions. Pour sauce over and
   serve garnished with scallions.

4 entrée servings

Serving Suggestions: Serve with a plate of grilled radicchio (see "To grill radicchio"
on page 247) and shiitake mushrooms lightly sautéed with Garlic Ghee (page 236).
The sauce is also delicious served alongside Basic Pilaf with Nutty Vermicelli Threads
(page 177) or as a topping for steamed Swiss chard or broccoflower.

✳ Rice Noodles, Black Beans, and ✳ Spring Greens Soup

EAST ASIA

San Francisco is jammed with Asian eateries, and "a movie and a bowl of noodles afterward" was a typical weekend diversion for me when I lived there. Gentle rice noodles are conducive to late-night suppers, and I like spicing them with rich, meaty Western black beans. These beans seem designed for Asian-style spicing, although they are rarely seen under the Pacific sun except in a fermented form. East Asians season a relatively bland noodle soup at the table by mixing soy sauce, Chinese sesame oil, and fish sauce in small individual saucers and pouring this sharp condiment mixture over their soup. The same process is used here, except I extend the range of sauces.

In India a whole red chile that has been toasted in oil is often added to a dish for flavor but not fieriness. Adapting that usage, here I dry-roast a red chile and add it to the soup at the beginning of cooking.

This easy one-dish meal has almost everything you could ask for—protein, carbohydrate, and vitamins. It also has an especially lulling quality.

8   cups (2 liters) Vegetable Stock (page 41) or canned vegetable broth

1   toasted dried red chile (see *Note 1*)

$1/4$ teaspoon (1 ml) asafetida powder

1   small onion, thinly sliced

2   large garlic cloves, slivered

$1/2$ pound (250 g) carrots, about 2 small, thinly sliced

1   medium-sized red bell pepper, thinly sliced

$1/2$ cup (125 ml) freshly cooked or canned black beans (preferably an organic brand from a natural-food store)

$1/2$ pound (250 g) dried rice noodles (preferably the $1/4$-inch [6-mm] wide, flat ribbonlike variety rather than a very thin type)

3   scallions, thinly sliced

2   cups (500 ml) firmly packed, shredded fresh spinach leaves

1   cup (250 ml) mung bean sprouts

Toasted dried fish (optional; see *Note 2*)

The seasonings:

    Salt and white pepper to taste

  1   tablespoon (15 ml) Chinese sesame oil

  ¹/₄ teaspoon (1 ml) fish sauce (to taste)

  ¹/₂ teaspoon (2 ml) shrimp powder (optional)

Bring stock, red chile, asafetida, onion, garlic, and carrots to a boil. Lower heat and simmer, covered, 5 minutes. Add bell pepper, black beans, and noodles. Simmer, covered, 3 to 4 minutes or just until the noodles are soft. Don't overcook. Add scallions, spinach, bean sprouts, and dried fish. As soon as spinach has wilted slightly, remove from heat. Add salt, pepper, sesame oil, fish sauce, and shrimp powder. It's ready to serve.

2 to 4 entrée servings

Note 1: For an added pungency, toast the chile on an ungreased skillet over low heat until blackened on all sides.

Note 2: These tiny dried fish are available in packages in Asian markets. Place them on an ungreased skillet over low heat and toast until lightly browned. Count on 3 to 4 fish per person, allowing a guest the option of omitting it.

Serving Suggestions: This dish is a meal in itself when offered with Five Fundamental Seasonings (page 203). In an individual saucer, whisk together sambal oeleck, Chinese sesame oil, and fish sauce and offer this as well for guests to mix in with the soup. For accompaniments consider Piquant Salad in Shades of Green (page 258) and possibly a basket of toasted French bread.

✳ Chile and Lime-Spiced Saifun Salad ✳
CHINA

For the lightest of vegetarian pasta salads, I offer this dish made with curly, delicate mung bean threads. The intense taste comes from the thin, oil-free dressing made with chile, lime, asafetida, and other spices. Its visual appeal is the result of a tantalizing mixture of shimmering noodles and deep red chile paste, flecked with bright green bits of scallions and cilantro. These noodles taste best when eaten with chopsticks.

3.85-ounce (110-g) package mung bean threads (*saifun*; see *Note*)
1   tablespoon (15 ml) Chinese sesame oil
    Chile-Lime Dressing (page 231)
1   jalapeño, seeded, thinly sliced (to taste)
1   small red bell pepper, finely chopped
1   tablespoon (15 ml) chopped cilantro
1 to 2   tablespoons (15 to 30 ml) choppped peanuts

Garnish:

Chopped fresh Thai basil or regular basil
Thinly sliced scallions (green part only)
Lime wedges

1. To prepare the mung bean threads: The package directions do not always indicate how to prepare them for a salad dish, so follow these instructions. Pour water into a large pan to come to about 1 inch (2.5 cm) deep. Bring water to a boil. Remove from heat and ease the mung bean threads into the water, working with a pair of chopsticks to keep them immersed. As soon as they soften and acquire a translucent color, about 1 minute, drain them in a large sieve over a basin. Run cold water over the sieve to stop the cooking. Place the noodles in a large deep bowl. If desired, cut them in smaller pieces using a pair of kitchen scissors.

2. Toss noodles with sesame oil. Gradually mix in the Chile-Lime Dressing using a pair of chopsticks, stopping when all the noodles have been thoroughly moistened. You may not need to use all the dressing. Toss the noodles with jalapeño, bell pepper, cilantro, and peanuts. Serve garnished with basil, scallions, and lime wedges.

4 side dish servings

Note: If bean threads are not available, substitute any wheat noodle.

Serving Suggestions: Noodles are a symbol of longevity in China, so consider celebrating a birthday with this dish. My favorite way to serve them is as an appetizer followed by Mango-Marinated Fish with Dried Tomato Sauce (page 110) and Peanutty Napa Cabbage (page 90). Or serve at a brunch with Gai Lan with Balsamic Vinaigrette (page 70) followed by a cup of barley tea. These colorful noodles are a hit at potlucks.

CHICKEN OR SHRIMP VARIATION: For a more substantial salad, in Step 2 just prior to garnishing, mix in ¾ cup (185 ml) cooked and cubed boneless chicken breast or ¼ pound (100 g) sautéed shrimp (sprinkled with a little Chile-Lime Dressing, reserved specifically for this purpose).

"New" and Ancient Grains

●●●●●●●●●●●●●●●●●●●●●●●●

My sister and I happily gobbled up the fresh fruits and vegetables our aunt offered us for lunch. But when we returned home, I told my mother, "We didn't eat much. She had no rice." For in India, having a meal means having rice. We ate it for lunch, dinner, and sometimes even for dessert, as rice pudding. I never tired of it.

In most Asian cultures, rice symbolizes prosperity. An affluent person is sometimes said to have an "abundance of rice." Years ago, Europeans similarly depended on wheat, their primary cereal for survival; for pre-Columbian Indians it was corn. The fate of nations was embodied in a tiny grain.

While rice, wheat, and corn have played dominant roles in the development of civilizations around the world, other equally nutritious grains have almost completely disappeared. Millet, a tiny, round, nutty-tasting grain, was a staple in parts of Africa in ancient times. Now other starches, such as maize and yuca, have replaced it. Quinoa, similar in appearance to millet but superior in protein content, sustained people of the Andes mountains for centuries. When the Inca civilization collapsed, quinoa disappeared from the world harvest for several hundred growing seasons.

Fortunately, because of their light, fluffy texture, pleasant nutlike aroma, and nutritional density, millet and quinoa are enjoying a resurgence in the West. While traveling and living abroad, I discovered these "new" grains as well as others not used in India. As a result of many culinary experiments, they now share the reverence I used to have only for rice.

One frigid winter morning I arrived in the Inner Mongolian region of China just in time for breakfast. With a cold wind scouring my face, I walked across a vast courtyard to a dilapidated, unheated dining hall, where I was served a steaming bowl of millet, laced with nuts and dried fruits and accompanied by a small pitcher of hot milk. Just one mouthful and I was warmed clear through. Such a fragrant porridge was a luxury in that vast, barren land. It has remained a favorite.

On another occasion, in a small Paris restaurant run by a Moroccan immigrant, I first tasted couscous, a wheat derivative of North African origin. As I had arrived before the main dinner crowd and was curious, the chef showed me how to cook this grain to perfection. He used a *couscousière*, a large two-sectioned pot similar to a double boiler. The top pan had a finely perforated bottom that allowed steam from a rich meat stock to rise into the upper chamber. He rubbed the couscous kernels between his palms over the upper pot, gradually filling the steaming chamber. When he brought the meat ragout in the lower chamber to a simmer, the steam permeated the couscous with the flavor of the rich stock. As he monitored the progress of the dish, he told me stories of his youth. His tales were simple, his couscous sophisticated. Once again my eyes were opened to the possibilities of including other grains on my own table.

Many traditional grain cooking techniques from India helped me vary my preparations. The most elaborate of all rice cooking techniques in northern India is *biriyani*, one that includes the finest of rice and rich, whole spices. South Indians snack on *uppama*, a light wheat dish spiced simply with black mustard and curry leaves. *Khichuri*, a method of cooking rice and legumes together, produces a one-dish casserole, popular all over India. Unfortunately, quinoa, kasha, barley, and millet are either unknown in India or used in a limited manner, and thus have not been used in preparing a *biriyani*, *uppama*, or *khichuri*. Since coming to the West, I have learned to cook these grains, using Indian spices and techniques, with considerable success. They are equally at home as the centerpiece of a meal or as a savory accompaniment to Indian-inspired main dishes.

Quinoa has a mild but distinct taste that is enhanced by pungent spices such as black mustard. Kasha's robust flavor is improved but not overpowered when seasoned with a fiery curry powder. Couscous, with its light, feathery texture, tastes delicious with cumin-infused sauces. And wild rice, actually a form of grass, acquires an exotic flavor when sautéed with turmeric and black cardamom before simmering.

Now I can enjoy saffron-colored millet pudding for breakfast, tamarind-tinged bulgur salad for lunch, and quinoa cooked with curry leaves for dinner. With a wealth of such grains and a vast number of spices and techniques at my disposal, I have a feast of flavors every day.

Spiced in this manner, these grains can set the mood for a meal with their unique color, texture, and aroma. Matching them imaginatively with Indian-inspired fish, meat, or vegetable dishes offers infinite possibilities. Nutritionally, and in spirit, I feel enriched. ✳

Going with the Grain

✳ Because of their drier consistency, grain-based dishes suggest to me the need for fruit sauces, salsas, or herb chutneys as accompaniments. Each recipe in this chapter includes several choices. Look for other alternatives in the Chutneys, Sauces, and Dressings chapter.

✳ Top these cooked grains with seeds, nuts, or dried fruits. Toasted seeds such as sunflower or pumpkin are a delicious addition to, and in many cases complement, the protein of the grain. Chopped dried fruits such as apples, cranberries, or raisins also work well with many grains.

✳ Combine leftover cooked grains with romaine and other raw or cooked vegetables for a salad. Rice, quinoa, and millet are especially good this way. You'll find several delicious grain salad recipes in this chapter.

✳ *To plain-cook grains:* When teaming with highly seasoned dishes, I prefer plain rice, millet, kasha, couscous, or bulgur. Before cooking, rinse quinoa and Basmati rice several times. You can toast millet and quinoa to impart a nutty flavor and to speed up cooking. If toasting quinoa, rinse it after roasting (or rinse it before and allow it to dry for an hour before roasting). Cook the grains, covered, with double the amount of hot water or, for an improved flavor, chicken or vegetable broth, until all liquid is absorbed and they are light and fluffy. If still crunchy, add a little hot water and cook for a few more minutes. Most grains take 10 to 30 minutes. Grains such as barley or brown Basmati rice will take longer, 45 to 55 minutes. Add salt. Note that couscous sold in the United States is instant and cooks in a matter of minutes.

✳ Picnic Squash Pullao ✳
EASTERN INDIA

The word "picnic" in the Bengali language literally translates to "sharing rice with the sparrows." In this traditional dish from Bengal, where there are many bright picnic days, yellow rice and orange butternut squash laced with ginger, green chile, and whole black peppercorns make a spectacular presentation—one that will entice guests and the sparrows alike.

1 1/2 tablespoons (22 ml) mustard oil
1 bay leaf
2 tablespoons (30 ml) minced gingerroot
1 jalapeño, seeded, chopped (to taste)
5 whole black peppercorns (do not grind)
1/4 teaspoon (1 ml) turmeric
1/2 teaspoon (2 ml) salt
1 teaspoon (5 ml) sugar
1 cup (500 ml) white Basmati rice (rinsed several times), or other fine long-grain white rice
1 1/2 cups (375 ml) water
1 1/2 cups (375 ml) butternut squash, peeled, cut into 3/4-inch (2-cm) cubes
1/2 teaspoon (2 ml) garam masala
A sprinkling of ghee (optional)

Garnish:
Toasted raw cashew halves or toasted slivered almonds
Chopped cilantro

1. Heat oil in a large, deep pan over moderate heat. Add bay leaf, gingerroot, and jalapeño and fry for a few seconds. Stir in peppercorns, turmeric, salt, sugar, and rice and cook until rice turns opaque, about 2 minutes, stirring often. Add water and squash. Cover and bring to a boil. Lower heat.
2. Simmer, covered, 15 to 20 minutes or until all water is absorbed and both rice and squash are tender. Remove from heat. Let stand, covered, for a few minutes to help develop flavor. Discard whole spices (or warn guests). Mix in garam masala and ghee. Serve garnished with cashews and cilantro.

2 to 4 side dish servings

Serving Suggestions: Bring the flavors of Bengal to your table by serving Indian Spiced Brussels Sprouts (page 74) and Fish Korma (page 108). For a light summer meal on the patio, team with Onion Yogurt Relish (page 209) and Piquant Salad in Shades of Green (page 258).

SHELLFISH VARIATION: SHRIMP AND SQUASH PULLAO The inclusion of shrimp makes a splendid one-dish meal. You can either partially cook the shrimp in a little oil first for a richer flavor and/or add it at the last moment.

  2　teaspoons (10 ml) mustard oil or canola oil (optional)
  1/2　pound (250 g) bay shrimp, fresh or thawed frozen

Do this optional step before you begin the recipe for Picnic Squash Pullao. Heat oil in a small skillet over moderate heat. Add shrimp and fry just until it changes to a pink color. Transfer shrimp and any accumulated juices to a medium bowl and set aside.

Arrange shrimp (whether sautéed or not) on top of rice during the last 3 minutes of cooking in Step 2. Pour any juice over rice. (Do not stir rice until just before serving.) Omit the garnish of cashews or almonds in this case but scatter cilantro on top.

✳ Bengali Crab Risotto ✳
EASTERN INDIA/ITALY

Risotto, a creamy Italian rice, is enormously popular in northern Italy. There, like pasta, it precedes the main dish. In the United States, this rice is served more often these days as part of a main meal. Risotto can accommodate a wide variety of Indian seasonings, including turmeric, asafetida, and black mustard seeds. Add crab meat for a sensuous touch.

A few tips will help in preparing risotto. First, the dish is cooked uncovered, so the broth becomes concentrated. It can become overly salty and can affect the finished dish unless you use homemade unsalted chicken or fish stock or canned low-salt chicken broth. Second, risotto needs frequent stirring to prevent sticking and to make the result creamier. Finally, to keep the fat calories down, I forgo the traditional complement of cheese. If you prefer, you can sprinkle grated Parmesan (or Romano or another hard cheese) over the risotto before serving.

  1 1/2　tablespoons (22 ml) mustard oil, butter, or Garlic Ghee (page 236)
  1/4　teaspoon (1 ml) black mustard seeds

    1 cup (250 ml) finely chopped onion
 $^1/_4$ teaspoon (1 ml) turmeric
    1 cup (250 ml) *superfino* arborio rice
    2 cups (500 ml) Chicken Stock (page 44), or 14 $^1/_2$-ounce (411-g) can low-salt
       chicken broth, defatted, heated to boiling (see "To defat canned chicken
       broth," page 45)
    3 cups-plus (750 ml) boiling water
6 to 8 ounces (170 to 225 g) crab meat
       Salt
1 to 2 ounces (25 to 50 g) grated Parmesan, Romano, or other hard cheese
       (optional)

Garnish: Chopped cilantro

1. Heat oil in a medium pan over moderate heat. (See "Choosing a pan for risotto"
   on page xx.) Add mustard seeds and fry until the seeds start to pop. (Keep the pan
   partially covered to prevent the seeds from flying out. The remainder of the time,
   this dish is cooked entirely without a cover.) Add onion and cook, stirring often,
   until it is richly browned but not burnt, 8 to 10 minutes. Add turmeric and rice;
   stir for a minute.

2. Add chicken stock, about $^1/_2$ cup (125 ml) at a time, and cook, stirring, until the
   liquid is absorbed. Continue adding stock this way until all the stock has been
   used up. Add boiling water, 1 cup (250 ml) at a time, and cook as before; stir
   more frequently as the liquid is absorbed to prevent sticking. The entire process
   will take about 30 minutes. (See *Do-ahead Note.*) When the rice is tender to the
   bite and the mixture is creamy, add crab meat. Heat the mixture through, adding
   a little more hot water if necessary for a soft, creamy texture. Add salt and cheese.
   Remove from heat. Serve garnished with cilantro.

4 to 6 side dish servings

Do-ahead Note: Risotto is best served immediately. You can, however, make part of
the recipe ahead of time. In Step 2, cook for about 20 minutes and refrigerate. Just
before serving, cook for the remaining 10 minutes.

Serving Suggestions: To dine around the globe, serve Peanuts, Seaweed, and Red
Chile Flakes (page 220) from China as an appetizer. Follow with Simple Pleasure
Zucchini Sauté (page 88) from the United States, Greens Ratatouille (page 94) from
France, and Lime-Grilled Chicken (page 125) from Africa.

✳ Saffron-Scented Millet ✳

NORTH INDIA

Here is an exotic millet dish that employs the 500-year-old *moghlai* cooking style of the royal courts of India, known for its rich, lavish quality. Rice, the grain of choice, would be sautéed with whole spices such as cardamom, cinnamon, and cloves along with cashews and raisins to add aroma and flavor. Saffron tinted the grains a brilliant yellow color, and caramelized onion provided a rich, sweet topping. Browned meat would be layered on top of the rice during steaming to moisten it with flavorful juices—a step that brings the meat to fork-tender doneness.

This simpler millet version of the classic *biriyani* dish includes the expected nuts, raisins, and the spices but no meat. It's superb for potlucks, buffets, or family dinners.

  1   cup (500 ml) millet
2 1/2   tablespoons (37 ml) canola oil
  1   cup (500 ml) thinly sliced onion
  1   bay leaf
  5   whole cardamom pods, bruised
      2-inch (5-cm) cinnamon stick
  2   whole cloves
 1/4   teaspoon (1 ml) cumin seeds
  1   tablespoon (15 ml) minced gingerroot
  1   jalapeño, seeded, chopped (to taste)
  4   ounces (100 g), Roma tomatoes, 2 medium, unpeeled, finely chopped
 1/2   teaspoon (2 ml) salt
 1/2   teaspoon (2 ml) sugar
  2   cups (500 ml) water
  2   tablespoons (30 ml) raw cashew halves
  2   tablespoons (30 ml) golden raisins
 1/2   teaspoon (2 ml) saffron threads, ground to a powder, mixed with 1 table-
      spoon (15 ml) warm water and allowed to stand 15 minutes
  2   cups (500 ml) cauliflower florets, about 1 inch (2.5 cm) in diameter
 1/4   cup (60 ml) fresh peas or thawed frozen peas

1. Toast the millet on an ungreased griddle or skillet over low heat until it is slightly brownish, turning often to prevent burning. Transfer to a medium bowl.

2. Heat 1 $^1/_2$ tablespoons (22 ml) oil in a small pan over moderate heat. Add onion and cook, stirring intermittently, until it is richly browned but not burnt, 8 to 12 minutes. Transfer to a small bowl.

3. Heat the remaining 1 tablespoon (15 ml) oil in a large, deep pan over moderate heat. Fry bay leaf, cardamom, cinnamon, cloves, and cumin seeds for a few seconds. Add gingerroot and jalapeño and fry for a minute or so. Add tomatoes and cook, stirring, for another minute. Add millet, salt, sugar, and water. Add cashews, raisins, and the saffron with its soaking liquid. Cover and bring to a boil.

4. Simmer, covered, 5 minutes. Arrange cauliflower on top, but don't stir the millet. Simmer, covered, 15 minutes. Place peas on top and simmer, covered, another 3 to 5 minutes. Remove from heat and let stand, covered, for a few minutes. Serve topped with onions.

4 side dish servings

Serving Suggestions: For a savory dinner, combine with grilled butternut squash (or sweet potato) and Mint-Basil Chutney (page 224). Garlic-Glazed Tofu (page 67) or Soy- and Mirin-Glazed Salmon (page 99) provides the protein.

✳ Hazelnut Kasha with Red Pepper Cream ✳
RUSSIA/ITALY

The first time I ate kasha—in a Jewish restaurant in Chicago—I knew I had met a superior grain. Actually kasha is not a grain, but the triangular fruit of the buckwheat plant. A Russian *babushka* told me she believes kasha to be a high-energy food and throws a handful of it into every soup, stew, and casserole she cooks for her family.

In this recipe, besides complementing the protein, hazelnuts and chick-peas add crunch and firmness to the softened kasha kernels. Sun-dried tomatoes, so beloved by Italians, infuse the dish with the sharp sunny taste reminiscent of Mediterranean afternoons.

   1 cup (250 ml) whole-grain kasha
   1 large egg, lightly beaten (optional; see *Note*)
1 $^1/_2$ cups (375 ml) chick-pea liquid or chicken broth, defatted (see "To defat canned chicken broth," page 45)

1 cup (250 ml) fresh cooked chick-peas or canned chick-peas (part of a
15^1/$_2$-ounce [430-g] can), drained, cooking or can liquid saved
Salt
2 tablespoons (30 ml) olive oil
1 cup (250 ml) thinly sliced onion
^{1}/$_4$ cup (60 ml) toasted and finely chopped hazelnuts
Sun-Dried Tomato and Red Pepper Cream (page 226)

1. Place kasha on a large skillet over moderate heat. Add the egg, stirring briskly for a few seconds to coat the grains. When the egg has been absorbed, add the chick-pea liquid. With the back of a spoon, press the kasha kernels so they lie under the liquid. Place chick-peas on top without disturbing the kasha. Cover and bring to a boil. Lower the heat, cover, and simmer 18 to 25 minutes or until all water is absorbed and kasha is light and fluffy. (Kasha cooks in 10 minutes, but this slow simmer helps release its full flavor.) Remove from heat. Add salt.
2. Meanwhile, brown-fry the onion: Heat oil in a small 7-inch (17.5-cm) skillet over moderate heat. Add onion and fry, stirring often, until it is richly browned but not burnt, 8 to 10 minutes. Transfer to a small bowl.
3. Arrange onion on top of kasha. Sprinkle with hazelnuts. Serve hot with the Sun-Dried Tomato and Red Pepper Cream on the side.

2 entrée or 6 side dish servings

Note: The egg coats the kasha kernels, keeping them separate, and imparts a richer flavor and fluffier texture to the dish. Omit it if you like.

Serving Suggestions: This grain-and-legume combination is a meal in itself. Lace the top lightly with the green-colored Cilantro Splash (page 223) to contrast with the red hue of Sun-Dried Tomato and Red Pepper Cream. Serve Date and Nut-Filled Meatballs (page 135) as an appetizer and fresh ripe peaches for dessert.

✳ Couscous and Smoked Oysters ✳

INTERNATIONAL

Unite couscous, smoked oysters, and Indian seasonings in this dauntless dish. Raise its taste to the highest pitch by using double-concentrated tomato paste (such as the Italian brand Ortolina) rather than the usual canned supermarket variety. Bake the dish in an attractive heat-proof casserole, then serve from it.

2	tablespoons (30 ml) olive oil
1	cup (250 ml) finely chopped onion
1/4	teaspoon (1 ml) turmeric
1	teaspoon (5 ml) ground cumin
1	teaspoon (5 ml) ground coriander
2	tablespoons (30 ml) tomato paste (preferably an Italian brand)
2	cups (500 ml) hot water
1	cup (250 ml) couscous or whole-grain kasha
	4-ounce (100-g) can smoked oysters, drained
1/2	cup (125 ml) thawed frozen peas

Garnish: (see *Note*)

Sweet onion rings

Seeded, coarsely chopped tomatoes

Chopped cilantro

1. Preheat oven to 350°F (180°C, gas marks 4). Heat oil in a large skillet over moderate heat. Add onion and cook, stirring intermittently, until it is richly browned but not burnt, 8 to 10 minutes. Add turmeric, cumin, and coriander and mix well. Add tomato paste and water. Bring to a boil. Remove from heat.

2. Place couscous and oysters in a lightly oiled ovenproof casserole dish. Pour the spice mixture over them. Arrange peas on top. Cover tightly with aluminum foil. Bake for 10 to 15 minutes or until all water is absorbed and couscous is light and fluffy.

2 to 4 side dish servings

Note: These fresh raw garnishes are essential to the dish to balance the smoky flavor of the oysters.

Serving Suggestions: Serve as a main course along with some stir-fried baby bok choy and Chilied Mango Chutney (page 205). The dish works equally well with Onion Yogurt Relish (page 209) and shredded Napa cabbage sprinkled with Sesame-Tamarind Dressing (page 233).

FISH VARIATION: Though it lacks the punch of smoked food, this variation still makes a hearty meal. Replace smoked oysters with $1/2$ pound (250 g) freshly poached fish or leftover cooked fish. Flake the fish with a fork before adding in Step 2. Remove from oven as soon as couscous is done so as not to overcook fish.

✳ Tabbouleh Plus ✳
THE MIDDLE EAST

A deli in my neighborhood was known for its Middle Eastern food, especially tabbouleh. After I learned how much oil was in the salad, I decided to prepare a lighter version. A fat-free Lime-Tamarind Dressing is the result. With the sharp touch of sundried tomatoes, the salad doesn't need help, but for extra flavor I sometimes fold in a little extra-virgin olive oil at the end. Or I divide the salad into two bowls, add oil to one and leave the other oil-free, letting my guests choose.

A man from the Middle East told me he used a native variety of sesame oil, not olive, for this grain dish. You may find Chinese sesame oil to be an exotic alternative.

1	cup (250 ml) fine bulgur
$3/4$	pound (375 g) Roma tomatoes, about 6 medium, peeled, seeded, and chopped
3	large garlic cloves, forced through a garlic press
$1/4$ to $1/2$	cup (60 to 125 ml) finely shredded arugula or chopped scallions
$1/4$	cup (60 ml) chopped fresh mint leaves
$1/4$	cup (60 ml) chopped cilantro or parsley
	Lime-Tamarind Dressing (page 232)
	Salt
1 to 2	tablespoons (15 to 30 ml) extra-virgin olive oil (or substitute Chinese sesame oil for part of the olive oil)

1. Rinse bulgur. Cover with boiling water to come up to $1/2$ inch (1 cm) above the grains, and let stand for 30 minutes or until softened. Drain in a sieve or colander lined with several layers of cheesecloth, and press out water.
2. In a large bowl, combine tomatoes, garlic, arugula, mint, and cilantro. Mix in the bulgur. Add the Lime-Tamarind Dressing and stir to blend in with the ingredients. Add salt. Fold in oil. Serve at room temperature.

4 to 6 side dish servings

Serving Suggestions: For a flexible meal that can accommodate many different dietary preferences, prepare this carbo-rich grain salad. Then surround it with one or more protein platters such as broiled chicken, tuna chunks, marinated tofu, plain cooked beans, or poached fish. Offer a tray of Five Fundamental Seasonings (page 203) and a plethora of sauces, such as fish sauce, Chinese sesame oil, or Dream Yogurt (page 212). You can joyfully share from such a table and at the same time create your own unique dining experience. I call such a meal a "celebration of differences."

❋ Basic Pilaf with Nutty Vermicelli Threads ❋
THE MIDDLE EAST

Although plain cooked grains go best with spicy dishes, for festive occasions I prepare a more elaborate pilaf, called pullao in India. Indians choose rice as their grain for this purpose, but you can prepare a pilaf with couscous, quinoa, millet, or other grains.

In this basic recipe, green peas, blushing carrots, and bright yellow turmeric combine with your choice of grain to make an easy but superlative pilaf. Using a Middle Eastern technique, I brown a few strands of vermicelli in a little oil before adding them to the grain. The threads decorate the pilaf while adding a textural contrast.

At those busy times when the stove is crowded with many pots, an electric rice cooker can come in handy for preparing this grain dish. This frees a burner and lets you concentrate on other dishes. If you own such a cooker, after you've sautéed the aromatics and readied other ingredients, finish the pilaf in it, following manufacturer's directions. The pilaf is light, fluffy, and either ready in time or stays warm for 20 or so minutes.

3/4 cup (185 ml) carrots, diced into 1/2-inch (1-cm) cubes (see *Note for the Gardener*)

1 1/2 tablespoons (22 ml) canola oil

10 to 12 strands vermicelli, broken into 2-inch (5-cm) pieces (use supermarket vermicelli, not the needle-thin variety sold in Indian groceries) (see *Note 1*)

1/4 teaspoon (1 ml) cumin seeds

1/2 cup (125 ml) finely chopped shallot or onion

1 tablespoon (15 ml) minced garlic

1 jalapeño, seeded, chopped (to taste)

1/4 teaspoon (1 ml) turmeric

1 cup (250 ml) grain of choice (see *Note 2*)

$^{1}/_{2}$ teaspoon (2 ml) salt

Hot water (see *Note 3*)

$^{1}/_{4}$ cup (60 ml) fresh or thawed frozen peas

1 tablespoon (15 ml) toasted, unsalted cashew halves

Garnish:

Honey-Glazed Onions (page 218) or browned potatoes (see "To brown potatoes," page 113)

Shredded arugula or fresh basil

1. Steam the carrots for 5 minutes. They need to be only partially cooked at this
   stage as they will be cooked more later.
2. In a small skillet, heat $^{1}/_{2}$ tablespoon (7 ml) oil and cook vermicelli until it browns
   lightly, less than a minute. Remove with a slotted spoon and drain on paper towels.
3. Heat the remaining 1 tablespoon (15 ml) oil in a large skillet over moderate heat.
   Add cumin seeds and fry until they are lightly browned. Add shallot, garlic, and
   jalapeño and fry until shallot is translucent. Stir in turmeric. Add grain, salt, vermicelli, and hot water, making sure the grain lies under water. Arrange carrots and
   fresh peas on top of grain. Bring to a boil.
4. Lower heat and simmer, covered, until all water is absorbed and the grains are
   plump. If using frozen peas, add them during the last 5 minutes of cooking. Let
   stand, covered, for a few minutes to make the grains fluffier. Add cashews and
   toss with a fork. Garnish with onions or potatoes and arugula.

4 side dish servings

Note for the Gardener: For a taste variation, use golden-orange beets instead of carrots. They don't "bleed" like regular purple beets and offer a carrotlike sweet flavor.

Note 1: An alternative to vermicelli is orzo. In Step 2, sauté 1 tablespoon (15 ml)
orzo for 1 to 2 minutes until medium brown.

Note 2: Use couscous, bulgur, quinoa, millet, or an aromatic rice like Basmati or
jasmine.

Note 3: See "To plain-cook grains" (page 168) for the amount of water and timing.

Serving Suggestions: Over the years, this savory pilaf has become a constant companion to my fish, meat, and vegetable dishes. Some favorite entrées are: Fish Swimming
in Three Flavors (page 102), Indian Chicken Salad (page 131), and Sweet and Spicy
Sancoche (page 68). For a starter, offer some grilled radicchio, dressed with Cumin
Vinaigrette (page 233) (see "To grill radicchio," page 247).

* Curried Quinoa, Olive, and Romaine Salad *

GREECE

Using olives to perk up a salad is a tip I gathered in Greece. The countryside is dotted with ancient olive trees and the stores there display the widest variety of olives I've ever seen. Often the fruit is shrunken and lusterless from sun-drying, not shiny and smooth as when cured in vinegar or oil, but it is always full of flavor.

Olives go well with quinoa, an import from Peru, cooked with a touch of curry. Romaine, the most nutritious variety of lettuce commonly found in supermarkets, makes this grain salad a light meal in itself.

The quinoa:

- 1/2 cup (125 ml) quinoa
- 1 tablespoon (15 ml) olive oil or canola oil
- 1/2 cup (125 ml) finely chopped onion
- 1/2 teaspoon (2 ml) curry powder (see "Selecting curry powder," page 10)
- 1 cup (250 ml) hot water
- 1 medium-sized red bell pepper, chopped into 1/2-inch (1-cm) pieces

The salad:

- 2 tablespoons (30 ml) slivered Kalamata olives
- 1/2 cup (125 ml) thinly sliced mild red or other sweet onion
- 4 cups (1 liter) shredded romaine lettuce (or a combination of romaine, arugula, and other salad greens of choice)
  Cumin Vinaigrette (page 233)

1. To toast quinoa: Place quinoa on an ungreased skillet over low heat for several minutes or until it browns lightly and a faint nutty smell is noticeable. Hold the cover over the skillet as the grains start to pop and fly out. Remove from heat. Rinse quinoa very thoroughly by placing in a large sieve and running cold water through it while stirring the grains with your fingers. Set aside to drain.
2. Heat oil in a large skillet over moderate heat. Cook onion until it is translucent and slightly soft, about 2 minutes. Add curry powder and stir a few times. Add quinoa and hot water. Bring to a boil. Cover and simmer for 15 to 20 minutes or until all water is absorbed and quinoa is light and fluffy. Place bell pepper on top of quinoa during the last 10 to 12 minutes of cooking. Remove from the heat and allow to cool slightly.

3. Combine quinoa with olive slivers (saving a few olive slivers for topping) and mound the mixture in the center of a large serving platter or on individual serving plates. Decorate with the remaining olive slivers and onion slices. Toss lettuce with Cumin Vinaigrette. Arrange lettuce in a circle around the quinoa and serve.

4 side dish servings

Serving Suggestions: Serve as a salad course along with grilled chicken or beef. Or serve as a light one-dish meal accompanied by Lime and Papaya Milk (page 294). Also splendid with a side dish of mung bean sauce as prepared in Shanghai Noodles with Mung Beans, Zucchini, and Lily Flowers (page 161). Look for other ideas in the Serving Suggestions for Tabbouleh Plus (page 177).

✳ Quinoa Uppama ✳
SOUTH INDIA

Visit South India and you are likely to find *uppama* (also spelled as *uppma*), a feathery grain dish, on your breakfast tray or as a snack. *Uppama* supplies the morning carbohydrate and is usually made of farina, which is similar to Cream of Wheat. I have substituted quinoa, a New World import, for wheat and find this nutritious high-protein grain to be a pleasant dinnertime alternative. The nutty taste of this dish is enhanced by black mustard seeds and curry leaves—a common South Indian spice combination.

1	cup (250 ml) quinoa
2	tablespoons (30 ml) canola oil
1/4	teaspoon (1 ml) black mustard seeds
5 to 6	curry leaves, crushed
1	cup (250 ml) finely chopped onion
1	jalapeño, seeded, chopped (to taste)
1/4	teaspoon (1 ml) turmeric
2	cups (500 ml) hot water
1/4	pound (100 g) carrot, about 1 medium, diced into 1/2-inch (1-cm) cubes
1	small red bell pepper, finely chopped
2	tablespoons to 1/4 cup (30 to 60 ml) unsalted raw cashew halves
1/2	cup (125 ml) fresh or thawed, frozen peas
	Salt
2	tablespoons (30 ml) fresh lemon juice

1. To toast quinoa: Place quinoa on an ungreased skillet over low heat for several minutes or until it browns lightly and a faint nutty smell is noticeable. Hold the cover over the skillet as the grains start to pop and fly out. Remove from heat. Rinse quinoa very thoroughly by placing in a large sieve and running cold water through it while stirring the grains with your fingers. Set aside to drain.
2. Heat oil over moderate heat in a large skillet. Add mustard seeds and curry leaves and fry until the seeds start to pop. (You may keep the skillet partially covered to keep the seeds from flying out.) Add onion and fry until it is lightly browned. Add jalapeño and turmeric. Add hot water and bring to a boil.
3. Add drained quinoa and press with the back of a spoon so that it lies under water. Gently place the carrot, bell pepper, cashews, and fresh peas on top without disturbing the quinoa. Cover and simmer until all water is absorbed and quinoa is light and fluffy, 20 to 30 minutes. Add frozen peas during the last 3 to 4 minutes of cooking. Let stand, covered, a few minutes to allow the grains to become even more fluffy. Add salt. Sprinkle lemon juice on top and toss with a fork.

4 side dish servings

Serving Suggestions: Top with two Indian favorites, Green Mango Chutney (page 206) and Cilantro Splash (page 223). Continue the Indian theme by serving Fish Swimming in Three Flavors (page 102) and Golden Squash Cream (page 87). This *uppama* also makes a satisfying meal when served with the eggplant sauce as prepared in Soba Noodles with Tahini Eggplant (page 158) and some steamed broccoli.

✳ Barley, Wild Rice, and Azuki Beans Khichuri ✳
INDIA/UNITED STATES/EAST ASIA

There's something heart-warming about *khichuri*, the classic Indian grain-and-legume stew. In rainy weather, Indians serve this easy, hearty one-dish meal at home, using whatever vegetables are on hand. In large temples, especially in the south where thousands of devotees are fed daily, the food must be kept simple. *Khichuri*, a protein-balanced dish, is often on the menu. This casserole pleases prince and peasant alike and a variation exists for each taste. One simple variation is named *fakir*, originally an Arabic word for "poor," which has come to mean a religious ascetic who has taken vows of poverty. A more elaborate one, called *badshahi*, or "royal," is layered lavishly with cashews and eggs, two pricey food items in India.

I have deviated from the tradition by using wild rice and barley instead of rice, and East Asian azuki beans instead of a dal. Chaat Powder and not garam masala is my final spice blend. This international adaptation packs just as much nutritional punch as its Indian cousin.

The beans and grains:
- 1/2 cup (125 ml) azuki beans, soaked in 4 cups (1 liter) water overnight (reserve liquid)
- 1/2 cup (125 ml) pearl barley
- 1/2 cup (125 ml) wild rice
- 2 cups (500 ml) Chicken Stock (page 44) or a 14 1/2-ounce (411-g) can chicken broth, defatted (see "To defat canned chicken broth," page 45)
- 1 cup (250 ml) bean cooking liquid or water, or a combination

The simmering spices:
- 2 bay leaves
- 1/4 teaspoon (1 ml) turmeric
- 1 teaspoon (5 ml) ground cumin
- 1 jalapeño, seeded, finely chopped (to taste)
- 1 tablespoon (15 ml) minced gingerroot
- 1 whole black cardamom pod (optional)
- 3/4 teaspoon (3 ml) salt

The vegetables:
- 1/2 pound (250 g) Roma tomatoes, about 4 medium, finely chopped
- 1 medium carrot, about 1/4 pound (100 g), diced
- 1/4 pound (100 g) (about 1/2 medium) kohlrabi, turnip, or rutabaga, or a whole unpeeled medium potato, diced
- 3/4 cup (185 ml) fresh peas or thawed frozen peas

The finishing spices:
- 1/2 teaspoon (2 ml) Chaat Powder (see page 8)
- 2 tablespoons (30 ml) lemon juice
  A sprinkling of ghee (optional)
- 2 tablespoons (30 ml) unrefined safflower oil or canola oil
- 1/4 teaspoon (1 ml) cumin seeds
- 1 medium onion, thinly sliced

Garnish: Toasted pumpkin seeds

1. Cook the azuki beans in soaking water for 1 hour or until tender to the bite. Check the water level and add more during cooking if necessary. Drain, reserving the bean liquid. Set the beans aside.

2. Combine barley, wild rice, chicken stock, and bean liquid. Place the simmering spices, tomatoes, carrot, and kohlrabi on top. (Make sure barley and wild rice remain under the liquid.) Cover and bring to a boil.

3. Simmer, covered, 40 to 50 minutes or until all liquid is absorbed and both barley and wild rice are tender. Add fresh peas during the last 10 minutes of cooking. (If using frozen peas, add during the last 3 to 5 minutes.) Add azuki beans also at this time. Remove from heat. Mix in Chaat Powder, lemon juice, and ghee. Taste for salt. Let stand, covered, for 10 minutes to let the grains absorb the rest of the steam and to develop flavor.

4. In small skillet, heat oil and fry cumin seeds until lightly browned. Add onion and cook, stirring often, until richly browned but not burnt, 8 to 15 minutes. Sprinkle this spice mixture over the grain-and-bean mixture. Serve garnished with pumpkin seeds.

2 entrée or 4 to 6 side dish servings

Serving Suggestions: This grain dish is filling enough for a meal when paired with sautéed shiitake mushrooms or button mushrooms, Roasted Banana Raita (page 210), and a crisp green salad. For another glorious meal, try with Sweet and Sour Plantain Sauce (page 222) and some baked papads. Serve any leftovers for lunch with Dream Yogurt (page 212).

FRESH CORN VARIATION: A speedier alternative. Instead of azuki beans use ¹/₂ cup (125 ml) fresh corn or thawed frozen corn. Add in Step 3 along with frozen peas.

✻ Leeks and Barley with Glazed Onions ✻ and Rosemary

TURKEY

I was once entranced by a Turkish dish in which leek, a most elegant vegetable, was cooked with aromatic rice. While being braised, the leek exuded a delicately sweet juice that was absorbed by the rice; the result was captivating.

In this recipe, barley is my substitution for rice. Since this grain is strongly flavored, I match it with bold rosemary and equally assertive caramelized onions. A small amount of Basmati rice soaks up any excess liquid while imparting fragrance. Potatoes add texture and more body. This grain-and-vegetable combination makes for a most appealing dish.

- 2 tablespoons (30 ml) olive oil
- 1 cup (250 ml) thinly sliced onion
- 1 teaspoon (5 ml) sugar
- 1/4 teaspoon (1 ml) turmeric
- 3 tablespoons (45 ml) pearl barley
- 1 tablespoon (15 ml) Basmati or other long-grain white rice
- 2 cups (500 ml) Chicken Stock (page 44) or 14 1/2-ounce (411-g) can chicken broth, defatted (see "To defat canned chicken broth," page 45; also see *Note 1*)
- 1 tablespoon (15 ml) fresh rosemary or 1 teaspoon (5 ml) dried rosemary
- 1/2 teaspoon (2 ml) salt
- 1 pound (500 g) leeks (see *Note for the Gardener*)

The potatoes:

- 1 pound (500 g) new potatoes, about 4 medium, unpeeled, cut into 1-inch (2.5-cm) cubes
- 1 tablespoon (15 ml) olive oil
- 1 whole dried red chile

Garnish: (see *Note 2*)

- Chopped parsley
- Sweet onion rings

1. Heat oil in a large skillet or ovenproof casserole over moderate heat until a light haze forms. Add onion and fry, stirring often, until it is richly browned but not burnt, 8 to 12 minutes. Stir in sugar and turmeric. Add barley and rice. Add chicken stock, rosemary, and salt. Cover and bring to a boil. Simmer, covered, 30 minutes.

2. Meanwhile, prepare the leeks. Trim off the rootlets and any coarse or withered green top ends. Slice into rounds 1 inch (2.5 cm) thick. Wash the cut pieces thoroughly to remove any dirt that often accumulates between the layers. You can slit a few of the outer layers to expose any soil. You can also soak them in a bowl of water for 5 or so minutes to draw out any remaining dirt.

3. Arrange leeks on top of the barley and make sure barley stays under the liquid. Simmer, covered, another 20 to 30 minutes or until both barley and leeks are tender.

4. To prepare the potatoes: Steam potatoes until tender, about 15 minutes. In medium skillet in hot oil, fry red chile until it is blackened. Add potatoes and cook over medium heat until richly browned, 5 to 8 minutes, turning often but gently to cook all sides. Remove from heat, discard red chile, and keep covered.

5. To thicken the sauce: Remove the vegetables and as much of the grains as possible with a slotted spoon, leaving the sauce in the casserole. Over medium heat, cook sauce, uncovered, for a few minutes until thick. Return the vegetables and grains to the skillet. Add the potatoes. Taste for salt. Remove from heat. Serve garnished with parsley and onion rings.

2 entrée or 4 to 6 side dish servings

Note 1: For best results use homemade Chicken Stock. If using canned chicken broth, which is already salted, adjust the amount of salt.

Note 2: Garnishing is essential to enhance the pale yellowish-green color of this dish.

Note for the Gardener: Chop some bright green leek tops and add to the dish for color. These tops also add flavor to soups of root vegetables such as potatoes or carrots.

Serving Suggestions: This makes a delicious presentation when accompanied by Fish Korma (page 108). Or go vegetarian by serving Peanutty Napa Cabbage (page 90) and Zippy Tomato Relish (page 228).

Pizzas and Tea Breads

·········· ······

During festive occasions when I was growing up in eastern India, the meal would consist of a rice pullao and elaborate flat breads. The rice would be served first with fish or vegetables. Flat breads came later as a delicious accompaniment to thick dal or meat sauces. "*Luchis* are coming," someone would yell. We would raise our eyes from the plate to see the arrival of small, dome-shaped breads, crispy and golden on the top, cooked just minutes before.

In the arid plains of northern or western India where wheat is the primary grain, flat breads are more common than rice and are served at most meals. One could travel to various localities in this area just to taste the different types of breads. Besides wheat, Indians use barley, millet, chick-peas, and occasionally grains that are not found elsewhere. A Gujarati man informed me that a typical lunch in his village consisted of coarse millet *roti* spread with peanut chutney, a side dish of yogurt, and a pickle. Simple though it was, he fondly remembered that lunch years later because of the robust taste of the bread.

Flat breads take well to a wide variety of chutneys, salsas, and condiments. Along with an assortment of fish, meat, or vegetable preparations and several sauces, my international table often features grilled tortillas, chapatis, or quick Western-style breads. My guests individualize their meal by spreading a sauce of choice on a piece of bread, then topping with one of the main ingredients.

But the ultimate flat breads are pizzas, a most universal food. Though pizzas originated in medieval Italy, practically any food can top a pizza—wild mushrooms, Kung Pao chicken, grilled vegetables, or meat. Although I have tasted many types of pizzas in restaurants, none has included the flavors of my youth. So I make "Indian" pizzas in my own kitchen.

My familiarity with flat bread preparation has helped. I may scatter my pizza crusts with cumin, kalonji, or green chiles. The sauce is zesty. Spiced vegetables or smoked curried fish adorn the top. Given the breadth of Indian cuisine, the possibilities for creating new pizza sauces and toppings are endless. Indian pizzas are great for entertaining because much of the preparation can be done ahead of time. They are also frivolous, fun, and a bit out of the ordinary.

On busy days, I bake quick bread substitutes such as biscuits, scones, and polenta. Indian cuisine doesn't include these types of breads but contains other similar savory and sweet breads. *Samosas*, triangular, deep-fried pastries stuffed with spicy potatoes or meat, are commonly served at teatime in India and appear on the menus of most Indian restaurants in the West as an appetizer. My favorite has always been the sweet version of *samosa*, a flaky-crusted dumpling filled with nutty, thickened milk and made only at home. The preparation is time-consuming, so instead I serve scones with a rich, gingery milk sauce, reminiscent of a sweet *samosa* stuffing. When in a mood for polenta with a different twist, I reach for gingerroot, asafetida, and cumin. These old Indian standbys transform the plain cornmeal squares into a savory bread, suitable for tea or a main meal.

More than many other dishes, basic foods like bread or pizza show the care and attention of the cook. The dough responds to a loving touch as if it were a living thing. The sauce must be chosen carefully to complement the bread's taste and texture without obscuring it. The ensemble should be served fresh out of the oven when the bread is at its peak in flavor, while the aroma of baking still permeates the home. This personal touch is what many of us crave, and that is why a meal featuring bread or pizza is so memorable. ✳

✳ Grilled Tortillas with Sauces ✳

MEXICO

You can have a fiesta anytime by serving ready-made flat breads topped with savory sauces and condiments. Grill or broil the sauced breads, then sprinkle liberally with freshly chopped aromatics—cilantro, scallions, and sweet onion.

1   package corn tortillas or whole wheat chapatis (see *Note*)

Sauces: (Choose from one or more below; look for other ideas in Chutneys, Sauces, and Dressings chapter)

> Cilantro Splash (page 223)
> Tamarind-Date Chutney (page208)
> Sun-Dried Tomato and Sweet Red Pepper Cream (page 226)
> Rustic Salsa Pasilla (page 214)

Some suggested condiments:

> Five Fundamental Seasonings (page 203)
> Sambal oeleck
> Chopped sweet onion
> Chopped scallions
> Chopped arugula
> Chopped peanuts

Spread each tortilla lightly but evenly with sauce. Grill or broil sauced side up, just until heated through, less than a minute. Longer broiling will harden the tortilla and burn the sauce. Sprinkle with a condiment of your choice, then roll like a burrito with the sauced face inside. Toothpick each piece so it holds together. Arrange on a large platter and serve with the remaining sauces and condiments on the side.

10 to 12 servings

Note: Supermarket flour tortillas often contain hydrogenated oil or preservatives, so I buy corn tortillas or chapatis instead.

Serving Suggestions: Accompany with grilled fish or meat at brunch; let the remaining sauces serve double purpose as a dip for the main ingredients. A large bowl of salad is all you'll need to satisfy your guests. For a quick evening meal that serves four to five, you can also fill the insides of the tortillas with steamed broccoli (sprinkled with lime juice) and grilled tofu before rolling. If you can find it, five-spice tofu makes for an interesting variation.

Pizza Pointers

✳ These spicy pizzas should not be overwhelmed with too much cheese, but a small amount sprinkled on top before baking can enhance them.

✳ When filling the pizza crust, leave the center underfilled; otherwise the pizza may become soggy.

✳ *To serve pizzas:* Serve these Indian pizzas as an appetizer at a main meal. Or serve as a main course with a green salad; a platter of raw vegetables such as red or yellow bell pepper, cauliflower, radishes, and sweet onion slivers; steamed vegetables such as asparagus, green beans, carrots, and broccoli; and grilled vegetables such as zucchini, eggplant, and tomatoes.

✳ Basic Pizza Dough ✳
INTERNATIONAL

Kalonji and jalapeño enliven this pizza crust.

2 teaspoons (10 ml) sugar

2/3 cup (160 ml) lukewarm water (110 to 115°F [40 to 45°C])

1 package (1/4-ounce [7-g]) quick-rise, active dry yeast

1 1/2 cups (375 ml) unbleached white flour plus additional flour for dredging

1 tablespoon (15 ml) olive oil

3/4 teaspoon (3 ml) salt

Canola oil for the bowl

1/2 teaspoon (2 ml) kalonji or cumin seeds

1 jalapeño, seeded, chopped (to taste)

Olive oil for the pizza pan and for brushing

Coarse cornmeal for dusting

1. Combine sugar and lukewarm water in a large, deep bowl, stirring until sugar dissolves. (For accuracy in reading the water temperature, use an instant thermometer or a meat thermometer.) Sprinkle yeast over this mixture. Stir gently to dissolve yeast and remove any lumps. Let stand in a warm place until a smooth, beige layer forms on top, about 5 minutes. This indicates that the yeast is working. (Be particularly careful that the water is at the right temperature and the yeast is fresh.)

2. Stir flour, olive oil, and salt into the yeast mixture. Beat vigorously with a wooden spoon until a dough forms. On a lightly floured board, knead for 10 to 12 minutes, adding a little more flour if necessary. The dough should be soft and slightly sticky.

3. Place dough in a deep warmed and lightly oiled bowl. Cover the bowl with a plastic wrap. Let dough rise in a warm, draft-free place, 75 to 85°F (25 to 30°C) until it has doubled in volume, 45 to 60 minutes. (If you don't have such a spot, turn the oven on to lowest heat for 5 minutes or so. Turn it off, check the temperature inside with a thermometer if possible, and wait until it reaches the desired degree of warmth. Do this ahead of time so that the oven will be heated when the dough is ready to rise. Place the bowl in the oven. Remove when it has doubled in volume.) While dough is rising, prepare the sauce of your choice from the recipes that follow.

4. Preheat oven to 500°F (240°C, gas marks 9). Generously oil a 12-inch (30-cm) pizza pan and sprinkle it with cornmeal. Punch the dough down. Roll out on a lightly floured board to a 12-inch (30-cm) round. Or roll dough out partially, then stretch it out with lightly floured hands. Fit into the pizza pan, pressing it up the sides. Sprinkle with kalonji and jalapeño. Prick all over with a fork. Brush the entire surface with olive oil. Let rest for another 5 to 10 minutes.

5. Ladle sauce over the crust, carefully avoiding the edges. (You may not need to use all of the sauce.) Sprinkle with cheese. Bake for 20 to 30 minutes or until the crust is crisp and nicely browned and the topping is piping hot. (Baking time may vary; start to check after 20 minutes and check frequently after that. Overbaking will harden the crust.) Consult each recipe for garnishing suggestions and serving sizes.

Using baking tiles for pizza: Ceramic tiles produce the crispiest crust. Following manufacturer's directions, place the tiles in the oven. Preheat the tiles for 1 hour. Place the pizzas on them and bake. Or follow this tip, which will cut down on cleaning: Fit a pizza pan with a piece of aluminum foil that is slightly larger than the pan. Oil the surface of the foil and crimp the edges to stand slightly higher than the edges of the pan itself. Now place the dough on this foil and complete the rest of Step 4. When ready to bake, wearing oven mittens, carefully lift the foil and the pizza off the pizza pan with both hands, and place on the hot tiles.

WHOLE WHEAT VARIATION: Use 1 cup (250 ml) unbleached white flour and ¹/2 cup (125 ml) whole wheat flour.

✳ Roasted Garlic, Sweet Red Pepper, ✳ and Squash Pizza

INTERNATIONAL

Pattypan or yellow crookneck squash, full of sweet natural juices, is perfect as a pizza topping during summer when you crave light fare. Turmeric and red chile paste give a slight Indian accent to this unusual pizza topping.

Basic Pizza Dough (page 189)

The sauce:

1	whole head of garlic
	Olive oil for sprinkling (optional)
4	large red bell peppers
1	tablespoon (15 ml) sambal oeleck (to taste; best if there is a slight hint of hotness)
1	tablespoon (15 ml) olive oil
1/2	cup (125 ml) finely chopped onion
1/4	teaspoon (1 ml) turmeric
4	ounces (100 g) Roma tomatoes, seeded, diced
1	cup (250 ml) diced pattypan or yellow crookneck squash (or zucchini)
1	tablespoon (15 ml) chopped arugula or cilantro
	Salt and freshly ground black pepper
1/4 to 1/2	cup (60 to 125 ml) your favorite hard cheese, grated (optional)

Garnish: Chopped cilantro

1. To roast the garlic head: Preheat oven to 450°F (230°C, gas marks 8). You can roast the garlic head as is, or optionally sprinkle it with olive oil before baking, which will impart a richer taste to the finished dish. To do so, chop off the top of the head of the garlic with a knife to expose the tops of the cloves. (You will lose a bit of flesh from each clove.) Drizzle a little olive oil over the cloves. Place the garlic head on an ungreased baking sheet and bake for 25 to 35 minutes or until soft to the touch. (The garlic will emit a strong aroma.) Check frequently and don't overbake as it can make the garlic bitter. When cool enough to handle, peel and discard the outer skin.

2. To roast the bell peppers: Broil the peppers for 5 to 7 minutes or until the skin is charred, turning it once or twice. Place the peppers in a paper bag and close the top.

Let stand for 10 minutes. Take the peppers out of the bag. When cool to the touch, peel and discard the skin, stem, seeds, and inner ribs. Chop the flesh coarsely.

3. Puree the roasted garlic and roasted bell peppers in a blender or food processor until smooth. Add sambal oeleck. If the mixture is too thick for the machine to puree, add a little water. The resulting mixture should be smooth and thick, but pourable.

4. Heat 1 tablespoon (15 ml) oil in a large skillet over moderate heat. Add onion and cook until it is translucent, about 2 minutes. Add the garlic-pepper puree and turmeric. Lower the heat, cover, and bring to a simmer. Add tomatoes and squash. Cover and simmer 3 to 5 minutes. Stir in arugula. Remove from heat. (The vegetables need not be completely done; they will be baked later.) Add salt and black pepper.

5. Assemble and bake pizza as described in Steps 4, 5, and 6 of Basic Pizza Dough, adding grated cheese if desired. Sprinkle the baked pizza with cilantro, cut with a pizza wheel or a knife, and serve immediately.

Makes one 12-inch (30-cm) pizza, 4 appetizer or 2 entrée servings

✳ Smoked Seafood and Shiitake Mushroom Pizza ✳

INTERNATIONAL

The smoky, earthy flavors of this pizza remind me of both spring and autumn in the Pacific Northwest, when the rain-soaked earth yields a bounty of wild mushrooms. Asafetida adds a new dimension to the woodsy flavor of the mushrooms.

	Basic Pizza Dough (page 189)
1	Anaheim chile

Tomato-Tamarind Sauce: (see *Note*)

1 1/2 to 2	tablespoons (22 to 30 ml) olive oil
1/2	teaspoon (2 ml) asafetida powder
1	medium onion, coarsely chopped
6 to 8	garlic cloves, coarsely chopped
1	pound (500 g) Roma tomatoes, peeled, seeded, chopped
1/2	cup (125 ml) chopped cilantro (or a combination of cilantro and fresh mint)

Salt
1 teaspoon (5 ml) tamarind concentrate
Honey-Glazed Onions (page 218)

The topping:

1 to 2 tablespoons (15 to 30 ml) canola oil, ghee, or butter (or a mixture of oil
and ghee)
1/4 teaspoon (1 ml) asafetida powder
5 large garlic cloves, slivered
4 ounces (100 g) fresh shiitake mushrooms (or reconstituted dried shiitake) or chanterelle mushrooms, woody stems removed, thinly sliced
1 tablespoon-plus (15 ml) canned chicken broth
1/2 cup (125 ml) mild red or other sweet onion, thinly sliced
Up to 4 ounces (100 g) smoked salmon or other smoked fish (trout,
cod, etc.)
4-ounce (100-g) can smoked mussels, drained
1/4 to 1/2 cup (60 to 125 ml) your favorite hard cheese, grated (optional)

Garnish: Chopped cilantro

1. To roast the chile: Broil for 6 to 10 minutes or until thoroughly charred. Place the chile in a paper bag and close the top. Let stand for 10 minutes. Take the chile out of the bag. When cool to the touch, peel and discard the skin, stem, seeds, and the inner ribs. Sliver the flesh.

2. To prepare Tomato-Tamarind Sauce: Heat oil in a large saucepan or steep-sided skillet over moderate heat. Sprinkle asafetida over oil. Add onion and garlic and cook until onion is translucent, about 2 minutes. Add tomatoes. Simmer, covered, 30 minutes. Process the mixture in a blender or food processor until smooth and creamy. Return mixture to the pan over low heat. Add cilantro, salt, and tamarind and stir until tamarind dissolves. Add the Honey-Glazed Onions and most of the Anaheim slivers (reserving a few for topping). Remove from heat.

3. To prepare the topping: Heat oil in a medium skillet over moderate heat. Sprinkle asafetida over the oil. Add garlic and cook until it is lightly browned. Add mush-rooms; stir gently to coat with the oil. Cook for 3 to 5 minutes, or until they soften a bit. Add chicken broth, a teaspoon (5 ml) at a time, if the bottom of the pan starts to become dry to avoid burning the mixture. Take off heat.

4. Assemble pizza as described in Step 4 of Basic Pizza Dough. When the pizza crust is ready, spread with the Tomato-Tamarind Sauce and layer with mushroom

mixture, onion, and smoked fish and mussels. Sprinkle on cheese if desired and follow Steps 5 and 6 of Basic Pizza Dough to bake. Scatter cilantro on top of the baked pizza, cut with a pizza wheel or a knife, and serve immediately.

Makes one 12-inch (30-cm) pizza, 4 appetizer or 2 entrée servings

Note: You can prepare this tasty sauce separately and use as you would any tomato sauce.

Other Pizza Sauce and Topping Ideas

You'll find additional ideas for pizza sauces and toppings in the following chapters: Pasta and Noodles; Fish and Seafood; Poultry and Meat; Chutneys, Sauces, and Dressings. Here are a few suggestions.

PEPPERY SQUID (page 122): Prepare up to Step 2. In Step 3, cook the squid for 5 to 8 minutes. Remove from heat. Spread sauce over pizza and bake. Don't overbake as squid will toughen.

UNIVERSAL VINDALOO (page 140): In preparing the recipe, cut the pork and vegetables into smaller sizes, 1/2-inch (1-cm) cubes. Since this vindaloo is not abundant with sauce, layer the crust with Tomato-Tamarind Sauce (page 192) or your favorite tomato sauce, top with the pork and vegetable mixture, then bake.

PASTA PUTTANESCA INTERNATIONAL (page 156): Spread this intense sauce (prepared without the noodles) over the crust. Top with a sautée of chopped onions, sliced fresh mushrooms, and red bell pepper strips before baking.

✻ Quick Indian Pizza ✻

INDIA

Papads or papadams, paper-thin, round lentil wafers, are an ideal meal starter when served with a chutney. These wafers can also act as a base for a quick pizza when layered with a sauce, sprinkled with a topping, then baked briefly. Purchase your favorite papad from an Indian grocery; Patira's Tastee brand, a rich, dense, somewhat flexible variety, works especially well as a mini-pizza.

1 dozen papads (see *Note*)

The sauces: (Choose one or more below or others from Chutneys, Sauces, and Dressings chapter; best if not watery)
 Tamarind-Date Chutney (page 208)
 Rustic Salsa Pasilla (page 214)
 Sweet and Hot Peanut-Lime Sambal (page 219)

The toppings:
 Shredded pecorino, Parmesan, or other hard cheese suitable for grating, or a
  soy cheese

One or more of the following:
 Minced mild red or other sweet onions
 Minced garlic
 Chopped cooked seafood or chicken meat
1 jalapeño, seeded, minced (a red one if available)

1. Preheat oven to 450°F (230°C, gas marks 8). Brush the surface of a papad lightly with a sauce. (Too much sauce will make it soggy.) Handle the papad very gently; it is brittle and cracks easily. Scatter with one of the topping ingredients. Place 3 to 4 papads, prepared this way, on an ungreased cookie sheet. Bake for 2 to 5 minutes or until crisp. Check often and don't let them burn. (Sauce each set of papads just before baking or else they might become limp.)

Makes 12 mini-pizzas, 4 small servings

Note: When buying papads, check the package carefully to ensure that they haven't been broken by rough handling.

Serving Suggestions: Exciting as an appetizer, especially before a vegetarian meal. For a tasty lunch, serve with Roasted Tikka Potatoes (page 243) and Honey Ginger Tea (page 292).

❋ Jalapeño-Rosemary Biscuits ❋

UNITED STATES

For spur-of-the moment entertaining or whenever you want to prepare fresh breads in a hurry, try this recipe. A small amount of cornmeal gives these chewy rounds a grainier texture and heartier taste than conventional biscuits. The flavor comes from fresh chiles, kalonji seeds, and rosemary. Another surprise ingredient is chapati flour, a soft wheat flour sold in Indian groceries and used to make flat breads. It lends itself well to this type of Western-style baking.

- 1 cup (250 ml) chapati flour (*atta*), or whole wheat pastry flour
- 1 cup (250 ml) unbleached white flour
- 1 tablespoon (15 ml) coarse cornmeal
- 2 teaspoons (10 ml) sugar
- 1/2 teaspoon (2 ml) salt
- 2 teaspoons (10 ml) baking powder
- 1/2 teaspoon (2 ml) baking soda
- 1 teaspoon (5 ml) fresh rosemary, or 1/2 teaspoon (1 ml) dried rosemary
- 1/4 teaspoon (1 ml) kalonji seeds
- 1 tablespoon (15 ml) chopped cilantro
- 1 teaspoon (5 ml) seeded and chopped jalapeño (use a red one if available)
- 2 teaspoons (10ml) canola oil
- 3/4 cup-plus (185 ml) lowfat buttermilk (don't substitute)

1. Preheat oven to 450°F (230°C, gas marks 8). Sift together the flours, cornmeal, sugar, salt, baking powder, and baking soda in a large bowl. Add rosemary, kalonji, cilantro, and jalapeño and mix until uniform. Make a well in the center and pour in oil and 3/4 cup buttermilk. Stir with a fork only until the ingredients are moistened and dough leaves the sides of the bowl. Add a little extra buttermilk if necessary. Turn onto a lightly floured board and knead lightly, about 15 strokes. Pat to a 1/2-inch (1-cm) thickness. Cut with a floured biscuit cutter. Gather up the rest of the dough to the same thickness and cut again as before. With any leftovers, prepare breadsticks. (See Spicy or Sweet Biscuitsticks Variation below.)

2. Place on an ungreased baking sheet, about 1 inch (2.5 cm) apart. Bake for 10 to 12 minutes or until a toothpick inserted in the center comes out clean. Immediately transfer to a serving platter.

Yields 8 biscuits plus a few biscuitsticks

Serving Suggestions: These spicy biscuits go well with any meal, particularly one that features fish or meat. Sop up the tasty sauce of Peppery Squid (page 122) or Kheema with Kale and Chinese Five-Spice (page 136). Or enjoy with Dream Yogurt (page 212). For an exotic mini-sandwich, slice a biscuit in half and fill with Sweet and Spicy Sancoche (page 68) and some alfalfa sprouts.

VARIATION: SWEET GINGER-FENNEL BISCUITS These aromatic biscuits can be served with a main meal or with Soy Chai (page 293) at breakfast or teatime. Omit kalonji, cilantro, and jalapeño, but add $1/2$ teaspoon (2 ml) fennel seeds and 1 teaspoon (5 ml) ginger powder. Increase the amount of sugar to $1/3$ cup (75 ml). Sprinkle the top with regular or maple sugar before baking. Use any leftover dough to make Sweet Biscuitsticks below.

VARIATION: SPICY OR SWEET BISCUITSTICKS For those who like to nibble on bread throughout a meal, these biscuitsticks are a daintier alternative. Use leftover dough pieces or reserve some specifically for this purpose. Roll them into "ropes" $1/2$ inch (1 cm) wide and 3 to 4 inches (7.5 to 10 cm) long. Brush the entire surface lightly with olive oil. Bake these sticks along with the biscuits for the same amount of time.

✳ Tea Scones with Ginger Kheer ✳

SCOTLAND

Scones are a favorite of my husband, so for years I have served a spicy version for breakfast, with tea, or as a snack. Instead of marmalades or clotted cream, I accompany them with *kheer* or *khoya*, creamy Indian sauce, made with lowfat milk. They taste utterly delicious this way and can be served as a light dessert as well. A cup of tea is an ideal mate, two good selections being green tea and orange spice tea.

$3/4$ cup (185 ml) unbleached white flour
$3/4$ cup (185 ml) whole wheat flour or chapati flour (*atta*; see *Note*)
  2 teaspoons (10 ml) baking powder
  1 tablespoon (15 ml) garam masala
$1/3$ cup (75 ml) sugar
  3 tablespoons (45 ml) canola oil
  2 large eggs or 4 egg whites, lightly beaten
$1/4$ to $1/3$ cup (60 to 75 ml) lowfat buttermilk (don't substitute)
$1/2$ cup (125 ml) chopped dried cranberries or raisins
    Ginger Kheer (page 287)

Preheat oven to 425°F (220°C, gas marks 7). Sift together the flours and baking pow-der in a large bowl. Add garam masala and sugar and mix until uniform. Add oil and stir with a fork until the mixture is mealy. Reserve 1 tablespoon (15 ml) of the eggs. Add the remaining eggs, 1/4 cup (60 ml) buttermilk, and cranberries to the dry ingre-dients. Stir until all ingredients are thoroughly mixed and hold together, adding the remaining buttermilk, a little at a time, if necessary. Pat into a circle about 3/4 inch (2 cm) thick. Cut into 8 wedges and place on a large, lightly oiled baking sheet, leav-ing about 1 inch (2.5 cm) of space between the pieces to allow for expansion during baking. Brush the wedges with remaining egg. Bake for 18 to 22 minutes or until richly browned. Serve with warmed Ginger Kheer.

Makes 8 scones

Note: Chapati flour makes light, delicious scones. Use slightly less buttermilk in this case.

VARIATION: TEA SCONES WITH GHEE-SCENTED MAPLE SYRUP Instead of (or along with) Ginger Kheer, serve the scones with a little of this rich syrup. Heat 1/4 cup (60 ml) pure maple syrup. When it comes to a bubble add 1 tablespoon (15 ml) ghee. Gently heat the mixture. Don't let it boil.

✳ Savory Indian Polenta ✳
ITALY/ROMANIA

Here polenta, the cornmeal pudding that is a staple in Italy and popular in Eastern Europe, is influenced by *dhoka* or *dhokla*, a spicy legume bar that Indian vegetarians love. The square or diamond-shaped *dhokla* come from the western Indian state of Gujarat, where vegetarian cooking has been elevated to an art form. The word *dhokla* means "to fool someone." The dish is so called because, although vegetarian, it has a meaty quality derived from a ground chick-pea batter that has been fermented. In Gujarat you'll find shops that specialize in *dhokla*. People line up as the shopkeeper lays out steaming trays of these savory cakes.

By preparing *dhokla* with cornmeal instead of chick-peas, I have eliminated the time-consuming process of grinding and fermentation. Yet by using the same season-ings, I can enjoy the spiciness that is the hallmark of *dhoklas*. All in all this is a good polenta dish that can be served in place of bread or grains in most meals.

The spice paste:

2 tablespoons (30 ml) coarsely chopped gingerroot

1 jalapeño, seeded, chopped (to taste)

$1/4$ cup (60 ml) water

$1/2$ teaspoon (2 ml) asafetida powder

$1/4$ teaspoon (1 ml) turmeric

1 teaspoon (5 ml) ground cumin

1 teaspoon (5 ml) ground coriander

1 teaspoon (5 ml) sugar

$3/4$ teaspoon (3 ml) salt

The polenta:

$1 1/2$ cups (375 ml) water

$1/2$ cup (125 ml) polenta (see *Note*)

2 tablespoons (30 ml) fresh lemon juice

$1/2$ cup (125 ml) chopped cilantro

$1/2$ teaspoon (2 ml) dried thyme

1 tablespoon (15 ml) Indian sesame oil (*gingely*), or canola oil

$1/2$ teaspoon (2 ml) black mustard seeds

1 tablespoon (15 ml) sesame seeds

Garnish:

Honey-Glazed Onions (page 218)

Chopped cilantro

Tomato-Tamarind Sauce (page 192) or your favorite tomato sauce (optional)

1. To prepare the spice paste: Process gingerroot, jalapeño, and $1/4$ cup (60 ml) water in a blender or food processor until relatively smooth. Transfer to a small bowl and add asafetida, turmeric, cumin, coriander, sugar, and salt.

2. To prepare polenta: Bring $1 1/2$ cups (375 ml) water to a boil in a large steep-sided pan or skillet. Add polenta gradually, stirring constantly. Add the spice paste. Cook, uncovered, stirring often, until the mixture becomes thick and forms a lump around the spoon, 12 to 30 minutes. (The timing will vary with the type of polenta.) Remove from heat. Add lemon juice, cilantro, and thyme.

3. Heat oil in a small 7-inch (17.5-cm) saucepan over moderate heat. Add mustard and sesame seeds and cook until the mustard seeds pop and the sesame seeds turn light brown. Hold cover (or a splatter screen) over the pan, otherwise the

seeds might splatter. Remove from heat and add to the polenta mixture. Adjust seasonings. You can serve polenta at this time as a savory pudding or go to Step 4 to let it set. To serve, mound it on the center of a serving plate, top with Honey-Glazed Onions and cilantro, and spoon a thin layer of tomato sauce all around the sides.

4. Optional: By allowing polenta to set, you can cut it into square or diamond shapes. Turn it out into a lightly oiled 8-inch (20-cm) square baking pan. Let rest in the refrigerator for an hour or until stiff. Preheat oven to 400°F (200°C, gas marks 6). Bake for 5 to 10 minutes or until thoroughly heated. Cut into desired shapes. Serve sprinkled with Honey-Glazed Onions and cilantro.

6 to 8 side dish servings

Note: Instant polenta cooks faster in Step 2 (about 5 minutes), but has a soft, mushy quality. Use regular polenta or yellow corn grits for a more solid texture.

Serving Suggestions: I like to offer this spicy polenta at a main meal with Sweet and Nutty Carrot-Turnip Soup (page 49) or Indian Chicken Soup (page 59). When cut into squares, it can be served as a tea bread accompanied by Mint-Basil Chutney (page 224) and a cup of *genmaicha* (green tea with roasted brown rice, sold in Asian markets). These polenta pieces are easy to transport, wrapped in several layers of aluminum foil, to a potluck, picnic, or hike. Spread a little chutney on top before packing.

Chutneys, Sauces, and Dressings

Once on the night of North India's most popular celebration of the year, *Diwali*, the Festival of Light, I was visiting Bombay. Chowpatty Beach, washed by the Arabian Sea, teemed with hungry people, and the food vendors did a brisk trade. One man, wearing a red scarf around his forehead, was outselling the others. His fare was basic and simple: thick round slices of boiled potatoes layered with a tangy yogurt sauce, topped with a spicy tamarind chutney and sprinkled with fragrant, roasted cumin seeds. *Alu chaat*, his finished dish, was tart, sweet, hot, and cooling all in the same mouthful. It was extraordinary. The sauces made it so.

Table sauces like chutneys, pickles, and fresh aromatics allow the diner a wide range of choices in mixing and matching flavors: sweet, sour, salty, pungent, or bitter, either singly or in combination. This is why Mexicans have their salsas and marinated jalapeños, Chinese their soy sauce and sesame oil, Americans their mustard and ketchup.

For those who wish to reduce their intake of fat, oil or butter can be wholly or partially replaced by intensely flavored condiments such as Chilied Mango Chutney or Mint-Tamarind Pesto when basting meat, dressing a salad or pasta, or filling dumplings.

In much of the world, condiments play a prominent role in peasant homes. The food is often sparse and lacks variety; as a result, people have come to depend on numerous simple sauces and pickles to add zest to their meals. Southeast Asian farmers eat mainly rice accompanied by vegetables and a few slivers of fish. A fresh chile, a spicy pickle, or a dash of fish sauce picks up the meal considerably.

Even elaborate fare can benefit from condiments. In the Netherlands I discovered the renowned Dutch Indonesian meal *rijstafel*, or rice table. The *rijstafel* comprises twenty or more small servings of fish, meat, and vegetables. The meal always includes a number of condiments, such as crushed roasted peanuts, shrimp chips, marinated vegetables, and shredded fresh coconut. The diners mix them with rice, sprinkle over vegetables, or use as a palate-cleanser between courses. They are an integral part of the meal.

Inspired by *rijstafel*, I now place a platter of simply prepared fish, meat, vegetables, or bread on the table surrounded by a multitude of condiments. Tarragon-Poached Chicken, for example, becomes irresistible when dipped into Sweet and Hot Peanut-Lime Sambal and scattered with chopped sweet onions. This book contains many other suggestions for enhancing your dining pleasure through the imaginative combination of condiments and main dishes.

In India, I ate onion, garlic, gingerroot, chile, and lime so often that I considered them essentials. Now I place these Five Fundamental Seasonings on the table for sprinkling over main or side dishes. Chutneys are another indispensable component of a meal in India, where people often finish their dinner with the highly seasoned taste of chutneys rather than a dessert. This is another reason why the serving suggestions throughout this book include one or more chutneys, salsas, or sauces as accompaniments.

Many traditional Indian sauces acquire a refreshingly new taste when combined with ingredients and techniques from other cultures. A tamarind chutney, for example, benefits from a dash of Southeast Asian fish sauce. Basil, which is considered sacred in India and not eaten, gives a fresh twist to the familiar mint chutney. When preparing a yogurt-based raita, I sometimes substitute roasted banana for raw banana to impart a rich mellowness.

In the course of developing the recipes for this book, condiments played a vital role either as ingredients or as accompaniments to the finished dishes at the table. Though their sources may be widespread, condiments speak a universal language. They bring the flavors of the world into any kitchen. ✳

Saucy Ideas

✴ The Serving Suggestions in this chapter include not only specific recipes but also more informal suggestions. You'll find these condiments referred to in the other chapters of this book as well.

✴ You can make these condiments ahead of time and refrigerate them for a few days. Allow them to come to room temperature before serving to bring out their flavor.

✴ Five Fundamental Seasonings ✴

INDIA

A small tray of onion, gingerroot, garlic, green chile, and lime can usually be found on my table at mealtime. These aromatics impart an interesting new accent to fish, meat, and vegetable dishes when sprinkled according to taste.

1/4 cup (60 ml) finely chopped mild red or other sweet onion
2 tablespoons (30 ml) minced garlic
2 tablespoons (30 ml) minced gingerroot
1 jalapeño, seeded, chopped (see *Note*)
   Lime or lemon wedges

Place each item in an individual bowl or saucer and let the diners help themselves.

4 small servings

Note: In the West, fresh green chiles are usually cooked or processed with other ingredients. In India, however, whole or chopped fresh green chile is as common a sight on the table as a salt shaker in the West. Indians often mash small bits of chile into a dal or a vegetable preparation during dining. Chiles impart fieriness and a clean taste to a dish. They are also rich in vitamins.

VARIATION: OTHER SPICY IDEAS At the table you can also provide chopped sun-dried tomatoes, slivered Kalamata olives, nori, soy sauce, fish sauce, Chinese sesame oil, sambal oeleck (or red chile paste), and chile oil.

❋ Leaf Scoops ❋
SOUTHEAST ASIA

They say that old habits die hard. At dinnertime I look for something to scoop food with, the way I used chapatis in my childhood. A new option for me is leafy greens. The custom comes from Southeast Asia, where vendors encase tasty shrimp or vegetable fillings in lettuce-like leaves, rolling them like a burrito. Adapting this technique, I now serve an assortment of leafy greens at the table to scoop up bits of spiced vegetable, fish, or meat.

Crispy, crunchy, semirigid romaine leaves make a sturdy base and are among the most nutritious of all lettuce. Spinach and Napa cabbage also work well. Combine a variety of leaves as well as seaweed for a multiflavored scoop; for instance, top a Napa cabbage leaf with mint, cilantro, or strips of slightly bitter arugula, followed by a butterhead lettuce leaf and a sheet of toasted, seasoned nori.

You can use flat bread such as pita for a "scoop inside a scoop." Start with the pita, then arrange some leaves in layers within the pocket.

Note for the Gardener: Japanese shiso (perilla) or edible chrysanthemum leaves could be part of the tray as well.

Serving Suggestions: Create an international food experience by serving a platter of grilled or barbecued fish, meat, and vegetables, and leaf scoops as described below.

Grilled lamb, chicken, or beef served with Five Fundamental Seasonings (page 203) and Roasted Banana Raita (page 210): Recommended greens are mint, cilantro, Napa cabbage, romaine, and arugula.

Grilled shrimp or fish partnered with chopped cilantro, Five Fundamental Seasonings (page 203), lime juice, and fish sauce: Recommended greens are butterhead or red leaf lettuce, arugula, and shiso leaves. Warmed chapatis or tortillas will also go well in this case.

Grilled vegetables (zucchini, tomato, tofu, eggplant, onion) teamed with sambal oeleck, Five Fundamental Seasonings (page 203), and Chilied Mango Chutney (page 205): Recommended greens are cilantro, any type of lettuce, and arugula. For a portable snack, wrap some softened rice papers around the vegetables. See "To soften rice paper for wrapping" (page 251).

✳ Chilied Mango Chutney ✳

SOUTH INDIA

As a fruit, a mango is unparalleled; as a cooking ingredient, it is versatile. When green, it can be dried into a tart powder known as *aamchoor*. When fully ripe, it can be simmered with thickened milk to form an ambrosial pudding, or tossed with hot chiles to form a spicy sweet chutney as in the recipe that follows.

Unlike most mango chutneys, which are highly spiced, this version is seasoned lightly in the South Indian manner with black mustard seeds and curry leaves and is sweetened gently. Use fresh mangoes, not canned, when preparing this chutney; the taste is far superior.

4 to 5	medium-sized ripe mangoes
2	teaspoons (10 ml) canola oil
$^1/_4$	teaspoon (1 ml) asafetida powder
$^1/_4$	teaspoon (1 ml) black mustard seeds
6 to 8	curry leaves, torn into small pieces
1	small jalapeño, finely chopped (to taste; retain a few seeds for a hint of hotness)
$^3/_4$	teaspoon (3 ml) salt
2	teaspoons (10 ml) sugar (adjusted according to the sweetness of the mango)

1. Peel and slice off the flesh of the mangoes and discard the pits. Dice the flesh into sugar-cube–sized pieces. They should measure about 4 cups (1 liter).
2. Heat oil in a small or medium skillet over moderate heat. Sprinkle asafetida over the oil. Add mustard seeds and curry leaves and fry until the seeds pop. (You may need to cover the skillet partially for a few seconds to prevent the seeds from flying out.) Add mango pulp, jalapeño, salt, and sugar. Cook, covered, for a few minutes to heat the mixture through. Taste for sweetness and, if necessary, add more sugar. The sauce should be fiery-hot and pleasantly sweet. Adjust the seasoning. Remove from heat. Serve warm or at room temperature. It will keep in the refrigerator for 2 to 3 days.

6 to 8 servings

Serving Suggestions: This versatile chutney is a welcome adddition to any meal. It goes particularly well with Saffron-Scented Millet (page 172), with pork or legume dishes, and over rice. Served with Karhi-Sauced Penne (page 154), it makes a good lunch. Spread this chutney also over papads or between the layers of a sandwich.

✳ Green Mango Chutney ✳

INDIA

Every part of the mango tree is revered in India. The large, sprawling branches shade people from the burning summer sun. The ripe, nutritious fruit is practically a staple during the intense heat of the Indian summer, when many lose their taste for heavier food. The mango leaf has been exalted in ancient Indian writing: "Her skin glistened like a mango leaf does in the morning dew."

As a child, I enjoyed young green mangoes eaten raw, adding a pinch of salt to counteract the tartness. Another use for green mango is as a chutney ingredient. They make a subtle spicy chutney that goes well with fish or grains. You can buy them, either fresh or in jars, in Asian (particularly Thai and Vietnamese) markets.

Prepare this easy chutney also with semiripe or ripe mangoes. Just adjust the amount of sugar so the finished dish is lightly sweetened.

2   medium-sized green mangoes or a 12-ounce (drained weight) (326-g) jar of
     green mangoes
2   teaspoons (10 ml) mustard oil or canola oil
1   whole dried red chile
1/4 teaspoon (1 ml) Indian five-spice
1/4 teaspoon (1 ml) turmeric
1   tablespoon (15 ml) sugar
1/4 teaspoon (1 ml) salt

1. If using fresh mangoes, peel, slice off the flesh, and discard the pits. Dice the flesh into sugar-cube–sized pieces. If using mangoes from a jar, drain and cube the pulp.
2. Heat oil over moderate heat in a large skillet. Add red chile and five-spice and fry for a few seconds. Sprinkle turmeric over the spices. Stir in mangoes. Simmer, covered, until mangoes are tender to the bite but not mushy, 10 to 12 minutes. Add sugar and salt. Remove from heat. Let stand, covered, for 15 minutes. Serve at room temperature. It will keep in the refrigerator for 2 to 3 days.

4 small servings

Serving Suggestions: This chutney can be served with any meal but is particularly good with one that features seafood. Some good entrée choices are Fish Korma (page 108), Velvet Fish (page 111), and Vietnamese Salmon Burrito (page 251).

✳ Prune and Date Chutney ✳

THE MIDDLE EAST

In an Arabian-nights type story I read as an adolescent, the heroine sat in her garden pining for her lost lover, nibbling on dried dates and plums as a warm, dry breeze blew. He came back and the story had a happy ending. Ever since then dried fruits have stayed in my mind as a symbol of romance.

Dried fruits were the food of royalty in India centuries ago. They are pricey even now and a luxury for us commoners. You can use them to make fine chutneys. When bathed in a sauce they plump up, their intense taste mellowing as they simmer. Dates impart a rich sweetness that you can't achieve by using sugar alone.

$^1/_2$ cup (125 ml) pitted prunes, soaked in 1 cup (250 ml) hot water in a small
      bowl for 30 minutes or longer
1   tablespoon (15 ml) mustard oil or canola oil
2   whole dried red chiles
$^1/_2$ teaspoon (2 ml) black mustard seeds
3   large cloves garlic, forced through a garlic press
$^1/_4$ pound (100 g) tomato, 2 medium Roma or $^1/_2$ a regular tomato, seeded,
      sliced (see *Note 1*)
1   jalapeño, seeded, chopped (to taste)
1   teaspoon (5 ml) ground cumin (see *Note 2*)
$^1/_2$ teaspoon (2 ml) salt
$^3/_4$ cup (375 ml) prune soaking liquid or water
1   teaspoon (5 ml) sugar
    Ground red pepper (to taste; start with a scant pinch)
$^1/_4$ cup (60 ml) pitted chopped dates (or a combination of 2 tablespoons [30 ml]
      pitted chopped dates and 2 tablespoons [30 ml] raisins)
1   tablespoon (15 ml) fresh lemon juice

1. Drain the prunes, reserving the soaking liquid. Chop the prunes coarsely and set them aside.
2. Heat oil in a skillet over moderate heat. Fry red chiles and black mustard seeds until the mustard seeds start popping. Add garlic and cook, stirring often, until it is richly browned but not burnt, about 2 minutes.
3. Add tomato, jalapeño, cumin, salt, and soaking liquid. Simmer, covered, 2 to 3 minutes or until tomatoes are tender. Stir in sugar, red pepper, dates, and prunes.

Simmer, covered, another 5 to 7 minutes. Uncover and stir once during this period, mashing the fruits and tomato with the back of a spoon to mix with the sauce. Taste for sugar. Remove from heat and add lemon juice. Let stand, covered, for a few minutes to help thicken the sauce and develop its flavors further. Discard red chiles. Serve immediately or at room temperature. It will keep in the refrigerator for 2 to 3 days.

4 small servings

Note 1: For best results, toast and grind ¹/₂ teaspoon (2 ml) cumin seeds just before using. Their rich, roasted flavor goes particularly well with this chutney.

Note 2: I don't peel the tomatoes; their skin forms a color pattern in an otherwise dark chutney. You can peel them if you like for a smoother texture.

Serving Suggestions: Excellent as a companion to seafood, poultry, and mixed vegetable dishes such as Soy- and Mirin-Glazed Salmon (page 99), Lime-Grilled Chicken (page 125), or Sweet and Spicy Sancoche (page 68). Also goes well with brown rice or other cooked grains.

✳ Tamarind-Date Chutney ✳
INDIA

Most traditional tamarind chutney recipes require soaking a block of tamarind in water and extracting the sour pulp. Once when pressed for time, I used the ready-to-use tamarind concentrate and found the result to be just as tasty but much quicker. In this blender-made version, dates help reduce the amount of sugar, and fish sauce, the ubiquitous Southeast Asian condiment, adds depth.

- 2 tablespoons (30 ml) tamarind concentrate
- 4 pitted dates, finely chopped
- ¹/₂ cup (125 ml) water
- ¹/₂ teaspoon (2 ml) ground cumin (see *Note*)
- 2 tablespoons (30 ml) sugar
- ¹/₂ teaspoon (2 ml) salt
- ¹/₂ teaspoon (2 ml) fish sauce

Place all the ingredients in a blender container. Whirl until smooth. Add more sugar if necessary for a mostly sour and mildly sweet taste. Serve immediately or store in a nonmetallic container in the refrigerator. It will last for 2 to 3 days.

Yields ²/₃ cup (150 ml)

Note: For best flavor, roast ¹/₄ teaspoon (1 ml) cumin seeds and grind just before using.

Serving Suggestions: This sauce is most useful; it stimulates your palate and enlivens plain vegetables, cooked chicken, or grains. It's excellent as a dip for crackers and corn chips. Brush a little on pita bread or papads when using either as a mini-pizza crust. Serve also with Leeks and Barley with Glazed Onions and Rosemary (page 184).

* Onion Yogurt Relish *

SOUTH INDIA/CHINA

In South India, Hindu wedding feasts follow the long tradition of vegetarian dishes. A South Indian man, who had invited more than a thousand people to his daughter's wedding, told me whispering with glee that he had kept to the tradition because "it's also economical." South Indian wedding meals are generally served on individual banana leaves. The first course is a small confection such as *jelabi* (a sweet pretzel) or a *laddoo* (a small, sweet ball made of coconut or lentils). Servers walk in procession, placing the remaining nine or so courses each on banana leaves in front of guests: assorted pickles; six or more vegetable preparations; *pachadi*, a saucy salad; and finally rice pudding.

Onion *pachadi* is both an everyday dish and a wedding condiment. It's similar to raita, a yogurt-based salad from North India, but has the distinction of having coconut as a flavorer. This recipe has a Chinese flair that comes from a touch of fragrant Szechuan pepper.

    1   cup (250 ml) plain nonfat yogurt, lightly beaten until smooth
        Salt
    1   teaspoon (5 ml) grated gingerroot
  ¹/₂   small jalapeño, finely chopped
    1   tablespoon (15 ml) finely chopped cilantro
    1   tablespoon (15 ml) dried sweetened flaked coconut

1 to 1 1/2   tablespoons (15 to 22 ml) Indian sesame oil (*gingely*), or canola oil
    1/4   teaspoon (1 ml) black mustard seeds
    1   medium onion, finely chopped
    1/4   teaspoon (1 ml) ground Szechuan pepper

1. Combine yogurt, salt, ginger, jalapeño, cilantro, and coconut in a large bowl.
2. Heat oil in a small skillet over moderate heat. Sauté black mustard seeds until they start to crackle. Add onion and fry until it is translucent and soft but still has a little crunch. Remove from heat and add to the yogurt mixture. Sprinkle Szechuan pepper on top. Refrigerate for 30 minutes. Serve chilled. Will keep in the refrigerator for a day or two.

4 small servings

Serving Suggestions: Enjoy time and again with any main course. Some suggestions are Fragrant Fish Pullao (page 103), Tarragon-Poached Chicken with Sauces (page 128), Shrimp-Scented Cabbage (page 92), and Gujarati Potato Boats (page 64).

✳ Roasted Banana Raita ✳

INDIA/THE CARIBBEAN

In this raita, the gentle sweetness of banana and coconut contrasts with the heat of green chile. For a taste variation, I first roast the banana in the Caribbean style, which creates in the fruit a rich mellowness that is utterly delicious.

This salad can be served anytime during the year, but I find it especially refreshing on a hot day.

    1   large, very ripe unpeeled banana
    1/4   cup (60 ml) dried, sweetened flaked coconut, ground to a coarse powder in a blender or food processor
    1   cup (250 ml) plain nonfat yogurt
    1   jalapeño, seeded, finely chopped (to taste; see *Note*)
    1/4   teaspoon (1 ml) salt

1   teaspoon (5 ml) mustard oil
1   whole dried red chile
$^1/_2$ teaspoon (2 ml) black mustard seeds

Garnish: Hungarian sweet paprika

1. To roast the banana: Place the unpeeled fruit on a cookie sheet lined with aluminum foil. Bake in a 350°F (180°C, gas marks 4) oven for 10 to 15 minutes or until deep brown in color, turning it once halfway through. Don't overbake, as banana juice will start to ooze out. Remove from the oven and allow to cool to room tempearture. Peel the banana and chop the flesh finely. Reserve any accumulated juice.

2. In a medium bowl combine coconut, yogurt, jalapeño, and salt. Add banana flesh and any accumulated juice and stir gently.

3. Heat oil in a small 6-inch (15-cm) skillet over moderate heat. Add red chile and fry until it blackens. Add black mustard seeds. As soon as the seeds start to pop, remove from heat. Discard red chile. Pour the remaining oil and spice blend over the yogurt mixture and stir. Refrigerate for at least 30 minutes to allow the flavor to develop further. Sprinkle paprika on top (making a crisscross design on the surface if you like). Serve lightly chilled. Will keep for a day or two in the refrigerator.

4 small servings

Note: This salad tastes best when fiery-hot, so use a little more jalapeño than usual or incorporate a few of the seeds.

Serving Suggestions: Goes well with grain and vegetable dishes. Some suggestions are Barley, Wild Rice, and Azuki Beans Khichuri (page 181); Curried Quinoa, Olive, and Romaine Salad (page 179); and Spicy Seoul Cucumber (page 76).

FRESH BANANA ALTERNATIVE: If time does not allow you to roast the banana, use it fresh to prepare a quicker raita. Thinly slice a medium-sized ripe banana crosswise and add to the yogurt mixture toward the end of Step 2 after the oil and spices have been incorporated. Serve immediately or chilled.

✳ Dream Yogurt ✳

NORTH INDIA

To me yogurt is not just a snack. It's a side dish or a sauce that goes beautifully with vegetables, grains, or legumes. Quite often, it has led me to interesting places. While living in Iran, I ate yogurt daily along with freshly made flat bread. Even the poorest peasant there could afford this nourishing snack.

But the yogurt that has stayed freshest in my memory is the one I had in Chandigarh, a young city in North India built after India's independence in 1947. In an obscure shopping area, I found a small snack shop run by a tall, impassive, turbaned Sikh with a flowing white beard who looked peaceful and ancient, like someone from another era. After he served me, he sat by the door and resumed reading from his holy book almost in a murmur. I munched on the vegetable fritters and tasted the accompanying sauce—homemade, sweet, dense yogurt with a buttery layer on top, so thick you almost had to cut it with a knife. The yogurt had a rich, dreamy quality and each spoonful dissolved sensuously on my palate. I wanted another helping but wasn't about to disturb the old man. Just then, he raised his eyes and without my asking got up to bring me another plate of yogurt. I ate the second helping slowly, wondering if it was the quality of the milk, the fermentation technique, or his spirit that made it so tasty. Or was it all of those things?

Using commercial yogurt, you can drain out the water and prepare a thickened version that can be used as a delicious side dish or sauce or as a dip for papads.

  1   cup (250 ml) plain lowfat or nonfat yogurt
  1   tablespoon to $^1/_4$ cup (15 to 60 ml) regular sugar, turbinado sugar, or sucanat
       (to taste; see *Note*)
$^1/_2$ teaspoon (2 ml) ground ginger
$^1/_4$ teaspoon (1 ml) ground cardamom

Combine yogurt, sugar, ginger, and cardamom in a medium bowl and stir with a fork. Place the mixture in a large sieve lined with several layers of cheesecloth to drain out the water. (You can also use a gadget called Yogurt Strainer, which is a fine sieve, available in kitchen shops.) Cover the top with a piece of plastic wrap. Put the sieve over the rim of a deep bowl in such a way that the sieve bottom is raised above the bottom of the bowl. Let rest in the refrigerator at least overnight or up to 36 hours. Transfer yogurt to a medium bowl, beat lightly with a fork, and serve as a savory sauce. Use the small amount of nutrient-rich water (whey) that has collected at the bottom of the bowl in preparing soups or fruit juice blends.

2 servings

Note: The sugar is added to offset the tartness of plain yogurt and should be barely noticeable. Since each brand of yogurt is different, adjust the amount of sweetener accordingly.

SWEET VARIATION: The combination of maple syrup, lime juice, and balsamic vinegar makes an interesting topping for this thickened yogurt when serving as a light dessert.

- 1 tablespoon (15 ml) maple syrup
- 2 tablespoons (30 ml) fresh lime juice
- 1/2 teaspoon (2 ml) balsamic vinegar

Combine the topping ingredients in a small bowl. At the table, drizzle over Dream Yogurt decoratively. (Don't stir it in before serving as it will darken the yogurt.)

PICKLED VARIATION: The custom of adding pickles to yogurt comes from Eastern Europe. Omit the sugar and spices in this case. Add a small amount of finely chopped pickle of your choice to the thickened yogurt. My favorite is lime or mango pickle, sold in Indian groceries.

✳ Salsa Maharaja ✳

MEXICO

Salsa in Mexico is a sauce or relish. Mexicans have a bowl of salsa on the table at all times. They spread salsa over eggs, beans, and sliced pork or beef. They roll it into their tacos or dip a tortilla in it before eating. They baste chicken with salsa before cooking.

To me salsas are the Mexican equivalent of chutney and I frequently place them next to Indian dishes. This particular Mexican sauce, *salsa cruda* or uncooked salsa, is a mélange of chopped tomatoes, chiles, onion, and cilantro. The seasonings of cumin, lime, and tamarind give it a richer, more complex flavor. I also use vinegar for tartness. Different vinegars will impart a different overall taste. For example, balsamic vinegar, which is aged longer than other vinegars, is warm and powerful; rice vinegar is mild and gentle.

This Indian-influenced salsa would please a maharaja, a great king.

1   pound (500 g) Roma tomatoes, about 5 medium, peeled, seeded, and finely
       chopped
¼   cup (60 ml) minced red or other mild onion
1   tablespoon (15 ml) minced garlic
2   teaspoons (10 ml) balsamic or rice vinegar
1½ tablespoons (22 ml) fresh lime juice
½   teaspoon (2 ml) ground cumin
¼   teaspoon (1 ml) salt
2   tablespoons (30 ml) chopped cilantro
1   tablespoon (15 ml) tamarind puree (see "To prepare tamarind puree," page
       18; preferred; or use 1½ teaspoons (7 ml) tamarind concentrate, adjusted
       according to taste)

Combine all the ingredients in a large bowl. Cover and chill in the refrigerator for at least 2 hours. Will keep in the refrigerator for a few days.

Yields about 2 cups (500 ml)

✳ Rustic Salsa Pasilla ✳
MEXICO

I've always been fascinated by the varieties of dried chiles available in Latin American markets, such as pasilla, árbol, and chipotle. The long thin pasilla pods (also called chile negro) have a wrinkled black skin. I was warned by a storekeeper that they possess a scorching flavor and need to be treated with respect. I wanted to know more about them, so I asked Gela Gibbons, a Mexican friend. She laughed a bit wickedly and said, "Allow me to introduce it to you." I knew I was in for a surprise.

I braved my way to Gela's house one day after she had promised to share with me her family salsa recipe. She taught me to temper the chile with tomatoes and orange juice. She had another secret: chicken bouillon powder. The resulting sauce had a rich, deep brown color, was hot to the taste, and had a pleasant fruity overtone.

I later introduced a dash of cumin to give this sauce even more character.

7	dried pasilla chiles or a mixture of chiles (see *Note 1*)
1/2	cup (125 ml) frozen concentrated orange juice, thawed
1	large garlic clove, coarsely chopped
1	tablespoon (15 ml) finely chopped onion
1/2	pound (250 g) vine-ripened tomatoes or 2 canned tomatoes (see *Note 2*)
1/4	teaspoon (1 ml) salt
1/2	teaspoon (2 ml) chicken bouillon powder
1/8	teaspoon (0.5 ml) ground cumin
1/4	cup (60 ml) water

1. On an ungreased griddle over a low flame, lightly toast the chiles until they soften and exude a pungent aroma. Watch carefully and don't let them burn, as they will turn bitter. Soak them in a bowl of hot water for 20 to 30 minutes or until very soft. (If not thoroughly softened, they will not blend properly in the next step.)
2. Remove and discard the stems, seeds, and inner ribs. Place the flesh and the remaining ingredients in a blender. Blend until a smooth sauce results. Serve immediately or, better yet, allow to stand in the refrigerator for 2 hours to develop flavor. Bring to room temperature before serving. Will keep in the refrigerator for a few days.

Yields 1 1/2 cups (375 ml)

Note 1: Since pasilla chile used alone can make this dish very hot, I substitute half the amount with other milder dried chiles such as ancho.

Note 2: I find that unless the tomatoes are vine-ripened they don't produce as good a result as the canned ones. Use Italian-style canned tomatoes.

Serving Suggestions: Serve in a bowl accompanied by papads or corn chips or alongside a main meal, especially one that features pork. Spread over poached eggs or on the inside of an omelet. I particularly like this salsa over brown rice.

✳ Roasted Tomato-Chile Salsa ✳

MEXICO

Broiled tomatoes give this salsa a rich, mellow flavor. Roasted chiles add a kick and asafetida an Indian touch.

1 to 4　whole dried red chiles (see *Note*)
3/4　pound (375 g) vine-ripened tomatoes or Roma tomatoes
1/2　cup (125 ml) coarsely chopped onion
3　large garlic cloves, coarsely chopped
1　tablespoon (15 ml) chopped cilantro
1/4　teaspoon (1 ml) asafetida powder
1/2　teaspoon (2 ml) ground cumin
1/4　teaspoon (1 ml) sugar
　　Salt

1. Roast the chiles on an ungreased skillet over low heat until they blacken and give off a pungent aroma. Remove from heat and allow to cool to room temperature. Discard the seeds and inner membranes, and chop the flesh coarsely.

2. To roast the tomatoes: Place the tomatoes on an ungreased baking sheet and broil for 8 to 12 minutes or until the skin is charred and the body looks shrunken. Remove from the broiler and allow to cool to room temperature. Place the tomatoes and any accumulated juice in the container of a blender or food processor along with onion, garlic, cilantro, asafetida, cumin, and sugar. Process until smooth. Add the roasted chiles, a small amount at first, and whirl again. Taste for hotness and add more chile if necessary. This salsa should be slightly hot. Add salt. Serve immediately or, better yet, store in the refrigerator for 2 hours to develop the flavor further. Bring back to room temperature before serving. Will keep in the refrigerator for a few days.

Yields over 1 cup (250 ml)

Note: Use the slender red cayenne-type chiles, sold in supermarkets and in Asian and Latin American markets.

Serving Suggestions: Excellent over steamed vegetables such as potatoes, zucchini, or broccoli. Or spread on a warmed tortilla, sprinkle with chopped chicken or steamed broccoli, and roll like a burrito. Drizzle over cooked pasta; it is particularly good over ravioli. Can be an accompaniment to a legume dish such as Hearty Lentils and Udon (page 160) or Chick-pea Ragout (page 56). Also good over grilled fish, chicken, pork, or beef.

✳ Roasted Chile Slivers ✳
MEXICO

These roasted chiles with their sweet, smoky, and hot flavors perk up an ordinary meal. Use them as a condiment at the table or to top a potato salad or a vegetable preparation. Puree them with a little olive oil and use as a sauce for pasta or grains. Use milder, larger stuffing chiles such as Anaheim for this dish.

6 to 8   Anaheim chiles, also known as California chiles (see *Note for the Gardener*)
         Chaat Powder (page 8; optional)

1. Follow one of the three methods below.

   Stove-top smoker method: If you have a stove-top smoker, follow manufacturer's directions to smoke the chiles.

   Stove-top toasting method: Place the chiles on an ungreased griddle or skillet over low heat. Cook until the skin is charred, turning them several times. This is a more energy-efficient method than broiling.

   Broiler method: Broil them for 6 to 10 minutes or until thoroughly charred. The smoky flavor will be more pronounced than in the toasting method.

2. Place the charred chiles in a paper bag and close the top. After 10 or so minutes, remove them and peel off the skin. Discard skin, seeds, inner ribs, and any charred flesh. Cut the remaining flesh into thin slivers. Dust with Chaat Powder.

4 small servings

Note for the Gardener: Hungarian Hot Wax is a hot (but not overwhelmingly so) stuffing pepper with a smooth yellow skin that I sometimes substitute for Anaheim in this dish.

✳ Honey-Glazed Onions ✳

INDIA

In North India, brown-fried onion is a rich garnish for elaborate pullaos, dals, and meat dishes. This tasty topping enhances many other dishes on my international table and also serves as a side dish or condiment. It is particularly good over roasted eggplant and can be tossed with cooked grains or scrambled eggs.

1 tablespoon (15 ml) olive oil
2 cups (500 ml) mild red or other sweet onion, sliced 1/4 inch to 1/2 inch
     (6 mm to 1 cm) thick (see *Note*)
1/2 teaspoon (2 ml) honey

For this you'll need a small, 7-inch (17.5-cm) or similar sized nonstick skillet or saucepan. (With a pan of this size, you'll need less oil.) Heat oil over moderate heat until a light haze forms. Add onion and cook, stirring often, for 5 to 7 minutes, or until onion starts to turn brown. Adjust heat to prevent burning. Add honey. Continue to cook until the onion turns rich brown in color, a few more minutes, stirring often. Remove from heat and turn it out on a plate.

4 garnish or 2 side dish servings

Note: For serving over dal or vegetables, these onions look best when thinly sliced. For use as a topping for meat dishes, wider slices are more appropriate. If sweet onion is not available, use regular yellow onion. Because these onions are drier, you might need a little more oil.

VARIATION: GLAZED ONION-GARLIC MEDLEY Add 5 medium cloves of garlic, cut in thin slivers, after the onion has cooked for about 3 minutes. Follow the rest of the recipe. Stir often to make sure garlic doesn't burn.

✳ Sweet and Hot Peanut-Lime Sambal ✳

EAST ASIA

You could travel all over East Asia exploring different types of peanut sauce. Soy sauce is the predominant flavor in one from China, while coconut milk enlivens a Malaysian sauce. Usually the sauce ingredients are simply combined, but in Singapore they are heated together for a more refined effect.

This cooked peanut sauce, which is from India, is soy and coconut free but rich in lime, garlic, and black salt. An extra dab of red pepper adds fire.

The word *sambal* is in the vocabulary of many Indians and Southeast Asians, and is now heard in a number of other countries as well. *Sambal* means a sauce, a condiment, or in some instances, a salad. I grew up knowing *sambal* to be a highly spiced relish that excites the palate.

1/2 cup (125 ml) peanut butter (see *Note 1*)
1/2 cup (125 ml) water
2 teaspoons (10 ml) canola oil
1/4 teaspoon (1 ml) asafetida powder
1 tablespoon (15 ml) minced garlic
1/4 teaspoon (1 ml) black salt
2 teaspoons (10 ml) sugar
   Ground red pepper (to taste; start with a scant pinch; best if there is a hint of hotness)
   Salt (optional)
1/4 cup (60 ml) fresh lime juice (see *Note 2*)

Place peanut butter in a medium bowl. Add water gradually, stirring with a fork until smooth. Heat oil in a medium skillet over moderate heat. Sprinkle asafetida over the oil. Add garlic and fry until it is lightly browned. Add peanut butter mixture, black salt, sugar, and red pepper; stir. Lower the heat slightly. Cook for a few minutes to thicken the sauce a bit more. Take off heat. Taste for salt. Add lime juice. The sauce should have a gently sweet, fiery-hot, and limey flavor. Let stand, covered, for a few minutes to help develop the flavor and thicken the sauce more. Serve warm or at room temperature. Will keep in the refrigerator for a few days.

Yields over 1 cup (250 ml)

Note 1: Choose a brand that is made only with peanuts or buy freshly ground peanut butter from natural-food stores. Although peanut butter is easier to use, I sometimes roast ¹/₄ cup (60 ml) raw, red-skinned peanuts in a 350°F (180°C, gas marks 4) oven for 15 to 18 minutes or until chewy and slightly darker in color, and then grind them in a blender. These freshly roasted nuts are simply more flavorful. Their skin provides extra nutrients and a slightly pinkish tint to the sauce.

Note 2: Lemon can be substituted for lime but will not provide as rich or complex a flavor.

Serving Suggestions: This sambal perks up the flavors of a roasted acorn or butternut squash; steamed potatoes and green beans; and sautéed or steamed leafy greens (Swiss chard, fresh spinach, kale). Use as a dressing for Piquant Salad in Shades of Green (page 258). Serve over grilled fish or grilled chicken breasts. Spread it over cooked pasta or on crackers and papads.

✳ Peanuts, Seaweed, and Red Chili Flakes ✳
CHINA

Peanuts serve not only as a snack in China but also as a basic food. They add protein to the diet, and the Chinese consume them with their breakfast rice soup (congee) and at other meals. Mixed with slivered seaweed, and sometimes small, dried fish, they become a condiment or a side dish. The plate looks pretty with the red-skinned peanuts, purplish-black nori, and crushed red pepper. Black salt complements this mélange.

3 to 4   seasoned nori (seaweed) sheets, toasted, thinly slivered
     1   cup (250 ml) dry-roasted, unsalted peanuts
          Red pepper flakes (to taste)
          Black salt (to taste)

Combine all ingredients in a medium bowl. Serve in small individual saucers.

2 servings

Serving Suggestions: As a condiment it perks up rice, millet, or quinoa at a main meal. Offer also as an appetizer preceding a vegetarian meal. It can be a lunch companion to Basmati Rice Congee (page 30) and stir-fried baby bok choy.

✳ Roasted Garlic Spread ✳

INTERNATIONAL

Garlic chutney, made of raw garlic, is popular in the western part of India. In this recipe, I follow the method an Indian neighbor taught me but deviate from tradition by roasting the garlic first, a technique I learned in the West. Roasting the garlic mellows its powerful aromatic flavor and also softens its texture. The result has a thick, smooth, spreadable consistency.

 4 garlic heads, unpeeled
   Olive oil for drizzling (optional)
 1/4 teaspoon (1 ml) ground cumin
 1 tablespoon (15 ml) seeded, chopped jalapeño
 2 tablespoons (30 ml) olive oil
 1/3 cup (75 ml) water
   Salt

1. To roast the garlic: Preheat oven to 450°F (230°C, gas marks 8). You can optionally drizzle the garlic heads with olive oil before baking to impart a richer taste. To do so, chop the top off each garlic head with a knife in such a way as to expose the tops of the cloves. (You will lose a bit of flesh from each clove.) Drizzle a little olive oil over the cloves. Place the garlic heads on an ungreased baking sheet and bake for 30 to 40 minutes or until soft to the touch. (The garlic will emit a strong aroma.) Check frequently and don't overbake, as the garlic might turn bitter. When cool enough to handle, peel and discard the outer skins.
2. Process garlic, cumin, jalapeño, 2 tablespoons (30 ml) oil, and water in a blender to a thick, smooth puree, adding a little extra water if necessary. Add salt. Serve at room temperature. Will keep in the refrigerator for a few days.

Yields over 1 cup (250 ml)

Serving Suggestions: Serve as a topping for baked potato, yam, or steamed cauliflower; spoon over roast chicken or grilled fish; toss with cooked whole wheat spaghetti or, better yet, whole spelt spaghetti. (Spelt is an ancient grain that is making a comeback; buy spelt pasta in natural-food stores.) Also excellent brushed on Jalapeño-Rosemary Biscuits (page 196), on toasted sourdough bread, or with papads. Spread this garlic puree on one half of an omelet being cooked and fold the other half over. Drizzle over baked oysters.

✳ Sweet and Sour Plantain Sauce ✳

THE CARIBBEAN

"A small plantain is better than none" is a "bird in the hand" type of saying from Jamaica, where plantain is a common accompaniment to many meals. Plantain now appears often in Western supermarkets. Once when serving rice, I offered this interesting sauce, which has a smooth texture, gentle banana sweetness, and a limey tartness. My guests finished it all before they touched the rice.

3/4   pound (375 g), 1 large ripe plantain (yellowish-brown, not green)

6   ounces (175 g), 1 medium-sized very ripe banana, peeled

1/4   cup (60 ml) fresh lime or lemon juice

1   teaspoon (5 ml) canola oil

1/4   teaspoon (1 ml) black mustard seeds

Crushed red pepper flakes (to taste)

Salt

1. Cover unpeeled plantain with water in a large pan. Bring to a boil. Lower heat slightly and simmer, covered, 40 to 60 minutes. Drain. Reserve the liquid for use in soups or vegetable dishes. Allow plantain to cool. Using a knife, peel, then cut the flesh in chunks. Discard the skin. Whirl plantain chunks, banana, and 2 tablespoons (30 ml) lime juice in a blender until smooth. Pour into a pan, cover, and bring to a simmer over moderate heat. Remove from heat.

2. Heat oil in a small 7-inch (17.5-cm) skillet over moderate heat until sizzling. Add mustard seeds and pepper flakes and fry until the mustard seeds pop. (Cover the pan partially to prevent the seeds from flying out.) Remove from heat, pour this spice mixture over the plantain-banana puree, and stir well. Add the remaining lime juice and salt. Serve warm or at room temperature. Can be kept in the refrigerator for a day and reheated gently.

6 small servings

Serving Suggestions: Goes well as an accompaniment to grains. It is also substantial enough to be served as a side dish just as you would a vegetable puree. In this case, team with brown rice (preferably the short-grained, sweet, glutinous type from Asian markets that cooks to a sticky mass), Parsee Chicken in Fragrant Coconut Gravy (page 133), and Eggplant Caponata International (page 78).

✳ Cilantro Splash ✳

INDIA

The first plant I grew as a child was cilantro. The few coriander seeds I planted sprouted into a plant whose frilly leaves were most aromatic. Although I never did let anyone snip them, cilantro has innumerable uses in an Indian kitchen: as a vegetable, garnish, or chutney ingredient.

Many variations of cilantro chutney exist. The sharp, clean taste of this version is derived from lime juice and mango powder. It's made quickly in the blender and adds zip to any meal.

1¹/₂ cups (375 ml) firmly packed cilantro leaves (see *Note*)
¹/₂ cup (125 ml) coarsely chopped onion
1 teaspoon (5 ml) seeded, chopped jalapeño
¹/₄ cup (60 ml) fresh lime or lemon juice
1 teaspoon (5 ml) ground cumin
¹/₂ teaspoon (2 ml) mango powder (*amchoor*)
2 teaspoons (10 ml) sugar
¹/₄ teaspoon (1 ml) salt
¹/₄ cup (60 ml) water

Whirl all the ingredients in a blender to a relatively smooth consistency, adding a bit more water if necessary. Serve immediately or refrigerate for several hours to develop flavor. It will keep in the refrigerator for a day or two.

Yields 1 cup (250 ml)

Note: Use the leaves only and not the stems. The stems can make the chutney bitter.

Serving Suggestions: For a light lunch, spread over cooked pasta, tossed with Herbed Butter-Oil Dip (page 235). This versatile chutney can also be served alongside rice, quinoa, or millet; over a baked sweet potato; with poached fish; on top of a potato and mushroom sauté; or as a dip for steamed cauliflower or raw jícama slices.

✳ Mint-Basil Chutney ✳

INTERNATIONAL

Here I add a new twist to the traditional Indian mint chutney by substituting basil for part of the mint. Basil has an equally pronounced flavor and the combination makes an even more exciting chutney.

1/2 cup (125 ml) firmly packed fresh mint leaves
1/4 cup (60 ml) firmly packed fresh basil leaves
1/4 cup (60 ml) coarsely chopped onion
1 large clove garlic, coarsely chopped
1/2 teaspoon (2 ml) salt
1 teaspoon (5 ml) sugar
1/4 cup (60 ml) fresh lime juice
1 1/2 tablespoons (22 ml) water
1/2 teaspoon (2 ml) garam masala

Combine all the ingredients in a blender container. Process until smooth, adding 1 tablespoon (15 ml) or so of water if necessary. Serve immediately. Will keep in the refrigerator for a day or two.

Yields 1 cup (250 ml)

Serving Suggestions: Serve as a dip with papads (especially good with red chile papads) or as a side dish to a main meal. You can make finger sandwiches by spreading this chutney on one slice of bread and Sun-Dried Tomato and Sweet Red Pepper Cream (page 226) on the other. The red and green sauces, peeking through the sides, are a delightful contrast in both color and flavor and bring a festive look to the table. You can also toss this chutney with cooked pasta to create an international *pasta al pesto*.

* Mint-Tamarind Pesto *

ITALY

Pesto, Italy's most famous sauce, got its start in Genoa, where people would pound fresh basil, pine nuts, and Parmesan cheese with olive oil. They used a mortar and pestle, hence the name. Today a blender does the job, but purists insist the color of the sauce is greener if pounded by hand.

This Indian-style pesto leaves out the customary Parmesan cheese (lowering the fat content), but includes tamarind for a sense of warmth and tartness. Pecans add a Western touch.

2   cups (500 ml) firmly packed fresh mint leaves, rinsed, towel-dried
2   large cloves garlic, coarsely chopped
2   tablespoons (30 ml) chopped pecans
2   tablespoons (30 ml) fresh lime or lemon juice
1   teaspoon (5 ml) tamarind concentrate
1/4   teaspoon (1 ml) salt

Whirl all the ingredients together in a blender or food processor until relatively smooth. Adjust seasonings. Will keep in the refrigerator for a day or two.

Yields about 1 cup (250 ml)

Serving Suggestions: Serve atop cooked pasta tossed with a little olive oil, ghee, or butter. Or serve alongside Fettuccine and Crab in Silky Black Mustard-Poppy Seed Sauce (page 147). Use this pesto to dress a potato salad, or dab on grilled fish. Sauce up grilled squash or steamed potatoes with it.

✴ Sun-Dried Tomato and Sweet Red Pepper Cream ✴

ITALY

Red is an auspicious color in India. A visiting foreign dignitary may be greeted with a red garland. In Bengal, a bride wears a red sari on her wedding day. Once married, she places a red dot on her forehead every morning. So at dinner a deep red-brown puree like this lends a lucky charm to the rest of the meal for me. Along with the color, I also appreciate the warm mellow flavors of sun-dried tomatoes and the smoky bouquet of the roasted bell peppers.

Though this sauce has a creamy quality, it is fat-free. It's never out of place at an international table.

      1   cup (250 ml) boiling water
      9   sun-dried tomatoes
      1   large red bell pepper
 1 to 2   teaspoons (5 to 10 ml) ground cumin
    1/4   teaspoon (1 ml) black salt
          Salt and freshly ground pepper

1. Pour boiling water over the sun-dried tomatoes. Let stand 5 to 10 minutes or until softened. Remove the tomatoes from water, reserving the soaking water. Use this water in cooking grains, preparing soups, or in place of water in vegetable preparations, especially those that call for tomatoes.

2. Broil the bell pepper for 5 to 7 minutes or until the skin is charred, turning it once or twice. Place the pepper in a paper bag and close the top. Let stand for 10 minutes, then take the pepper out of the bag. When cool to the touch, peel and discard the skin. Remove and discard the stem, seeds, and inner membranes, and chop the flesh coarsely. Place in a blender or food processor along with the tomatoes and process until smooth, using a little of the soaking liquid. Add cumin, black salt, regular salt, and pepper. Serve at room temperature. If not ready to serve yet, chill it, but bring to room temperature before serving. Will keep in the refrigerator for a few days.

Yields 1 cup (250 ml)

Serving Suggestions: This flavorful sauce is excellent alongside Basic Pilaf with Nutty Vermicelli Threads (page 177) or with roasted potatoes and steamed green beans. Toss with pasta. Spread it on a warm tortilla, fill with shredded chicken and romaine lettuce, and roll like a soft taco. It's also good on your morning toast. A special dinnertime treat is to brush it on toasted garlic bread.

✳ Fish Aïoli ✳

FRANCE

Many French cooks prepare mayonnaise by hand rather than buy it from the store. I, too, learned to prepare it using only egg, oil, and salt when I attended a cooking school in France. Once you master the technique, you can vary the basic recipe infinitely. An example is this fish mayonnaise, which I put together one day when I had some leftover cooked fish on hand. The fish gave the sauce more body, reduced the amount of oil, and, together with asafetida and cilantro, added extra flavor. For best results, bring all the ingredients to room temperature.

1/4	cup (60 ml) plain poached or steamed fish (see *Note*)
3	cloves garlic, coarsely chopped
1/4	teaspoon (1 ml) asafetida powder
1	large egg
2	teaspoons (10 ml) chopped cilantro
1/4 to 1/2	cup (60 to 125 ml) olive oil
	Salt and white pepper

Place fish, garlic, asafetida, egg, and cilantro in a blender. Process to a relatively smooth puree. With the motor running, drizzle oil through the central opening on top, a drop at a time at first, until the mixture starts to thicken. Then pour the rest of the oil in a slow, steady stream. Transfer to a small bowl. Add salt and pepper. The mayonnaise can be served immediately. Or store in the refrigerator for an hour or so, which will thicken it further. It will keep in the refrigerator for a day or two.

Yields up to 3/4 cup (175 ml)

Note: Use a fish of your choice. Mild white fish will produce a subdued effect, while a fish such as swordfish, fresh tuna, or salmon will impart its own pronounced flavor.

Serving Suggestions: There are innumerable uses for this luscious dip. Served alongside Gujarati Potato Boats (page 64), this mayonnaise makes a delicious first course. Toss with cooked fish slivers for a fish salad. Spread over scrambled eggs. Brush on crackers or toasted Italian coarse bread. Dip into it grilled eggplant, zucchini, or summer squash, as well as steamed potatoes, cauliflower, or snow peas. It also goes well as a dressing for salad Niçoise.

✳ Zippy Tomato Relish ✳
INTERNATIONAL

You fly over many national boundaries when you taste this spicy relish and garnish: India, Italy, Southeast Asia. The dish looks particularly pretty arranged over steamed salmon or other plain cooked fish. Or, after you have sauced a pasta dish, border it with this colorful mixture. With its chaat-tart dressing, the relish also stands on its own as a grain accompaniment.

The sauce:
- 1/3　cup (75 ml) rice vinegar
- 1　teaspoon (5 ml) Chaat Powder (see page 8)
- 1　tablespoon (15 ml) chopped cilantro (or equal parts of cilantro and fresh basil)
- 1　teaspoon (5 ml) sambal oeleck (to taste)

The tomato:
- 3/4　pound (375 g) Roma or regular tomatoes, seeded, finely chopped

Combine all the sauce ingredients in a medium bowl, adjusting the amount of sambal oeleck according to taste. Add tomatoes and marinate at room temperature for 15 to 30 minutes. Best if served the same day it's made.

4 small servings

✳ Indian Apple Butter ✳

INDIA

During late summer or early autumn when I harvest tart apples in my garden, I prepare this dish, which is similar to applesauce except that it is a bit thicker and has a deep brown color reminiscent of apple butter. I leave the apples unpeeled and sweeten them gently with a hint of maple sugar. Cinnamon, cardamom, and cloves as well as tamarind give the fat-free sauce a rich, warm flavor.

This sauce is a welcome addition to the table on cold evenings. You can use it also in baking just as you would applesauce.

    2   pounds (1 kg) tart apples, 4 medium (Granny Smith, Northern Spy, Graven-
        stein, etc.)
    3   tablespoons (45 ml) water
 $1/2$ teaspoon (2 ml) ground cinnamon
    1   teaspoon (5 ml) ground cardamom
 $1/4$ teaspoon (1 ml) ground cloves
    3   tablespoons-plus (45 ml) dark brown sugar (adjusted according to the tartness
        of the apples; see *Note 1*)
$1^{1}/2$ teaspoons (7 ml) tamarind concentrate (see *Note 2*)

Core the unpeeled apples and chop them coarsely. In a medium saucepan, place the apples, water, cinnamon, cardamom, cloves, and sugar. Cover and cook gently until the apples are very tender, 12 to 16 minutes. Process in a blender or food processor until smooth. Stir in tamarind. Taste for sugar. Best served warm, but can also be served at room temperature. Will keep in the refrigerator for a few days.

Yields about 2 cups (500 ml)

Note 1: For a deeper flavor, use maple sugar or palm sugar. Palm sugar is sold in cans in Asian markets.

Note 2: Omit the tamarind if you plan to use the mixture in baking (in place of applesauce or some other liquid), or for topping a cake or bar cookie.

Serving Suggestions: The uses of this sauce are endless. Serve with baked sweet potato, roast pork, dark turkey, or chicken meat. Spread on top of Spiced Fruit Bars (page 278) or between layers of a cake. Offer alongside a quinoa, millet, or rice dish. Drizzle over toasted bread or pancakes. Dip gingerbread or other cookies into it. The sauce also makes a fine gift; it will last in the refrigerator for several days.

Salad Dressings

A gourmet friend once told me he could always tell a cook by the salad dressing. Since then I have tried to select my dressing carefully, varying it to complement not only the salad ingredients but also other dishes in the meal. For diversity and a more complex taste, I may use two dressings for the same salad: an oil-based one such as Cumin Vinaigrette to lightly coat the leaves, then Cilantro Splash or the hot and spicy Chile-Lime Dressing for sprinkling.

An oil-and-vinegar dressing has many uses. In addition to gracing a salad, it can coat cooked pasta or act as a marinade for fish or meat to be grilled. When used to moisten leftover cooked grains tossed with lettuce and raw or steamed vegetables, it can transform leftovers into a substantial main dish.

Although Indians don't commonly use Western-style salad dressings, I have discovered that a few drops of Indian cooking oils such as sesame or mustard or a dash of spices such as garam masala add a new twist to many vinaigrettes. Another way to perk up a dressing is to add commercial Indian pickles. Try mango, lime, garlic, or other pickles that are sold in Indian groceries. Chop finely and use only a dab as they tend to be highly seasoned.

The secret of preparing a good vinaigrette is in blending the ingredients thoroughly. This causes the oil to emulsify. It also traps the vinegar and other spices in richly flavored droplets that adhere to the main ingredients. Let the dressing stand for an hour or more before serving to allow the flavors to intensify; during this time, the oil and other ingredients will separate; shake thoroughly before using.

Count on 1 tablespoon (15 ml) of dressing per person.

✳ Lime-Ginger Dressing ✳
EAST ASIA

This nonfat, all-purpose dressing is good for fruit and vegetable salads. You can use it to sauce cooked grains or thin pieces of peeled cucumber, and for dipping steamed greens.

1/2　cup (125 ml) fresh lime or lemon juice

1　teaspoon (5 ml) finely minced gingerroot

¹/₄ teaspoon (1 ml) seeded, chopped jalapeño (or to taste; best if there is a hint
     of hotness)
¹/₄ teaspoon (1 ml) salt
  2 teaspoons (10 ml) sugar
  1 teaspoon (5 ml) toasted sesame seeds (optional)

Place all the ingredients in a small screw-top jar. Cover and shake thoroughly. Chill
dressing until needed.

Yields ¹/₂ cup (125 ml)

SESAME OIL VARIATION: Add 1 teaspoon (5 ml) Chinese sesame oil along with the
other ingredients for a warm flavor.

✳ Chile-Lime Dressing ✳
INTERNATIONAL

A thin, sharp, fat-free dressing with the lovely color and flavor of red chiles. It's great
over cooked pasta (especially udon, Shanghai noodles, or any other wheat noodles
that have been tossed with a little olive oil or avocado oil) or cooked grains, and as a
dressing for fresh fruits.

¹/₂ cup (125 ml) fresh lime juice (juice of about 3 limes)
  1 tablespoon (15 ml) fish sauce
  1 teaspoon (5 ml) sambal oeleck
¹/₄ teaspoon (1 ml) asafetida powder
¹/₂ teaspoon (2 ml) salt
  1 teaspoon (5 ml) sugar

Whisk all the ingredients together in a small bowl until smooth. Chill dressing until
needed.

Yields ²/₃ cup (150 ml)

✳ Lime-Tamarind Dressing ✳

INDIA

A lovely dressing to sprinkle over grains or to moisten fruit salads.

- $1/2$　teaspoon (2 ml) tamarind concentrate
- 5　teaspoons (20 ml) sugar
- 6　tablespoons (90 ml) lime juice (juice of 2 to 3 limes)

Combine tamarind and sugar with a little of the lime juice and stir until smooth. Add the remaining lime juice and mix well. Chill until needed.

Yields $1/3$ cup (75 ml)

✳ Sesame-Garlic Vinaigrette ✳

EAST ASIA

T oss a green salad with this robust dressing redolent with the warm flavors of Chinese sesame oil and garam masala. Or serve as a light dip for raw, steamed, or grilled vegetables.

- 2　tablespoons (30 ml) rice vinegar
- 2　tablespoons (30 ml) unrefined safflower oil or canola oil
- 1　teaspoon (5 ml) fresh lime juice
- 1　large clove garlic, minced
- 1　large clove garlic, halved
- $1/4$　teaspoon (1 ml) Chinese sesame oil
- $1/8$　teaspoon (0.5 ml) garam masala
- $1/8$　teaspoon (0.5 ml) salt

Combine vinegar, oil, lime juice, minced garlic, and garlic halves in a small screw-top jar. Cover and shake thoroughly several times. Add sesame oil, garam masala, and salt and shake again. Let stand in the refrigerator for 1 hour before serving. If you like, remove the garlic halves, chop them, and sprinkle them on top of the salad.

Yields $1/4$ cup (60 ml)

✳ Sesame-Tamarind Dressing ✳

INTERNATIONAL

A flavorful dressing that perks up a romaine salad; serve also as a dip for steamed greens and grilled vegetables.

  3 large garlic cloves, forced through a garlic press
  2 tablespoons (30 ml) Chinese sesame oil
  1 tablespoon (15 ml) chopped cilantro
  1 tablespoon (15 ml) low-sodium soy sauce
  1 tablespoon (15 ml) rice vinegar
 1/4 teaspoon (1 ml) salt
 1/4 teaspoon (1 ml) black salt
  3 tablespoons (45 ml) tamarind puree (see "To prepare tamarind puree,"
      page 18), or 1 to 2 teaspoons (5 to 10 ml) tamarind concentrate, adjusted
      to taste
  1 teaspoon (5 ml) sugar

Whisk together all the ingredients in a small nonmetallic bowl until smooth. Cover and allow to stand for 30 minutes in the refrigerator for the flavor to develop.

Yields 1/2 cup (125 ml)

✳ Cumin Vinaigrette ✳

INTERNATIONAL

An all-purpose tart dressing for vegetable salads. For an extra spiciness, add a dash of finely chopped lime or garlic pickle (sold in Indian groceries).

 1/4 cup (60 ml) rice vinegar
 1/2 teaspoon (2 ml) Dijon-style mustard
  2 tablespoons (30 ml) extra-virgin olive oil or hazelnut oil
 1/8 teaspoon (0.5 ml) ground cumin
      Dash Indian pickle (lime or garlic; optional)

Place vinegar and mustard in a screw-top jar and mix together with a fork. Add oil and cumin, cover, and shake vigorously. Add pickle. Chill dressing until needed.

Yields 1/4 cup (60 ml)

✸ Curry-Walnut Dressing ✸

INTERNATIONAL

A dressing for crisp greens and other vegetables. The curry flavor becomes more noticeable if the dressing is allowed to sit overnight.

- 2 tablespoons (30 ml) walnut oil
- 2 tablespoons (30 ml) rice vinegar
- 3 tablespoons (45 ml) orange juice, preferably freshly squeezed
- 1/4 teaspoon (1 ml) salt
  Freshly ground black pepper
- 1/4 teaspoon (1 ml) curry powder (see "Selecting curry powder," page 10)

Whisk all the dressing ingredients in a medium bowl until well-mixed. Cover and chill until needed.

Yields about 1/2 cup (125 ml)

✸ Tamari-Wasabi Dressing ✸

INTERNATIONAL

O ffer this sharp dip with roasted and steamed vegetables, as a dressing for greens, and as a sauce for cooked pasta.

- 3 tablespoons (45 ml) tamari-wasabi mustard (see *Note*)
- 1 tablespoon (15 ml) balsamic vinegar
- 4 teaspoons (20 ml) rice vinegar
- 2 tablespoons (30 ml) Chinese sesame oil
  A few drops of mustard oil (optional)
- 3 tablespoons (45 ml) plain nonfat yogurt
- 1 teaspoon (5 ml) sugar
  Salt

Whisk together mustard and the two vinegars in a medium bowl until smooth. Stir in oil(s). Add yogurt, sugar, and salt and mix until smooth. Cover and chill until needed.

Yields about 1 cup (250 ml)

Note: This mustard is sold in natural-food stores.

✳ Olive Oil and Fresh Herb Dip ✳

ITALY

Visit the neighborhood bakery for the freshest baguette or Italian country bread and serve with this dip as an elegant meal starter. Chaat Powder adds an extra zip to this oil-and-herb base.

  1 cup (250 ml) extra-virgin olive oil
  1 tablespoon (15 ml) finely chopped fresh herbs (a combination of basil,
        oregano, thyme, tarragon, and sage)
  1/4 teaspoon (1 ml) Chaat Powder (see page 8)
     Salt and freshly ground black pepper

Combine oil, herbs, and Chaat Powder in a medium bowl. Add salt and pepper to taste. Let stand, covered, overnight in the refrigerator for the flavor to develop.

Yields 1 cup (250 ml)

✳ Herbed Butter-Oil Dip ✳

INTERNATIONAL

A delightful dip for steamed or grilled vegetables and grilled fish. Also splendid when tossed with cooked pasta or drizzled over cooked grains. To enhance its versatility, divide the dip into two bowls; prepare the East Asian variation with one half and serve the other half as is.

     4-ounce (113-g) stick butter, softened at room temperature (see *Note*)
  1/4 cup-plus (60 ml) fresh lime juice (juice of 1 to 2 limes)
  2 large garlic cloves, coarsely chopped
  1/2 teaspoon (2 ml) asafetida powder
  1 tablespoon (15 ml) coarsely chopped cilantro
     Freshly ground black pepper
  1/2 cup-plus (125 ml) avocado oil or olive oil
     A few drops of mustard oil or Indian sesame oil (*gingely*) (optional)

Place butter, lime juice, garlic, asafetida, cilantro, and black pepper in a blender or food processor and process until smooth. Transfer to a medium bowl. Add oil gradually, whisking with a fork or wire whisk until a mayonnaise-like consistency results, finishing with a few drops of mustard oil. Add a little more lime juice if necessary to have a limey flavor and adjust the other seasonings. Serve at room temperature. Refrigerate any leftovers, but allow it to soften at room temperature before serving.

Yields 3/4 cup (185 ml) or more

Note: For best results, leave the butter at room temperature for several hours or until very soft. I use unsalted butter and add a little black salt for flavor.

EAST ASIAN VARIATION: A splendid dip with a bold chile-sesame fragrance. Drizzle 1 teaspoon (5 ml) Chinese sesame oil and a few drops each of chile oil and fish sauce over the finished dish and stir to mix well. All three ingredients are available in Asian markets.

✳ Garlic Ghee ✳

INDIA

Use this multipurpose, flavored ghee in cooking and as a dip for steamed vegetables; toss it with cooked pasta; or drizzle over cooked grains. Best when served hot.

1/2 cup (125 ml) ghee (see "To prepare ghee," page 11)
2 to 3 large garlic cloves, forced through a garlic press

Melt ghee in a small saucepan over low heat. Add garlic and cook just until lightly browned. Remove from heat and serve immediately.

Yields 1/2 cup (125 ml)

VARIATIONS: You can flavor this ghee further with a pinch of asafetida powder, ground red pepper, or Chaat Powder (see page 8). Add to melted hot ghee and serve immediately.

Street Foods:
Snacks, Salads, and Other Savories

India is a snack culture. Indians eat breakfast and dinner at home, but lunch is usually a sampler selected from a wide variety of snack foods available at tea shops or from street vendors and eaten in a more social context.

The streets of India teem with pedestrians, hawkers, and cars, stray dogs, goats, and cows. Every bit of space is crowded. A hustle of activities occurs simultaneously: A serious book seller sets up shop on the sidewalk; rickshaw pullers zigzag through traffic; political slogans pour forth from loudspeakers on a passing truck. As I wander, I pass food vendors creating magic in their pushcarts on tiny oil stoves from a few basic ingredients.

There's an art to enjoying street food. Of most importance is noting the type of food and how it's prepared. When traveling in many parts of the world, one needs to pay attention to potential sanitary problems. I do this by looking for hot foods and fresh fruits and vegetables sliced only minutes before. Once a vendor passes my health inspection, I am comfortable eating at open-air places, where I mingle with the locals and feel the throb of everyday life.

With such a wide variety of finger foods displayed, I select the right snack for my mood. Do I crave something chewy or delicate, bland or fragrant, sweet or savory? Before I can make up my mind, a vendor, who has noticed my curious glances, calls out, "*Didi* (Sister), why do you just look? Why don't you try a little *chaat*?"

"Only if you make it fresh," I reply. The man smiles knowingly, then gets busy. He shakes a jar of his own special spice mix and sprinkles some over freshly cut fruits and vegetables. With a final, theatrical squeeze of lime, he creates a visually perfect fruit-and-vegetable salad that would please the most fastidious eater anywhere. This vendor proves himself both a fast-food artist and a master chef.

While the Sweet and Sour Salad costs only a few rupees, it is worth lingering over each bite to savor the artful combination of taste and texture. I feel an immediate, immense pleasure. This mini-meal not only satisfies my hunger but also lifts my spirit by returning me to the roots of the diverse and ancient culture that is distinctly India.

I've encountered other delicious fast foods from street vendors in Malaysia and Singapore. I have spent entire evenings strolling through the streets of Singapore, stopping at one food stall after another, sampling tastes unique to Asia: tiny dried fish in a pungent sauce, crispy grilled vegetables, and spicy seafood tidbits over rice.

I now prepare many of these snacks at home when I exercise. Running is my favorite form of workout, and since it is such a strenuous activity, it puts eating in a different perspective. If I am going to run in three hours, I say to myself, "I can't eat a big meal, but I really should have a bite of something."

I steam some potatoes and sprinkle Chaat Powder over them, or spread a few rice cakes with Sun-Dried Tomato and Sweet Red Pepper Cream. After running I want nothing heavy, perhaps a spicy Indo-Chinese Bean Salad or Carrot Cashew Koftas. Snacks, which I once considered to be treats, are now a vital part of my life-style.

This chapter is a collection of street classics from around the world. Black salt, tamarind, or roasted cumin powder from a street vendor's bag of tricks add an exotic Indian touch. These savories can double as appetizers or brown bag lunches. They complement other dishes at picnics, buffets, and cocktail parties.

While these snack ideas tempt the tongue, they don't deny the fulfillment of a meal. On some evenings, a number of such dishes make a light supper for me. Simple snacking becomes joyous and nutritious eating. ✳

✳ Sweet and Sour Salad ✳

INDIA/MALAYSIA

Mention *chaat* and many Indian mouths begin to water. *Chaat* is a snack-style veg-etable salad that can be combined with fruits. What makes it unique is its dressing, which is sharply tart and gently sweet. A spice mix called *chaat* masala, specially ground for this purpose, is sprinkled over the ingredients at the end. In India, street vendors selling *chaat* do brisk business with pedestrians who are tempted to delay their errands for a bite of this colorful salad.

In food stalls in Malaysia, I came across a similar fruit-and-vegetable salad called *rojak*, which is believed to have originated in Indonesia, a country once ruled by Indian conquerors. This recipe exhibits influences from both cultures. Tropical fruits such as papaya and pineapple typically adorn such a salad, but I find fruits of cooler climates—apple or, better yet, Asian pear—go just as well. Traditionally the ingredi-ents are cut in large chunks, about 1 1/2-inch (4-cm) cubes. They can be cut in smaller sizes if desired.

The dressing:
- 1/2 cup (125 ml) rice vinegar
- 1/4 teaspoon (1 ml) salt
- 1 teaspoon (5 ml) sugar
- 1/8 teaspoon (0.5 ml) sambal oeleck (or red chile paste)

The salad:
- 1/2 pound (250 g), 1 medium Asian pear or a sweet apple, cored but not peeled, cubed
- 1/2 pound (250 g) grapes
- 1/2 pound (250 g), 1 medium cucumber, peeled, halved, seeded, and cubed (or English cucumber, cubed)
- 1/2 large mild red or other sweet onion, coarsely chopped
- 1/4 pound (100 g), 2 medium Roma tomatoes, seeded, chopped
  Black salt or regular salt
  Chaat Powder (see page 8; start with 1/8 teaspoon [0.5 ml])
  Tamarind-Date Chutney (page 208)
- 1 tablespoon (15 ml) finely chopped cilantro
- 1 teaspoon (5 ml) finely chopped fresh dill or 1/4 teaspoon (1 ml) dried dill

1. Place all the dressing ingredients in a small saucepan and bring to a boil. Remove from heat. Transfer to a small bowl and allow to cool. This can be done ahead of time. About an hour or so before serving, combine Asian pear, grapes, cucumber, onion, and tomatoes in a medium bowl. Pour the dressing over mixture. Let stand in the refrigerator, stirring gently once or twice.
2. Just before serving, drain, reserving the dressing (see Serving Suggestions). Dust the mixture lightly with black salt and Chaat Powder. Drizzle Tamarind-Date Chutney decoratively on top. (Don't mix it in as it will darken the salad.) Serve decorated with cilantro and dill.

4 servings

Serving Suggestions: Enjoy as a snack with a glass of Yogurt Borhani (page 295). Serve as an appetizer followed by Couscous and Smoked Oysters (page 175) and Savory Sprouts Stir-Fry (page 77). The leftover dressing, which has extra flavors imparted by the fruits and vegetables, can be served on the side or refrigerated and used in another meal to drizzle over steamed beet greens, Swiss chard, or spinach.

VARIATION: For an alternative selection of fruits and vegetables, try papaya (1 medium, 1/2 pound [250 g]), cucumber (1 medium, 1/2 pound [250 g]), fresh pineapple (1 cup [250 ml]), and cooked potatoes (2 medium, 1/2 pound [250 g]).

✳ Vegetable Chaat ✳
INDIA

One of the first words a Westerner learns in India is *wallah*. The word is actually a suffix, and when placed at the end of a name of a commodity, it means the seller or producer of that product. For example, a *sabji wallah* is a vegetable vendor (*sabji* means vegetables). In Calcutta, we call the vendor of this invigorating salad *chaat wallah*. He combines corn and tomatoes and serves them with a nippy, sweet-sour dressing.

I add other vegetables, such as carrots and black-eyed peas for variety and texture, and capers and sweet red bell pepper for a touch of the West. Though sold as a snack by our *chaat wallah*, this dish is filling enough to be the main course of a simple meal.

   1   ear fresh corn, or 1 cup (250 ml) frozen corn kernels
1/2   pound (250 g) carrots, 2 small, diced

4 to 5 large romaine leaves

1/2 cup (125 ml) freshly cooked black-eyed peas (follow cooking instructions in
Indo-Chinese Bean Salad, page 248) or canned black-eyed peas

1/2 pound (250 g), 1/2 a large mild red or other sweet onion, sliced

8 cherry tomatoes, quartered, or 1 cup (250 ml) seeded, coarsely chopped
regular tomatoes

1 medium-sized red bell pepper, seeded, coarsely chopped (see *Note for the
Gardener*)

1 tablespoon (15 ml) capers, drained, rinsed

1 tablespoon (15 ml) finely chopped cilantro

Lime-Ginger Dressing (page 230)

Chaat Powder (see page 8)

Tamarind-Date Chutney (page 208)

1. If using fresh corn on the cob, steam it whole for 4 to 7 minutes or until tender.
With a knife, cut off the kernels and discard the cob. Separate the kernels gently
with a knife if they clump together. Steam frozen corn until tender to the bite,
2 to 5 minutes.

2. Steam the carrots for 10 to 15 minutes or until fork-tender. Arrange lettuce leaves
on individual serving plates. Combine corn, carrots, black-eyed peas, onion, tomatoes, bell pepper, capers, and cilantro in a bowl. Pour Lime-Ginger Dressing over
the vegetables. Spoon vegetables over lettuce leaves, sprinkle with Chaat Powder,
then drizzle Tamarind-Date Chutney on top. The salad tastes best if served immediately while still a little warm or shortly after at room temperature. If made
ahead and refrigerated, bring it to room temperature before serving.

4 to 6 servings

Note for the Gardener: For an extra dash of color, substitute 1/2 of the red bell pepper with Purple Beauty, a dark purple bell pepper. (This pepper, however, loses its
color when cooked.)

Serving Suggestions: Savor these rainbow vegetables at snacktime with warm whole
wheat pita wedges and a glass of Lime and Papaya Milk (page 294). Or accompany at
a brunch with Quick Indian Pizza (page 195) and Shah Jahani Flan (page 270).

POTATO VARIATION: Substitute boiled potatoes (1 medium, 1/4 pound [125 g]) for
corn, in which case, add 1/2 cup (125 ml) cooked fresh peas (or thawed frozen peas)
or steamed green beans for color.

✳ Sweet Potato Salad with ✳ Sesame-Tamarind Dressing

JAPAN

Once in Honolulu, choosing to eat on the beach, I visited a Japanese department store known for its wide array of freshly cooked delicacies. It was one of those dazzling Hawaiian days when I was tempted to dash into the store, fill my picnic basket with edibles, and leave as fast as possible. But, like some of the Japanese shoppers, I lingered to read the labels of various luscious-looking items. I ultimately bought a zippy dish—a sweet potato salad enhanced by a salty soy dressing and some cold soba noodles. My picnic was perfect. Later, in re-creating this salad, I augmented the soy dressing with tamarind and black salt to give it an Indo-Japanese flavor.

1   pound (500 g) peeled or unpeeled sweet potatoes or yams, cut into 1¹/₂-inch
     (4-cm) cubes (see *Note for the Gardener*)
     Sesame-Tamarind Dressing (page 233)

Garnish: Minced gingerroot

Steam the sweet potatoes for 12 to 18 minutes or until tender but firm. Immediately add Sesame-Tamarind Dressing. Allow to cool to room temperature. Serve garnished with minced gingerroot.

4 servings

Note for the Gardener: Natalie Ng, an artist and expert cook, told me that sweet potato leaves are appreciated as a stir-fry vegetable in her homeland, mainland China. If you grow sweet potatoes, harvest the leaves after the plant has stopped producing so as not to impact the growth of the vegetables. Snip off a handful, then stir-fry in 2 teaspoons (10 ml) olive or canola oil in a wok or skillet over medium heat. As soon as the leaves start to become limp, add ¹/₂ teaspoon (2 ml) low-sodium soy sauce and ¹/₂ teaspoon (2 ml) sambal oeleck, adjusted according to taste. Serve piping hot with rice or other plain-cooked grains, or as a salad at room temperature.

Serving Suggestions: This salad is delicious served at a main meal with barley, millet, or brown rice, or cooked soba noodles tossed with Chinese sesame oil. Serve Garlic-Glazed Tofu (page 67) for protein. A small dish of Peanuts, Seaweed, and Red Chile Flakes (page 220) makes a good beginning and sliced kiwis a delightful conclusion.

KALONJI VARIATION: Dry-roast ¼ teaspoon (1 ml) kalonji seeds on an ungreased skillet over low heat for a few minutes. Grind the seeds, then sprinkle over the salad for an exotic onion flavor.

✳ Roasted Tikka Potatoes ✳
NORTH INDIA/ITALY

Tikka, or chunky, highly seasoned potatoes, are popular throughout North India. They can be enjoyed as a snack and are especially good after a run or workout when you "carbo-crave." Here I pair them with a sauce made of sun-dried tomatoes, an Italian import, and they make a perfect match. These potatoes are also good served without the sauce.

Choose Yellow Finn, Yukon Gold, or other yellow-fleshed potatoes, if they are available, for this dish.

      2 pounds (1 kg) peeled new potatoes, 7 to 8 medium, cut into 2-inch
         (5-cm) cubes (see *Note* and *Note for the Gardener*)
1 ½ to 2 tablespoons (22 to 30 ml) mustard oil
      2 tablespoons (30 ml) fresh lime or lemon juice
      1 tablespoon (15 ml) coarsely chopped garlic
     ½ teaspoon (2 ml) asafetida powder
     ½ teaspoon (2 ml) turmeric
      1 tablespoon (15 ml) ground cumin
         Ground red pepper (to taste; start with a scant pinch; best if there is a
         hint of hotness)
     ¼ teaspoon (1 ml) black salt
     ½ teaspoon (2 ml) salt
         Sun-Dried Tomato and Sweet Red Pepper Cream (page 226; optional)

1. Steam the potatoes until tender, 15 to 20 minutes. Towel dry.
2. Preheat oven to 450°F (230°C, gas marks 8). Place oil, lime juice, garlic, asafetida, turmeric, cumin, red pepper, black salt, and salt in a blender container. Whirl until smooth. Gently toss the potatoes with this spice mixture, making sure each piece is well-coated. Place the potatoes cut side up on an aluminum foil-wrapped cookie sheet. Bake for 15 to 20 minutes. Place under the broiler for a minute or

two to brown them lightly. Remove from the broiler. Adjust seasonings. Place a dollop of Sun-Dried Tomato and Sweet Red Pepper Cream on top and serve immediately. Serve any leftover sauce on the side.

6 servings

Note: The potatoes are cut in large chunks for eye appeal and also because they are easier to steam this way.

Note for the Gardener: Several years ago I went to a garden show and bought some Desiree seed potatoes. Those were the days when supermarkets carried only a few varieties of potatoes. The farmer who sold them told me the seeds were of a flavorful stock that came from Europe "where potatoes aren't grown only for French fries." Ever since, the red-skinned, waxy, and creamy-textured Desiree potatoes from Holland have grown in my garden. Every autumn I save a few choice potatoes as seeds to plant the following year. Desiree is a good choice for roasting or sautéeing, or for salads.

Serving Suggestions: With white Basmati rice, Vegetable Sunburst (page 254), Cilantro Splash (page 223), and some baked papads, you have a perfect dinner for the family. As an appetizer, side dish, or a party buffet, these potatoes go well with Honey-Glazed Onions (page 218), Roasted Garlic Spread (page 221), and Mint-Basil Chutney (page 224). For an afternoon tea or snack, team them with Spiced Fruit Bars (page 278) and Honey Ginger Tea (page 292).

✳ Chicken-Flavored Baby Potatoes ✳
INTERNATIONAL

I accidentally made these twice-cooked potatoes one day when I had some home-made chicken stock on hand. First I poached tender new potatoes in the stock, and they were exquisite. The next day I took the few leftover potatoes out of the stock and browned them lightly in a little olive oil. The home-fries, infused with the flavors of chicken stock and spices, were delicious, and I now prepare them regularly.

1 1/2   pounds (750 g) small new potatoes, about 10 or 12, peeled or unpeeled, cut in quarters; or 6 medium potatoes, cut in 1 1/2-inch (4-cm) cubes (see *Note for the Gardener*)

2   cups (500 ml) Chicken Stock (page 44), or a 14 1/2-ounce (411-g) can chicken broth, defatted (see "To defat canned chicken broth," page 45)

$^1/_2$ teaspoon (2 ml) black salt or regular salt

2 tablespoons (30 ml) olive oil

$^1/_2$ teaspoon (2 ml) asafetida powder

3 large garlic cloves, forced through a garlic press (to taste)

   Ground red pepper (to taste; start with a scant pinch)

1 teaspoon (5 ml) dehydrated garlic flakes, toasted and ground (optional;
   see *Note*)

   A few kale leaves

Garnish: Lime wedges

1. Place the potatoes and the stock in a large pan over moderate heat. Cover and bring to a boil. Lower heat and simmer, covered, until the potatoes are tender but not breaking, 12 to 20 minutes. Remove from heat. Transfer stock and potatoes to a large bowl and allow to stand, covered, in the refrigerator several hours or overnight. (The potatoes, however, can be sautéed immediately if you're pressed for time.) Drain, retaining the stock for use in soups or cooking grains. Dust potatoes lightly with black salt.

2. Heat oil in a 12-inch (30-cm) skillet over medium-high heat. Sprinkle asafetida over the oil. Add garlic and red pepper and cook for a few seconds. Add the potatoes and cook, turning them gently several times, until richly browned, 6 to 12 minutes. Sprinkle with half the toasted garlic crumbs. Remove from heat. Taste for salt and red pepper. Keep covered until the kale is ready.

3. Steam the kale leaves until tender, about 5 minutes. Overcooking will discolor them and make them very limp. Place the potatoes on top of kale, squeeze lime juice over them, and sprinkle with the remaining garlic crumbs. Arrange the remaining lime wedges around the kale.

4 servings

Note: To prepare toasted garlic crumbs: Dehydrated garlic flakes, sold in Asian markets, have an intense garlic flavor and are delicious when toasted and used as a topping. (An alternative is to buy garlic chips, sold in some supermarkets.) To toast dried garlic, place flakes on an ungreased griddle or skillet over low heat and cook until slightly darker, turning them often. Watch carefully and don't let them burn. Grind them to a coarse powder in a blender or food processor. Sprinkle over cooked grains, vegetable dishes, and over green salads.

Note for the Gardener: During the months of July and August, I unearth fresh potatoes from the garden to prepare this dish. I use a mixture of Red Gold, Yukon Gold,

German Butterball, and Rote Erstling. Some of the soft-textured potatoes break slightly during cooking, creating an interesting texture.

Serving Suggestions: These potatoes are perfect on a buffet table and also go well with most main courses. Three possible selections are Blackened Chicken (page 126), Fish Swimming in Three Flavors (page 102), and Egg and Cauliflower Whimsy (page 115).

POMEGRANATE VARIATION: The seeds of a special variety of pomegranate are used in India to impart a slight sweet-sour lift to dishes. These seeds are sold in Indian stores under the name of *anardana.* Take a teaspoon (5 ml) of these seeds and grind to a paste in a mortar and pestle or in a spice grinder, adding a little water as necessary. When the potatoes are ready, remove about ³/₄ of them from the skillet and transfer to a large bowl. Keep covered. Add the paste to the remaining potatoes in the skillet and stir gently over low heat for a few seconds. The paste will impart a brownish color to the potatoes. Remove from heat. Combine with the rest of the potatoes and serve. This way, the potatoes will have a variety of flavors.

✹ Crisp Potato and Wilted Spinach Salad ✹
INTERNATIONAL

In Bengal, potatoes and greens are eaten together. Taking that example, I have created a spicy potato-spinach salad that requires little attention and is tasty and filling. The warmth of this salad heightens the appetite. The contrast of the richly browned potatoes and the brilliance of the steamed greens delight the eye.

2   tablespoons (30 ml) Indian sesame oil (*gingely*), or olive oil

¹/₄   teaspoon (1 ml) asafetida powder

¹/₂   teaspoon (2 ml) mango powder (*aamchoor*)

¹/₄   teaspoon (1 ml) black salt

¹/₄   teaspoon (1 ml) salt

Ground red pepper to taste (start with a scant pinch; best if there is a hint of hotness)

1¹/₂   pounds (750 g) peeled or unpeeled potatoes, about 6 medium, cut into 2-inch (5-cm) cubes

About ¹/₂ pound (250 g) fresh spinach leaves, 7 cups (1.75 liters), washed several times, stemmed and cut in wide strips (see *Note* and *Note for the Gardener*)

Curry-Walnut Dressing (page 234)

Feta, Gorgonzola, or other crumbly goat or sheep cheese (or a soy cheese)
for topping

1. Preheat oven to 425°F (220°C, gas marks 7). Combine oil, asafetida, mango powder, black salt, salt, and red pepper. Taste and adjust seasoning if necessary. Toss
   potatoes in this mixture so that each piece is well-coated. Line a large cookie
   sheet with a piece of lightly oiled aluminum foil. Place potatoes, skin side up, on
   this sheet. Bake for 30 to 35 minutes or until a toothpick inserted in the thickest
   part goes smoothly all the way through. The potatoes will be pale to medium
   brown in color. Remove from the oven. Turn the potatoes cut side up. Broil potatoes 2 to 3 minutes or until richly browned. Watch carefully and don't let them
   burn. Remove from the broiler and transfer to a large bowl. Keep covered.

2. Dip the spinach strips in hot water for a few seconds to wilt them just slightly.
   Drain in a sieve. Place them in a large bowl and toss with Curry-Walnut Dressing.
   Arrange on individual serving plates. Lay the potatoes on this spinach bed. (The
   potatoes are not dressed so they will retain their crispness.) Serve topped with
   crumbled cheese.

4 servings

Note: Use the freshest spinach leaves from a bunch. Add a few arugula leaves, if
available, for a pleasantly bitter taste.

Note for the Gardener: My favorite type of garden spinach is Mazurka, which has
large thick leaves and a sweet bite. I also add some Mizuna mustard and a few tender leaves of edible chrysanthemum for a peppery effect.

Serving Suggestions: This lovely salad can precede any meal. The potatoes are also
delicious alone as a snack or side dish; top with Roasted Chile Slivers (page 217) for
an exotic flavor.

VARIATION: POTATO RADICCHIO SALAD Add flair to this salad by replacing at least half
of the spinach with grilled radicchio for its bold, pleasantly bitter taste.

To grill radicchio: Trim the bases of 1 or 2 small radicchio heads. Separate each
leaf by hand and arrange them, not overlapping, on a large baking sheet. Brush the
leaves lightly with olive oil and dust with asafetida powder, black salt, and a touch
of ground red pepper. Grill or broil for a minute or two or just until the leaves are
wilted. Radicchio will lose some of its lovely color but will acquire an exotic roasted
flavor.

SWISS CHARD, KALE, OR BEET GREEN VARIATION: Use any one of these hearty greens or a combination instead of spinach. Steam these greens (instead of merely wilting as in the case of spinach) for about 5 minutes or just until tooth-tender. Overcooking will darken them. You can also serve these greens alone dressed with Curry-Walnut Dressing (page 234) as a nourishing side dish.

✳ Indo-Chinese Bean Salad ✳
INDIA/CHINA

Indian cooks do wondrous things with beans. Traveling farther north and then east to China, I find dried peas and beans are rarely eaten but dark sesame oil is used everywhere. In India, a milder-flavored sesame oil is used primarily in the south. The union of these two ingredients from two different cultures creates a colorful bean and vegetable salad with a bare hint of roasted sesame fragrance.

1¹/₂ cups (375 ml) black-eyed peas
  4 cups (1 liter) water
¹/₂ cup (125 ml) rice vinegar
¹/₂ pound (250 g) carrots, about 2 medium, diced
  1 cup (250 ml) mild red or other sweet onion, thinly sliced (see *Note*)
  1 medium green bell pepper, seeded, finely chopped
¹/₂ cup (125 ml) finely chopped cilantro
  2 scallions, finely chopped (green part only)
    Lime-Ginger Dressing with Sesame Oil Variation (page 230)
    Salt

Garnish: Toasted sesame seeds

1. Soak black-eyed peas in water for 6 to 8 hours (optional). Cook peas in the soaking water for about 20 minutes (40 to 50 minutes if not soaked) or until tender to the bite but not mushy. Drain, retaining the cooking water for making soups or cooking other vegetables. Immediately pour vinegar over the hot peas. Let stand until the other ingredients are ready.
2. Steam carrots until tender, then transfer to a medium bowl. Add the black-eyed peas. Add onion, bell pepper, cilantro, and scallion. Pour dressing over the mixture. Adjust the amount of salt. Garnish with sesame seeds. Best if

served immediately. If made ahead and refrigerated, bring to room temperature before serving.

4 to 6 servings

Note: If sweet onion is not available, use regular onion. Place the chopped onions in a sieve and rinse several times with boiling water to make them milder.

Serving Suggestions: At a brunch, serve with Savory Indian Polenta (page 198) and Yogurt Borhani (page 295). This hearty salad will also make a satisfying supper when accompanied by Indian Chicken Soup (page 59) and papads.

✳ Artichoke and Sweet Red Pepper Salad ✳
UNITED STATES/ITALY

When playing classical music, Indian musicians perform a few notes to set the mood before proceeding with the composition. This is called *alaap* or "first introduction." Some music fans judge a performance by its *alaap*. To me, an appetizer of fresh artichokes, in which each leaf is gently separated and dipped in a savory sauce, is the *alaap* of dinner. It is a graceful and leisurely way to step into a meal, with the promise that more serious courses will follow.

4 artichokes
1 medium-sized red bell pepper
   Cumin Vinaigrette (page 233)
   Fish Aïoli (page 227)
1 teaspoon (5 ml) capers, drained, rinsed, and chopped (optional)

1. To prepare artichokes: Peel the coarse outer layers from the stem. Remove tough outer leaves and lop off about $1/2$ inch (1 cm) from the top leaves. Place in a steamer and steam for 20 to 40 minutes or until the leaves can be pulled off easily and the bottom can be pierced with a fork.
2. To roast the bell pepper: Place the pepper under the broiler for 6 to 8 minutes, or until the skin is charred, turning it once. Place in a paper bag, close the top tightly, and let rest for 10 or so minutes. Remove, allow to cool to room temperature, then peel the skin off. Discard the skin, seeds, inner membranes, and any darkened flesh. Chop the remaining flesh into bite-sized pieces.

3. Remove the artichoke leaves and arrange them in a circle on one or more large serving plates (or on individual plates) with the pointed end on the outside. Place a small bowl containing the Cumin Vinaigrette in the center.

4. Chop the artichoke heart into bite-sized pieces. Combine with roasted red pepper, Fish Aïoli, and capers. Serve in a large bowl (or in individual bowls) along with the artichoke leaf platter.

4 small servings

Serving Suggestions: The best way to enjoy this dish is to share it with friends as a first course. Offer some Hindi Croutons (page 259) for dipping into the sauce. Follow with Barley, Wild Rice, and Azuki Beans Khichuri (page 181), and Soy- and Mirin-Glazed Salmon (page 99).

SPEEDY ALTERNATIVE: For a quicker but still tempting salad, substitute for the fresh artichoke two 9-ounce (250-g) cans of artichoke hearts, drained and rinsed. In this case you will not have the artichoke leaf plate, but only the peppery appetizer. Omit Cumin Vinaigrette and Steps 1 and 3 in this case.

✳ Salmon-Pasta Salad International ✳
INTERNATIONAL

After moving to America's Pacific Northwest, I learned that Pacific salmon is one of the most versatile of fishes. In this region of the country, salmon is especially fresh and comes in many varieties: Chinook, coho, steelhead. It is now widely available in other parts of the United States, and its richness and succulence make it well-suited for Indian and East Asian cooking. This recipe has a multicultural basis. The fish is from the North Pacific, and its sauce is a cross between an Indian salad dressing and a Thai-style dip. Pasta, of course, is universal.

Capers create a Mediterranean finale to this appetizer or brunch dish.

The fish:
   1   cup (250 ml) Fish Stock (page 42) or water
   1/2   pound (250 g) fresh salmon fillet

The sauce:
   1/2   cup (125 ml) fresh lime juice
   2   tablespoons plus 2 teaspoons (40 ml) sugar

Ground red pepper (to taste; start with a scant pinch; best if there is a hint
of hotness)

A few drops of fish sauce (to taste)

Salt (with a dash of black salt for flavor)

The pasta salad:

1/4 pound (100 g) rice noodles or linguine, cooked, drained, rinsed in cold water
and cooled to room temperature (see *Note*)

2 tablespoons (30 ml) capers, drained, rinsed, chopped

1/2 cup (125 ml) mild red or other sweet onion rings

1 tablespoon (15 ml) fresh chopped Thai basil or regular basil (or cilantro)

1 tablespoon (15 ml) toasted sesame seeds

1. Bring Fish Stock or water to a boil in a fish poacher or large pan over moderate
heat. Lower heat. Add fish and simmer, covered, 5 to 7 minutes or just until fish
is done. (A toothpick inserted in the thickest part should reveal an opaque color in
the fish.) With a slotted spatula, transfer fish to a medium bowl. (Reserve the
broth for cooking fish, vegetables, or soups.) Allow fish to cool slightly, then cut
into bite-sized pieces.

2. Combine lime juice, sugar, red pepper, fish sauce, and salt in a large bowl. Add
fish and gently mix in with the dressing. Cut the noodles into bite-sized strips and
add to the bowl; stir gently. Add capers. Place onion rings on top. Serve topped
with basil and sesame seeds.

4 small servings

Note: Use any variety of rice noodles, the best being the 1/4-inch (6-mm) wide ones.
For a warm, nutty flavor toss the cooked noodles (or linguine) with 2 teaspoons
(10 ml) Chinese sesame oil immediately after they have been drained and rinsed.

Serving Suggestions: At brunch begin with a green salad and conclude with Exotic
Fruits with Sweet Pecans and Sauce (page 285). You can also place the filling (without the noodles) on one half of an omelet and fold the other half over.

VARIATION: VIETNAMESE SALMON BURRITO For an elegant, easy-to-carry snack or

brown bag lunch, wrap the salmon salad (with or without the noodles) burrito-fashion
in rice paper. Packets of edible rice paper, made from glutinous rice, are available in
Asian (especially Thai and Vietnamese) markets.

To soften rice paper for wrapping: Separate the thin, transparent sheets and lightly
wet one at a time with hot water, using fingers or a pastry brush, to make it soft and

pliable. Alternatively, dip each sheet in hot water, contained in a large bowl. Place the sheet over a kitchen towel to absorb any excess moisture. Spoon some filling along the centerfold and roll neatly into a tube shape, tucking in both ends. (Make sure salmon pieces are on top so their pretty color shows through the wrapper.) Continue moistening and rolling until the filling is used up. Serve as an appetizer or as part of a light meal. The dry rice paper will keep indefinitely. As in Vietnam, you can fill these rice papers with any leftover fish, meat, or vegetables along with chopped fresh mint or cilantro and carry them to a picnic.

✳ Carrot Cashew Koftas ✳
INDIA/HUNGARY

Shopping for nuts and spices in India has a special charm because sampling, smelling, and drinking tea are part of the ritual. During a recent trip to India, I visited Calcutta's New Market to buy some cashews. Since cashews grow in India, they are especially fresh and flavorful there. The shopowner showed me his supply and let me sample a few plump cashews that glistened in the store's dim light. When I asked for a kilo, he offered me a cup of tea to drink while he wrapped the nuts in newspaper and talked about his family, his business, and the state of the country. Then, without my asking, he brought out a jar of *tej pata*, the Indian equivalent of bay leaf. He crushed a leaf, put it on a plate, and invited me to smell it. The leaves were so fragrant that I decided a buy a bunch. As I drank another cup of tea, he laid some Kashmiri chiles in front of me. These bell-shaped, dried red peppers are less piquant than other chile varieties. They are prized for their color and rich flavor like Hungarian paprika in the West. I was captivated by their vibrancy. After finishing my third cup of tea, I left this shop well-satisfied but with several more packages than I had anticipated.

Cashews and carrots, hot and sweet Hungarian paprika, and a few Indian staple spices form the tasty mixture from which these yellowish-orange koftas are made. Traditionalists deep-fry them, but I bake them oil-free and enjoy them just as much. The vegetable mixture is so tasty that I also serve it as a side dish as described in the variation below.

The koftas:

3/4 pound (375 g) carrots, about 3 medium, diced

3/4 pound (375 g) sweet potato, 1/2 of 1 large potato, peeled, diced

2 tablespoons (30 ml) Indian sesame oil (*gingely*), or canola oil

1/4 teaspoon (1 ml) asafetida powder

1 cup (250 ml) finely chopped onion

2 tablespoons (30 ml) minced gingerroot

1 jalapeño, seeded, chopped (to taste)

1/2 teaspoon (2 ml) turmeric

1 tablespoon (15 ml) ground cumin

1/4 teaspoon (1 ml) Hungarian sweet paprika

1/8 teaspoon (0.5 ml) Hungarian hot paprika (to taste)

1/2 teaspoon (2 ml) salt

3/4 teaspoon (3 ml) sugar

1 tablespoon (15 ml) white poppy seeds, lightly roasted

1 tablespoon (15 ml) fresh lime or lemon juice

1 tablespoon (15 ml) finely chopped cilantro

1/2 cup (125 ml) unsalted raw cashew halves, pulverized to a coarse powder in a blender or food processor

1/2 cup-plus (125 ml) bread crumbs (see "To prepare bread crumbs," page 85)

1. Steam the carrots for 15 to 18 minutes or until very tender. Mash with a fork until smooth. Steam the sweet potatoes for 12 to 16 minutes or until very tender. Mash them until smooth.

2. Heat oil in a large skillet over moderate heat until a light haze forms. Sprinkle asafetida over the oil. Add onion, gingerroot, and jalapeño and cook until onion is translucent and slightly soft, 4 to 5 minutes. Add turmeric, cumin, sweet paprika, hot paprika, salt, sugar, and poppy seeds and stir several times. Add carrots and sweet potato and cook for 5 minutes, stirring constantly. Remove from heat, transfer to a large bowl, and allow to cool. Add lime juice, cilantro, and cashew powder. Adjust seasoning if necessary.

3. To shape the koftas: Add bread crumbs to the vegetable mixture and mix well to form a dough that holds together. If too moist, add a bit more of the bread crumbs. Pinch off a portion and form into a ball about 1 1/2 inches (4 cm) in diameter by rolling between the palms of your hands. If using as a sandwich filling, flatten the ball into a patty about 1 3/4 inches (4.5 cm) in diameter and about 1/2 inch (1 cm) thick. Continue this way until you use up the vegetable mixture.

4. To bake the koftas: Preheat oven to 350°F (180°C, gas marks 4). Place the koftas on a lightly oiled baking sheet. Bake for 5 to 8 minutes or until they are thoroughly heated.

Makes 30 to 40 koftas, 4 entrée servings

Serving Suggestions: At tea or snacktime, two worthy companions are Dream Yogurt (page 212) and Chilied Mango Chutney (page 205). To use as an entrée, start with rice, millet, or quinoa, and follow with Gai Lan with Balsamic Vinaigrette (page 70) and Lychee Swirl (page 287). Fill warmed whole wheat pita halves with these koftas along with shredded lettuce, alfalfa sprouts, and sweet onion rings, and serve as a sandwich.

VARIATION: VEGETABLE SUNBURST Replace sweet potato with butternut squash; toast the cashews, but don't pulverize them; and omit bread crumbs. Don't mash the vegetables after they have been steamed. In Step 1, as soon as they have been removed from heat, add lime juice and cilantro, garnish with the toasted cashews, and serve.

6 side dish servings

Serving Suggestions: Can be partnered with plain-cooked grains or scooped up with flat breads; it is also complemented by Greens Ratatouille (page 94) or Roasted Tikka Potatoes (page 243).

❋ Plum-Rice Balls ❋

JAPAN

I once watched a Japanese-American friend prepare these balls for a picnic lunch. She wetted her palms for shaping the balls, and stuffed the center of each with *umeboshi,* pickled plums. The finished dish resembled sushi but was simpler to prepare. The story goes that centuries ago, people traveling in Japan carried cooked rice and *umeboshi* in a box, and the pickling of the plums helped preserve the rice for several days. Hence comes the custom of stuffing rice balls with *umeboshi.*

Since these rice balls are best served fresh, it's fun to let your guests participate. Lay out little saucers of the various stuffing choices and cruets of the dipping sauces. Then bring on the warm sushi rice for the guests to shape into balls. Dip and munch as you go along.

- ¹/₄ cup (60 ml) rice vinegar
- 4 teaspoons (20 ml) sugar
- ³/₄ teaspoon (3 ml) salt

  1 cup (250 ml) short-grain white rice (see *Note 1*)

1³/4 cups (435 ml) water

  1 whole black cardamom pod or 2 to 3 whole green cardamom pods

¹/4 cup (60 ml) toasted sesame seeds (see *Note 2*)

25 sheets of seasoned nori, 2 x 3¹/2 inches (5 x 9 cm)

For stuffing (choose one or more): salmon as prepared in Salmon-Pasta Salad International (page 250), without the noodles; canned smoked mussels or oysters; pitted and chopped olives; pickled plum or ginger (available in Asian markets); pickled lime, mango, or garlic (available in Indian groceries)

For dipping (choose one or more of these combinations): soy sauce and Japanese horseradish (wasabi) or regular horseradish; soy sauce, rice vinegar, and fish sauce; soy sauce and Chinese sesame oil

For topping (optional; choose one or more): slivered cucumber or avocado; fresh chopped basil

For dusting on top: Chaat Powder (see page 8)

1. Combine vinegar, sugar, and salt in a small bowl and stir to dissolve sugar and salt.
2. Place rice, water, and cardamom in a medium-sized pan. Cover and bring to a boil. Lower heat and simmer, covered. When rice and water are at the same level, about 5 minutes, uncover and stir the rice. This will loosen the starch and make the mixture creamier. Simmer, covered, until all water is absorbed and rice is tender, another 5 to 10 minutes. Remove from heat and allow to cool slightly. Discard cardamom. The rice will be sticky. Add the vinegar mixture to the rice and use while still warm. With wet palms, shape the rice into balls 1¹/2 inches (4 cm) in diameter. Stuff with a small amount of a filling of your choice, finely chopped. Close the ball.
3. Roll the balls in sesame seeds. (If packing these balls into a lunch or picnic box, omit the rest of this step.) On a small individual saucer, combine dipping sauce ingredients, tasting to adjust the spiciness. Toast the nori sheets by placing on an ungreased griddle over low heat for a few seconds until they change color. Watch carefully; they burn quickly. (If serving to guests, you can prepare the nori ahead of time.) Place a rice ball on top of a nori sheet. Wrap the nori around the ball, add a topping ingredient, dust with Chaat Powder, dip into the sauce, and enjoy. Best served soon after they are made.

Makes about 25 balls, 4 to 6 appetizer servings

Note 1: For best results use sushi rice, available in Asian markets and well-stocked supermarkets. Regular long- or short-grained brown rice doesn't hold together as well when shaped into balls. You can use short-grained sweet (glutinous) brown rice, which becomes sticky when cooked; it is available in natural-food stores. The cooking time of this rice is longer, 30 to 40 minutes.

Note 2: If available, use black sesame seeds rather than the common white variety for a contrast in color. They are sold in Asian markets.

Serving Suggestions: Place on a buffet table or carry along on a picnic or a day hike. Try these savory rice balls after a run or workout with a cup of roasted barley tea (available in Asian markets). Serve as an appetizer followed by Lime-Ginger Chicken (page 102) and steamed corn on the cob sprinkled with lime juice and Roasted Tomato-Chile Salsa (page 216).

✳ Plantain Fou-Fou ✳
AFRICA/THE CARIBBEAN

Fou-fous are walnut-sized plantain balls that are soft, sweet, and limey. I first experienced them at Islabelle, a Caribbean restaurant in Seattle, and seized the opportunity to talk to Chef Lorenzo. He told me the dish originated in Africa but is also found in his native Cuba, where it's more likely to be served as a big lump rather than as dainty balls.

Later I learned that fou-fou is the generic name for a starchy dish served daily in Africa. It's made with ground rice, plantain, or yuca. An African friend fondly recalled being awakened each dawn in his village home by the sounds of the women pounding fou-fou ingredients.

In adapting Chef Lorenzo's recipe, I couldn't resist adding turmeric for a slight pungency and color, and asafetida for a garlicky perfume. Fou-fous can be difficult to shape into balls, so I often serve the delicious puree as a vegetable side dish.

3/4 pound (375 g), 1 large unpeeled plantain, more yellow than green (see *Note*)
6   ounces (175 g) yam, peeled and cut into 1-inch (2.5-cm) cubes
1/4 cup (60 ml) fresh lime juice
1/2 cup (125 ml) or more plantain cooking water
     Romaine or radicchio leaves

The spices:

- 1   tablespoon (15 ml) olive oil
- ¼   teaspoon (1 ml) asafetida powder
- 6   large cloves garlic, finely minced
- 1   jalapeño, seeded, chopped (to taste)
- ⅛   teaspoon (0.5 ml) turmeric
- 1   small red or green bell pepper, minced
-     Salt
- ¼   teaspoon (1 ml) garam masala
- 1   tablespoon (15 ml) finely chopped cilantro

1. Place the plantain in a large, steep-sided pan. Add water to cover and bring to a boil. Lower heat and simmer, covered, for 25 to 40 minutes or until plantain is tender. (A toothpick inserted should go through easily.) Drain, reserving some of the cooking water. Using the tines of a fork, remove the skin and discard it. Also remove the dark thread in the center. Chop the flesh coarsely.
2. Steam the yam for 15 to 18 minutes or until tender.
3. Place the plantain, yam, and lime juice in a blender or food processor. Whirl until smooth, adding a bit of the cooking water if necessary. (Too much water will make the mixture soft and the fou-fous will not hold their shape.) Transfer to a large bowl.
4. Heat oil in a small skillet over moderate heat until it sizzles. Sprinkle asafetida over the oil. Add garlic and cook for a few seconds. Add jalapeño and turmeric. Add bell pepper. Cover and simmer until the bell pepper is tender, 8 to 12 minutes. Remove from heat. Add salt and garam masala.
5. Add the bell pepper mixture and cilantro to the plantain-yam puree and mix thoroughly. Serve immediately as a vegetable puree on romaine or radicchio cups. (For an exotic taste, grill the radicchio; see "To grill radicchio," page 247.)
6. If you want to shape fou-fou into balls, refrigerate the mixture for at least 2 hours or overnight. Scoop into balls using a melon scooper or a soup spoon. (Sometimes only a part of the mixture will be stiff enough to be shaped. Serve the remainder as a vegetable side dish.) For best flavor, bring to room temperature before serving.

Makes 20 or more balls, 4 to 6 side dish servings

Note: The consistency and taste of fou-fou depend on the ripeness of the plantain. If the plantain is yellowish brown with dark spots (which means they are very ripe), the resulting dish will be sweeter and have a more spreadable consistency.

Serving Suggestions: As an appetizer, serve 4 balls per person (or a ¹/2 cup [125 ml] portion) on a plate with Cilantro Splash (page 223) and Tamarind-Date Chutney (page 208) on the side. Or serve as a spread for raw vegetables or papads. For an excellent, low-cholesterol deviled egg, mound 1 tablespoon (15 ml) or so on top of a hard-boiled egg half (removing the yolk first). At a main meal serve with Cuban-Indian Cassoulet (page 84). Fou-fou is also an excellent accompaniment to most grain and bean dishes.

NONFAT ALTERNATIVE: For a simpler but still delicious fou-fou, omit the oil and spices. Add salt at the end of Step 3. Serve as in Step 5.

✻ Piquant Salad in Shades of Green ✻
INTERNATIONAL

The base of this salad is green vegetables of different shades and consistencies. You can serve it either as a stimulating starter or European-style as a palate cleanser after the main course. For a feast, compose a more substantial salad by adding yellow or orange vegetables; complex carbohydrates in the form of cooked pasta, potatoes, or whole grains; seaweed for trace elements; and protein-rich sprinkles such as tempeh, seeds, or nuts. Supplement the texture of the salad with Hindi Croutons (recipe follows). For such an elaborate salad, choose one or more ingredients from these lists. Allow 1¹/2 cups (375 ml) or more per person depending on the rest of the meal.

The green base: Baby romaine, endive, radicchio, chicory, arugula, purslane, spinach, Mizuna mustard; blanched greens such as bok choy, kale, collard, Swiss chard; steamed leeks or green beans. Chopped fresh basil, cilantro, or Italian parsley provides further variety and flavor.

Complementary vegetables: Dried tomato bits; pitted Kalamata olives; toasted, dehydrated garlic chips; canned palm hearts; wakame or other seaweed, softened; steamed golden beets or rutabaga.

Carbo additions: Cooked pasta; steamed potatoes; cooked brown rice, millet, quinoa, or barley.

Global garnishes: Enoki mushroom; toasted nori; pan-fried tempeh cubes; toasted pumpkin seeds; toasted pecans; crumbled goat or sheep cheese such as feta or Gorgonzola, or soy cheese.

Savory dressings: Ideas abound in the Chutneys, Sauces, and Dressings chapter and other chapters in this book. For a change, simply toss the leaves with fine extra-virgin olive oil, then mix in rice vinegar or a flavored vinegar. This custom of dressing a salad with oil and vinegar separately comes from Greece and the Middle East.

VARIATION: WINTER SALAD In cooler weather, for warmth and textural contrast, steam, roast, sauté, or wilt some of the vegetables. Some choices are grilled zucchini, roasted potatoes, sautéed gai lan, and wilted red cabbage. You can also prepare the same vegetable in two different ways; for example, steam some of the carrots, but add the remainder raw in grated form.

✳ Hindi Croutons ✳

THE MIDDLE EAST

These crispy wafers provide textural contrast to a salad but contain far less fat than most commercial croutons. Their spiciness and crunchy texture make them a wonderful snack as well.

3 to 4   whole wheat or white pita breads
         Olive oil for brushing

The spices (use one of these combinations):

1) Asafetida powder
   Ground red pepper
   Black salt

2) Chaat Powder (see page 8)

Preheat oven to 450°F (230°C, gas marks 8). Cut each pita in half. Separate two layers of each half. Place the 4 semicircles on an ungreased baking sheet with the inner side down. Bake for 3 minutes or just until slightly crisp. Brush the inner side with olive oil and sprinkle with spices. Cut each semicircle into 1-inch (2.5-cm) squares. (If using as a snack with a dip, cut them into chip-sized wedges.) Bake for another 3 to 5 minutes, inner side up, just until crisp and lightly browned. Take care not to burn them.

4 small servings

Serving Suggestions: These spicy croutons have innumerable uses. They are delicious sprinkled over a crisp green salad, particularly one made with butterhead lettuce. Topped with boiled potato chunks and drizzled with plain yogurt and Tamarind-Date

Chutney (page 208), they become a tempting appetizer. Crush and sprinkle a few croutons over Roasted Banana Raita (page 210) just before serving for a delicious crunch. They can also be served as a snack with dips, such as Plantain Fou-Fou (page 256) or Sun-Dried Tomato and Sweet Red Pepper Cream (page 226).

✳ Sweet Curry Pecans ✳
INTERNATIONAL

For years I've given these sweet pecans as a Christmas gift. Fine quality pecans, hot aromatic curry powder, and flavored sugar are the ingredients. I place the finished nuts in a colorful container, tie a bow around it, and place the recipe on top. My friends have always appreciated this gift.

Instead of pecans you can use walnuts.

1   cup (250 ml) pecans (or walnuts)
2   teaspoons (10 ml) canola oil (see *Note* on nonfat alternative)
1/4   teaspoon (1 ml) curry powder (preferably hot; see "Selecting curry powder," page 10)
1/4   cup (60 ml) sugar (or a combination of date or maple sugar and regular sugar)
1/4   cup (60 ml) water
1/4   teaspoon (1 ml) ginger powder (also known as ground ginger)
1/8   teaspoon (0.5 ml) salt
     Ground red pepper (to taste; start with a scant pinch)

1. To toast the pecans: Place the pecans on an ungreased griddle over low to medium-low heat until they are evenly browned, turning them once. If using walnuts, toast them slightly longer, turning them frequently to avoid burning. Transfer to a medium bowl as soon as each nut is done.
2. Heat oil in a medium skillet over moderate heat. Stir in curry powder. Add nuts and mix well. Cook for a minute or so. Remove from heat and transfer to a medium bowl.
3. Place sugar and water in a medium pan and bring to a boil. Lower the heat. Add ginger powder and salt and cook until the syrup starts to become sticky, a few minutes. Dust lightly with red pepper. Add the nuts and stir gently. As soon as the syrup has formed a coating around the nuts, remove from heat. Transfer to a large

plate lined with wax paper. Keep the nuts as far apart from each other as possible, as they will have a tendency to clump together. Allow to cool to room temperature. Separate those nuts that stick together. Serve at room temperature.

4 small servings

Note: For a nonfat alternative, omit oil and don't sauté the nuts in Step 2. In Step 3, add curry powder to the sugar mixture as it boils. Proceed as in the rest of the recipe.

Serving Suggestions: Serve as a snack alone or accompany with fresh fruits for dessert. Excellent when chopped and used as a garnish for cole slaw, apple salad, or rice pudding.

✻ Toasted Baby Sardines and ✻ Caramelized Peanuts
SINGAPORE/MALAYSIA

I first encountered *ikan bilis*, a delightful snack of tiny dried fish and sweet peanuts, in Singapore. There, on a lazy afternoon with the tropical sun still overhead, I wandered to an outdoor food stall where I noticed a man sitting at a table. He had in front of him a glass of sugarcane juice and a snack containing peanuts and fish. I was unfamiliar with this snack. As he sipped his beverage and nibbled leisurely on his food, he looked as though the sun, the sugarcane, and the snack were all in the whole world that mattered. I ordered some *ikan bilis* myself.

The appetizer is characterized by an intriguing combination of sweet, salty, and nutty flavors and is enhanced by the crunchiness of toasted fish. Singapore-returned tourists claim that the famed Raffles Hotel first served it with cocktails some years ago, promoting it as an afternoon ritual. But, according to residents of Singapore and Malaysia, *ikan bilis* dates back much further. They say that for as long as people can remember it has been eaten daily in homes with the morning rice as a protein-packed accompaniment.

Though it may seem exotic, *ikan bilis* can be easily prepared in Western kitchens, where peanuts are a common snack item. Baby sardines or other packaged, small dried fish can be obtained in Asian stores. Curry powder, not used in the Singapore version, spikes this recipe, while *sev*, a ready-to-eat chick-pea noodle, gives it an even more Indian character.

    2 teaspoons (10 ml) Indian sesame oil (*gingely*), or canola oil

    6 ounces (170 g) dry-roasted, unsalted peanuts (see *Note 1*)

  ¹/₄ cup (60 ml) dark brown sugar

1¹/₂ tablespoons (22 ml) water

    1 tablespoon (15 ml) low-sodium soy sauce

  ¹/₄ teaspoon (1 ml) curry powder

      Ground red pepper (to taste; start with a scant pinch)

  ¹/₄ teaspoon (1 ml) black salt

      Salt

4 to 5 ounces (100 to 150 g) dried baby sardines or other packaged small dried fish, 1 to 2 inches (2.5 to 5 cm) in length

    1 cup (250 ml) *sev*, chick-pea noodles (see *Note 2*)

1. Heat oil in a small skillet over medium heat. Add peanuts and cook for a minute or two or until slightly darkened, stirring often. Transfer to a medium bowl.

2. Combine sugar, water, and soy sauce in a small saucepan over medium heat and bring to a boil. Lower the heat and add curry powder, red pepper, and black salt. Cook, stirring often, until the sauce is very thick and starts to become sticky. Add peanuts and stir to mix well with the syrup. Add salt. Remove from heat and transfer to a large bowl. Keep covered.

3. If the fish are more than 1¹/₂ inches (4 cm) long, cut crosswise in halves. Toast the fish pieces on an ungreased skillet over low heat until lightly browned, 4 to 6 minutes, turning them frequently. Transfer to the bowl containing the caramelized peanuts. Add chick-pea noodles and gently toss the mixture. Best served while still warm but also good at room temperature.

4 to 6 servings

Note 1: For freshness, I buy raw peanuts (with their skin on) from natural-food stores and roast them in a 350°F (180°C, gas marks 4) oven for about 15 minutes or until crunchy and slightly darkened.

Note 2: These snack noodles come in pieces about 1 to 2 inches (2.5 to 5 cm) long and in different degrees of thickness. Choose the needle-thin variety if available.

Serving Suggestions: Munch at snacktime or serve as a condiment with a grain dish such as Basic Pilaf with Nutty Vermicelli Threads (page 177). Enjoy as a prelude to Crisp Potatoes and Wilted Spinach Salad (page 246) or Sesame Arugula and Squash (page 85).

Sweet Touches

● ● ● ● ● ● ● ● ● ● ●

In the western Indian state of Gujarat, a typical meal starts with a small sweet dish. "You get the most intense taste from that first bite. It sets the tone for the entire meal," said a Gujarati man. Sweets were not a regular part of our meals in Bengal except during festivals. On those special days, we savored a variety of milk-based confections, such as tiny dumplings made with fresh cheese and flavored with saffron, rose water, or kewra essence. On most occasions, however, sweet snacks consisted of fresh tropical fruits—mango, papaya, jackfruit, and lychees.

After moving to the United States, I found fruits were not only served fresh but also used in cooking. As I tried my hand at baking, I discovered wholesome, appetizing treats including such old-time favorites as cobblers and crisps. These fruit-filled delights not only look and taste delicious but also infuse the kitchen with a lovely aroma while they bake.

Later, I acquired more valuable knowledge about the use of fruits in desserts while staying with a family in the southwestern region of France, renowned for its cooking. During the summer, they gave informal classes on the French language, culture, and cuisine. On my first day, we visited a fine restaurant and feasted on a gourmet meal featuring such delicacies as truffles and goose liver pâtés. After dinner, I interviewed the chef and got some tips on making pâtés. It was a fine introduction to the regional cooking of France, but my real lesson started the next morning.

We studied French intensively for several hours and, just as Marcel Proust was remembering what it was like to dip a madeleine into a cup of tea, the teacher inter-rupted, "It's eleven o'clock. Time to prepare lunch." We rushed to the kitchen.

Within an hour she had prepared a delicious lunch that included an excellent fruit tart. She rolled out a thin crust and covered it attractively with slices of fresh ripe peaches bursting with nectar. Then she glazed the top lightly with melted fruit preserve, and finally placed the ensemble in the oven. Just as we finished lunch, a fragrance emanating from the oven announced that the tart was ready. The warm, brown tart was fruity-sweet and light, and enhanced the meal without overwhelm-ing it. Though I have long since forgotten the flavor of the pâté, I can still taste that peach tart.

Besides fruit desserts, I have taken a liking to Western milk-based desserts—cus-tards, bread puddings, and creamy dessert sauces. When preparing them, I often apply traditional Indian dessert cooking techniques such as thickening milk by slowly simmering it. Many sweet dishes in this chapter use this creamy, thick milk as a rich, nutty sauce or as a base.

Another popular Indian ingredient is freshly made cheese, *channa.* This cheese, which is a foundation for many Indian desserts, serves as an accompaniment to my fresh fruit platters. Crushed cashews and pistachios, indispensable to Indian sweet-makers, add elegance to puddings. I borrow the American technique of using pureed fruits when making Indian confections. This reduces the intense sweetness that many Westerners find overwhelming.

Many familiar Western desserts taste even better when appropriate ingredients from other cultures are used in their preparation. For instance, I add cardamom and coriander powder to an apple cake batter and top the finished cake with a warm honey-ricotta spread. Cardamom, cloves, and cinnamon intensify the flavor of Spiced Fruit Bars.

Lean, fresh, healthy sweets have an appeal greater than the sum of their diverse ethnic origins. They complement Indian-inspired meals beautifully. In this chapter, you'll find recipes for Spanish flan prepared with thickened lowfat milk, a lovely end-ing to a dinner. Italy's arborio rice, simmered in thickened milk and spices, Indian style, produces a rice pudding worthy of any multicultural table. A Caribbean yam cake, sweetened with pureed banana and spiced with cardamom and nutmeg, pro-vides an excellent counterpoint for steamed fish and vegetables.

The best dessert, I believe, is one that doesn't overpower—an accent, not a statement. And as is the custom in India, I serve desserts in small portions. Enlivened with fresh fruits, vegetables, and grains, the sweet touches found in this chapter will leave you with pleasant memories and good health. ✳

Sweet Hints

* When using baking powder or baking soda, I mix it thoroughly with flour so the rising action will take place evenly.

* I don't use salt in my baking and notice no difference in taste.

* In trying to minimize the use of sugar, I experiment with raw or flavored sugars, which also improve the quality of a dessert. Date sugar has a slight crunch and adds a bit of texture (because it doesn't dissolve completely) to an otherwise soft pudding. Flavorful maple sugar is best in a dessert where it's not overwhelmed by spices or other bolder ingredients. Brown rice syrup is gentle. Sucanat (raw cane sugar) has a robust, natural taste.

  Jaggery, unrefined palm sugar, sold in Indian groceries as solid dense blocks, is another flavorful alternative. It adds a new dimension to dessert recipes, especially those that are milk-based. I use it whenever I can. If not available, substitute regular palm sugar, also sold as a block in cans in Asian markets.

  Note that some of these sugars are darker and will change the color of the finished dish.

* A crack on the top of a loaf or a cake indicates it is done.

* When dusting with powdered sugar, I place the sugar in a fine sieve, then gently shake the sieve over the cake. This distributes the sugar finely and evenly over the surface.

* I have specified egg whites as substitutes for whole eggs whenever possible. Instead of eliminating egg yolks altogether, consider the option of adding $1/2$ an egg yolk or even a teaspoon of a beaten yolk along with the egg whites for a richer taste and color.

* You'll find a number of fruit cobblers, crunches, and crisps in this chapter. These simple, lowfat baked items have made a comeback in America. They go beautifully with most Indian-inspired meals.

✳ Risotto-Style Rice Pudding ✳
INDIA/ENGLAND/ITALY

In India, one speaks of rice pudding in the same breath as childhood's favorite kite or a first visit to a country fair. There, specially grown, tiny-grained rice is simmered slowly in milk on top of the stove with fragrant cardamom pods.

Rice pudding is also a standard in England. A British woman recalled how her mother would bake plain rice, eggs, milk, sugar, cinnamon, and nutmeg in an earthenware pot for several hours.

This recipe differs from the traditional Indian or English method and is also quicker. I first boil the milk for a short time in the Indian fashion to thicken it, then cook Italian arborio rice in it risotto style. The result is a creamy, velvety pudding fun to prepare and eat. A dash of rose water at the end adds a flowery aroma.

    5 cups (1.25 liters) 2% lowfat milk (don't use nonfat)
       Pinch saffron threads, soaked in 1 tablespoon (15 ml) warm milk or water
          for 15 minutes
2¹/₂ cups-plus (625 ml) boiling water
  ¹/₂ cup (125 ml) *superfino* arborio rice
    3 whole cardamom pods, bruised
  ¹/₄ cup (60 ml) sugar (to taste)
       A splash of rose water (optional)

1. Lightly oil the bottom and sides of a large, steep-sided pan to prevent milk from sticking. Bring milk to a boil over medium-high to high heat. Lower the heat immediately to prevent milk from boiling over and stir vigorously until foaming subsides. Turn heat to medium. Cook for 12 to 15 minutes or until reduced to about half of its volume. Stir often and mix in any thickened bits of milk into the liquid milk. Add saffron. Reduce heat to very low.

2. Bring ¹/₂ cup (125 ml) of the boiling water, rice, and cardamom pods to a boil in a medium pan over moderate heat (see *Note*). Lower the heat slightly and cook, uncovered, until all water is absorbed, stirring often. Add ¹/₂ cup (125 ml) more of the remaining hot water and cook, stirring often. Continue this way until all of the hot water is used up. At this point, rice should be firm and chewy but not hard at the center. If it is, add a little more hot water and cook. Taste an individual grain to make sure it's done.

3. Now add ½ cup (125 ml) of the hot milk and cook, uncovered, until the milk is absorbed, stirring constantly. Repeat until all milk is used up and the mixture becomes thick and creamy. (Be sure to turn off the heat under the pan containing the milk and remove the pan from the heat.) Add sugar and mix well. Remove from heat. Allow to cool to room temperature, discard cardamom pods, and sprinkle rose water on top. Serve immediately. You can also refrigerate and serve chilled, in which case the pudding will be slightly drier.

4 servings

Note: Choosing a pan for risotto: The choice of a pan is important in cooking risotto. With a wide pan, the liquid will evaporate quickly but the rice may not cook. Choose a pan that's heavy and deep, neither too narrow nor too wide.

Serving Suggestions: Surrounded with fresh ripe peaches, mangoes, or raspberries, this rice pudding can adorn any meal and is particularly good with seafood dishes. Try Soy- and Mirin-Glazed Salmon (page 99) or Steamed Fish in Lime-Ginger Sauce (page 101). For accompaniment I suggest warmed chapatis or baked papads, not rice.

JACKFRUIT VARIATION: Dried jackfruit, sweetened by its own juice, adds a marvelous flavor to this pudding. (If not available, use dried mango or another dried fruit of your choice.) Finely chop 3 or 4 pieces of the fruit and add to the milk in Step 1, after it has come to a boil for the first time.

✳ Sweet Yam Cake from Negril ✳
THE CARIBBEAN

At Negril Beach, located on the western coast of Jamaica, I came across a fine bakery offering fruit- and vegetable-based cakes that were delicious and never overwhelmingly sweet. I sampled a flourless yam cake with a puddinglike consistency. This, I was told, existed in many forms throughout the Caribbean. Coconut milk was the liquid they used, but my substitution of evaporated milk (similar to Indian thickened milk) works just as well.

The spices—cinnamon, cardamom, and nutmeg—impart a warm, breezy "island" feel, and their fragrance fills the house when I bake this rich brown cake. Since the yams are grated, the cake's texture is slightly chewy, not soft.

  2 large eggs or 4 egg whites, lightly beaten

1/2 cup (125 ml) light brown sugar or sucanat (raw cane sugar)

10 ounces (300 ml) evaporated skim milk

  1 teaspoon (5 ml) ground cinnamon

  1 teaspoon (5 ml) ground cardamom

  1 teaspoon (5 ml) ground nutmeg

18 ounces (500 g) yam or sweet potato, about 1 1/2 medium, grated

1/2 pound (250 g), 1 large very ripe banana, peeled, thoroughly mashed

1. Preheat oven to 400°F (200°C, gas marks 6). Beat eggs and sugar together in a large bowl until thoroughly mixed. Add milk, cinnamon, cardamom, and nutmeg and beat again. Add yam and banana. Pour into a lightly oiled, 9-inch (22.5-cm) square baking pan.
2. Bake for 40 to 45 minutes or until a toothpick inserted in the center comes out clean. Allow to cool, then cut in squares and serve. Or, refrigerate to develop the flavor and serve the next day.

10 servings

Serving Suggestions: This cake goes well with beef or pork dishes or with vegetable dishes containing dark leafy greens. I suggest Universal Vindaloo (page 140), Kheema with Kale and Chinese Five-Spice (page 136), or Greens Ratatouille (page 94).

✳ Royal Bread Pudding ✳
NORTH INDIA/UNITED STATES

One of my favorite American indulgences is bread pudding, which reminds me of its Indian equivalent, *shahi tukra*, "bread for the king." Unlike its American counterpart, the Indian version is eggless and requires no baking. It originated in the Mogul days, when the bread cubes were fried in fragrant ghee and wrapped in edible silver leaf before being dipped into a lush cream sauce. They were presented to the king in a gold filigreed bowl.

    This recipe is faster and simpler and uses techniques from both India and the United States, but stands royally on its own.

  4 cups (1 liter) 2% lowfat milk (preferable; or use nonfat milk) (see *Note 1*)

1/4 cup (60 ml) sugar

1   tablespoon (15 ml) unsalted raw cashew halves or slivered almonds
1   tablespoon (15 ml) unsalted raw pistachios
2   tablespoons (30 ml) golden raisins
$^1/_4$ teaspoon (1 ml) nutmeg
$^1/_2$ teaspoon (2 ml) ground cardamom
2   slices whole wheat, multigrain, or white bread about $^1/_2$ inch (1 cm) thick, cut into 1 × 1 inch (2.5 × 2.5 cm) pieces
$^1/_2$ cup (125 ml) water

Garnish: (mandatory; one of the following):
   Chopped dried cranberries or apricots
   Chopped fresh apples

1. Lightly oil the bottom and sides of a large, steep-sided, and preferably nonstick pan. Heat milk over medium-high heat. When it comes to a boil, turn heat to medium. Start timimg from this point. Watch carefully and do not allow the milk to boil over. Stir frequently and scrape the bottom and sides to loosen the milk solids and incorporate with the liquid milk. Cook until the milk reaches the consistency of heavy cream, 18 to 25 minutes. Stir in 1 tablespoon (15 ml) of the sugar, the cashews, pistachios, raisins, nutmeg, and cardamom. Remove from heat. Keep covered until Step 2 and Step 3 are done.

2. Preheat oven to 350°F (180°C, gas marks 4). Place the bread pieces on an ungreased cookie sheet. Bake until they are hard, browned, and crouton-like, 10 to 15 minutes. Take care not to burn. (See *Note 2*.)

3. Bring the remaining sugar and water to a boil. Cook for 7 to 10 minutes over moderate heat, until it acquires the consistency of a thin syrup. Remove from heat. Drop the bread croutons into this hot syrup. They will absorb the syrup immediately. Remove with a slotted spoon and add to the thickened milk mixture. Garnish liberally with one of the dried or fresh fruits to balance the dark color of the bread pieces. Serve warm or at room temperature. Best if eaten within a few hours. If allowed to stand overnight in the refrigerator, the bread cubes will "drink up" much of the sauce, although the dish will still taste delicious.

4 servings

Note 1: A richer and creamier alternative is to replace lowfat milk with whole milk. Or use lowfat milk but add 1 to 2 tablespoons (15 to 30 ml) whipping cream (not whipped) in Step 1 just before adding the sugar and the nuts. This will enrich the sauce without significantly increasing its fat content.

Note 2: For extra flavor, you can pan-fry the bread pieces instead of baking them. Heat 1 to 2 tablespoons (15 to 30 ml) oil, ghee, or butter in a small skillet over moderate heat. Fry the bread pieces, turning them often. They will absorb the oil quickly. Continue to cook them until they harden and turn medium brown, 3 to 5 minutes.

Serving Suggestions: Enjoy this treat for breakfast or as dessert, alone or accompanied by slices of fresh fruits—mangoes, peaches, bananas, raspberries, or strawberries. When served with Shrimp and Orzo Pullao (page 149), Hot Punjab Eggplant (page 80), and some grilled Hubbard squash, this dessert will bring you rave reviews.

VARIATION: PAPAYA BREAD PUDDING For an exotic fruity taste, add 6 tablespoons (90 ml) creamy papaya concentrate to the thickened milk just before adding the bread pieces in Step 3. You can buy this concentrate in natural-food stores.

✳ Shah Jahani Flan ✳
SPAIN

A Cuban cook once told me that he could prepare flan on short notice, because it calls for only three ingredients—eggs, milk, and sugar. "And you usually have them in your kitchen," he said.

I have taken flan lessons from many Spanish-speaking cooks and each one has taught me a unique and exciting variation. In this recipe, I add my own twist by thickening the milk first in the Indian fashion. The resulting custard has a delicate yet more solid texture.

- $1/4$ cup (60 ml) dark brown sugar
- 1 tablespoon (15 ml) water
- 3 cups (750 ml) 2% lowfat milk (don't use nonfat)
- 3 large eggs or 6 egg whites at room temperature (see *Note 1*)
- $1/4$ cup (60 ml) sugar
- 1 teaspoon (5 ml) vanilla extract (see *Note 2*)

1. Place brown sugar and water in a small saucepan over low heat. Cook for several minutes until sugar starts to form a sticky syrup that coats a spoon. Immediately pour equal amounts of this syrup into 6 custard cups. Swirl it around to coat the bottom and partway up the sides. The syrup will harden as it cools.
2. Lightly oil the bottom and sides of a large, steep-sided pan to prevent milk from sticking. Place milk in it and bring to a boil over medium-high heat. Stir vigorously

until the foaming subsides. Reduce the heat to medium and cook for 6 to 8 minutes, stirring often, until slightly thickened. Remove from heat.

3. Preheat oven to 350°F (180°C, gas marks 4). Beat eggs and sugar in a medium bowl until smooth and lemon-colored. (If using only egg whites, the color will be white.) Gradually mix the hot milk into the egg-sugar mixture, stirring constantly. Add vanilla. Divide into the custard cups.

4. In a larger baking pan (such as a 9 × 12 inch [22.5 × 30 cm] cake pan), pour very hot water to come to a height of $^1/_2$ to 1 inch (1 to 2.5 cm). This pan has to be deep enough to fit the custard cups without overflowing. Place the cups in this pan and bake for 40 to 55 minutes or just until a toothpick inserted in the center comes out clean. Don't overbake, as the custard will start to separate. Cool completely, then chill for at least 30 minutes.

5. Just before serving, pass a blunt knife around the inside of each cup. Place a serving plate on top. Invert the plate and the cup, and gently lift the cup. The custard should remain on the serving plate and the caramel sauce will ooze over. Hold cup over the custard to allow the remaining caramel sauce to drizzle over.

6 servings

Note 1: For those on a low-cholesterol diet, flan can be made with egg whites alone. The resulting dish will not have as solid a texture or as rich a color, although it will still be tasty.

Note 2: The quality of vanilla really shows through this flan. My favorite vanilla comes from the town of Papantla in Mexico.

Serving Suggestions: To show off the warm, beautiful colors of this custard, serve on a glass plate or a simple white plate. Accompany with fresh fruits—mangoes, strawberries, or chilled grapes. This versatile dessert goes well with any meal but has a particular affinity for simply prepared seafood. For a lively Spanish touch, serve with Peppery Squid (page 122) or Mussels Bedded on Saffron Rice (page 119). Or plan a summer luncheon with Siamese Ceviche with Jícama (page 98), Artichoke and Sweet Red Pepper Salad (page 249), and some Sweet Biscuitsticks (page 197).

SAFFRON VARIATION: Use saffron to impart a distinct bouquet and a brighter color to the finished dish. Grind $^1/_2$ teaspoon (2 ml) saffron threads to a powder. Soak in 1 tablespoon (15 ml) warm milk or water for 15 minutes. Combine with the milk and egg-sugar mixture in Step 3. Omit vanilla in this case.

✳ Maple Peanut Flan ✳

SPAIN

Nuts are a common dessert ingredient in India. In this contemporary flan, peanut butter forms a top layer and maple flavor permeates throughout. A pleasing finale to any meal.

- 3 tablespoons (45 ml) peanut butter
- 1/2 cup (125 ml) pure maple syrup
- 3 large eggs or 6 egg whites at room temperature, lightly beaten
- 2 cups (500 ml) lowfat milk (don't use nonfat)

1. Preheat oven to 350°F (180°C, gas marks 4). Mix peanut butter and maple syrup in a medium-sized bowl with a fork until smooth. Add eggs one a time, mixing after each addition.
2. Scald the milk in a medium pan. Pour the hot milk gradually over the egg mixture, stirring constantly. Divide into 6 custard cups. Fill a 9 × 13 inch (22.5 × 32.5 cm) baking pan with hot water that comes to a height of 1/2 inch to 1 inch (1 to 2.5 cm). This pan has to be deep enough to fit the custard cups without overflowing. Place the custard cups in this pan. Bake for 60 to 65 minutes, or until a toothpick inserted in the center comes out clean. Don't overbake. During baking, the peanut butter will separate and rise to the top, forming a thin layer. Serve warm or allow to cool to room temperature, then refrigerate for 1 hour and serve chilled.

6 servings

Serving Suggestions: It's best to serve this flan in the same custard cup it's been baked in. It has a softer, less solid texture than most flans and can't be inverted onto a plate. Arrange colorful slices of kiwi, papaya, and mandarin orange segments, along with some Italian biscotti on a platter around the cups for a dramatic effect. Entrée suggestions include Indian Chicken Salad (page 131), Karhi-Sauced Penne (page 154), and Braised Leeks with Elephant Garlic (page 72).

✳ Sweet Orzo Pullao ✳

PAKISTAN/THE MEDITERRANEAN

Jarda, sweetened rice, is a must at wedding feasts and religious festivals in Pakistan, Bangladesh, and northwestern India. This elaborate dessert is made of fine quality rice, ghee, cashews, raisins, and rose water. Because these items are expensive in those countries, *jarda* is considered a special treat. Even the raisins are chosen carefully. Raisins from Kabul, Afganistan, are considered to be the most flavorful of all and fetch a high price in Indian markets. Whenever I visit India, I bring back some *kabuli* raisins especially to make *jarda*.

I have made a few changes to the traditional recipe. Orzo, the tear-shaped Mediterranean pasta, takes the place of rice. I use less ghee. Crystallized ginger balances the gentle sweetness of this dish with a sharp spicy accent.

6	cups (1.5 liters) water
1	cup (250 ml) orzo
1 to 1¹/₂	tablespoons (15 to 22 ml) ghee or butter
5	whole cardamom pods, bruised
	2-inch (5-cm) cinnamon stick
5	whole cloves
1	tablespoon (15 ml) raw cashew halves
1	tablespoon (15 ml) golden raisins, soaked in warm water for 15 minutes
¹/₃	cup (75 ml) sugar
1	teaspoon (5 ml) ground cardamom

Garnish: Chopped crystallized ginger

1. To cook orzo: Bring water to a boil in a large pan. Lower heat slightly. Add orzo and cook, uncovered, stirring often to prevent sticking to the bottom, just until tender, 6 to 10 minutes. The best way to check for doneness is to taste. Drain and set orzo aside. (Reserve the cooking water for use in soups or vegetable dishes.)

2. Heat ghee in a large skillet over moderate heat. Add cardamom pods, cinnamon, and cloves and fry for a minute or so. Add orzo, cashews, and raisins. Cook for 2 minutes, stirring gently so as not to break the orzo. Add sugar and ground cardamom and cook until sugar is dissolved. Discard whole spices and serve immediately. If allowed to stand, orzo may become lumpy, although it will still taste good.

4 to 6 servings

Serving Suggestions: Serve at a brunch with Eggs in a Spinach Nest (page 33), fresh ripe apricots or strawberries, and a cup of Honey Ginger Tea (page 292). Pass a small plate of fennel seeds at the end for the guests to chew. This Indian spice is believed to aid digestion.

✳ Fresh Mango Brûlée ✳

FRANCE

Creme brûlée or "burnt cream" is a custard whose sugar-layered top is broiled to a rich bittersweet crust. In this recipe, my base isn't custard but ripe, juicy mango (or peach) chunks, topped with nut-enriched *khoya* or *kheer*, Indian-style thickened milk. The same caramelizing technique is employed here. The result is a simpler and healthier dish that I find irresistible.

Choose fruits that are lusciously ripe.

The milk sauce:
- 2   cups (500 ml) lowfat milk (don't use nonfat)
- 1   cup (250 ml) evaporated skim milk
- 2   tablespoons (30 ml) unsalted raw cashews or slivered almonds, ground to a coarse powder in a blender or food processor
- 1/4   teaspoon (1 ml) cardamom
- 2   teaspoons (10 ml) sugar

The fruit:
- 2   medium-sized ripe mangoes, or 3 to 4 medium-sized ripe peaches or 2 cups (500 ml) fresh raspberries
-     Dark brown sugar

1. To prepare the thickened milk: Lightly oil the bottom and sides of a large, steep-sided pan to prevent milk from sticking. Bring lowfat milk and evaporated milk to a boil over medium-high heat. Lower heat to medium and stir until foaming subsides. Cook until milk thickens, 10 to 15 minutes. Watch carefully as milk will try to rise over and over again. If it does, stir until it subsides. Stir the mixture frequently and scrape the bottom and the sides to loosen any milk solids and incorporate them into the liquid milk mixture. If any skin forms on the surface, gently stir it into the liquid mixture as well.

   Add cashews and cardamom and cook for a few minutes or until quite thick, stirring often. Mix in the 2 teaspoons (10 ml) sugar. Remove from heat, transfer to a small bowl, and allow to cool.

2. Peel the mangoes, remove the flesh from the pit, and dice the flesh. If using peaches, do the same but do not peel. Divide into 4 to 6 custard cups so that they are slightly over half full. Spoon a generous layer of thickened milk over the fruit, covering it completely. The sauce should come up to no higher than $1/4$ inch (6 mm) from the top. Chill for 30 minutes.

3. Create a "lid" with a generous layer of brown sugar, covering the milk sauce entirely. Broil for 2 to 3 minutes until the top bubbles and the sugar caramelizes to a deep brown color. Watch carefully; the sugar will burn very quickly. Serve hot. If not ready to serve yet, refrigerate. Bring to room temperature before serving.

4 to 6 servings

Serving Suggestions: Particularly good after a vegetarian, pasta, pork, or beef dinner. Select from Shrimp and Squash Pullao (page 170), Coconut-Sauced Beef (page 138), Scallops, Rotini, and Vegetables Malai (page 150), or Saffron-Scented Millet (page 172).

✳ Halwa Delight ✳
INDIA

H*alwa,* thick pudding, became popular in India during the reign of the Mogul kings. The original *halwas* were probably prepared with ground nuts, but Indians now cook this pudding by simmering cereals, fruits, or vegetables in milk, then decorating the top with jadelike bits of pistachio.

When I need an easy dessert that is sure to be a hit with guests, I prepare this dish. An extra garnish of dried cranberries adds a beautiful red accent, a pleasant sourness, and an American touch.

  2 cups (500 ml) 2% lowfat milk (don't use nonfat)
$1/2$ teaspoon (2 ml) ground cardamom
$1 1/2$ cups (375 ml) raw cashews or almonds, pulverized to a coarse
      powder in a blender or food processor
$1/4$ cup (60 ml) sugar

Garnish: Chopped raw pistachios and chopped dried cranberries (or chopped dried sour cherries)

1. Lightly oil the bottom and sides of a wide, steep-sided pan to prevent milk from sticking. Bring milk to a boil over medium to high heat. Turn heat to medium and stir until foaming subsides. Cook until milk thickens slightly, about 5 minutes.

Watch carefully, as milk will try to rise over and over again. If it does, stir until it subsides. Stir the mixture frequently and scrape the bottom and sides to loosen any milk solids and incorporate them into the liquid milk mixture. If any skin forms on the surface, gently stir it into the liquid mixture as well.

2. Add cardamom and cashew powder and cook until all milk is absorbed, stirring often. Stir in sugar. Remove from heat and garnish with pistachios and cranberries. Best served warm or at room temperature. If made ahead and refrigerated, bring to room temperature before serving.

6 servings

Serving Suggestions: Surround with slices of fresh mango, papaya, pineapple, strawberries, or raspberries. The rich taste of this *halwa* ends most meals on an elegant note. I love to serve it with Steamed Fish in Lime-Ginger Sauce (page 101) or Braised Leeks with Elephant Garlic (page 72).

SAFFRON VARIATION: For a delightful bouquet, add ¹/₄ teaspoon (1 ml) saffron threads, ground to a powder and mixed with 1 tablespoon (15 ml) warm milk or water, during the last few minutes of cooking. Saffron will impart a lovely yellow color and a delightful fragrance to the dish. Cardamom is optional in this case.

✳ Maple Caramel Bananas ✳

THAILAND

Bananas stewed in sugar syrup are served as a finale to many Thai meals. If you caramelize maple syrup and season the bananas with lime and cardamom, you will make this simple sweet even more elegant and tasty.

    2   ripe but firm bananas, peeled
  ¹/₄   cup (60 ml) pure maple syrup
  ¹/₄   teaspoon (1 ml) ground cardamom
        Lime wedges
        Ground cardamom for sprinkling

1. Cut the bananas crosswise into pieces 3 inches (7.5 cm) long. Halve each piece lengthwise.
2. Place maple syrup and cardamom in a medium skillet over moderate heat. When the mixture starts to bubble, lower the heat slightly. Cook until the mixture thickens, a few minutes. Place the bananas in this syrup and cook for a minute or so,

turning gently once to coat both sides with the syrup. Remove from heat. Place on individual serving plates. Squeeze lime juice over the top and sprinkle with cardamom. Serve immediately.

4 servings

Serving Suggestions: Try with Kheema with Kale and Chinese Five-Spice (page 136), Shrimp and Scallop Vatapa (page 115), Parsee Chicken in Fragrant Coconut Gravy (page 133), or Golden Squash Cream (page 87).

* Spicy Apple Cake *
UNITED STATES

Years ago my mother-in-law handed me this cherished family recipe. Although it has undergone changes in my hand, the basic recipe is still the same. I use less oil and sugar and several varieties of apples for a wealth of flavors. During late summer, when apples are plentiful in my garden, I can pick Golden Russet, Chehalis, and Holstein. Experiment with whatever tart apples are available to you.

The rich spiciness of this cake comes from cardamom, cinnamon, and coriander. It is a hit at parties and potlucks. You can make it a day or two ahead and refrigerate it.

  1 pound (500 g), 4 cups (1 liter) cored but unpeeled tart apples (Granny Smith, Northern Spy, Gravenstein, etc.), chopped into $^1/_2$-inch (1-cm) cubes
  2 tablespoons (30 ml) fresh lemon juice
$^3/_4$ cup (185 ml) sugar
  2 tablespoons (30 ml) raisins
  1 cup (250 ml) chopped walnuts
  3 cups (750 ml) unbleached white flour (see *Note*)
$^3/_4$ teaspoon (3 ml) baking soda
$^1/_2$ teaspoon (2 ml) ground cinnamon
  1 teaspoon (5 ml) ground cardamom
  1 teaspoon (5 ml) ground coriander
  2 large eggs or 4 egg whites, lightly beaten
$^1/_2$ cup (125 ml) canola oil
$^1/_4$ cup (60 ml) lowfat buttermilk (preferred; or plain nonfat yogurt)
     Powdered sugar or Honey Ricotta (page 288)

1. In a large, deep bowl combine apples, lemon juice, sugar, raisins, and walnuts. Let stand 1 hour, stirring once or twice during this period. The mixture will make its own juice.
2. Preheat oven to 350°F (180°C, gas marks 4). In a separate medium-sized bowl, sift together flour and baking soda. Add cinnamon, cardamom, and coriander. Add to the apple mixture and stir with a spoon to mix.
3. In another medium-sized bowl, beat eggs and oil together. Fold in buttermilk. Add to the flour-apple mixture and stir to combine the ingredients thoroughly. Place in an oiled cake pan or, better yet, an angel food cake pan, 9 inches (22.5 cm) in diameter. Bake for 50 to 60 minutes or until a toothpick inserted near the center comes out clean. Serve dusted with powdered sugar or spread with Honey Ricotta.

10 or more servings

Note: You can replace 1 cup (250 ml) unbleached white flour with whole wheat pastry flour.

Serving Suggestions: This versatile cake goes well with most meals. It's also excellent for celebrating a birthday, and at a potluck, tea party, or an open house. My own favorite summer meal is Artichoke and Sweet Red Pepper Salad (page 249), August Tomato Soup (page 47), some Italian panini bread, and a slice of this cake.

✳ Spiced Fruit Bars ✳
RUSSIA

These Russian-inspired bars are brimming with fresh fruits and Indian spices. Dried cranberries add a tempting tart taste and show their bright color through the bars.

The liquid mixture:
- 1/2 cup (125 ml) regular or maple sugar, or sucanat (raw cane sugar)
- 1/2 cup (125 ml) canola oil
- 2 large eggs or 4 egg whites
- 1/4 cup (60 ml) Indian Apple Butter (page 229) or applesauce (see *Note*)
- 1 medium-sized ripe banana, peeled, whirled to a smooth puree in a blender or food processor

The dry mixture:
- 1 cup (250 ml) whole wheat flour
- 1 cup (250 ml) unbleached white flour

2   teaspoons (10 ml) baking powder

1   teaspoon (5 ml) ground cinnamon

$^1/_2$ teaspoon (2 ml) ground cardamom

$^1/_2$ teaspoon (2 ml) ground cloves

2   tablespoons (30 ml) dried cranberries, dried sour cherries, or raisins

$^1/_2$ cup (125 ml) chopped walnuts

$^1/_2$ pound (250 g), 1 medium-sized tart apple (Granny Smith, Northern Spy, Gravenstein, etc.), cored but not peeled, chopped into $^1/_2$-inch (1-cm) cubes
    Powdered sugar (optional)

1. Preheat oven to 350°F (180°C, gas marks 4). To prepare the liquid mixture: In a large bowl, beat sugar and oil together. Add eggs one at a time, mixing well after each addition. Fold in Indian Apple Butter and banana puree.

2. In another large bowl, sift together whole wheat flour, unbleached white flour, and baking powder. Add cinnamon, cardamom, cloves, cranberries, walnuts, and apples. Add to the liquid mixture and stir until the dry ingredients are thoroughly moistened. Pour into an oiled 7 × 11 inch (17.5 × 27.5 cm) or similar sized baking pan. Bake for 40 to 50 minutes or until a toothpick inserted in the middle comes out clean. Dust with powdered sugar and cut into bars or squares.

10 servings

Note: For best results use the richly spiced Indian Apple Butter. If using applesauce, double the amount of cinnamon, cardamom, and cloves.

Serving Suggestions: Serve alone or spread with Basic Kheer Sauce (page 286). Accompany with a pot of Assam or Darjeeling tea. At suppertime, thse bars can be a companion to Indian Chicken Soup (page 59), Savory Indian Polenta (page 198), and some wilted red cabbage sprinkled with Curry-Walnut Dressing (page 234).

✳ Mango, Blueberry, and Toasted Pecan Cobbler ✳
UNITED STATES

According to an old Betty Crocker cookbook, the word cobbler comes from "cobble up," which means to slap together something in a hurry. Fruit cobblers are quicker to prepare than pies and less intimidating to many cooks because they don't have to make a pie crust. Cobblers contain fewer calories yet often have the same taste sensation as a pie. As a friend puts it, "They're yummy."

I usually bake this cobbler during dinner. A fruity scent permeates the air while we eat. The dessert's ready just as dinner ends.

The fruits:

   $^1/_2$ cup (125 ml) fresh or thawed frozen blueberries

   $^1/_2$ teaspoon (2 ml) cornstarch

   $^1/_4$ cup (60 ml) sugar

   4 cups (1 liter) fresh mango pulp, diced (see *Note*)

   1 tablespoon (15 ml) fresh lime or lemon juice

The liquid ingredients:

   2 tablespoons (30 ml) canola oil

   1 large egg or 2 egg whites, lightly beaten

   $^1/_4$ cup plus 2 tablespoons (90 ml) lowfat buttermilk

The dry ingredients:

   1 cup (250 ml) unbleached white flour

$1^1/_2$ teaspoons (7 ml) baking powder

   2 tablespoons (30 ml) toasted and chopped pecans

1. Preheat oven to 400°F (200°C, gas marks 6). Lightly oil a 9-inch (22.5-cm) square baking pan. Toss blueberries with cornstarch and 1 tablespoon (15 ml) sugar, then layer them in the baking pan. Combine mangoes and 1 tablespoon (15 ml) sugar in another large bowl. Arrange the mangoes above the berries in the baking pan. Sprinkle with lemon juice.

2. To prepare the liquid ingredients: Beat oil and egg together in a medium bowl until smooth. Fold in buttermilk.

3. To prepare the dry ingredients: Sift flour and baking powder together in a large bowl. Mix in the remaining 2 tablespoons (30 ml) sugar. Add pecans. Add the oil-egg mixture and stir just until the dry ingredients are thoroughly moistened. Pour over the fruits in the pan. Bake for 40 to 50 minutes or until a toothpick inserted in the center comes out clean and the top is lightly browned. Allow to cool for a few minutes to help settle the fruit at the bottom. Best served while still warm. Cut in squares and place in individual shallow bowls with the fruit side on top. Be sure to spoon any fruit mixture from the bottom of the pan over the top of the servings. Reheat any leftovers in a 350°F (180°C, gas marks 4) oven for 10 minutes or just until thoroughly heated.

6 to 8 servings

Serving Suggestions: Serve this cobbler plain or with Lychee Swirl (page 287). Its simplicity makes it appropriate for a family meal. Accompany with Roasted Garlic, Sweet Red Pepper, and Squash Pizza (page 191) and Piquant Salad in Shades of Green (page 258).

✳ Sour Cherry Hazelnut Cobbler ✳
UNITED STATES

In June the Montmorency sour cherry tree in our yard produces fruit in abundance. The cherries change color, darkening as they ripen to a deep ruby red. Rubies as stones are a passion with many Indians. An Indian, a descendant of a royal family, once spoke to me longingly about family rubies. These jewel-like cherries are just that to me. And harvesting them is fun. When I pick the fruit, I look up and all I can see is the red splash of the cherries against an impressionist blue Pacific Northwest sky.

Following a tip from my mother-in-law, I thicken the profusely juicy cherries with tapioca. As she says, tapioca, not cornstarch, thickened her baked goods during the '30s and '40s. If sour cherries are not available, use sweet cherries. Just adjust the amount of sugar.

The fruit filling:
- 3 pounds (1.5 kg) sour cherries, pitted (about 6 cups [1.5 liters] after removal of pits)
- 2 tablespoons (30 ml) quick-cooking tapioca
- 1/2 cup (125 ml) sugar (to taste)
- 3 tablespoons (45 ml) Amaretto or other almond liqueur (optional)
- 1/2 teaspoon (2 ml) pure almond extract

Hazelnut crust:
- 4 ounces (100 g), 3/4 cup (375 ml) hazelnuts, ground to a coarse powder in a blender or food processor
- 1/4 cup (60 ml) firmly packed dark brown sugar
- 2 tablespoons (30 ml) softened butter or canola oil

Biscuit top:
- 1 cup (250 ml) unbleached white flour
- 1 1/2 teaspoons (7 ml) baking powder
- 1 tablespoon (15 ml) sugar
- 2 tablespoons (30 ml) canola oil
- 1/2 cup (125 ml) lowfat buttermilk

1. Preheat oven to 400°F (200°C, gas marks 6). Combine cherries, tapioca, and sugar in a large bowl. Let stand 15 minutes. Add Amaretto and almond extract. Place the fruits in an ungreased steep baking dish such as a 9-inch (22.5-cm) square cake pan.

2. Combine the hazelnut crust ingredients in a medium bowl and stir until thoroughly mixed. Sprinkle over the fruits evenly.

3. In a large bowl, sift flour and baking powder together. Stir in sugar. Gradually add oil, mixing in with a spoon. Fold in buttermilk. Drop by spoonfuls over the fruit so that most of the top surface is covered. Bake for 40 to 50 minutes or until the biscuit top is lightly browned. The cherries will still be bubbly. Remove from the oven. Let stand for 15 minutes to allow the fruit mixture to settle and thicken. Best served warm, but also good at room temperature. Reheat any leftovers in a 350°F (180°C, gas marks 4) oven for 10 or so minutes or just until thoroughly heated.

6 to 8 servings

Serving Suggestions: Throw a summer buffet with Indian Fish Salad (page 132), Simple Pleasure Zucchini Sauté (page 88), Roasted Tomato-Chile Salsa (page 216), and a heap of baked papads.

✹ Cherry, Blueberry, and Mangosteen Crunch ✹
UNITED STATES

A crunch is similar to a cobbler except that, instead of a biscuit dough, it has a crisp top. This crunch contains an exotic combination of fruits: sour cherries, blueberries, and mangosteen. Mangosteen is a fruit from Southeast Asia with a purplish-red outer skin and juicy white flesh that tastes somewhat like a lychee. It's not yet available fresh, but the canned variety is an acceptable substitute.

I usually prepare this dessert during early July when the red, white, and blue colors of the fruits celebrate the Fourth.

The fruit filling:

1   pound (500 g) sour cherries, pitted (or sweet cherries)

3/4 cup (175 ml) fresh or thawed frozen blueberries

2 tablespoons (30 ml) quick-cooking tapioca

10-ounce (280-g) can mangosteen, drained, pits removed and flesh slivered

2 tablespoons (30 ml) sugar (to taste)

1 tablespoon (15 ml) Amaretto or other almond liqueur (optional)

1/2 teaspoon (1 ml) pure almond extract

The oat topping:

3/4 cup (175 ml) mixture of oat, rye, and triticale flakes, or regular oatmeal (see *Note 1*)

1/4 cup (60 ml) unbleached white flour

3 tablespoons (45 ml) sugar (see *Note 2*)

1 1/2 tablespoons (22 ml) melted ghee or softened butter

1. Preheat oven to 400°F (200°C, gas marks 6). Combine cherries, blueberries, and tapioca in a large bowl and let stand 15 minutes. Add mangosteen, sugar, Amaretto, and almond extract and mix well. Transfer the mixture to an ungreased steep baking dish such as a 9-inch (22.5-cm) square cake pan.

2. Combine oats, flour, and sugar in a large bowl. Stir in ghee or butter using a fork until the mixture becomes crumbly. Spread evenly over the fruits. Bake for 30 to 35 minutes or until the fruits are very soft and bubbly. (The red, white, and blue colors of the fruits will not remain distinct at this point.) Remove from the oven. Let stand for 15 minutes to allow the fruit mixture to settle and thicken. Best served warm, but can also be served at room temperature. Reheat any leftovers in a 350°F (180°C, gas marks 4) oven for 10 or so minutes or just until thoroughly heated.

6 to 8 servings

Note 1: You can buy these mixed flakes at natural-food stores. They offer a chewier texture and a wider range of nutrients than oatmeal alone.

Note 2: Substitute date or maple sugar to enhance the flavor.

Serving Suggestions: Serve following a gorgeous meal of Artichoke and Sweet Red Pepper Salad (page 249), Coconut-Sauced Beef (page 138), and Basmati rice.

✸ Asian Pear with Hazelnut Cream ✸

INTERNATIONAL

I first tasted an Asian pear while traveling in mainland China, where crisp, juicy, sweet slices of the fruit were served following a sumptuous dinner. Later I found that the Chinese not only enjoy this fruit fresh but also steam or bake it and often serve it as dessert. In this recipe, I bake the fruit, filling the hollowed-out central part with a mixture of Indian-style thickened milk and nuts.

An easy but elegant dessert.

The filling:

> About 1 ounce (25 g), $1/4$ cup (60 ml) hazelnuts ground to a coarse powder in a blender or food processor

$1^1/4$ tablespoons (22 ml) regular or maple sugar

$1/2$ teaspoon (2 ml) ground cardamom

$1/4$ teaspoon (1 ml) cinnamon

$1/4$ teaspoon (1 ml) nutmeg

1 cup (250 ml) 2% lowfat milk (preferred; or use nonfat milk)

6 Asian pears

Pure maple syrup for drizzling

Garnish: Chopped dried cranberries

1. To prepare the filling: Combine hazelnuts, sugar, cardamom, cinnamon, and nutmeg in a medium bowl. Set aside. Heat milk in a medium, steep-sided pan over medium to high heat. When it comes to a boil, lower heat, and stir vigorously until the foaming subsides. Turn heat to medium. Add the nut mixture. Cook for 7 to 10 minutes or until the mixture is very thick. Stir as often as necessary during this period to prevent the milk from boiling over. Scrape the sides and the bottom and incorporate any milk solids into the liquid milk. Transfer to a small bowl.

2. Preheat oven to 350°F (180°C, gas marks 4). Peel the skin from the top half of each pear. Core and remove seeds. Stuff the cavity with some of the filling. Drizzle a little maple syrup on top. Place the pears on a cookie sheet lined with aluminum foil. Bake for 15 to 18 minutes. (The pear skin will turn brown.) Best served immediately. To offset their deep brown color, garnish the top with bits of chopped cranberries. Serve any leftover filling, topped with the remaining cranberries, on the side.

6 servings

Serving Suggestions: To complement these baked pears, serve Chile and Lime-Spiced Saifun Salad (Shrimp Variation; page 165) and steamed broccoli drizzled with Tamarind-Date Chutney (page 208).

APPLE VARIATION: Apples are also tasty when baked this way. Don't overbake them, as their skin might crack.

✳ Exotic Fruits with Sweet Pecans and Sauce ✳
INTERNATIONAL

Having grown up in Bengal, with its abundance of fresh fruits, I developed a preference for fresh fruit, at its peak of ripeness, whenever I had a desire for something sweet. I like to combine fruits of varying textures and degrees of sweetness. Since I left India, the list of fruits has expanded considerably to include kiwis, strawberries, and Asian pears, to name a few.

When serving to company, I like to dress up the fruit platter with a few contrasting nibbles such as crunchy curry-carameled pecans; firm, brick-colored, nutty-sweet Norwegian gjetost cheese; or sweet balls made with fresh Indian cheese. I also like to surround the platter with a few dessert sauces. Dipping fruit chunks and other sweet nibbles into various sauces can be a most pleasant summer pastime.

The fruits and other nibbles:
    Assorted fresh fruits of your choice
    Sweet Curry Pecans (page 260)
    Gjetost cheese
    Indian Cheese Balls (see page 12)
    Sweet Biscuitsticks (page 197)

The dessert sauces (choose one or more):
    Lychee Swirl (page 287)
    Orange Kheer with Crushed Nuts (page 286)
    Honey Ricotta (page 288)
    Blood Orange and Lime Marinade (page 288)

Arrange fruits and other nibbles of your choice in a large platter. Surround with bowls of various sauces.

Dessert Sauces

Add a dab of a complementary sauce to raise desserts and baked goods to an even more ethereal plane. Some of these sauces are so delicious they can be served alone like a pudding as a sweet ending to a meal.

✳ Basic Kheer Sauce ✳

INDIA

Boiling milk and then cooking it slowly to thicken it is a technique that originated in India centuries ago, possibly as a way of preserving milk. Once thickened, the milk (called *kheer*, *khoya*, or *mawa*) could be used in various ways—as a base for confections, as a dessert sauce, or as a thickener for savory dishes.

Even fat-reduced milk tastes rich and delicious when cooked this Indian way. In this recipe, this sauce is gently sweetened. Use it as a pudding or as a dip for fresh fruits.

4   cups (1 liter) 2% lowfat milk (don't use nonfat)
2   tablespoons (30 ml) plus sugar

Lightly oil the bottom and sides of a large, steep-sided, and preferably nonstick pan to prevent milk from sticking. Bring milk to a boil over medium to high heat. Lower the heat to prevent milk from boiling over and stir vigorously until foaming subsides. Turn heat to medium. Cook until milk thickens to the consistency of heavy cream, 15 to 25 minutes. Watch carefully as milk will try to rise over and over again. If it does, stir until it subsides. Stir the mixture frequently and scrape the bottom and sides to loosen any milk solids and incorporate them into the liquid milk mixture. If any skin forms on the surface, gently stir it into the liquid mixture as well. Add sugar, adjusting the amount to your taste. Remove from heat.

Yields over 1 cup (250 ml), 4 small servings

VARIATION: ORANGE KHEER WITH CRUSHED NUTS Oranges are not taken for granted in India since they aren't available year-round. They come to the market in winter, small in size with a pale outer skin. Because they are sweet, juicy, and full of flavor, Indian cooks often incorporate them in their desserts. The flavor of freshly squeezed orange juice blends especially well with the Basic Kheer Sauce.

2 tablespoons (30 ml) juice and pulp of a fresh orange
2 tablespoons (30 ml) minced, unsalted pistachios

After removing the sweetened, thickened milk from the heat, mix in orange juice and pulp. Sprinkle with pistachios. Best when served chilled.

VARIATION: GINGER KHEER Add $\frac{1}{4}$ to $\frac{1}{2}$ teaspoon (1 to 2 ml) ground ginger (to taste) to the thickened milk along with sugar.

VARIATION: LYCHEE SWIRL Lychee was a common fruit when I was growing up in India, not at all the exotic item it is in the West. I've always loved its delicate juicy flesh and wish I could buy the fruit more often. Asian grocers occasionally stock a few. Once I came across a roadside vendor in Hawaii selling fresh lychees and bought all she had. It was the only time since I left India that I had enough lychees.

Even frozen or canned lychees impart a fine flavor to this creamy dip for fresh fruits. You can also serve it alone as a delicate pudding.

20 fresh peeled or canned lychees (part of a 20-ounce [565-g] can), or thawed
frozen lychees (reserve can liquid)
Apple juice or lychee can liquid (optional)

Whirl the lychees in a blender, adding a little apple juice or lychee can liquid if too thick to process. Add to the thickened milk after it has been removed from the heat. Serve at once or chilled.

4 small servings

GOAT'S MILK VARIATION: If you want a more robust-flavored sauce, substitute goat's milk for regular milk entirely or partly. Goats were one of the first animals in history to be domesticated, and the custom of using goat's milk is an ancient one. This milk is believed to be more easily digestible than cow's milk. As a child I frequently drank goat's milk.

Fresh goat's milk is sold in many natural-food stores and is rapidly becoming available in many supermarkets as well. If unavailable, substitute canned evaporated goat's milk, which is sold in large supermarkets. The fat content is higher, so you might simply want to add a tablespoon (15 ml) or so at the last stage of cooking the thickened milk, just before removing from the heat, for richness.

OTHER FRUITY VARIATIONS: Add chunks of fresh ripe peach or apricot to the thickened milk or arrange some raspberries on top. Chopped dried apricot or mango "leathers," added after the milk has come to a boil, also impart a fine flavor to this sauce.

✳ Honey Ricotta ✳
EASTERN INDIA/ITALY

This sauce derives its inspiration from a famed Bengali bar-type confection called *sandesh*, made simply with freshly prepared Indian cheese and sugar. (In my book, *The Healthy Cuisine of India: Recipes from the Bengal Region*, you'll find a recipe for *sandesh*, Silk and Satin Bars.) Italian ricotta cheese, somewhat similar in taste to Indian cheese, is a quicker alternative, and honey goes especially well with its creamy texture. Spread this sauce on top of cake slices or use as a dip for fresh fruits—strawberries, peaches, nectarines.

    1   pound (500 g) part-skim or lowfat ricotta cheese
    3   tablespoons (45 ml) honey (to taste)

Whisk together cheese and honey until smooth and place the mixture in a medium-sized heavy-bottomed pan over low heat. Cook for 5 to 10 minutes or until the mixture has a saucelike consistency, stirring often. Overcooking will make it dry. Serve immediately or at room temperature.

10 or more servings

✳ Blood Orange and Lime Marinade ✳
THE MEDITERRANEAN

In spring, I make a special trip to Seattle's Pike Place Market for flavorful blood oranges with their exotic flavor and pulp flecked with vivid-red streaks. These oranges are popular in Mediterranean countries but not used widely in the United States. Their dark red juice, which has a citrus tang, makes an exotic marinade for yellowish-orange fruits such as fresh ripe apricots, peaches, mangoes, and papayas. Fresh mint imparts a fragrant bouquet. As a marinade, pour over fresh fruit chunks—apricots, peaches, or papayas.

    1/2   cup (125 ml) blood orange juice, extracted from 1 to 3 blood oranges
          (depending on size and juiciness; see *Note*)
    2   teaspoons (10 ml) fresh lime juice (to taste)

Combine orange juice and lime juice in a small nonmetallic bowl. Serve immediately or chilled.

Yields 1/2 cup (125 ml)

Note: Don't worry about extra juice. It won't last long.

Thirst Quenchers

● ● ● ● ● ● ● ● ● ● ● ● ●

A Bangladeshi friend has escorted me from my hotel in the modern section of Dhaka, capital of Bangladesh, to the old quarter. I know this is where I'll see the real life of the Dhakans.

A wedding procession threads its way through the crowd. The women are attired in saris, their arms festooned with gold bracelets that flash in the sun. As the group passes, merchants seated behind piles of rice, turmeric, and mustard seeds hawk their wares. Craftsmen, who fashion bangles and jewelry by hand from conch shells and semiprecious stones, seem undisturbed by the noise.

The narrow, winding streets teem with people on foot, on bicycles, in three-wheel motorcycle taxis—movement by every method except cars. And the din continues—motorcycles thundering, rickshaws honking, people shouting. The effect is exotic, almost overpowering. I soon find myself deliriously thirsty.

"Let's have *lassi*," my friend suggests. "We'll find the best right here in Chalk-bazaar."

In Dhaka, people congregate in *lassi* houses for refreshment and conversation in much the same way Europeans gather at cafés in Paris and Amsterdam. *Lassi*, a soothing yogurt drink, is popular throughout the countries of the Indian subcontinent—India, Pakistan, and Bangladesh.

My friend takes me to a one-room shop lined with cushioned benches. The owner concentrates on preparing *lassi*, a specialty of his for years that he makes in only one flavor. He mixes homemade yogurt with a brilliant yellow, saffron-flavored sugar syrup that permeates the room with its rich scent. Next he pours the drink back and forth from one tall glass to another, making it light and frothy. Then he wraps a block of ice with a piece of cloth and crushes it by pounding it on the bare, concrete floor. He adds the crushed ice to the yogurt, producing a smooth, creamy drink, delicious and refreshing.

Throughout the Indian subcontinent, I have discovered *lassi* and tea made exotic by the addition of spices, aromatics, and other flavorings. These beverages not only satisfy one's thirst but also provide a reason for gathering with friends for a quiet moment to discuss events of the day.

I have incorporated many beverage ideas from India into my recipes. Plain yogurt is most often the main ingredient in Indian beverages, both for its cooling properties and as a protein source for many vegetarians. I often substitute buttermilk for its creamier texture, or soy milk when seeking a nondairy alternative. Some Indian beverages are sweet; others are blended with green chile, cumin, and coriander for a pleasant spicy effect. I use these seasonings in many Western-style coolers and punches.

Fresh fruits can make delicious drinks. In Iran, it's the custom on warm evenings to share fresh fruit drinks with friends. We often gathered around an outdoor juice bar, sipping a frothy banana milk or a pleasantly sour pomegranate juice as we chatted. When it was time to pay, several hands would go up. The vendor would pocket the money and smile. "One more round?" And we'd often delay dinner to stay longer.

This chapter contains beverage recipes that are inspired by the diverse cultures I have encountered. Among the offerings are a tea and apple juice blend that is perfect for cool-weather entertaining; a lime and papaya milk, a year-round treat; and a tamarind drink that is especially welcome on a hot summer afternoon.

You'll also find a number of tea recipes. Tea, in its many forms, is perhaps the most cherished social drink throughout the world. It's also a beverage to be enjoyed alone.

One afternoon while visiting Hong Kong, I ducked into a tea shop to escape a sudden storm. Alone in a corner, an elderly woman sipped a glass of tea and stared at a faded black-and-white photo. Her wrinkled face showed a deeply lined map of her life. She ignored the newspaper lying on the table and the rain-lashed street beyond the window. She sat with the tea and her memories. ✱

✳ Mulled Apple Tea ✳

INDIA/UNITED STATES

Introduce the complex fruity flavor of Darjeeling tea into this warming mixture of apple juice and spices. It is excellent for cool autumn and winter evenings. When entertaining large crowds, keep a kettle of this tea on the stove, just below simmer, and let the guests help themselves.

- 2 cups (500 ml) water
- 1/2 teaspoon (2 ml) ground cinnamon
- 1/2 teaspoon (2 ml) ground cardamom
- 2 teaspoons (10 ml) loose Darjeeling tea or 2 decaffeinated tea bags
- 2 cups (500 ml) apple juice
- 1/2 medium-sized sweet apple, thinly sliced

Place water, cinnamon, and cardamom in a large pan. Cover and bring to a boil. Lower heat and add tea. Cook uncovered from this point. As soon as the water has taken on an amber color, add apple juice and the apple slices. Allow the mixture to come to a gentle simmer, but don't let it boil. Remove from heat. Strain into cups and serve hot, adding an apple slice from the simmering tea in each cup if desired.

2 to 3 servings

Serving Suggestions: Perfect for holiday entertaining; offer to the guests along with some roasted Italian chestnuts as a meal starter. (To roast chestnuts, slash an "x" on the skin with a knife; bake at 350°F [180°C, gas marks 4] for 25 to 30 minutes.) Carry a thermos of this tea with you on a hike; or enjoy it with a slice of Date-Nut Squash Bread (page 35) on your afternoon break.

✳ Green Tea with Rice ✳

JAPAN

An intriguing Japanese custom is the pouring of green tea over a bowl of rice at the end of a meal and savoring it. I was told this cleans the palate before dessert. But, according to a Japanese woman, the custom arose because the hot liquid makes it easier to clean the rice bowl. Whatever the reason, this tea-rice course, eaten with a spoon, is a light way to end a meal.

Instead of the traditional short-grain Japanese rice, I use either Basmati or jasmine rice, made even more fragrant by the addition of a black cardamom pod.

$^1/_2$ cup (125 ml) Basmati rice or jasmine rice

1 cup (250 ml) water

1 whole black cardamom pod or 2 or 3 whole green cardamom pods, bruised

2 cups (500 ml) water

2 teaspoons (10 ml) loose green tea (to taste)

1. Place rice, 1 cup (250 ml) water, and cardamom in a medium-sized pan. Cover and bring to a boil. Simmer, covered, until all water is absorbed and rice is tender and fluffy, about 15 minutes. Discard cardamom.

2. Bring 2 cups (500 ml) water to a boil. Remove from heat and pour in a teapot that has been rinsed with hot water. Add green tea and let steep for a few minutes. Place rice in individual bowls and strain some tea over it. Pass the teapot around for extra helpings.

2 servings

Serving Suggestions: Serve following a seafood meal such as Tart Fish Soup (page 57). (Rice is a recommended side dish for this soup; prepare some extra for this dish.) Or try with the spectacular Shrimp and Scallop Vatapa (page 115) or its vegetarian equivalent, Cauliflower and Potato Vatapa (page 117).

✳ Honey Ginger Tea ✳

INTERNATIONAL

This light, gingery, caffeine-free beverage refreshes you any time you need a break, or after a strenuous run or a workout when your body craves liquids.

2-inch (5-cm) piece gingerroot, coarsely chopped

4 cups (1 liter) water

2-inch (5-cm) cinnamon stick

4 whole cardamom pods, bruised

A wedge of lime or lemon

Honey

Bring all the ingredients except lime and honey to a boil in a pan. Simmer, covered, 5 minutes. Stir well, add lime, and simmer, covered, another 5 minutes. Strain and serve hot, sweetened with honey.

4 servings

Serving Suggestions: This cold-weather favorite complements entrées with an Asian accent such as Soy- and Mirin-Glazed Salmon (page 99), Blackened Chicken (page 126), or Tofu-Mushroom Scramble (page 32). Enjoy with a slice of Spiced Fruit Bars (page 278) at snacktime.

✸ Soy Chai ✸
INDIA/UNITED STATES

A woman I encountered one day while shopping told me she had just finished reading my first book, *The Healthy Cuisine of India.* In it I have a recipe for Fragrant Milk Tea, *cha* or *chai* as it's called in India, which is prepared by brewing milk, tea, and fragrant spices together. But because her diet was dairy-free, she wanted a soy milk version of this tea, and she chided me for not providing it in that book. I mumbled some excuses, but went home and retested the recipe using soy milk. The tea tasted delicious, even a bit lighter than the original version. I noticed one difference: with regular milk, which is naturally sweet, one can omit the sugar, but because of the stronger, somewhat chalky flavor of soy milk, some sweetener is essential for the soy-based version. I remain grateful to that woman for leading me to this new variation.

 2 cups (500 ml) water
 2 teaspoons (10 ml) loose black tea (Darjeeling, Assam, or other fine variety),
   or 2 decaffeinated tea bags
 5 whole cardamom pods, bruised
   2-inch (5-cm) cinnamon stick
 5 whole cloves
 1 cup (250 ml) plain soy milk
   Sugar or other sweetener of choice

Combine water, tea, cardamom, cinnamon, and cloves in a large pot and bring to a boil. Lower heat and simmer, uncovered, 10 to 12 minutes or until the water is deep amber in color. Add soy milk and cook over low heat just until the mixture is heated through, another 10 to 15 minutes. Strain and pour into cups. Sweeten to taste.

2 servings

Serving Suggestions: Serve after any elaborate meal such as one that features Parsee Chicken in Fragrant Coconut Gravy (page 133) or Fragrant Fish Pullao (page 103). Enjoy this chai with snacks—Chicken-Flavored Baby Potatoes (page 244) or Quick Indian Pizza (page 195). Also delicious as a late-evening warming beverage (made with decaffeinated tea) and served with a slice of Sweet Yam Cake from Negril (page 267).

✳ Lime and Papaya Milk ✳

MEXICO

Indians delight in *lassi,* yogurt-based drinks, and Mexicans pride themselves on their *licuados,* tropical fruit blends. These beverages make a nourishing breakfast or after-workout snack. Here's a deliciously creamy papaya drink, a cross between the two, with a new twist of buttermilk.

        2   ripe papayas, peeled, seeded, coarsely chopped
     1/4   cup (60 ml) fresh lime juice
        2   cups (500 ml) lowfat buttermilk
1/2 to 1   teaspoon (2 to 5 ml) ground cardamom (to taste)
     1/4   cup (60 ml) sugar (to taste)
             Ice cubes

Place papaya, lime juice, buttermilk, cardamom, and sugar in the container of a blender. Process until smooth. Pour over ice cubes.

2 servings

Serving Suggestions: Although I usually serve water as the beverage with spicy meals, this fruity milk (and Yogurt Borhani, below) are exceptions. Some compatible entrées are: Savory Sprouts Stir-Fry (page 77), Curried Pasta and Fagioli (page 152), or Kale Spiced with Fish (page 107).

✻ Yogurt Borhani ✻
BANGLADESH

Sweet or salty *lassi* can quench everyday thirst, but for special occasions Bangladeshis bring out *borhani*, a spicy yogurt drink brightened by green chile, cumin, and coriander. This drink is a perfect accompaniment for richly flavored rice dishes of that country, I was told.

  1   cup (250 ml) plain nonfat yogurt
 ¹/₂   a small jalapeno, seeded, chopped (to taste)
  4   fresh mint leaves
 ¹/₂   teaspoon (2 ml) ground cumin
 ¹/₂   teaspoon (2 ml) ground coriander
       Dash black salt
       Dash salt
       Dash white pepper
       Ice cubes or crushed ice

Combine all the ingredients except ice in a blender container. Whirl until smooth. Adjust seasoning. Serve over ice in chilled glasses.

1 serving

Serving Suggestions: Sip a glass of *borhani* while snacking on Toasted Baby Sardines and Caramelized Peanuts (page 261) and some papads. At a main meal, serve alongside a grain dish such as Hazelnut Kasha with Red Pepper Cream (page 173) or Shrimp and Squash Pullao (page 170). For a light summer brunch, accompany with a crisp green salad, an herb omelet, and Gujarati Potato Boats (page 64) or some warmed chapatis.

❋ Tamarind Cooler ❋

INDIA/MEXICO

A tart taste is said to be especially cooling in hot weather, so the sour pulp of tamarind peps up many a beverage in tropical and semitropical climates.

    1   cup (250 ml) water
    1   teaspoon (5 ml) tamarind concentrate
    1/4 teaspoon (1 ml) garam masala
    1/8 teaspoon (0.5 ml) ground cumin
        Ground red pepper (start with a scant pinch)
        Dash black salt or regular salt
        Crushed ice

Garnish: Fresh mint leaf (optional)

Combine all the ingredients except ice and mint leaf in a blender container and whirl until smooth. Taste and adjust the amount of salt and red pepper. Chill for at least 30 minutes. Pour over crushed ice, float a mint leaf on top, and serve.

1 serving

Serving Suggestions: Goes particularly well with Carrot-Cashew Koftas (page 252), Plum-Rice Balls (page 254), or Fragrant Fish Pullao (page 103).

Suggested Menus

● ● ● ● ● ● ● ● ● ● ● ● ● ●

One Hour or Less Menu

Steamed Fish in Lime-Ginger Sauce (page 101)
or Lime-Ginger Chicken (page 102)
Simple Pleasure Zucchini Sauté (page 88)
Baked sweet potato

One Hour or Less Menu—Vegetarian

Basmati Rice Congee (page 30)
Savory Sprouts Stir-Fry (page 77)
Peanuts, Seaweed, and Red Chile Flakes (page 220)

Nonfat Dinner

Mango-Marinated Fish with Dried Tomato Sauce (page 110)
Brown Basmati rice
Steamed kale with Lime-Ginger Dressing (page 230)
Papads with Tamarind-Date Chutney (page 208)

Nonfat Dinner—Vegetarian

Garlic-Glazed Tofu (page 67)
Crispy Snow Peas (page 89)
Crusty bread with Mint-Tamarind Pesto (page 225)

Sunday Dinner

Artichoke and Sweet Red Pepper Salad (page 249)
Coconut-Sauced Beef (page 138)
or Parsee Chicken in Fragrant Coconut Gravy (page 133)
Jasmine rice
Baked butternut squash

Sunday Dinner—Vegetarian

Quinoa Uppama (page 180)
Sweet and Spicy Sancoche (page 68)
Onion Yogurt Relish (page 209)
Chilied Mango Chutney (page 205)

Brown-Bag Surprises #1

Indian Chicken Salad (page 131)
Roasted Tikka Potatoes (page 243)
Papads with Green Mango Chutney (page 206)

Brown-Bag Surprises #2

Vietnamese Salmon Burrito (page 251)
Piquant Salad in Shades of Green (page 258)
Soy Chai (page 293)

Brown-Bag Surprises – Vegetarian

Tabbouleh Plus (page 176)
Gujarati Potato Boats (page 64)
Honey Ginger Tea (page 292)

Teatime

Plum-Rice Balls (page 254)
Toasted Baby Sardines with Caramelized Peanuts (page 261)
Spiced Fruit Bars (page 278)
An assortment of teas

Party Fare

Sweet, Sour, and Smoky Potatoes (page 63)
Lime-Grilled Chicken (page 125)
Spicy Apple Cake (page 277)
Exotic Fruits with Sweet Pecans and Sauce (page 285)
Soy Chai (page 293)

Spring Celebration

Shrimp and Orzo Pullao (page 149)
or Picnic Squash Pullao (page 169; for vegetarians)
Chick-pea Ragout (page 56)
Potato Radicchio Salad (page 247)
Fresh Mango Brûlée (page 274)

Summer Brunch

South Indian Gazpacho (page 46)
Quick Indian Pizza (page 195)
Salmon-Pasta Salad International (page 250)
or Crisp Potatoes and Wilted Spinach Salad (page 246; for vegetarians)
Exotic Fruits with Sweet Pecans and Sauce (page 285)

Autumn Harvest Dinner

Sweet and Nutty Carrot-Turnip Soup (page 49)
Soy- and Mirin-Glazed Salmon (page 99)
or Garlic-Glazed Tofu (page 67; for vegetarians)
Basic Pilaf with Nutty Vermicelli Threads (page 177)
Greens Ratatouille (page 94)
Prune and Date Chutney (page 207)

Hearty Winter Fare

Universal Vindaloo (page 140)
or Hearty Lentils and Udon (page 160; for vegetarians)
Steamed broccoli with Sesame-Tamarind Dressing (page 233)
Winter Salad (page 259)

Food Gathering, Food Shopping: Mail-Order Sources

Cooking is part of the larger cycle of birth, growth, and regeneration. The sowing of seeds is followed by harvesting and gathering—or, more often, shopping and mail-ordering. Chopping, spicing, cooking, and eating culminate the process. I absorbed the basics of this approach to life when my family spent a few years in Bangladesh, where life was lived "close to the soil." Gas or electricity hadn't yet arrived in the town of Brahmanbaria, and most of the roads were simple dirt tracks. My mother cooked on a handmade clay oven fired by charcoal.

We shopped at a farmers' market where the growers, who lived only a few miles away, arrived every morning with baskets of produce. Fruits and vegetables were displayed without artifice. Some were tiny, a few oddly shaped. Snacks and sweets were sold. We children often got samples, a sticky brown lump of moist palm sugar, a ripe plum or two, or *pera*, a simple confection made of milk and sugar. Cows wandered, munching on leftover leaves and vegetable trimmings. A warm breeze blew. A fruit-seller fanned himself with a bamboo fan and watched us as we ran, laughing and screaming, between the stalls.

I've always felt this same excitement about all markets. When I visited modern, bustling Singapore, where cooking inspiration comes from China, India, and Malaysia, I found a huge Western-style supermarket. There the shelves displayed fresh and prepared food items—marmalade from Australia, muesli as the Swiss make it, grains and seasonal leafy greens from many parts of Asia. It was the same cycle as that in the little town in Bangladesh, but on a grander scale.

Ever since, whenever I travel to a new country, I visit the markets first. They serve as a "Yellow Pages" guide to the country's gastronomy, its economy, and its soul.

In Holland, the cities were neat and orderly and the streets clean. People tipped their hats to strangers in the park. The vegetables in the supermarkets were perfect and entirely predictable. But one day in Amsterdam I came across a boisterous farmers' market. Here was where the expatriates from Holland's colonial empire shopped. The merchants and customers conducted as much business in Indonesian and Chinese as in Dutch or English. The exotic items necessary to Asian cooking, which I'd been unable to locate in Dutch supermarkets, were here in abundance.

I found bright yellow turmeric root, something I hadn't seen since leaving India. Selling was animated. "Tatyana, do you think this is enough chile?" I heard a voice behind me. A woman was showing her friend a paper sack filled to the brim with bright red chiles. I couldn't place the accent, but understood the urgency in the question. My perceptions about Holland began to change.

On the Mendocino coast of Northern California, my food gathering took the form of mushroom picking. A group of us spent a few days at a friend's ranch. It was the beginning of autumn and the first rain of the season had fallen the night before. "We go mushroom hunting," said a Czech botanist who was staying with us. He made it sound as normal as going to the store. I had never picked mushrooms before.

We tiptoed through a pine forest like children hunting for Easter eggs. The botanist gave us a lesson so we'd be able to distinguish the edible mushrooms from the poisonous. Soon I recognized the boletus mushroom, a close cousin of that Italian delicacy, porcini. Boletus has a delicate brown color and is shaped like a hamburger bun. Once I found one, dozens appeared before my eyes.

Although we had planned to dine in one of the finer restaurants in Mendocino that night, we ended up cooking the food we had gathered. We traded some of the mushrooms with the farmer next door for vegetables from his garden, beets the size of large grapefruits and gigantic, sweet carrots. The hired hand invited us to his barn so we could watch him milk the cows. I returned with a bucket of fresh milk.

To top it all, my husband and others dived in the cold waters of the Pacific Ocean among slippery beds of kelp and returned with some twenty abalones. Our dinner that night consisted of strips of abalone sautéed with mushrooms. The next day we breakfasted on scrambled eggs and more mushrooms. Not since I had left Bangladesh had food tasted so good or satisfied so completely. I realized later this was because I had experienced food not merely in the context of a meal but as part of a larger process.

In the Pacific Northwest where I now live, I often find myself equally close to the source of food. The gentle climate is friendly to a wide range of plants. Here one can grow a wide variety of vegetables throughout the year. When the crocuses and daffodils bloom in early spring, we are out in our yard, shoveling and weeding. We plant leafy greens, spinach, and peas in March, and they yield by May. Beginning in April we sow seeds for the full range of warm-weather vegetables we harvest throughout summer and fall.

In late summer we make room in the garden for root vegetables: rutabaga, turnips, and carrots, as well as kale, cabbage, and cauliflower. They are available throughout the winter. Just before dinnertime, year-round, I visit my vegetable beds and pluck what I need. As I peel and chop, I collect all vegetable scraps and save them in a bag until the meal is over.

Then I compost it all. And the cycle begins again.

We cannot always gather food from the earth ourselves. To supplement garden produce, I shop at supermarkets, natural-food stores, and ethnic groceries. Once I received a box of pecans as a gift from a friend, sent from a mail-order house, and found them to be the best pecans I've ever tasted. Ever since I have regularly mail-ordered them.

For those who live away from a metropolis, some items mentioned in this book may be hard to find. Here's a list of mail-order companies that supply specialty products. A few companies ship perishable items overnight. Call or write for their catalogs or price lists.

Asian markets and health-food stores are becoming increasingly common, even in smaller towns. Many supermarkets carry natural foods and basic ingredients for Chinese cooking. I have omitted such items from my mail-order list below. ✳

Seed Companies

Ronniger's Seed Potatoes, Star Route, Moyie Springs, ID 83845.

Johnny's Selected Seeds, Foss Hill Road, Albion, ME 04910-9731; (207) 437-4301.

For seeds that grow west of the Cascades:

Territorial Seed Company, 20 Palmer Avenue, P.O. Box 157, Cottage Grove, OR 97424; (503) 942-9547.

Produce

For exotic fresh or dried produce such as yuca, Yellow Finnish potatoes, arugula, dried chile peppers, and mushrooms:

World Variety Produce, P.O. Box 21127, Los Angeles, CA 90021; 1-800-468-7111 or (213) 588-0151.

For exotic fruits, squash, dried mushrooms, herbs, and plants:

Frieda's by Mail, P.O. Box 58488, Los Angeles, CA 90058; 1-800-242-1771.

For Vidalia sweet onions:

Bland Farms, P.O. Box 506, Glennville, GA 30427-0506; 1-800-843-2542.

Rice Products

For sweet rice, rice syrup, and brown rice:

Lundberg Family Farms, P.O. Box 369, Richvale, CA 95974; (916) 882-4551.

For arborio, wild rice, polenta, and pastas:

Zingerman's Delicatessen, 422 Detroit Street, Ann Arbor, MI 48104-1118; (313) 663-3400.

Dried Fruit and Nuts

For fine quality pecans:

Goodbee Pecan Plantation, P.O. Box 3650, Albany, GA 31708.

For natural or roasted hazelnuts:

Holmquist Hazelnut Orchards, 9821 Holmquist Road, Lynden, WA 98264; (206) 988-9240.

For dried sour cherries, cranberries, and other berries:

Chukar Cherries, 320 Wine Country Road, P.O. Box 510, Prosser, WA 99350-0510; 1-800-624-9544 (outside Washington state), (509) 786-2055 (inside Washington state).

Teas

For loose teas, tea bags, and naturally flavored teas:

Robert and Joseph, Ltd., Drawer 100, Redgranite, WI 54970.

For a large selection of black, green, oolong, and herb teas:

Teahouse Kwan Yin, 1707 N. 45th Street, Seattle, WA 98103; (206) 632-2056.

For green teas:

Eden Foods, 701 Tecumseh Road, Clinton, MI 49236.

Oils and Vinegar

For organic olive oil, balsamic vinegar, and Italian pastas:

Gaeta Imports, 141 John Street, Babylon, NY 11702-2903; 1-800-669-2681 or (516) 661-2681.

For a selection of oils:

Spectrum Naturals, 113 Copeland Street, Petaluma, CA 94952; (707) 778-8900.

For raspberry vinegar and other berry products:

The Granger Berry Patch, 1731 Beam Road, Granger, WA 98932; 1-800-346-1417.

Smoked Seafood

Port Chatham, 632 N.W. 46th Street, Seattle, WA 98107; 1-800-872-5666.

Indian Spices and Ingredients

The following is a small sample of the large number of Indian groceries in the United States, arranged alphabetically. Consult the Yellow Pages of the city nearest you for other stores.

Bombay Emporium, 294 Craft Avenue, Pittsburgh, PA 15213; (412) 682-4965.

House of Spices, 76-17 Broadway, Jackson Heights, NY 11373; (718) 476-1577.

House of Spices, Inc., 13929 N. Central Expressway, Suite 419, Dallas, TX 75243; (214) 783-7544.

India Gifts and Foods, 1031 W. Belmont Avenue, Chicago, IL 60657; (312) 348-4393.

Indian Spice World, 126 Lexington Avenue, New York, NY 10016; (212) 686-2727.

Indian Spices & Grocery, 5891 W. Pico Boulevard, Los Angeles, CA 90019; (213) 931-4871.

Spice Club, 38242 Glenmoor Drive, Fremont, CA 94536; (510) 797-7423.

The Souk, 1916 Pike Place, N, Seattle, WA 98101; (206) 441-1666.

Index

•••••